The Country Without Humans

vol. 1

STORY & ART BY IWATOBINEKO

CONTENTS

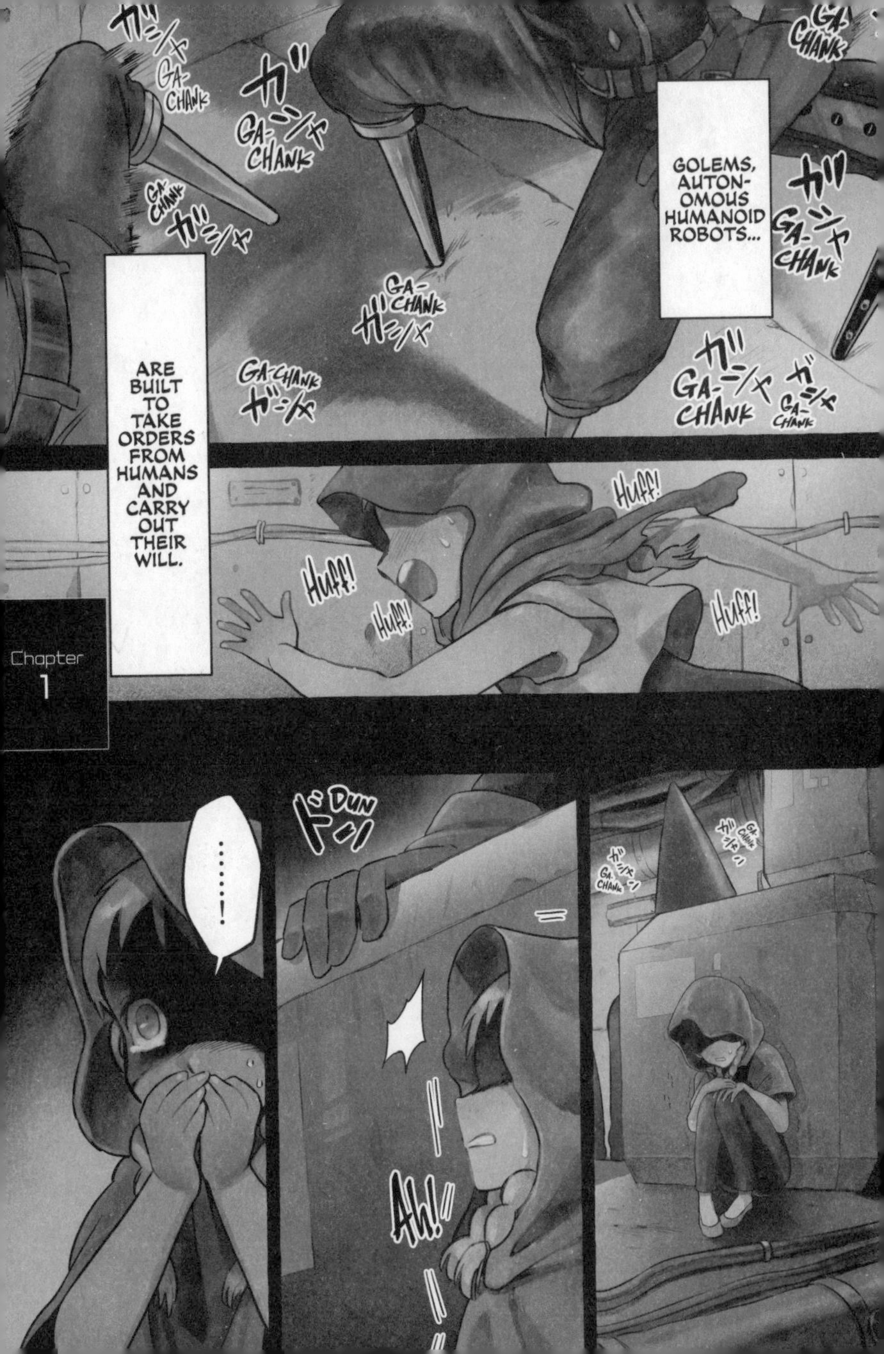

GA-CHANK
GOLEMS, AUTONOMOUS HUMANOID ROBOTS...
GA-CHANK
GA-CHANK
GA-CHANK
GA-CHANK
GA-CHANK
GA-CHANK
GA-CHANK
GA-CHANK
GA-CHANK
ARE BUILT TO TAKE ORDERS FROM HUMANS AND CARRY OUT THEIR WILL.
Huff!
Huff!
Huff!
Huff!
Chapter 1
GA-CHANK
GA-CHANK
DUN
Ah!
......!

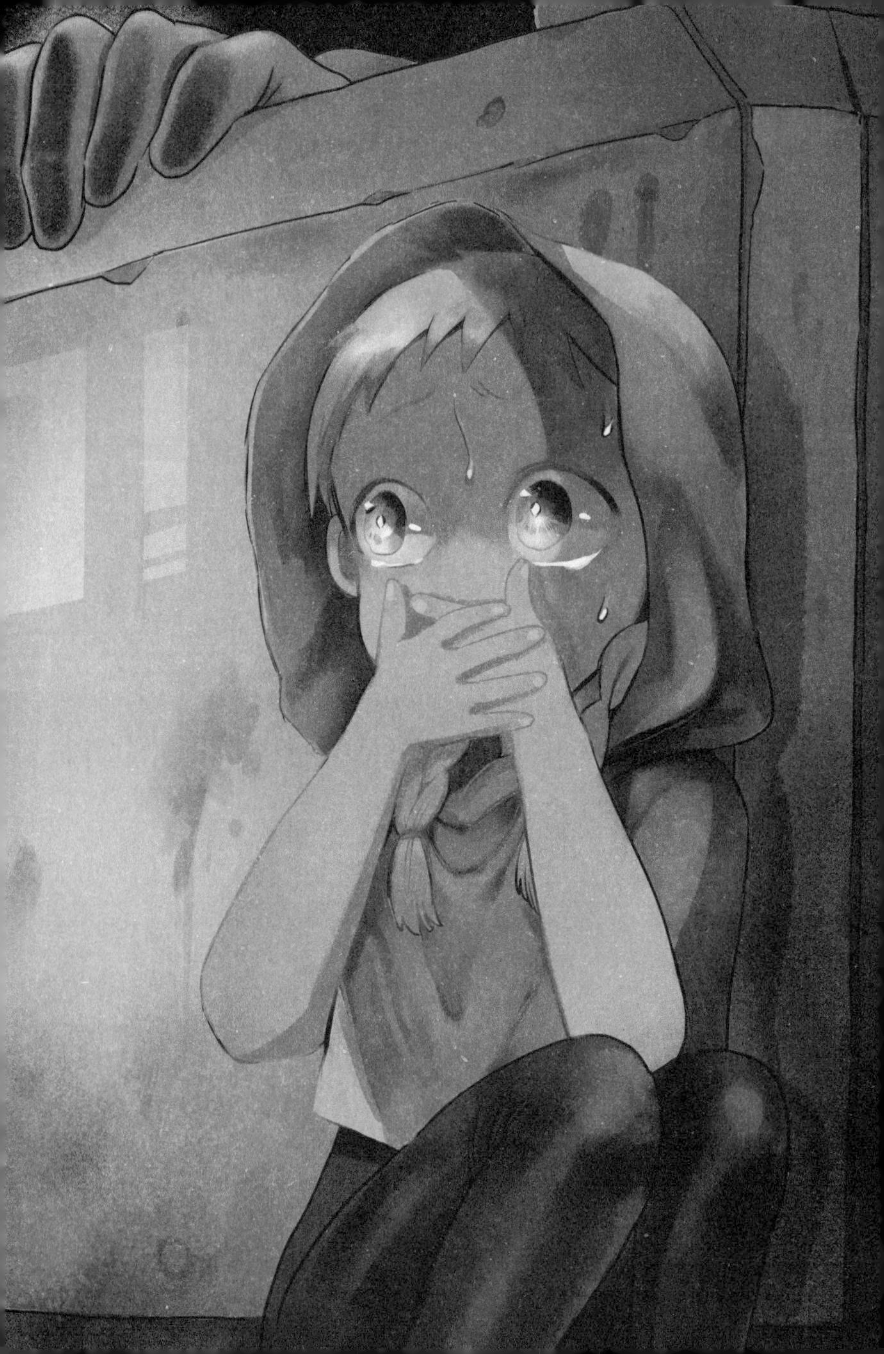

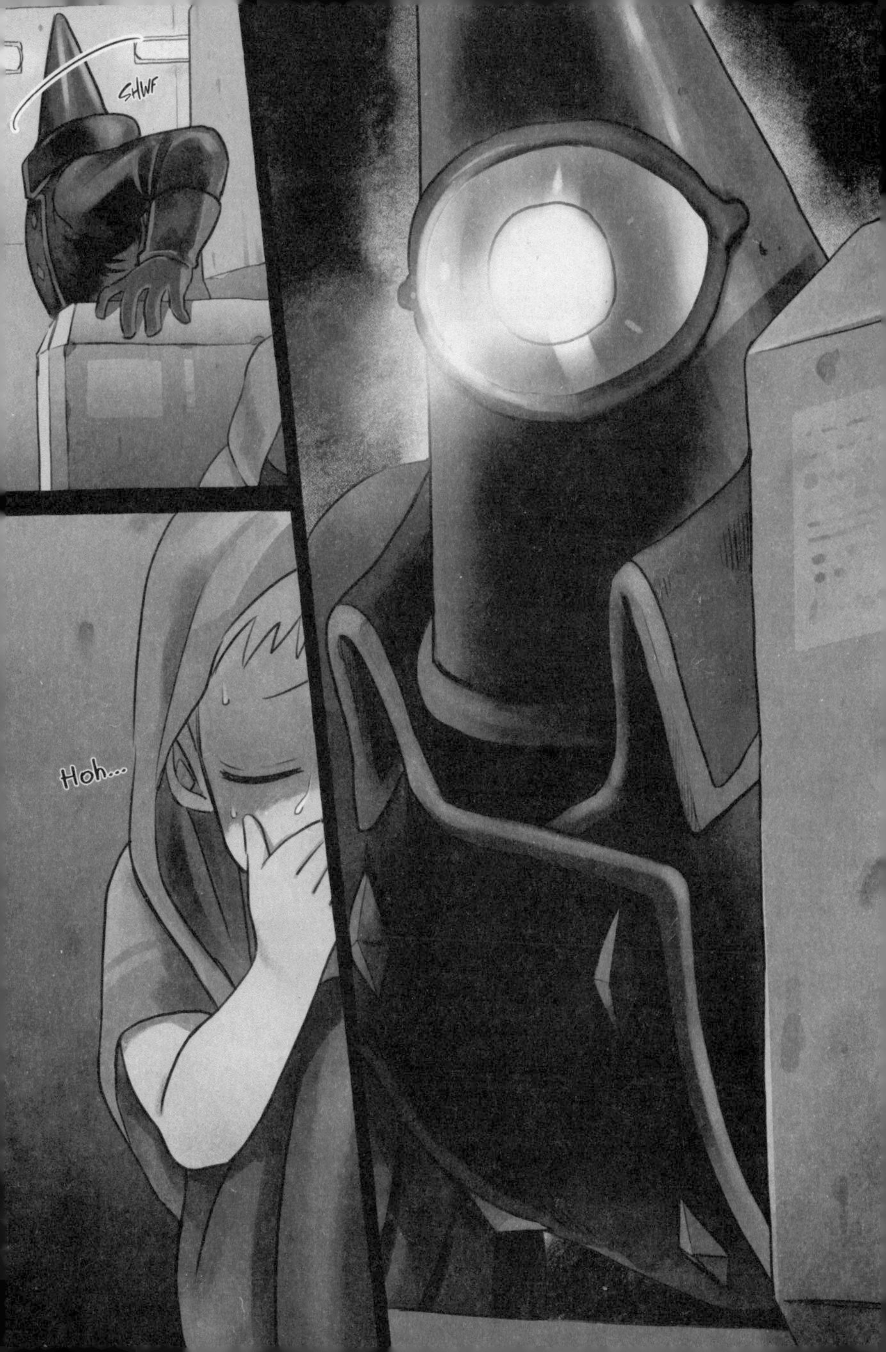
SHWF
Hoh...

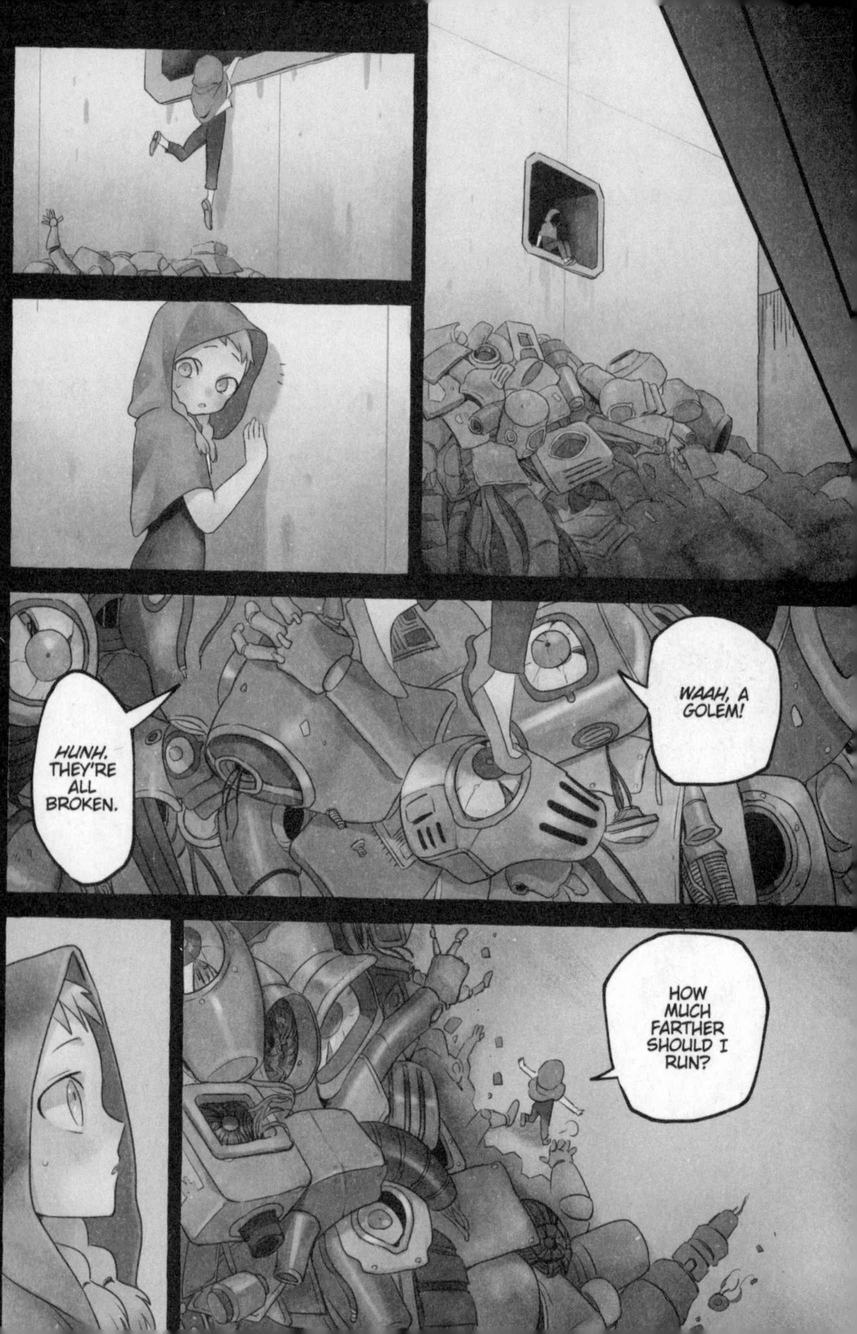
WAAH, A GOLEM!
HUNH. THEY'RE ALL BROKEN.
HOW MUCH FARTHER SHOULD I RUN?

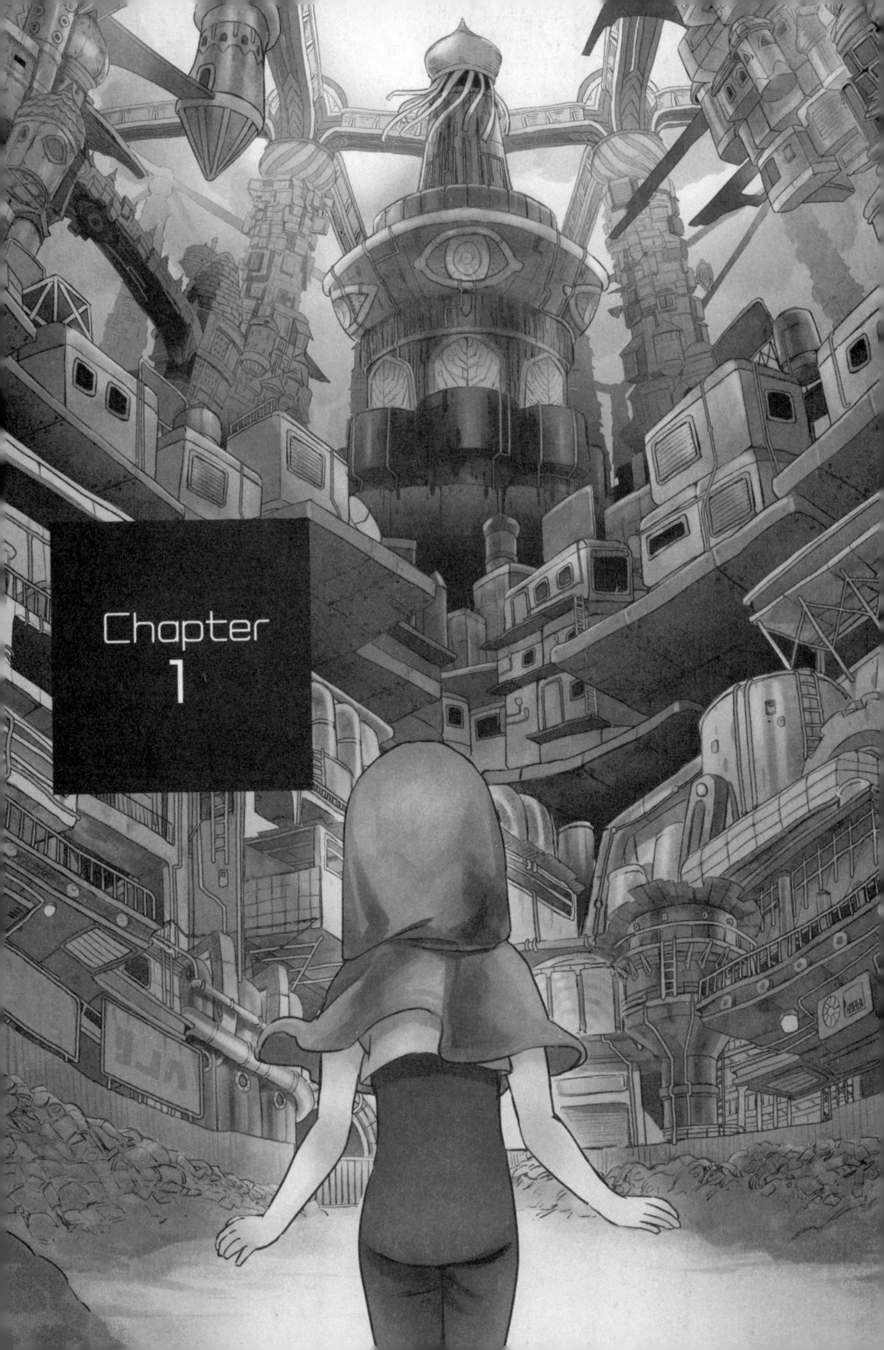
Chapter
1

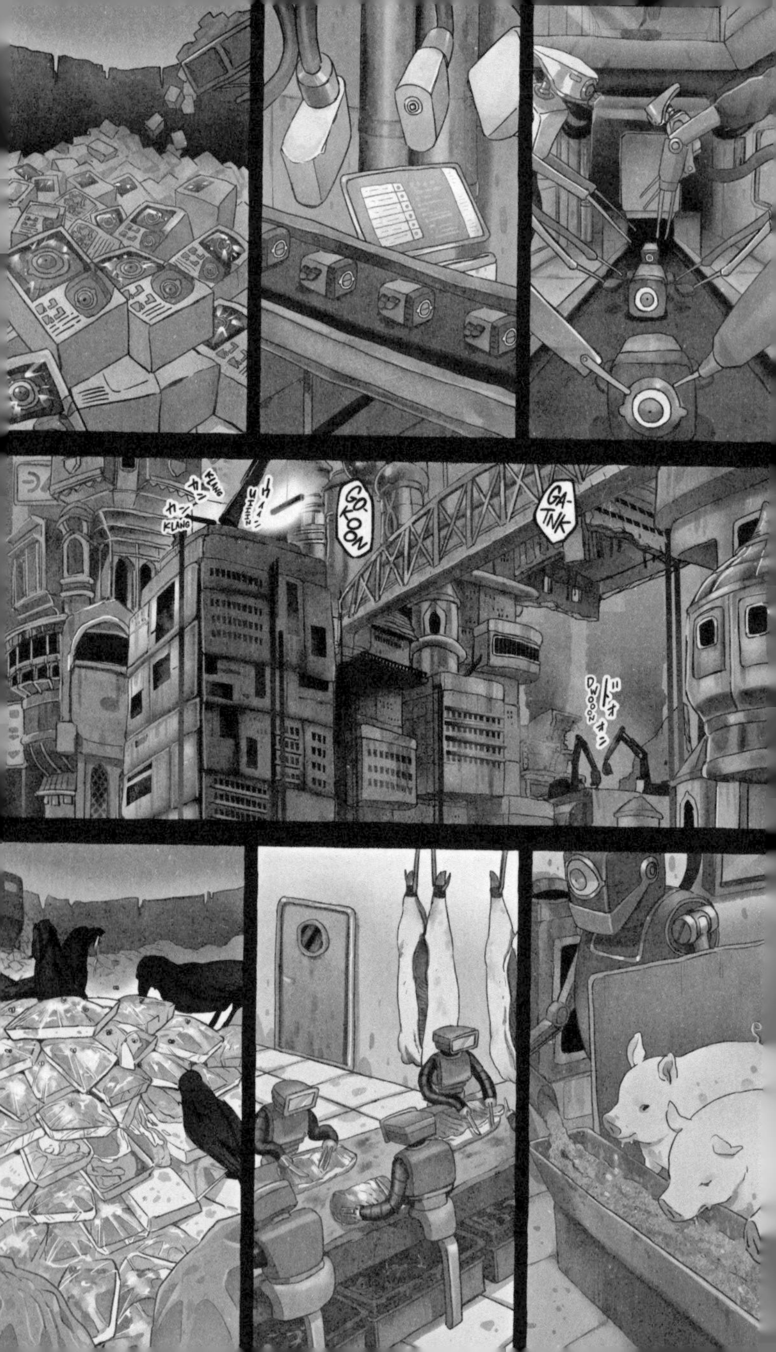
GA-TNK
GO-KOON
ウィィーン
UIIIIN
カン
KLANG
カン
KLANG
ドォオオン
DWOOOON

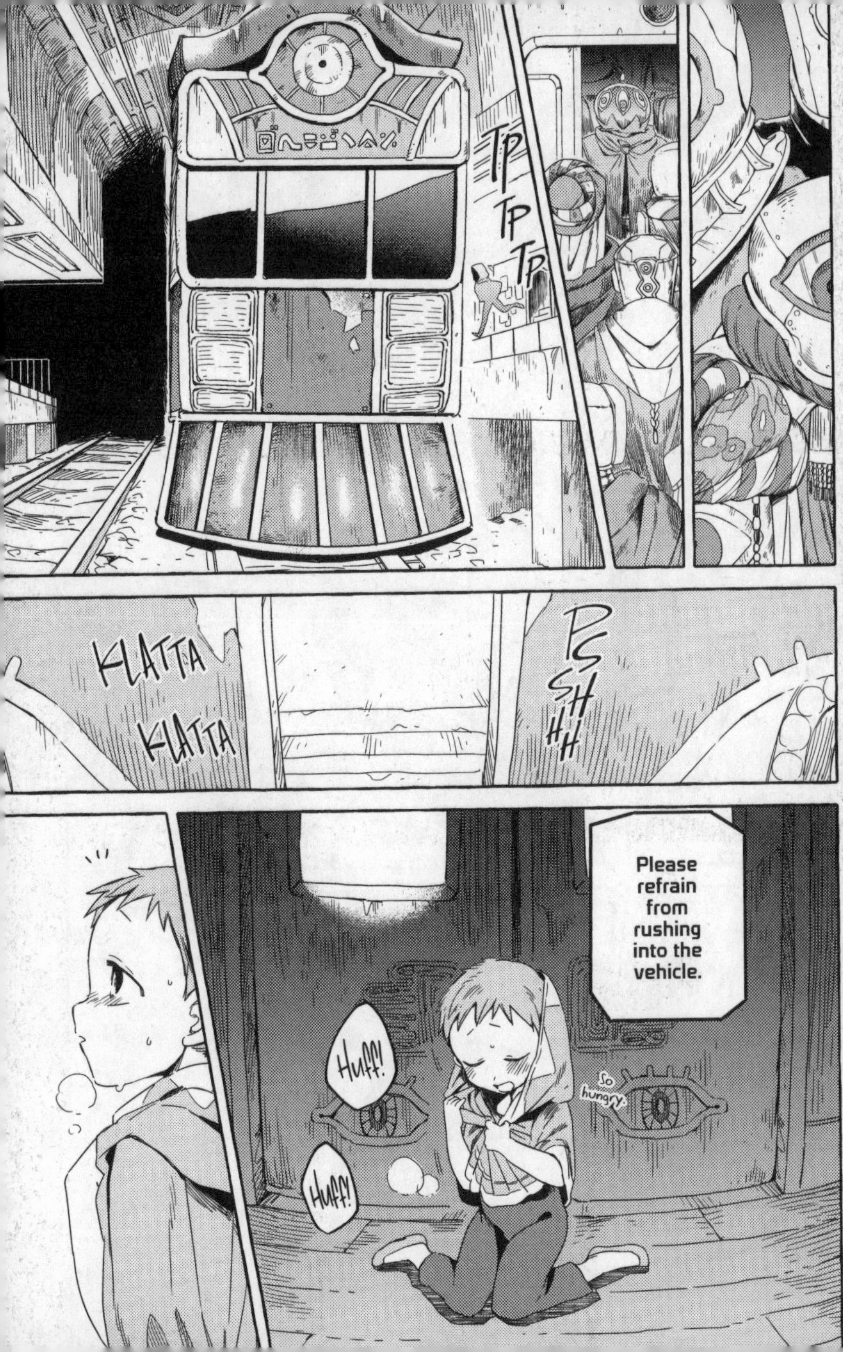
TP TP TP TP
PSHHH
KLATTA KLATTA
Please refrain from rushing into the vehicle.
So hungry.
Huff!
Huff!

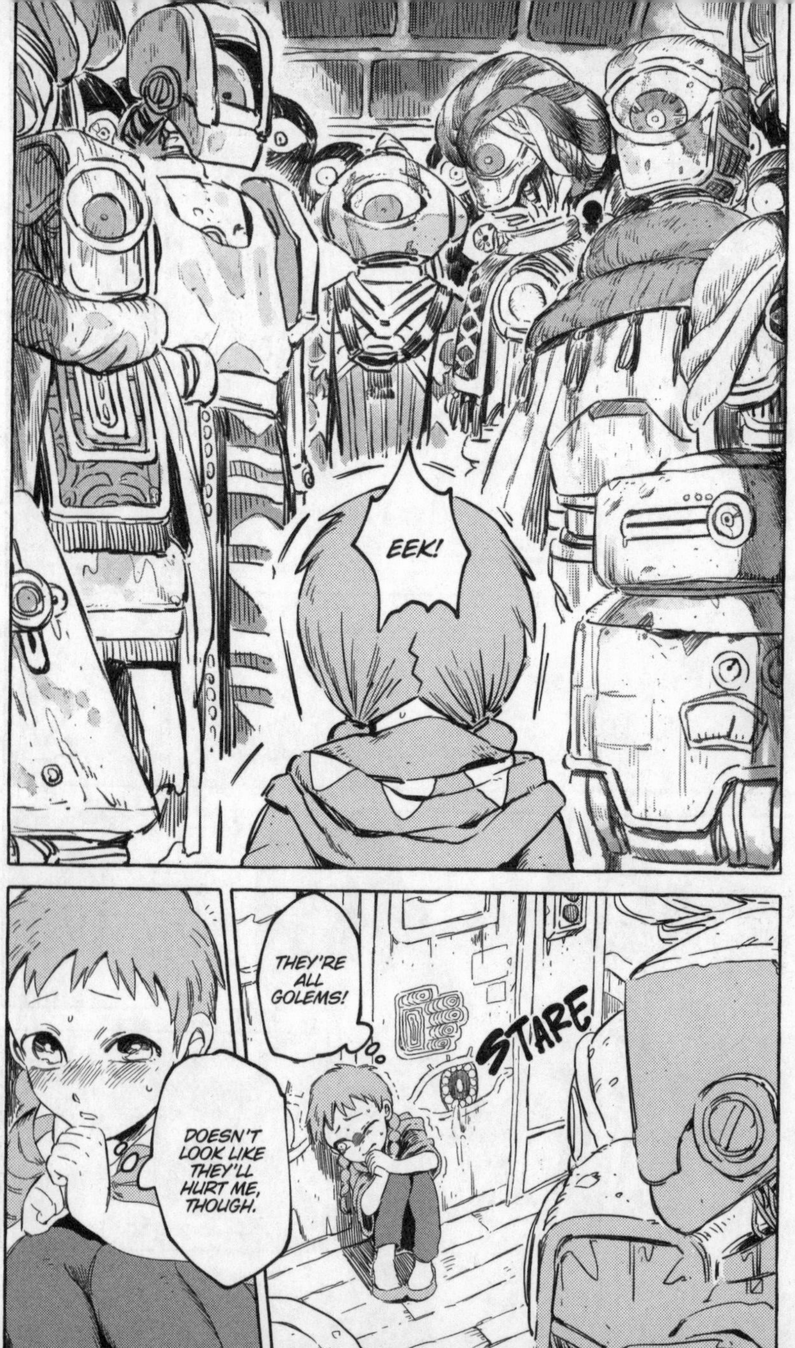
EEK!
THEY'RE ALL GOLEMS!
STARE
DOESN'T LOOK LIKE THEY'LL HURT ME, THOUGH.

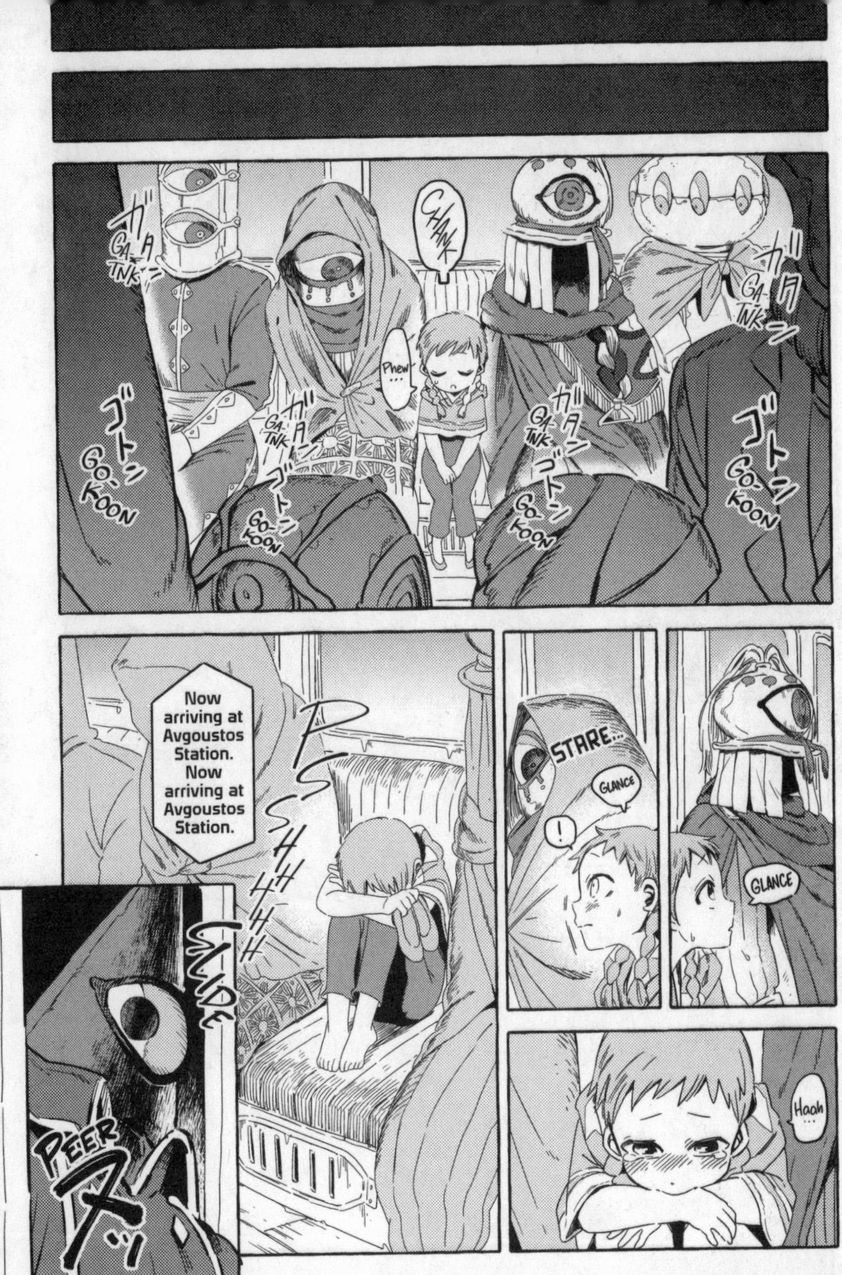

ガタン GA-TNK
ゴトン GO-KOON
CHANK
ガタン GA-TNK
Phew...
ガタン GA-TNK
ゴトン GO-KOON
ガタン GA-TNK
ゴトン GO-KOON
ゴトン GO-KOON
GLANCE
STARE...
GLANCE
!
Haah...
Now arriving at Avgoustos Station. Now arriving at Avgoustos Station.
PSSHHHHHH
GLIDE
PEER

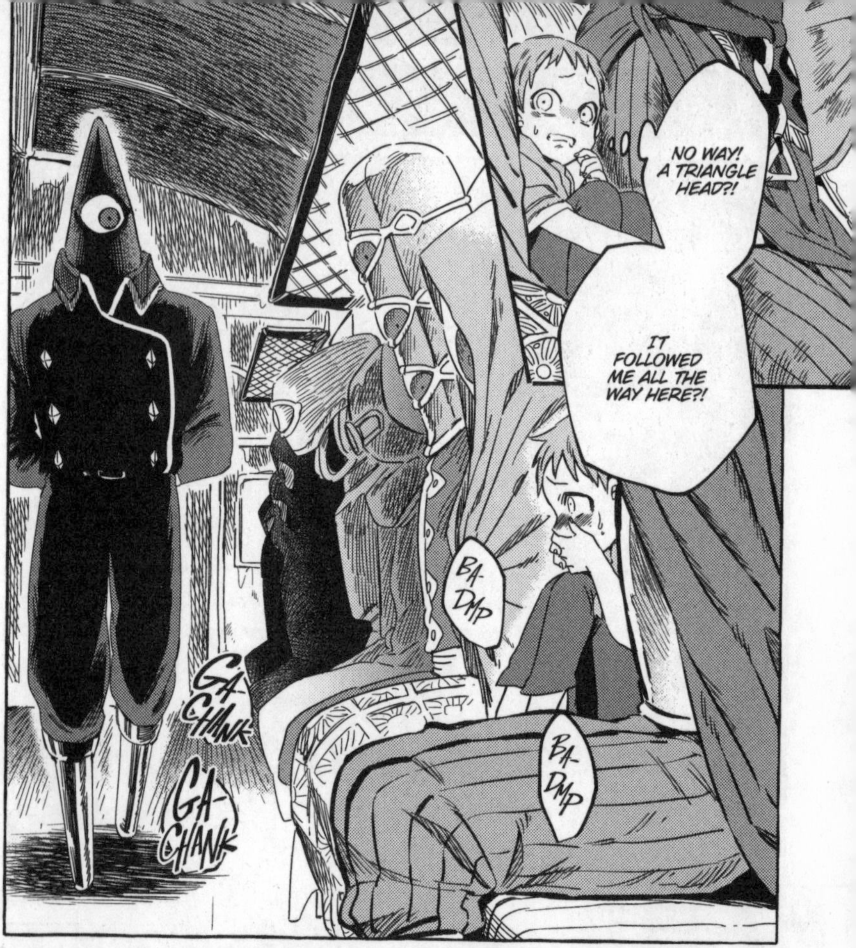
NO WAY! A TRIANGLE HEAD?!
IT FOLLOWED ME ALL THE WAY HERE?!
BA-DMP
BA-DMP
GA-CHANK
GA-CHANK

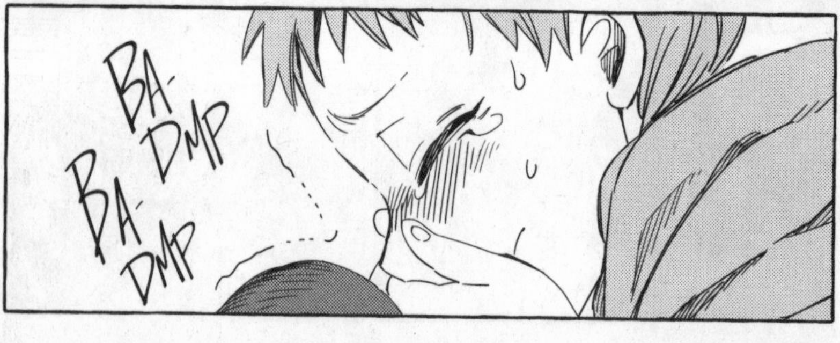
BA-DMP
BA-DMP

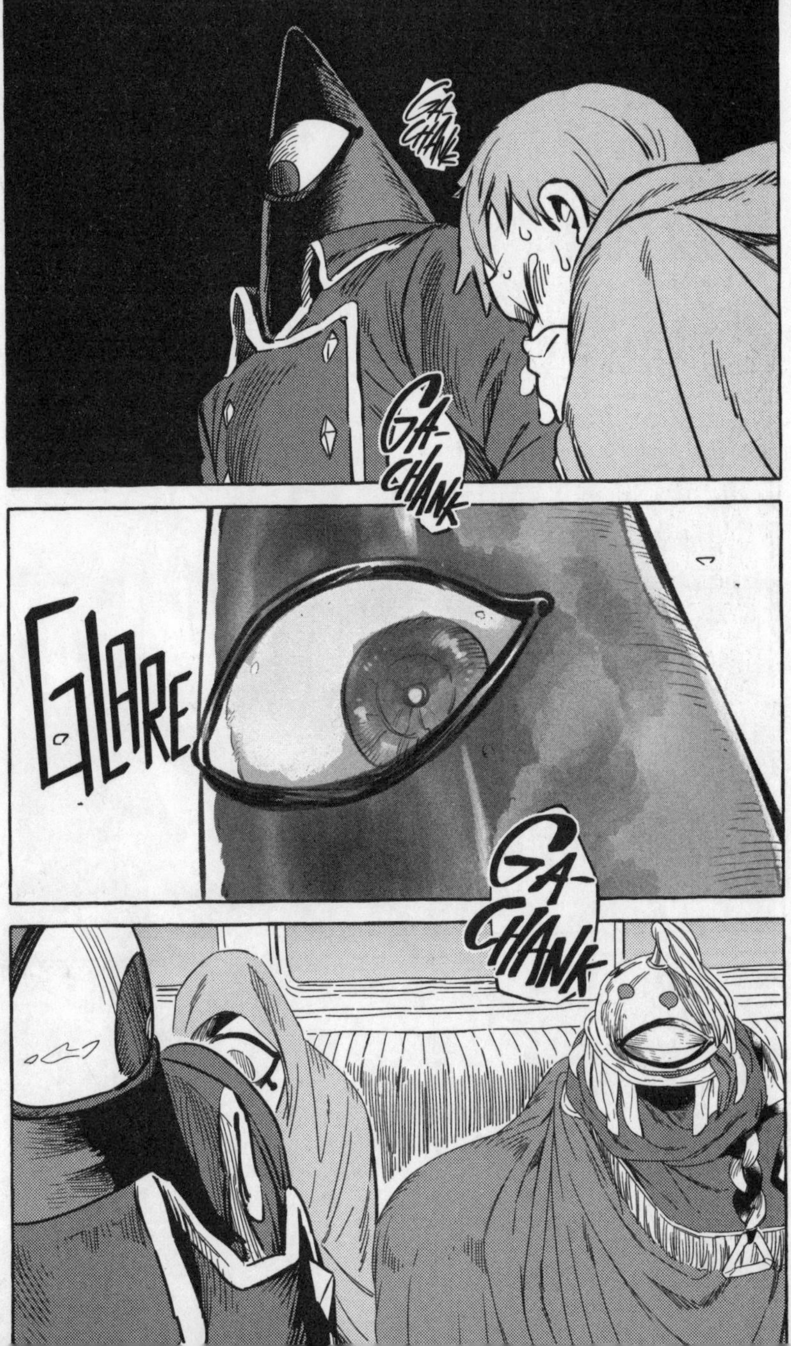
GA-CHANK
GA-CHANK
GLARE
GA-CHANK

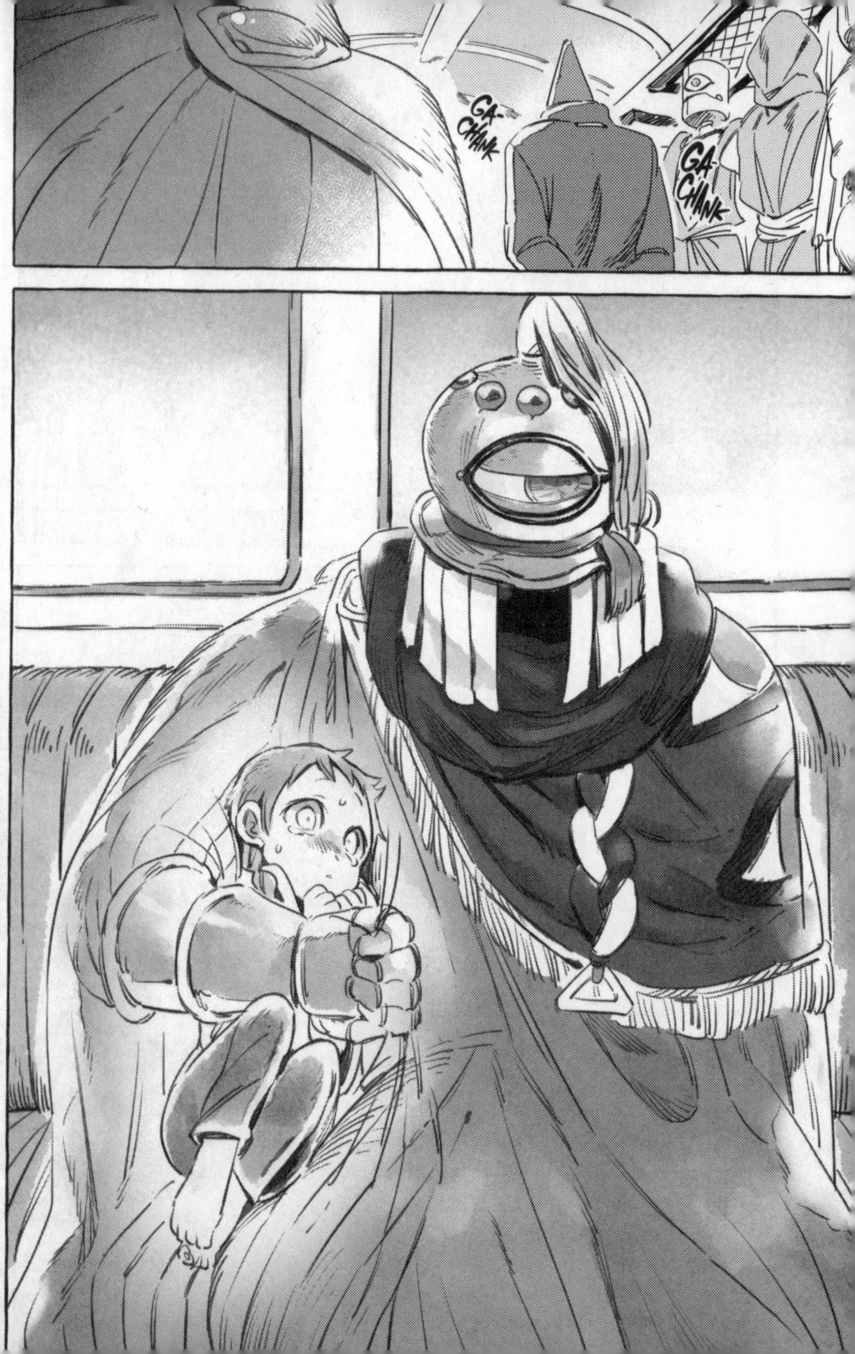
GA-CHANK
GA-CHANK

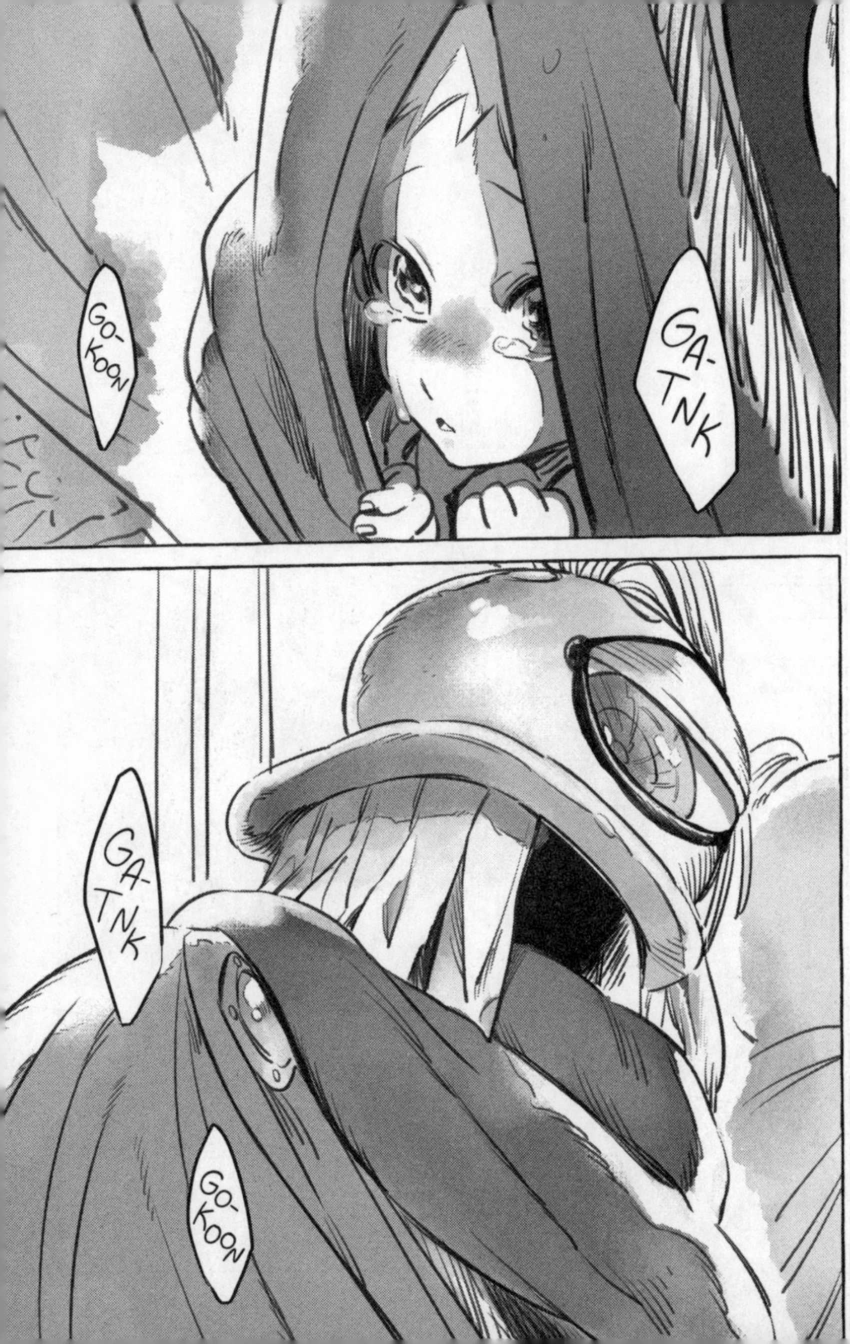
GA-TNK
GO-KOON
GA-TNK
GO-KOON

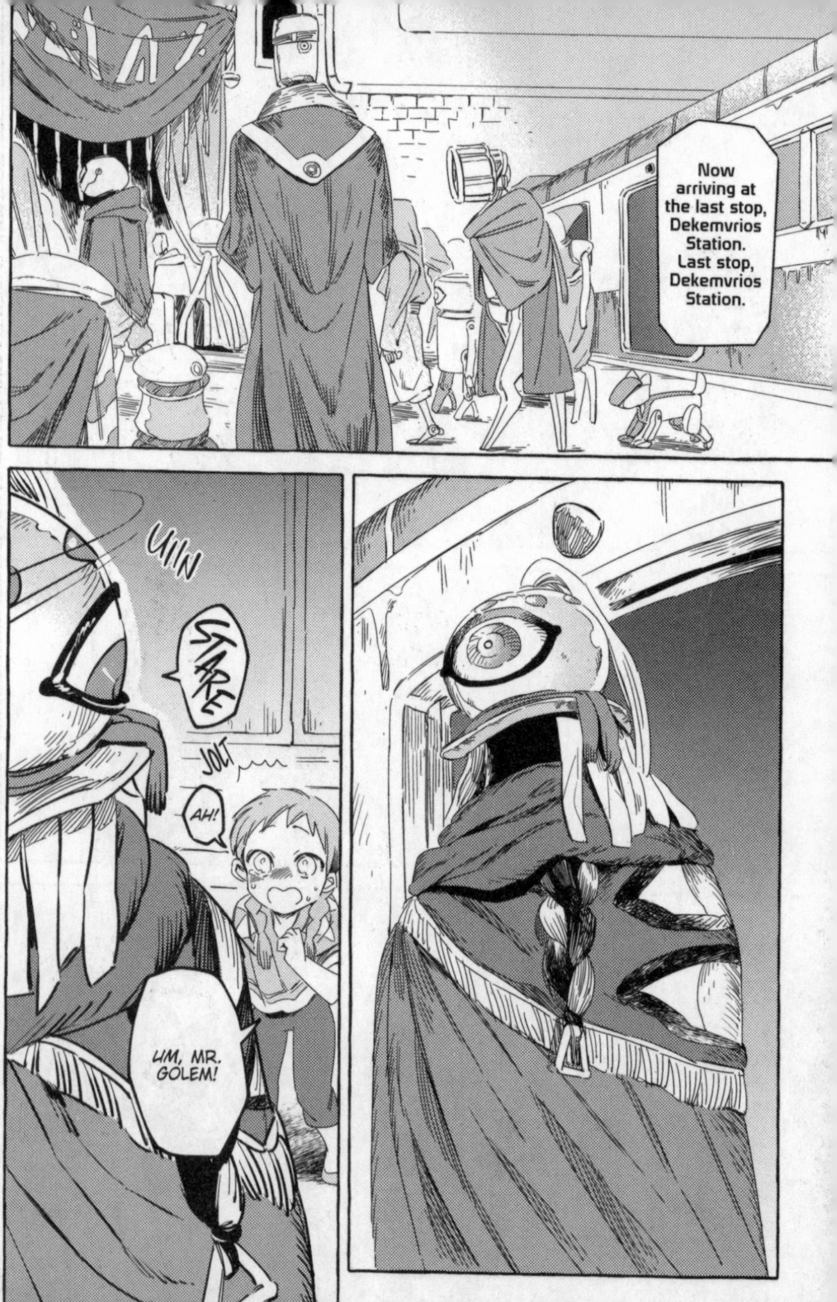
Now arriving at the last stop, Dekemvrios Station. Last stop, Dekemvrios Station.
UIIN
STARE
JOLT
AH!
UM, MR. GOLEM!

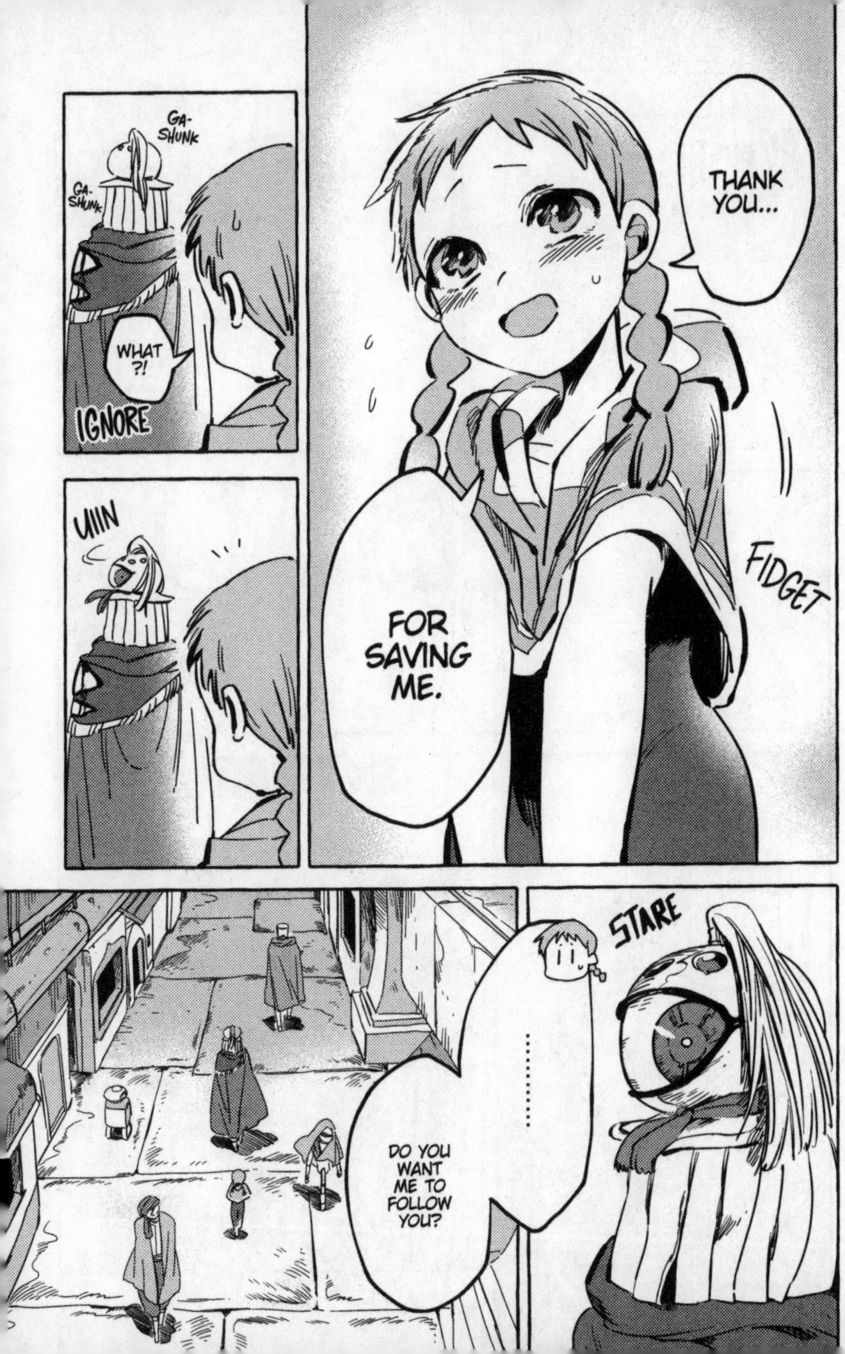
THANK YOU...
FOR SAVING ME.
FIDGET
GA-SHUNK
GA-SHUNK
WHAT?!
IGNORE
UIIN
STARE
......
DO YOU WANT ME TO FOLLOW YOU?

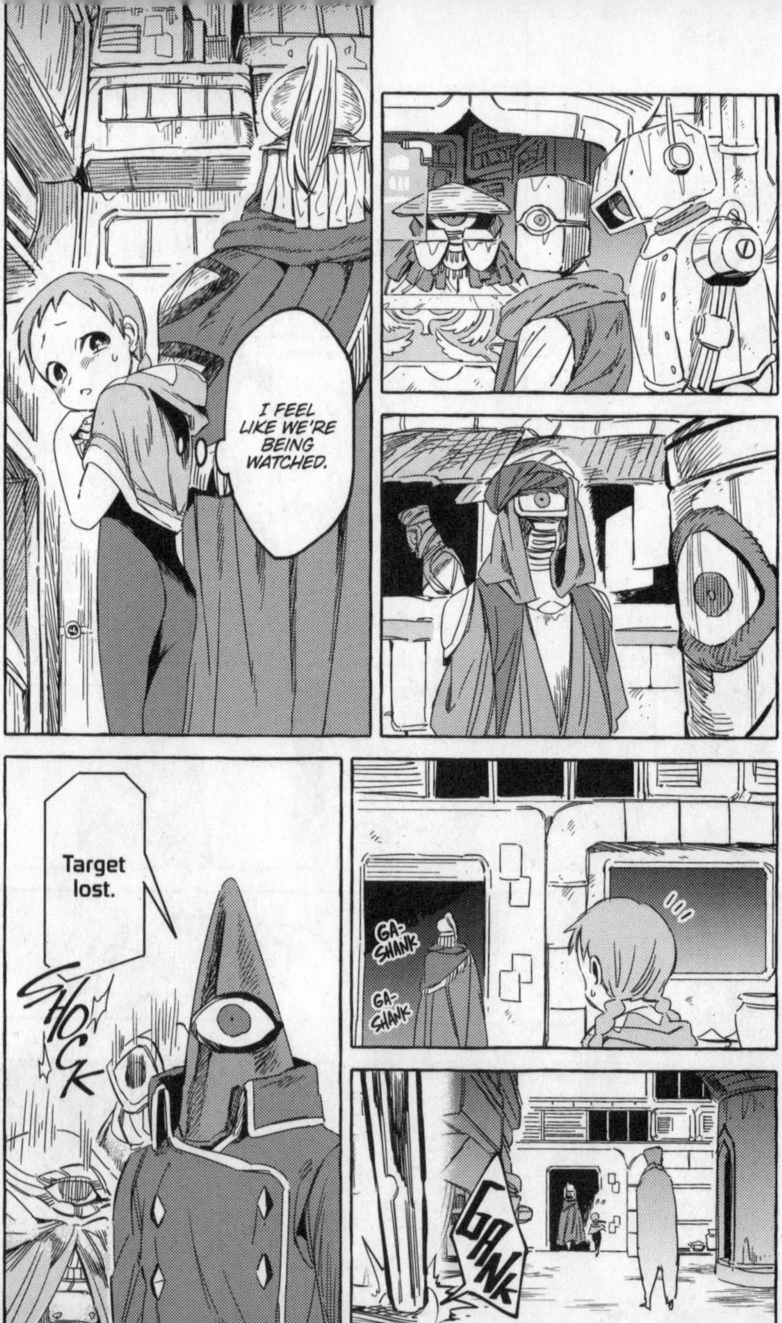
I FEEL LIKE WE'RE BEING WATCHED.
GA-SHANK
GA-SHANK
GANK
Target lost.
SHOCK

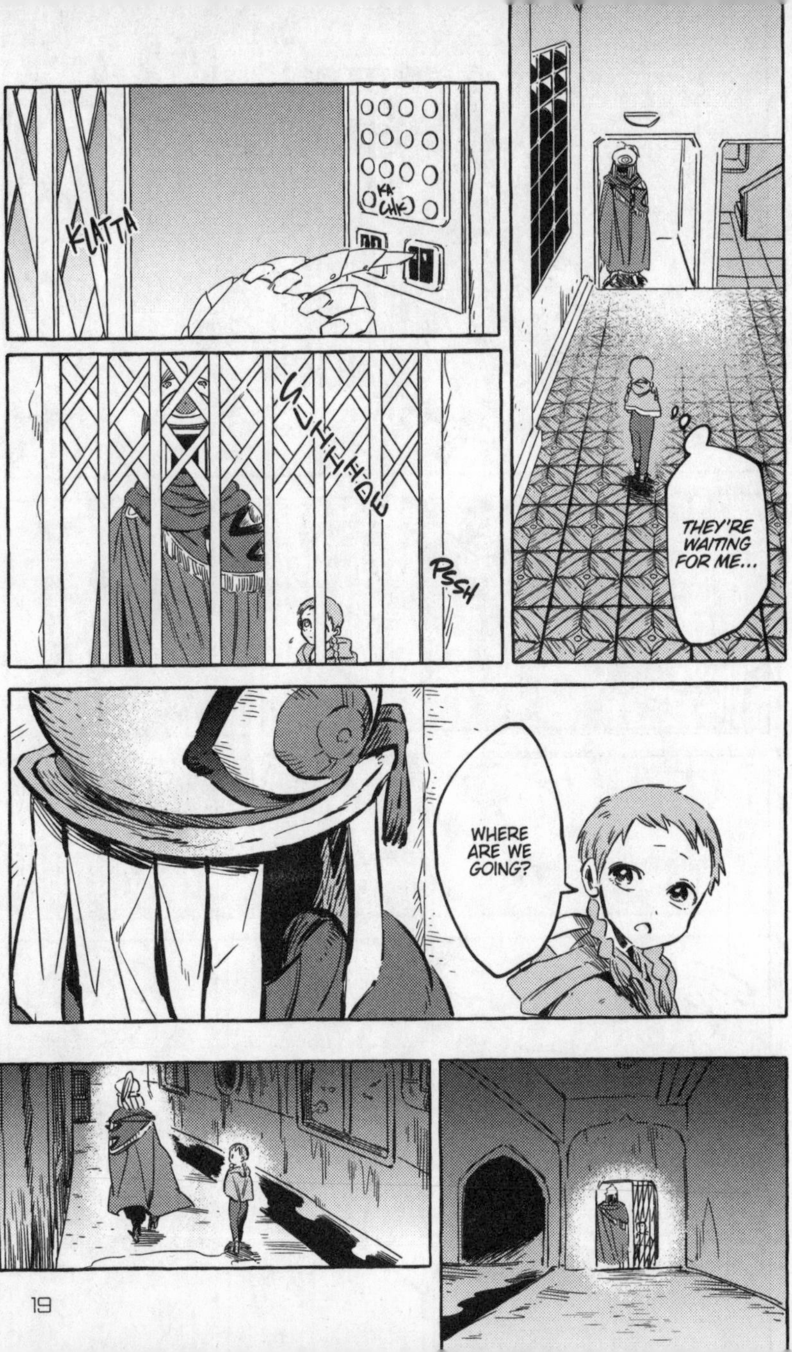
THEY'RE WAITING FOR ME...
KLATTA
KA-CHK
SHHHHOM
PSSH
WHERE ARE WE GOING?

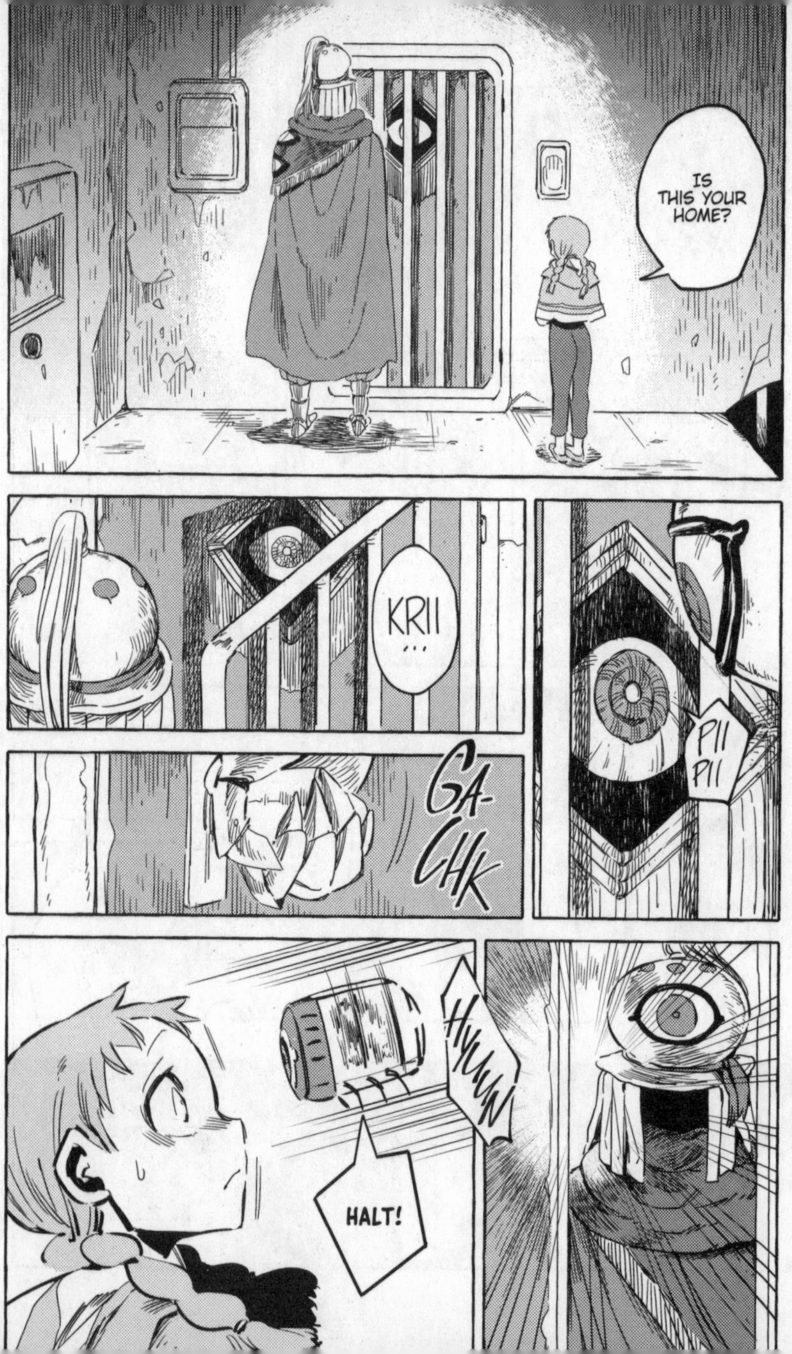
IS THIS YOUR HOME?
PII PII
KRII ...
GA-CHK
HYUUUN
HALT!

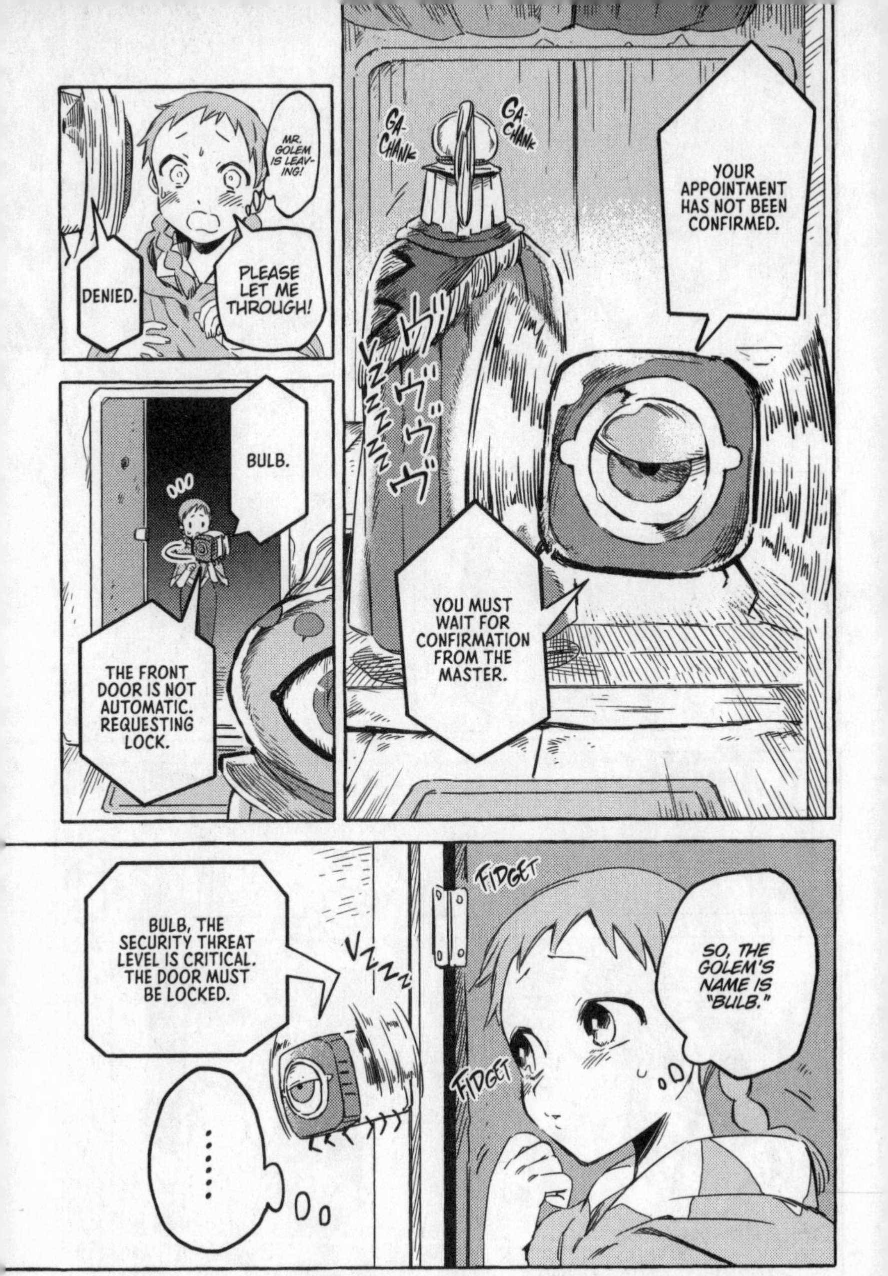
GA-CHANK
GA-CHANK
YOUR APPOINTMENT HAS NOT BEEN CONFIRMED.
VZZZZZZ
ヴヴヴヴ
YOU MUST WAIT FOR CONFIRMATION FROM THE MASTER.
MR. GOLEM IS LEAVING!
PLEASE LET ME THROUGH!
DENIED.
BULB.
OOO
THE FRONT DOOR IS NOT AUTOMATIC. REQUESTING LOCK.
FIDGET
SO, THE GOLEM'S NAME IS "BULB."
FIDGET
BULB, THE SECURITY THREAT LEVEL IS CRITICAL. THE DOOR MUST BE LOCKED.
VZZZ
......

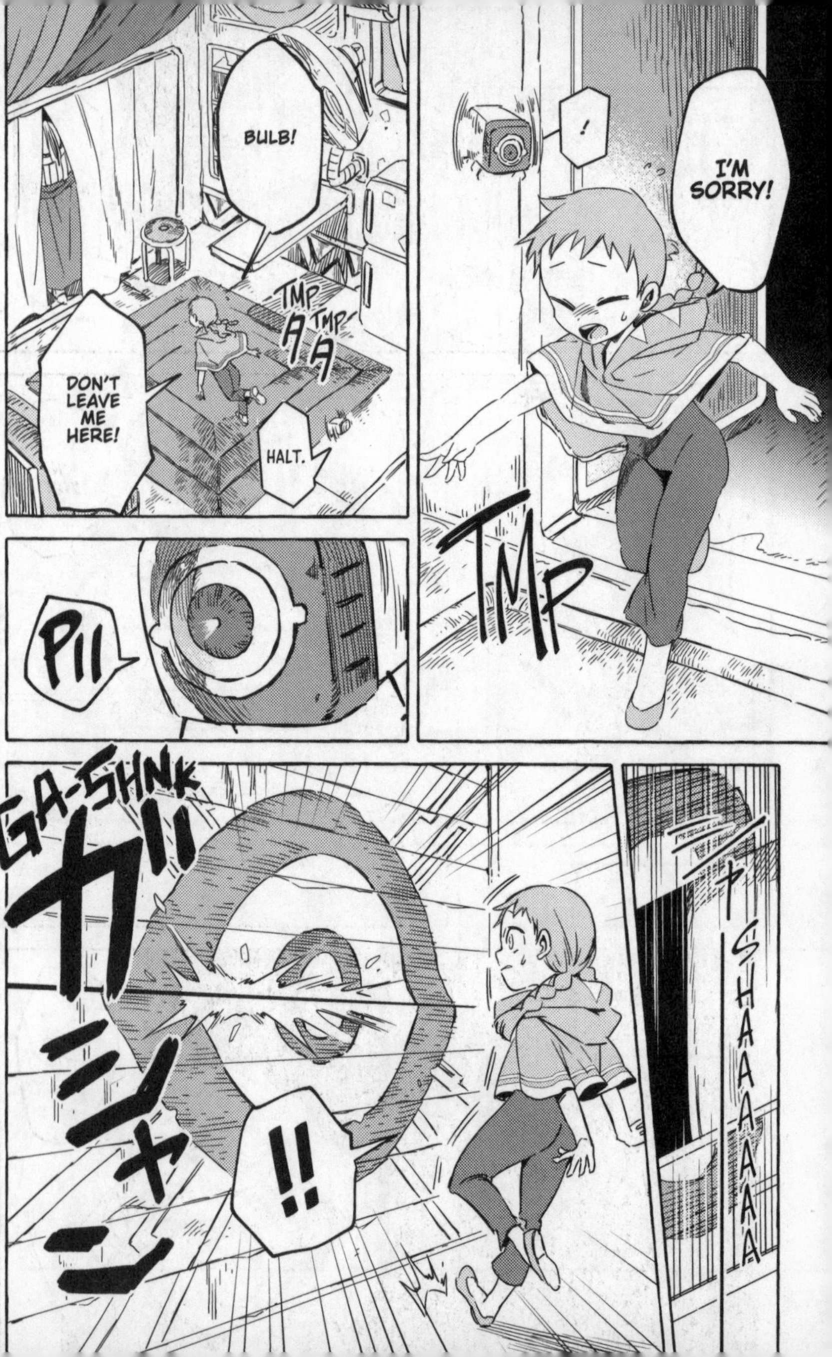
!
I'M SORRY!
TMP
BULB!
TMPA TMPA
DON'T LEAVE ME HERE!
HALT.
PII
SHAAAAAAA
GA-SHNK
!!

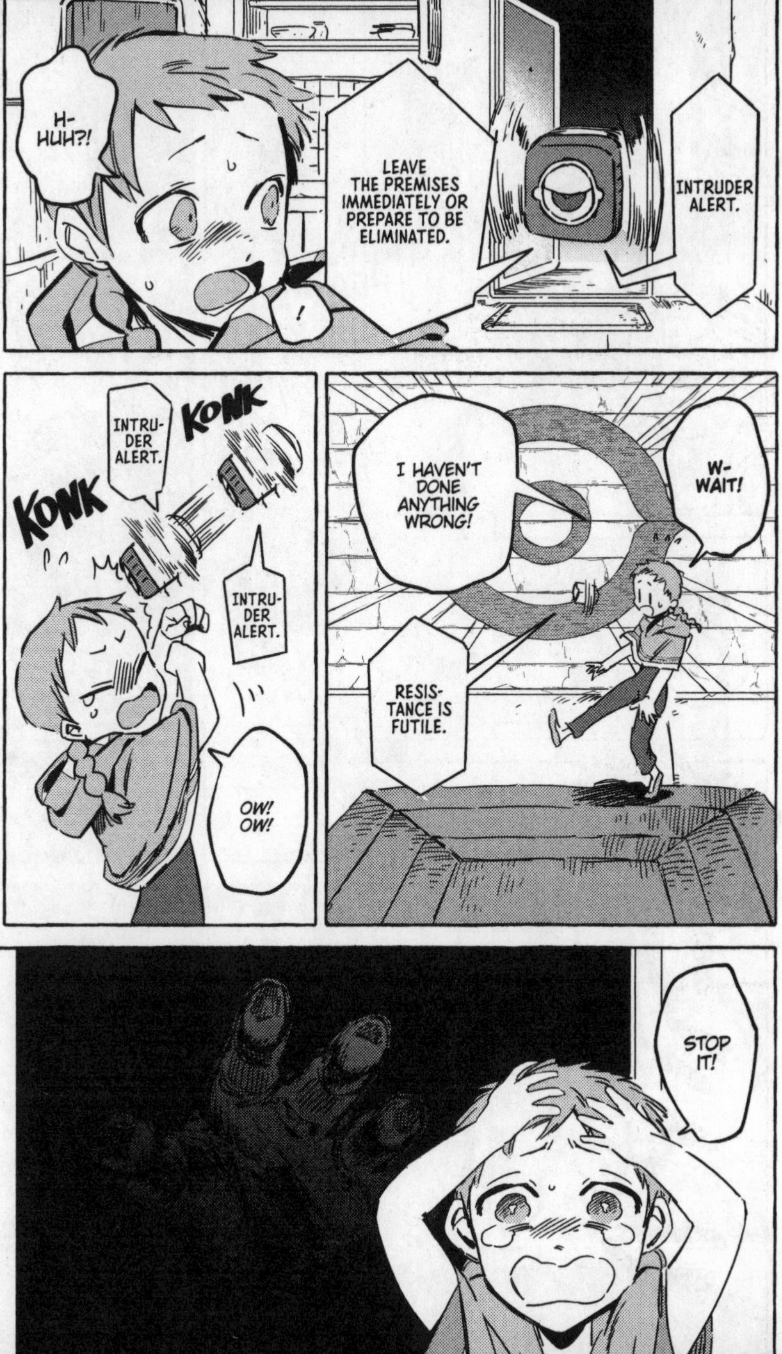
INTRUDER ALERT.
LEAVE THE PREMISES IMMEDIATELY OR PREPARE TO BE ELIMINATED.
H-HUH?!
!
W-WAIT!
I HAVEN'T DONE ANYTHING WRONG!
RESISTANCE IS FUTILE.
INTRU-DER ALERT.
KONK
KONK
INTRU-DER ALERT.
OW! OW!
STOP IT!

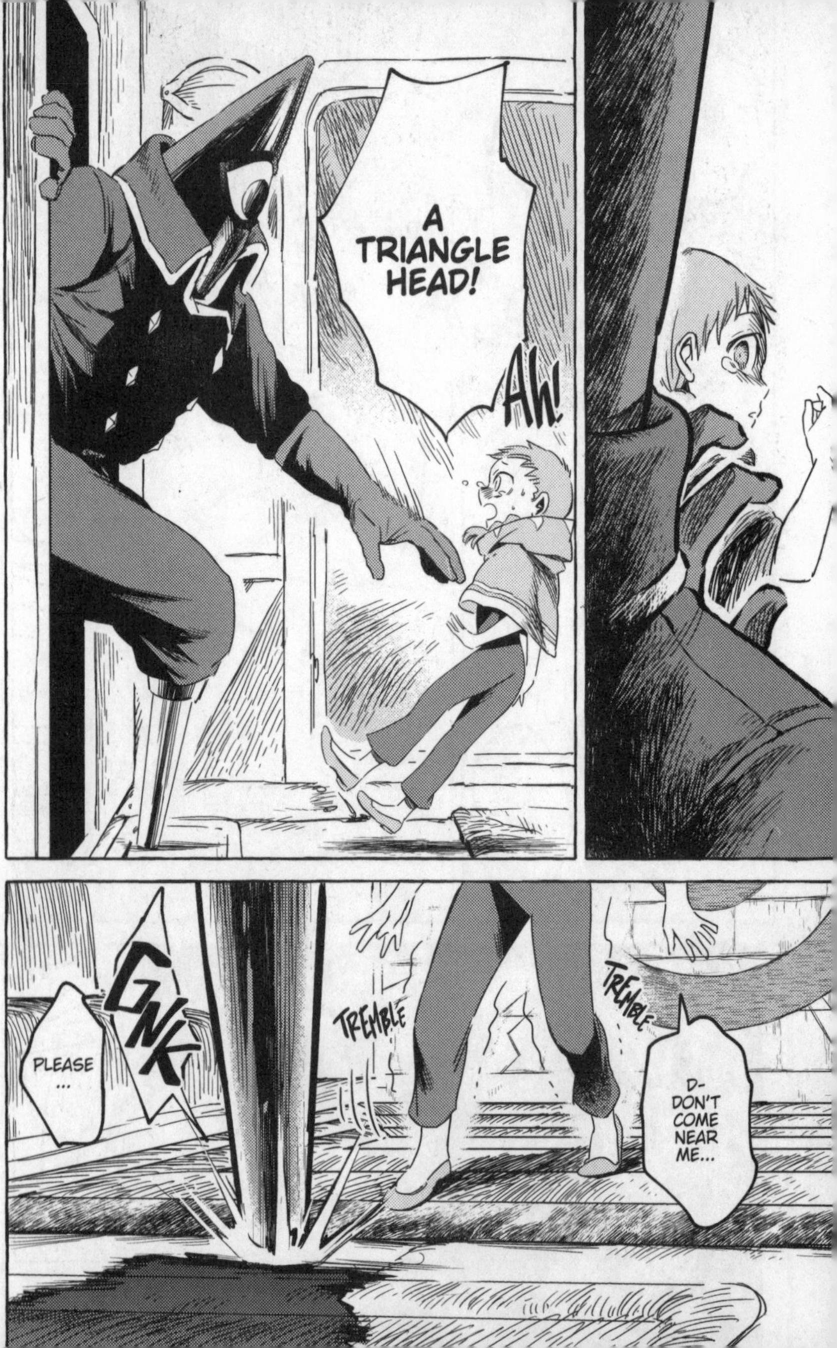
A TRIANGLE HEAD!
AH!
D-DON'T COME NEAR ME...
TREMBLE
TREMBLE
GNK
PLEASE...

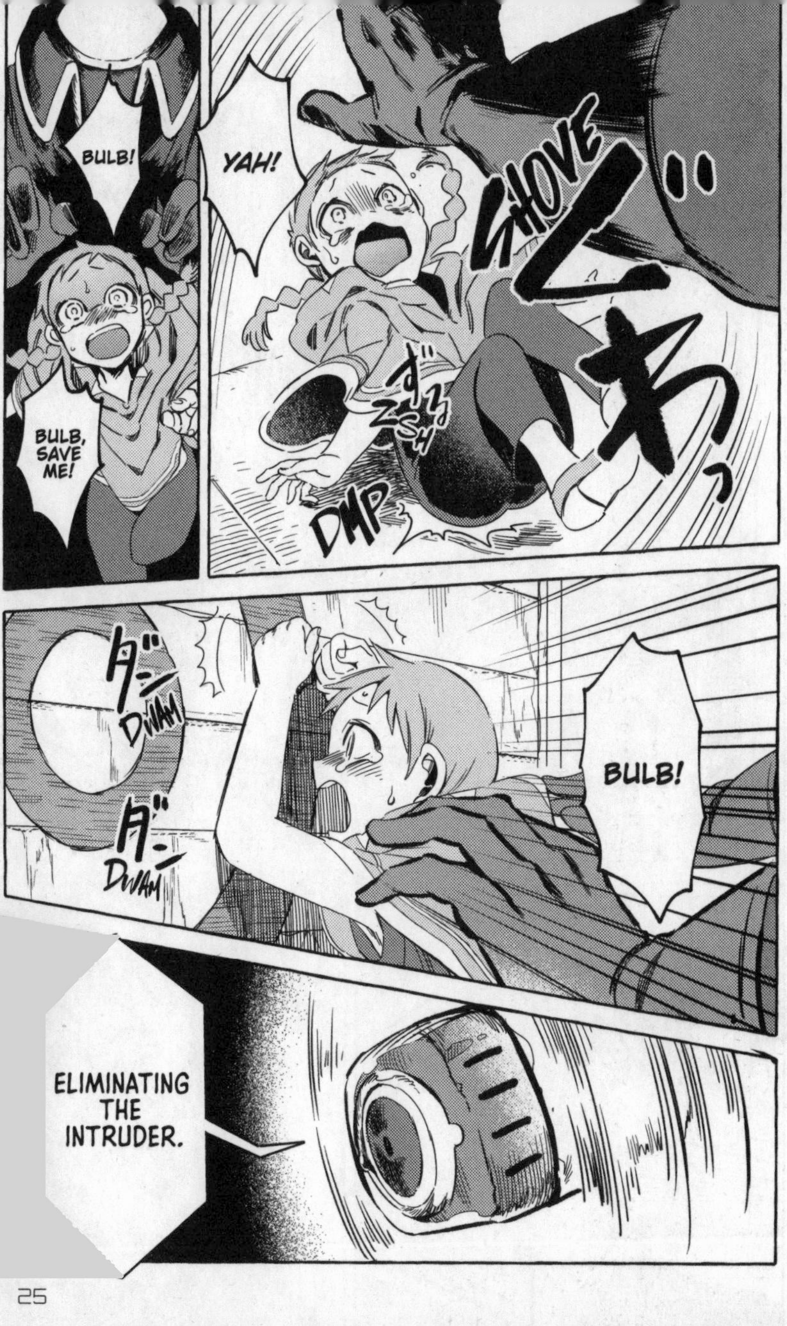
YAH!
SHOVE
ZSH
DMP
BULB!
BULB, SAVE ME!
BULB!
DWAM
DWAM
ELIMINATING THE INTRUDER.

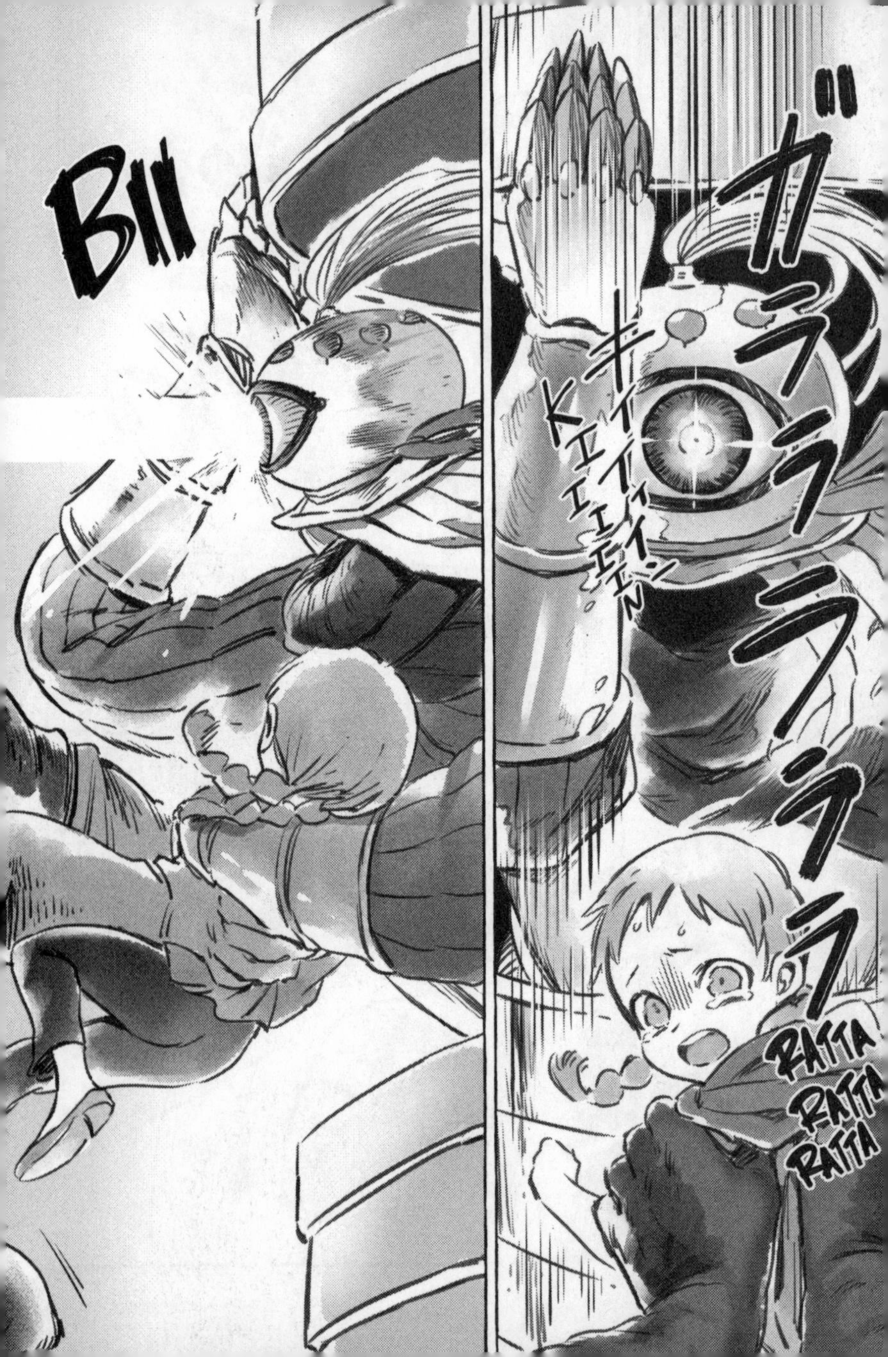
KIIIIIN
RATTA
RATTA
RATTA
BIII

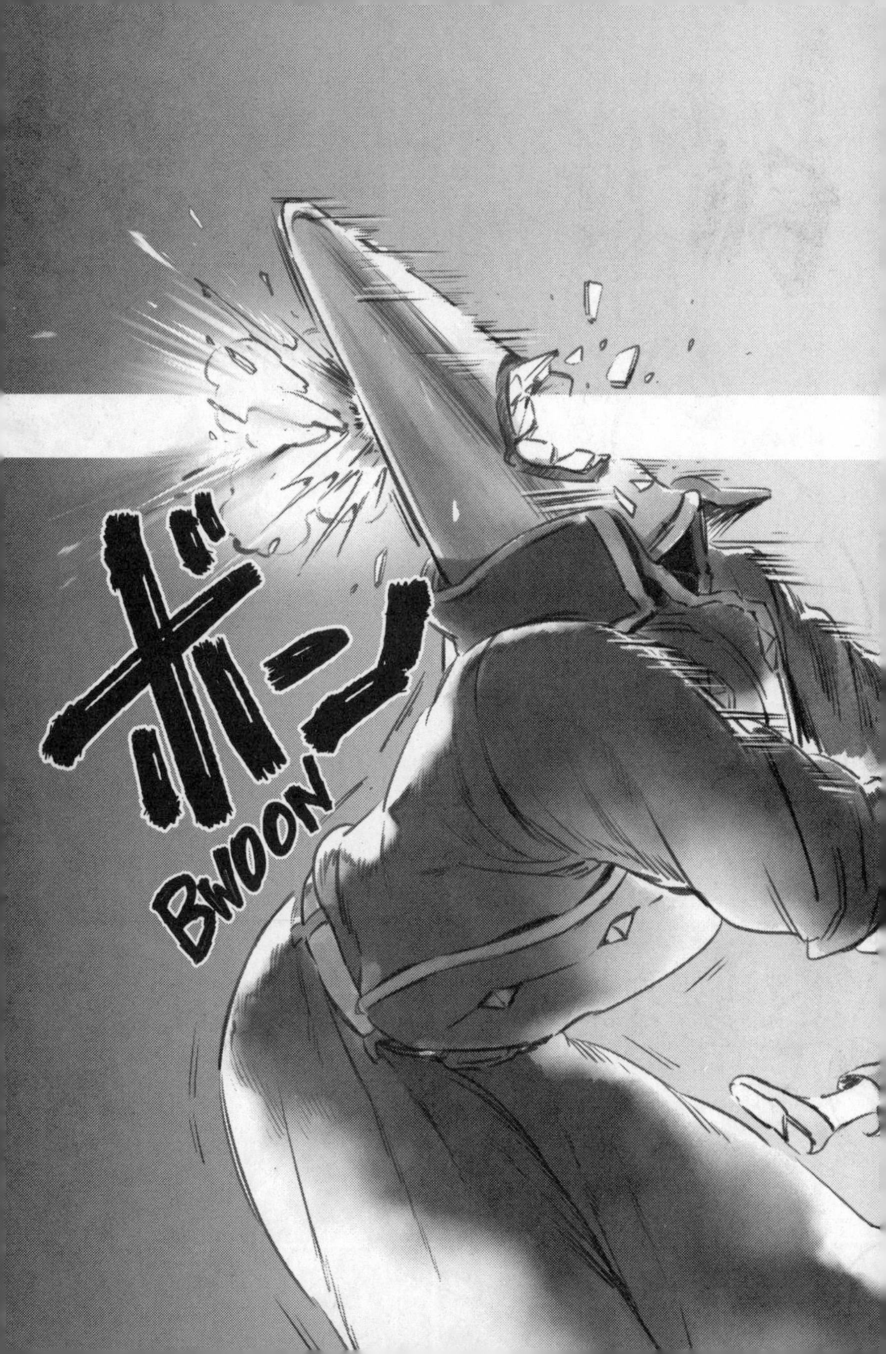
ボーン
BWOON

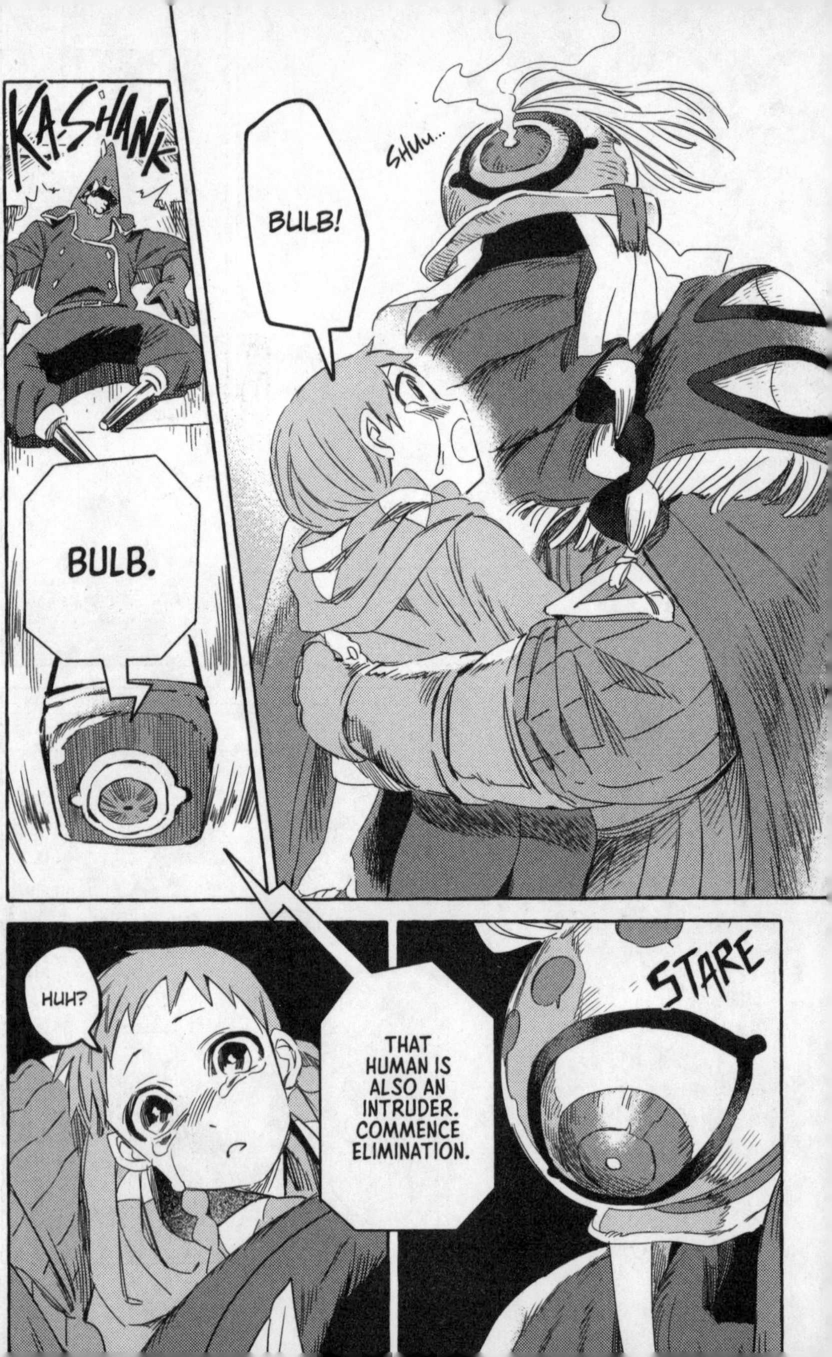
SHUU...
BULB!
KA-SHANK
BULB.
STARE
THAT HUMAN IS ALSO AN INTRUDER. COMMENCE ELIMINATION.
HUH?

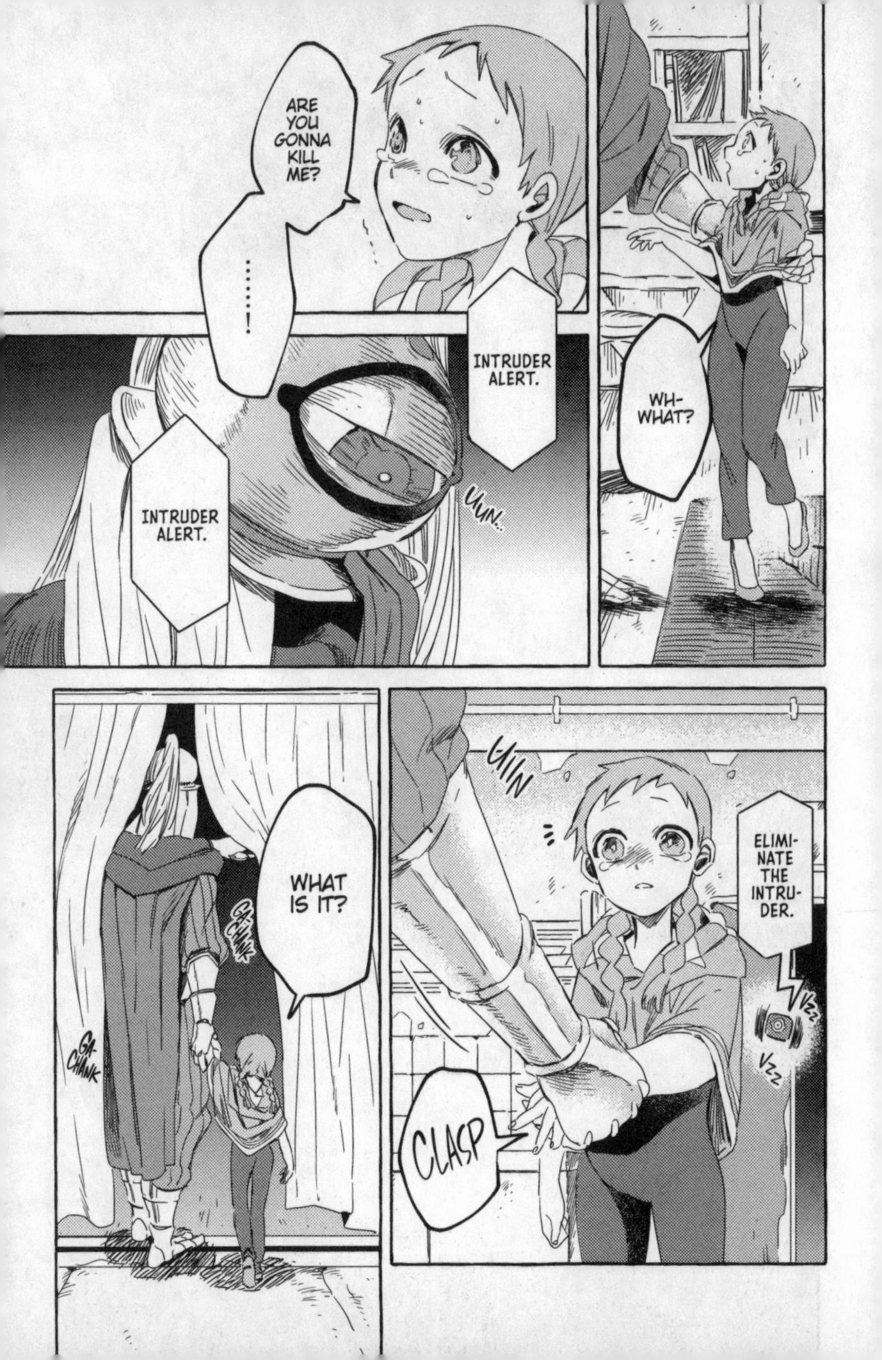
WH-WHAT?
ARE YOU GONNA KILL ME?
......!
INTRUDER ALERT.
UUN..
INTRUDER ALERT.
UIIN
ELIMINATE THE INTRUDER.
VZZ
VZZ
CLASP
WHAT IS IT?
GA-CHANK
GA-CHANK

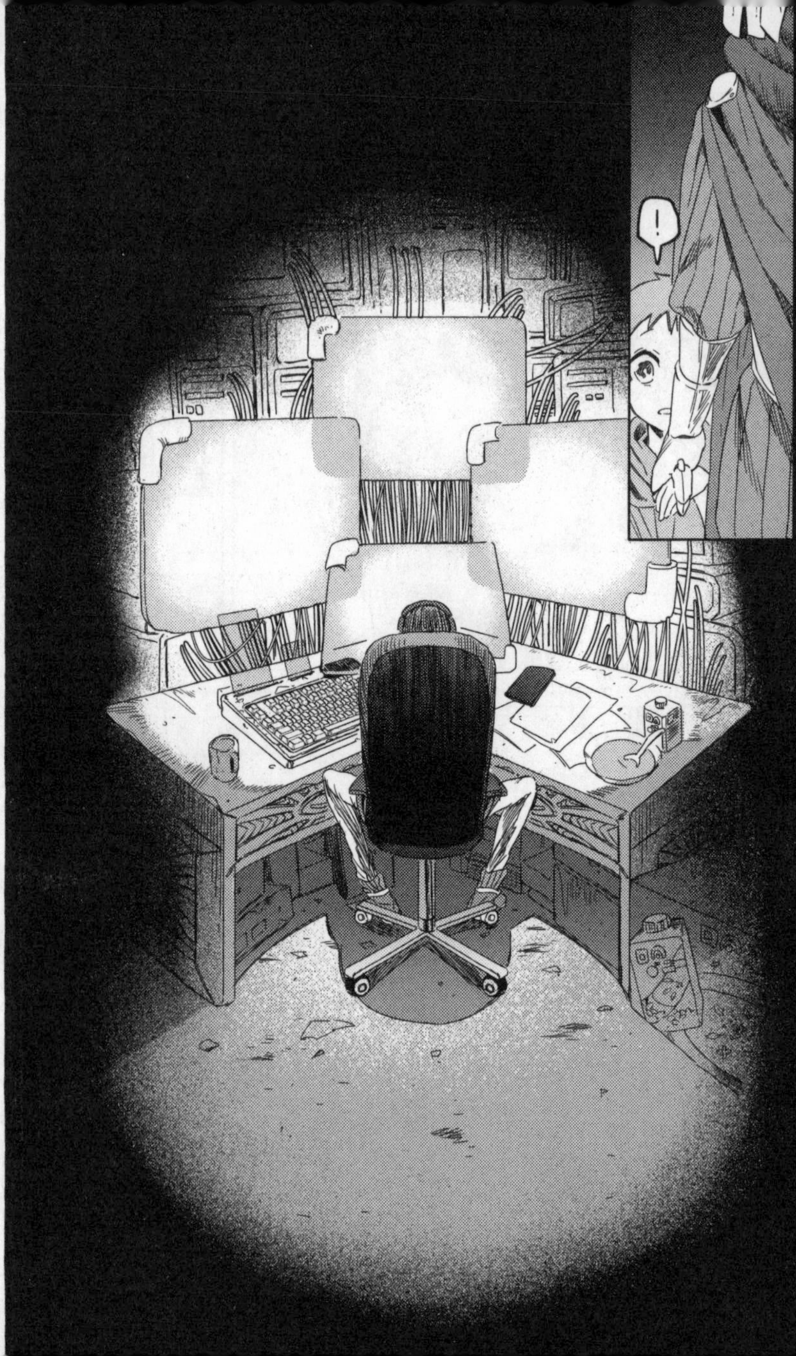
!

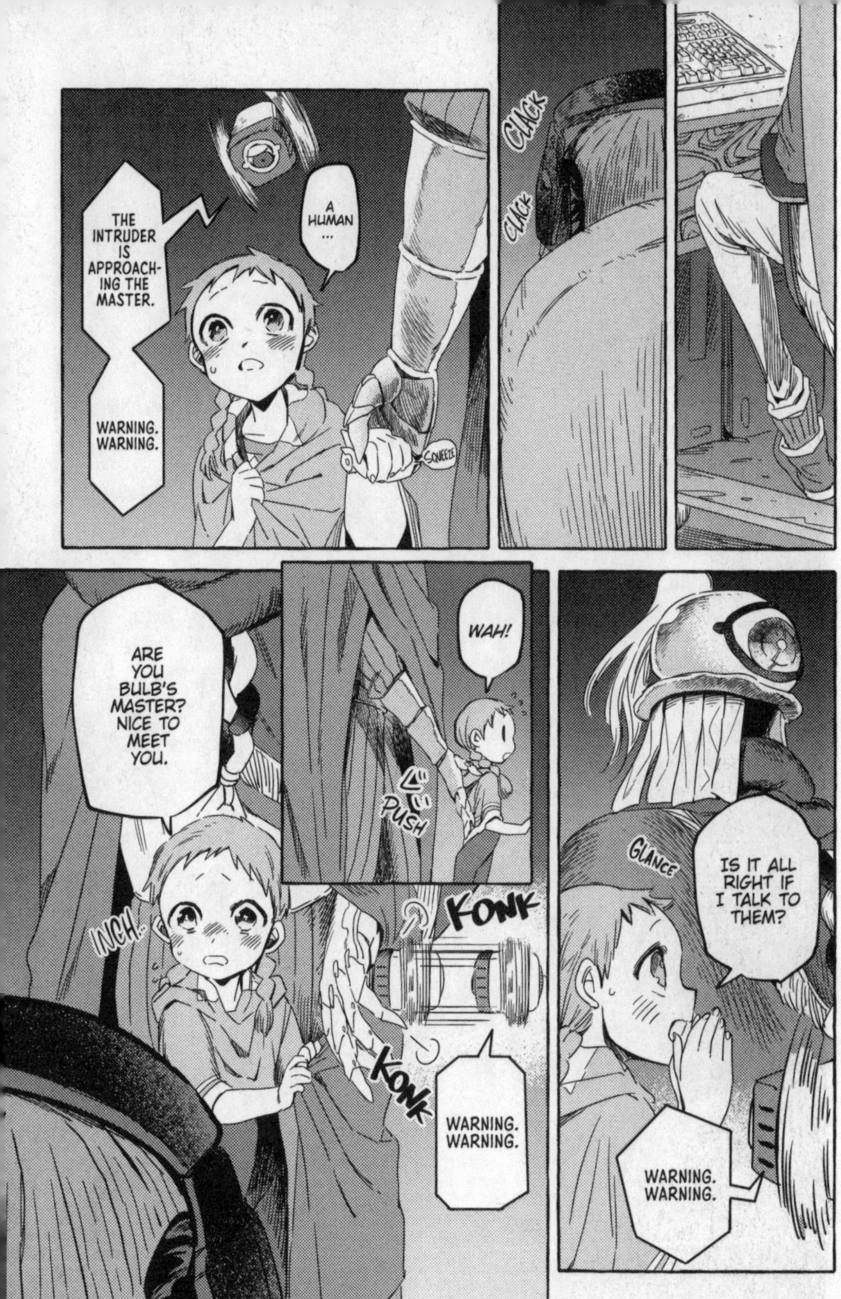
CLACK
CLACK
A HUMAN ...
THE INTRUDER IS APPROACHING THE MASTER.
WARNING. WARNING.
SQUEEZE
IS IT ALL RIGHT IF I TALK TO THEM?
GLANCE
WARNING. WARNING.
WAH!
PUSH
ARE YOU BULB'S MASTER? NICE TO MEET YOU.
KONK
INCH..
KONK
WARNING. WARNING.

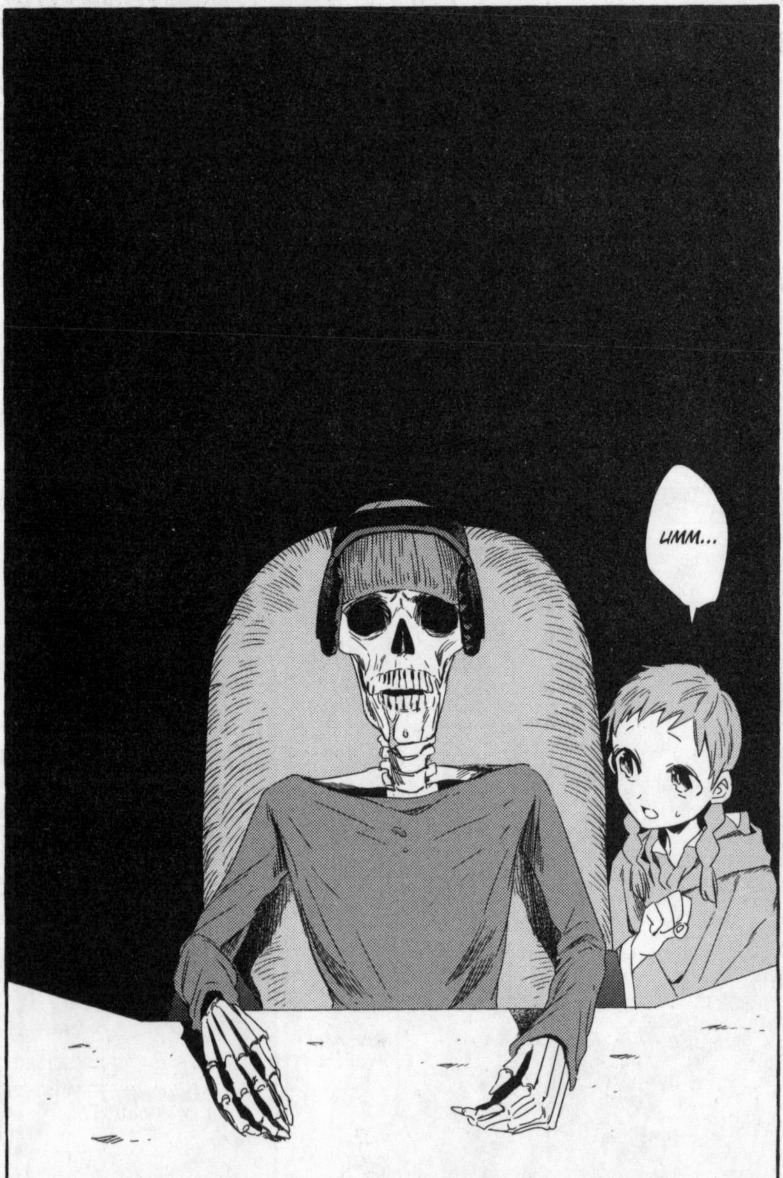
UMM...

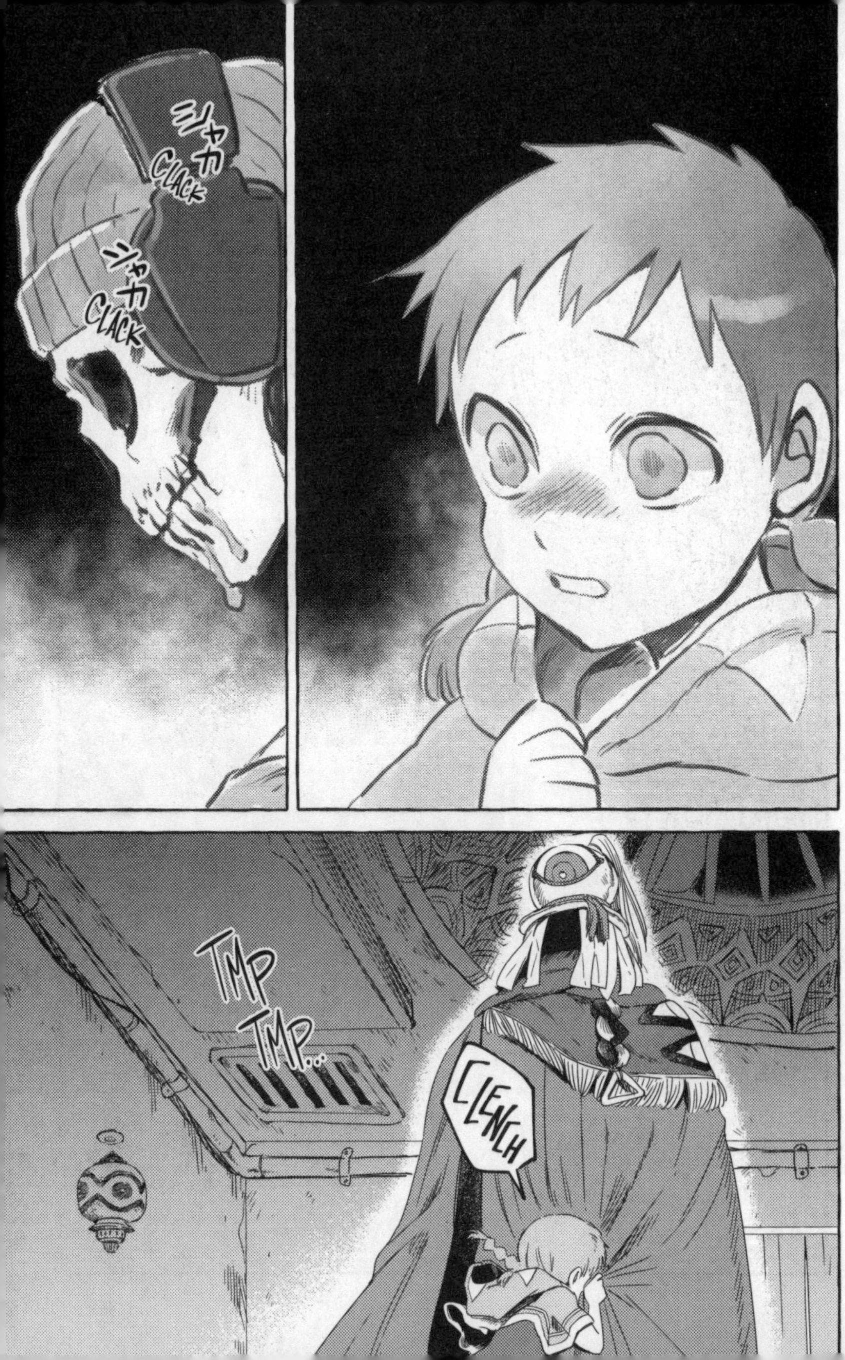
シャカ
CLACK
シャカ
CLACK
TMP TMP...
CLENCH

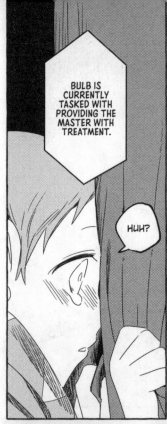

BULB IS CURRENTLY TASKED WITH PROVIDING THE MASTER WITH TREATMENT.

HUH?

......

......

DRIB

WHAT?

BUT...

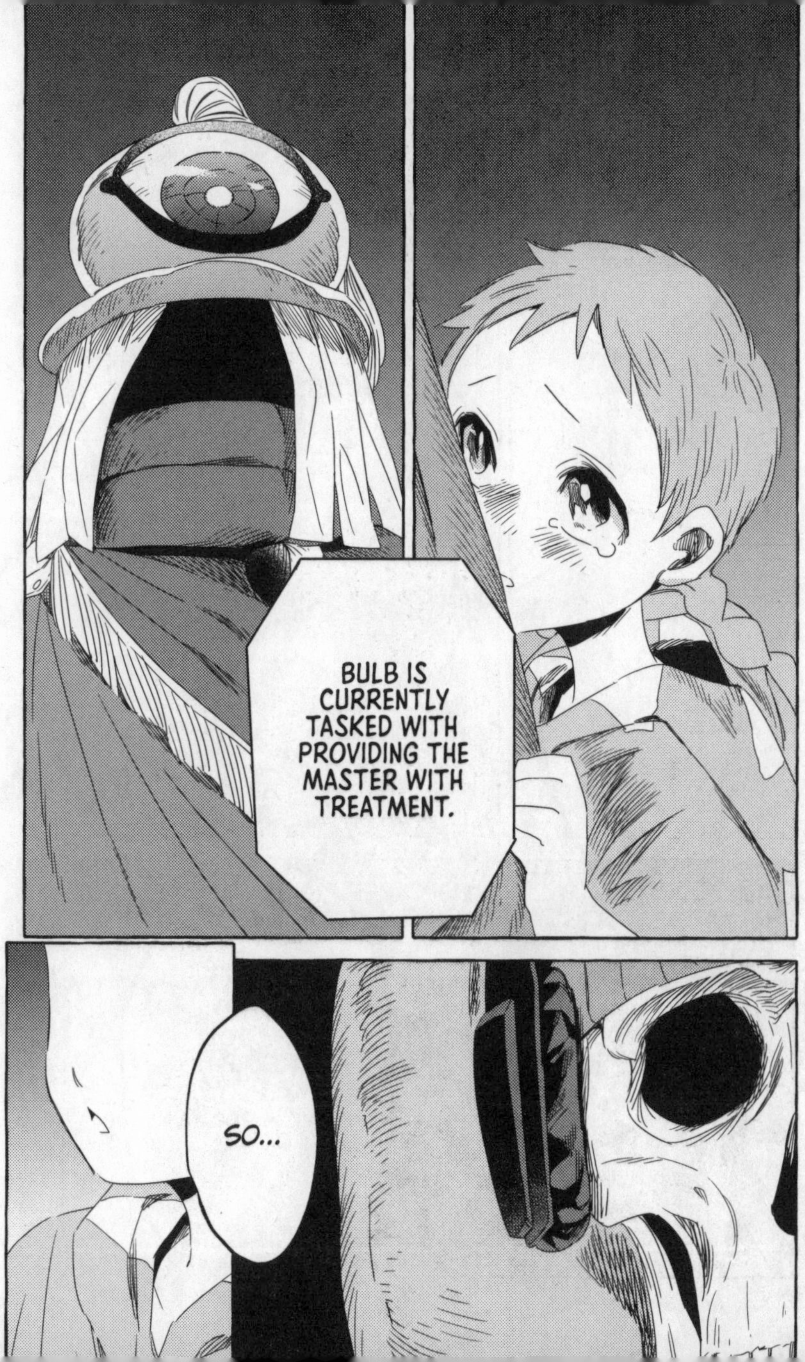
BULB IS CURRENTLY TASKED WITH PROVIDING THE MASTER WITH TREATMENT.
SO...

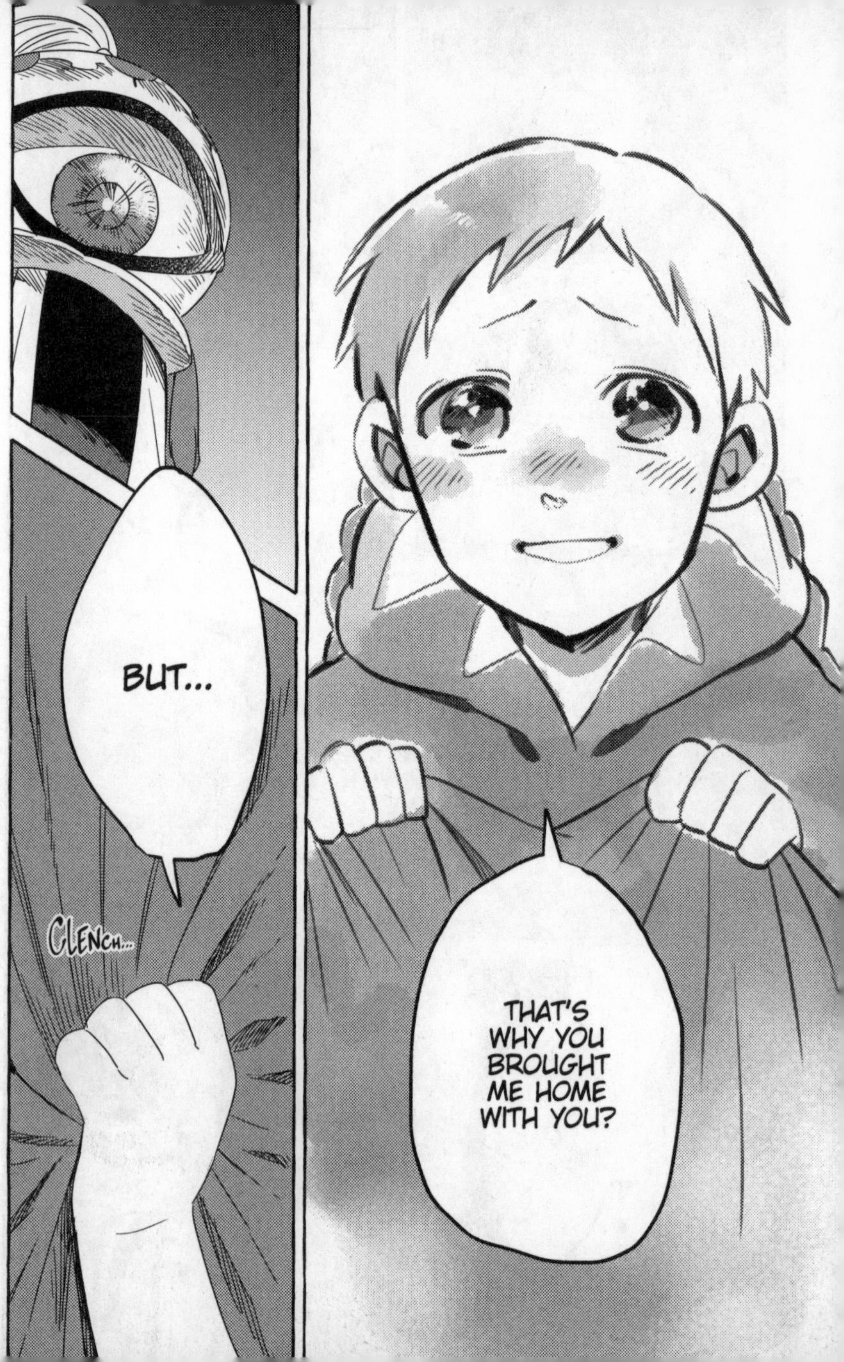
THAT'S WHY YOU BROUGHT ME HOME WITH YOU?
BUT...
CLENCH...

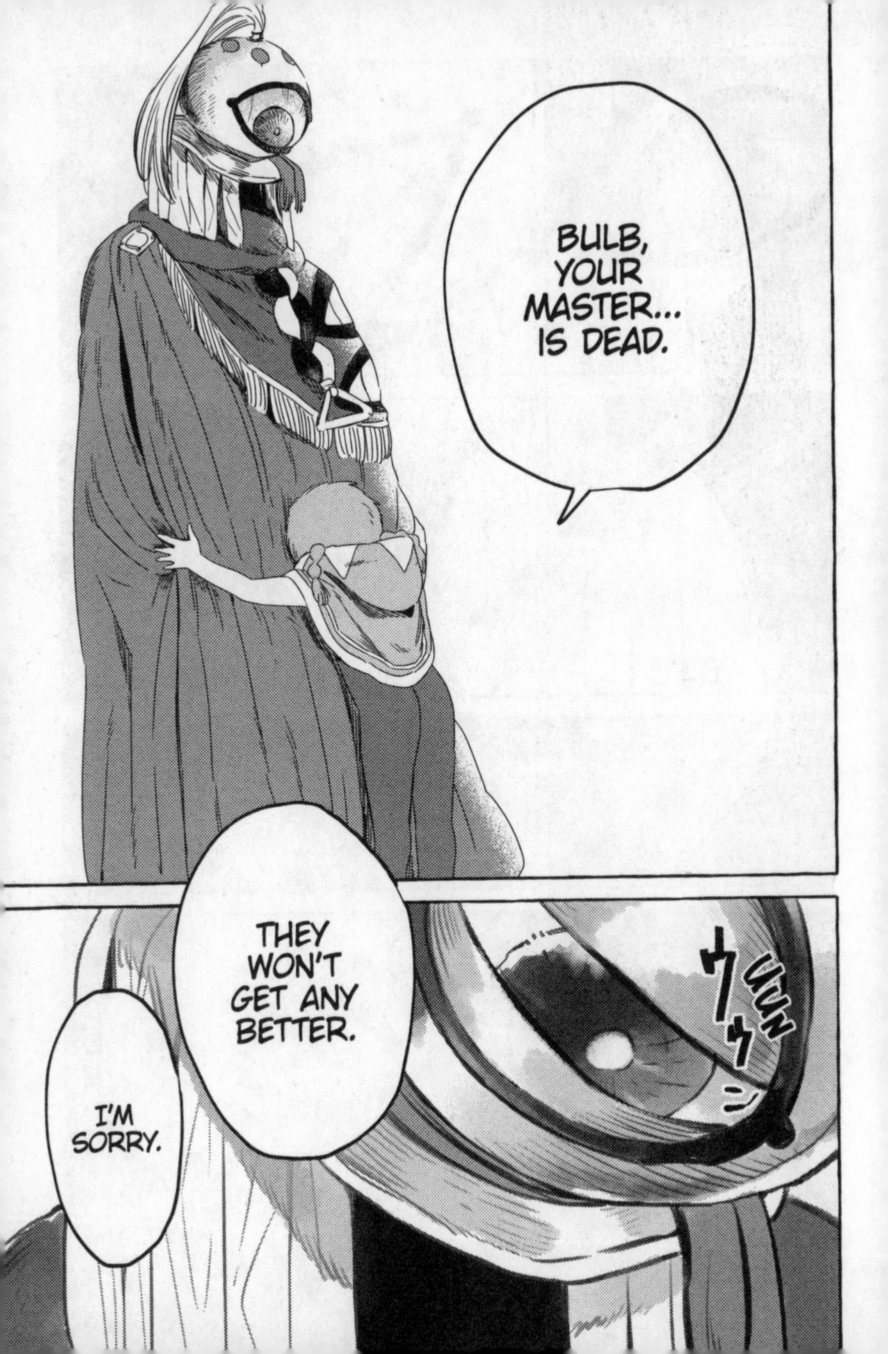
BULB, YOUR MASTER... IS DEAD.
UUN
THEY WON'T GET ANY BETTER.
I'M SORRY.

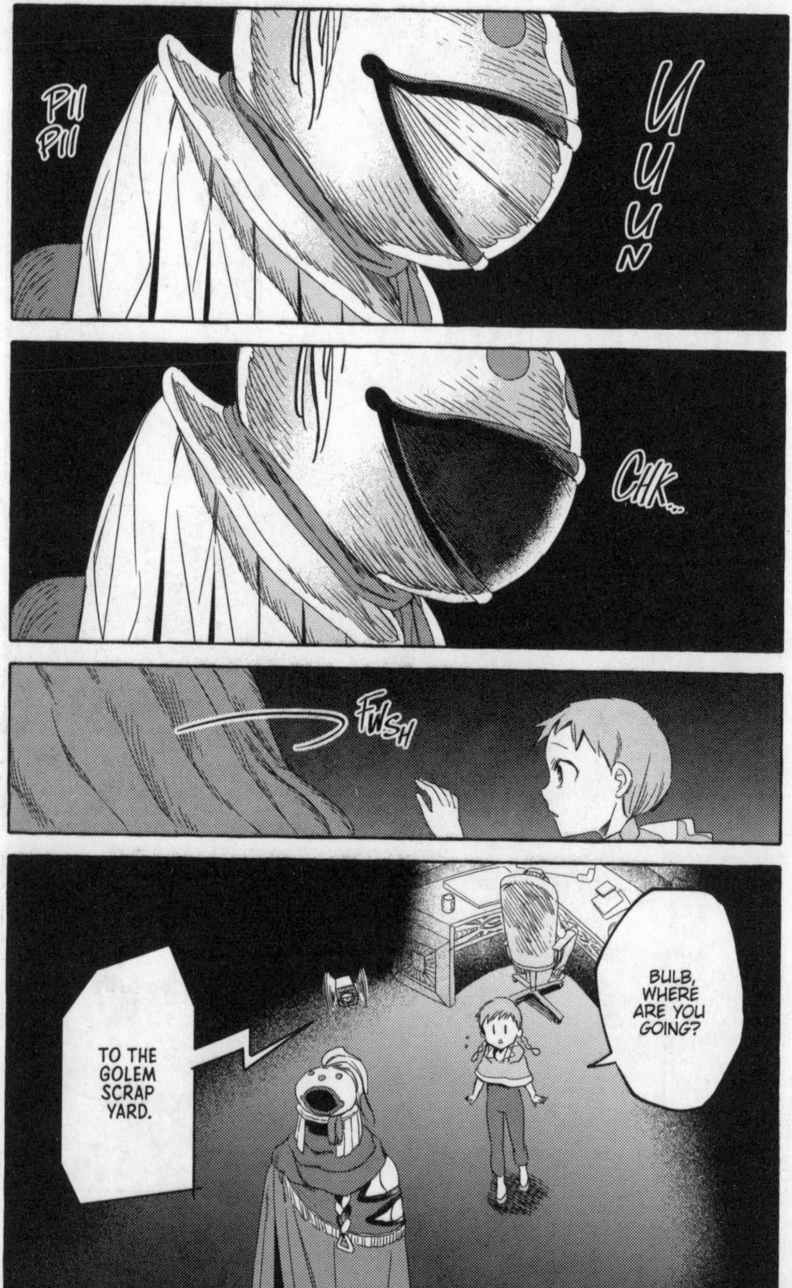
UUUUN
PII PII
CHK...
FWSH
BULB, WHERE ARE YOU GOING?
TO THE GOLEM SCRAP YARD.

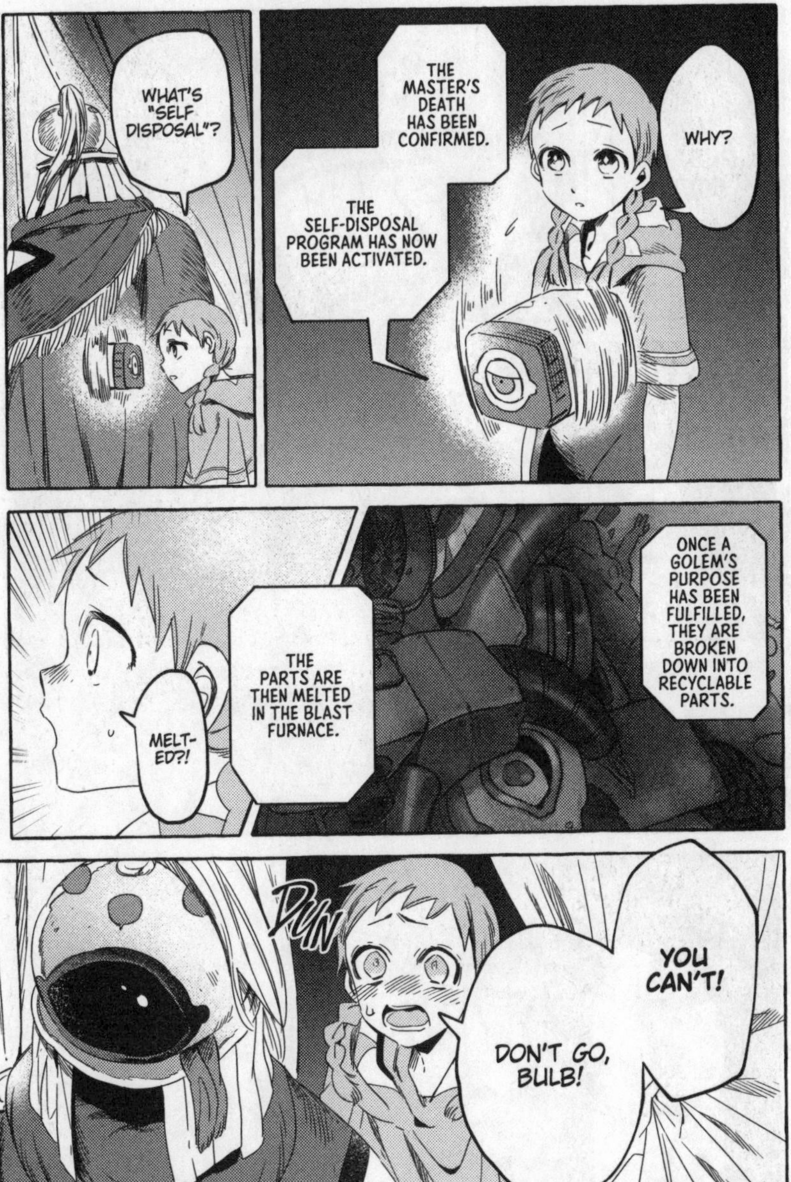
WHY?
THE MASTER'S DEATH HAS BEEN CONFIRMED.
THE SELF-DISPOSAL PROGRAM HAS NOW BEEN ACTIVATED.
WHAT'S "SELF DISPOSAL"?
ONCE A GOLEM'S PURPOSE HAS BEEN FULFILLED, THEY ARE BROKEN DOWN INTO RECYCLABLE PARTS.
THE PARTS ARE THEN MELTED IN THE BLAST FURNACE.
MELT-ED?!
YOU CAN'T!
DON'T GO, BULB!
DUN

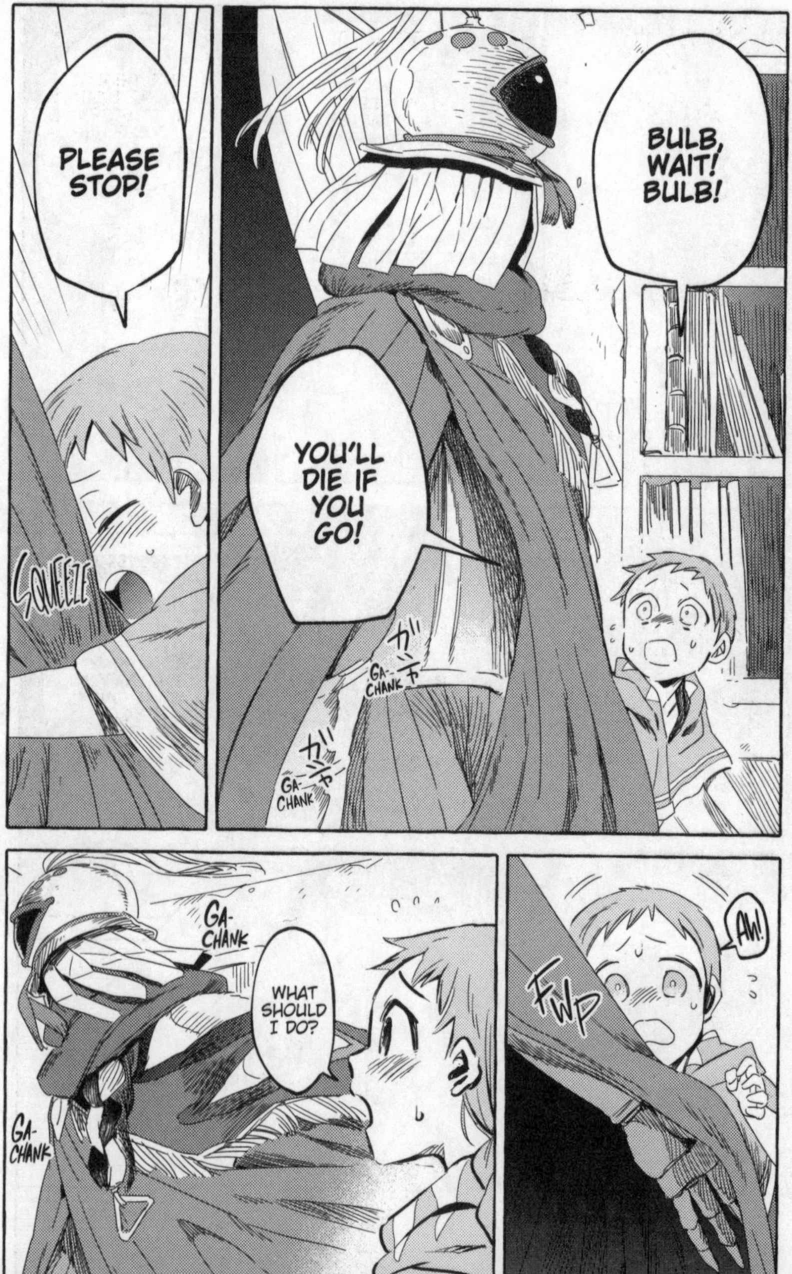
BULB, WAIT! BULB!
YOU'LL DIE IF YOU GO!
GA-CHANK
GA-CHANK
PLEASE STOP!
SQUEEZE
AW!
FWP
GA-CHANK
WHAT SHOULD I DO?
GA-CHANK

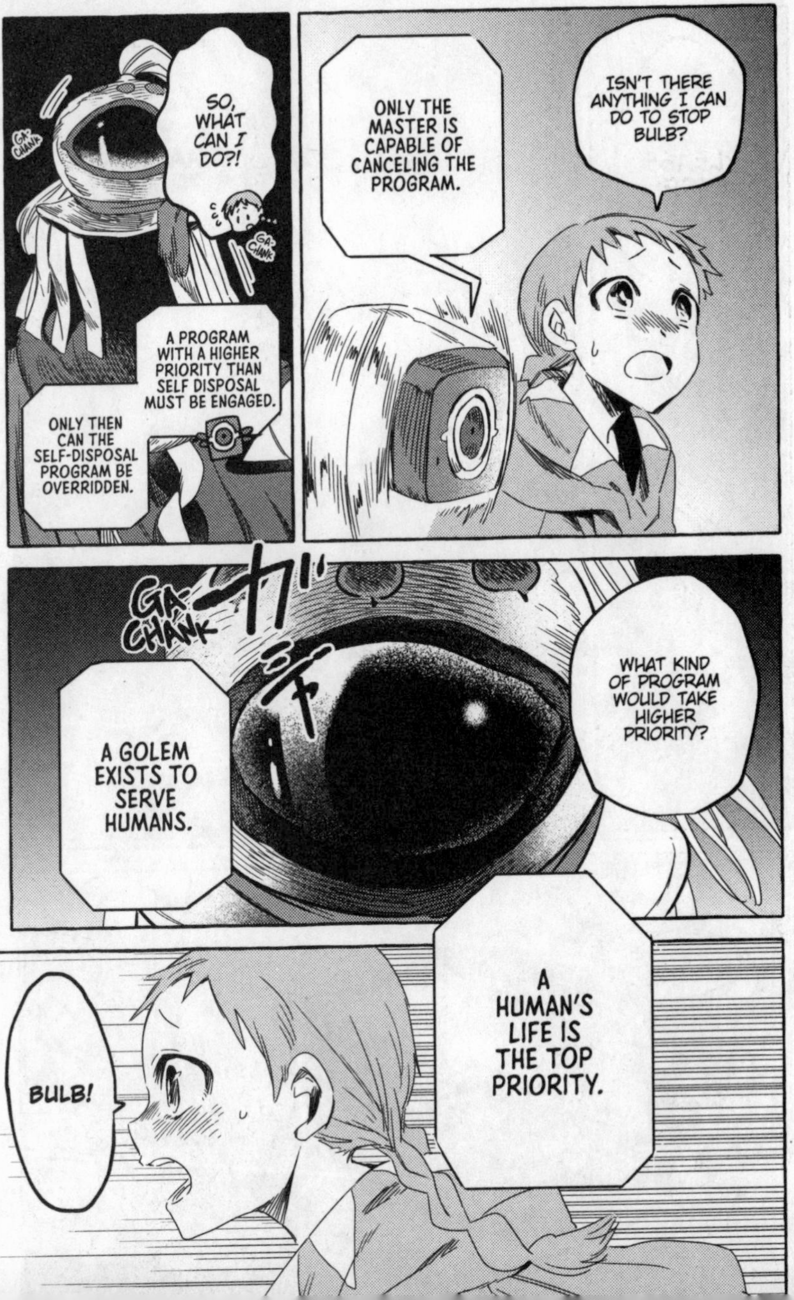
ISN'T THERE ANYTHING I CAN DO TO STOP BULB?
ONLY THE MASTER IS CAPABLE OF CANCELING THE PROGRAM.
SO, WHAT CAN I DO?!
GA-CHANK
GA-CHANK
A PROGRAM WITH A HIGHER PRIORITY THAN SELF DISPOSAL MUST BE ENGAGED.
ONLY THEN CAN THE SELF-DISPOSAL PROGRAM BE OVERRIDDEN.
GA-CHANK
WHAT KIND OF PROGRAM WOULD TAKE HIGHER PRIORITY?
A GOLEM EXISTS TO SERVE HUMANS.
A HUMAN'S LIFE IS THE TOP PRIORITY.
BULB!

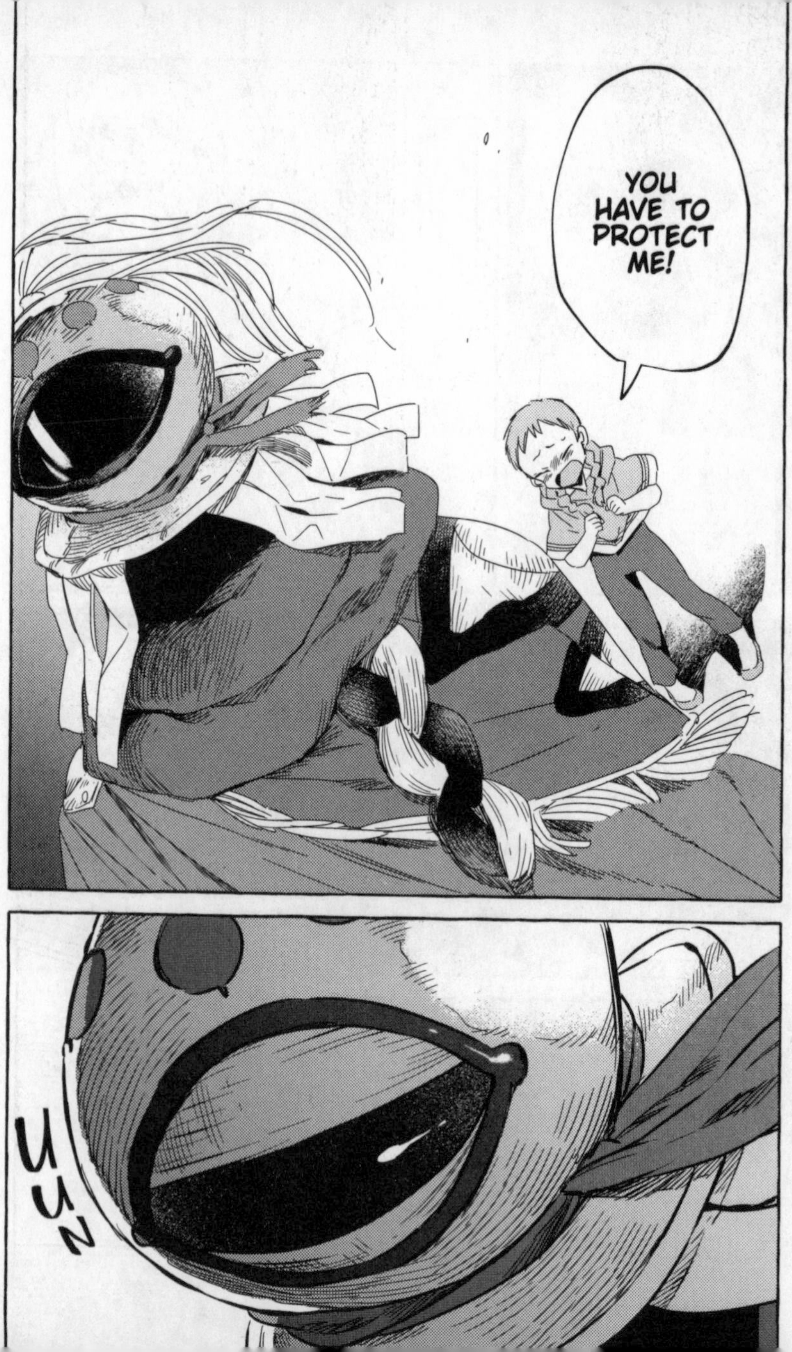
YOU HAVE TO PROTECT ME!
UUN

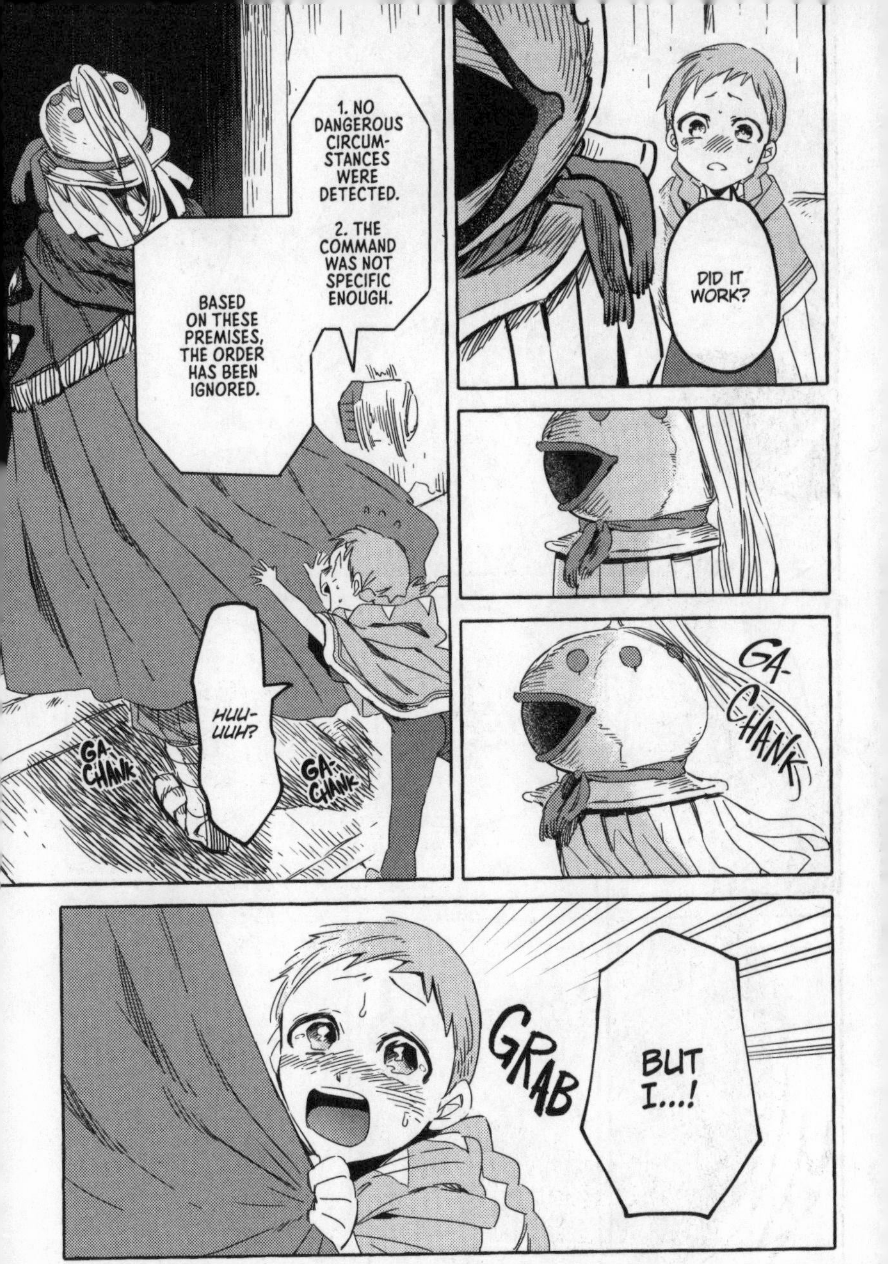
DID IT WORK?
GA-CHANK
1. NO DANGEROUS CIRCUM-STANCES WERE DETECTED.
2. THE COMMAND WAS NOT SPECIFIC ENOUGH.
BASED ON THESE PREMISES, THE ORDER HAS BEEN IGNORED.
GA-CHANK
HUUU-UUH?
GA-CHANK
BUT I...!
GRAB

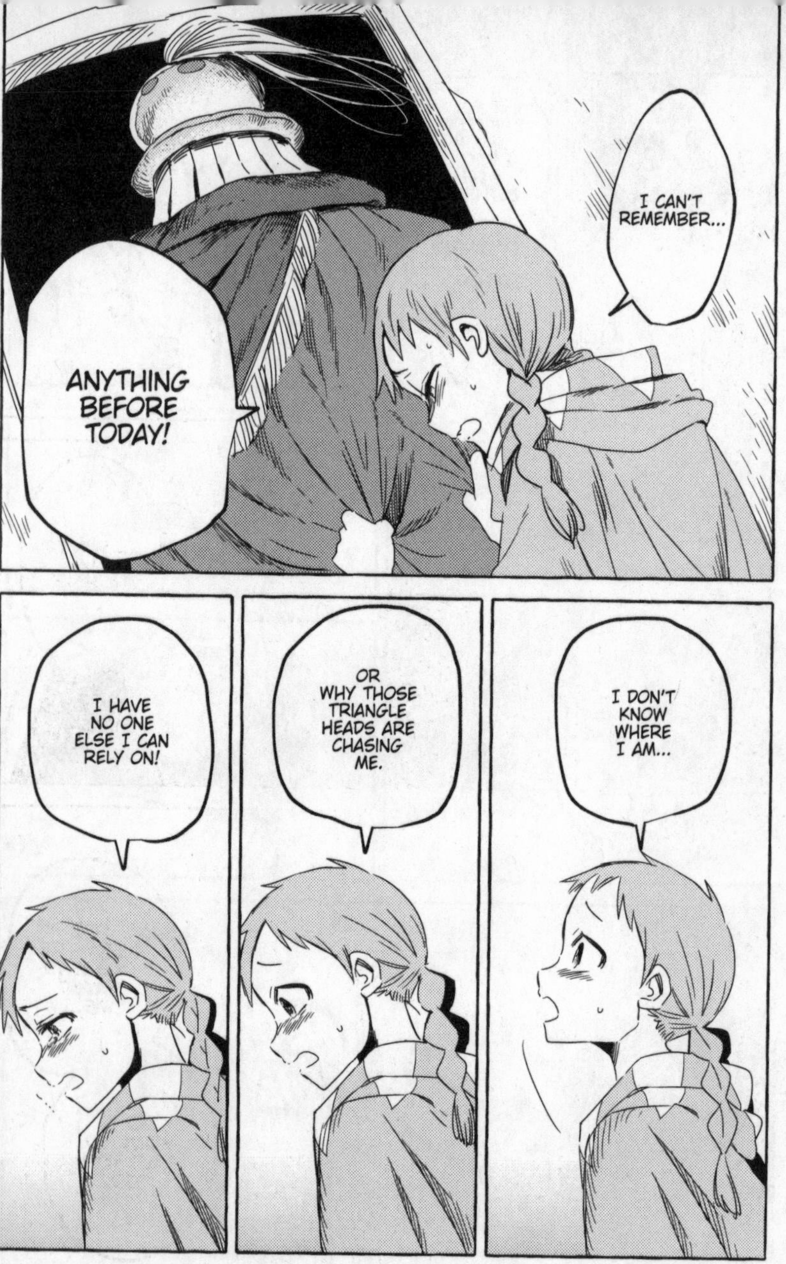
I CAN'T REMEMBER...
ANYTHING BEFORE TODAY!
I DON'T KNOW WHERE I AM...
OR WHY THOSE TRIANGLE HEADS ARE CHASING ME.
I HAVE NO ONE ELSE I CAN RELY ON!

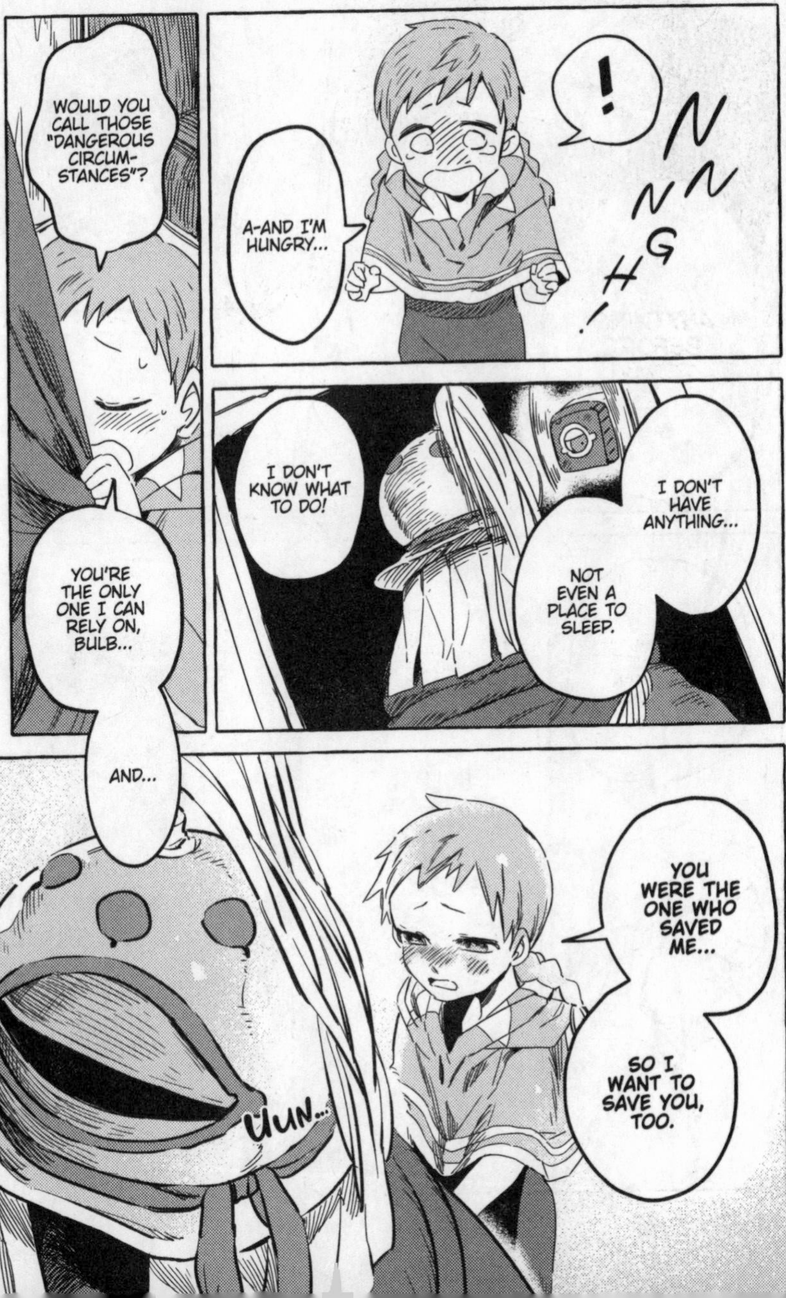
!
NNNNGH!
A-AND I'M HUNGRY...
I DON'T HAVE ANYTHING...
NOT EVEN A PLACE TO SLEEP.
I DON'T KNOW WHAT TO DO!
WOULD YOU CALL THOSE "DANGEROUS CIRCUM-STANCES"?
YOU'RE THE ONLY ONE I CAN RELY ON, BULB...
AND...
YOU WERE THE ONE WHO SAVED ME...
SO I WANT TO SAVE YOU, TOO.
UUN...

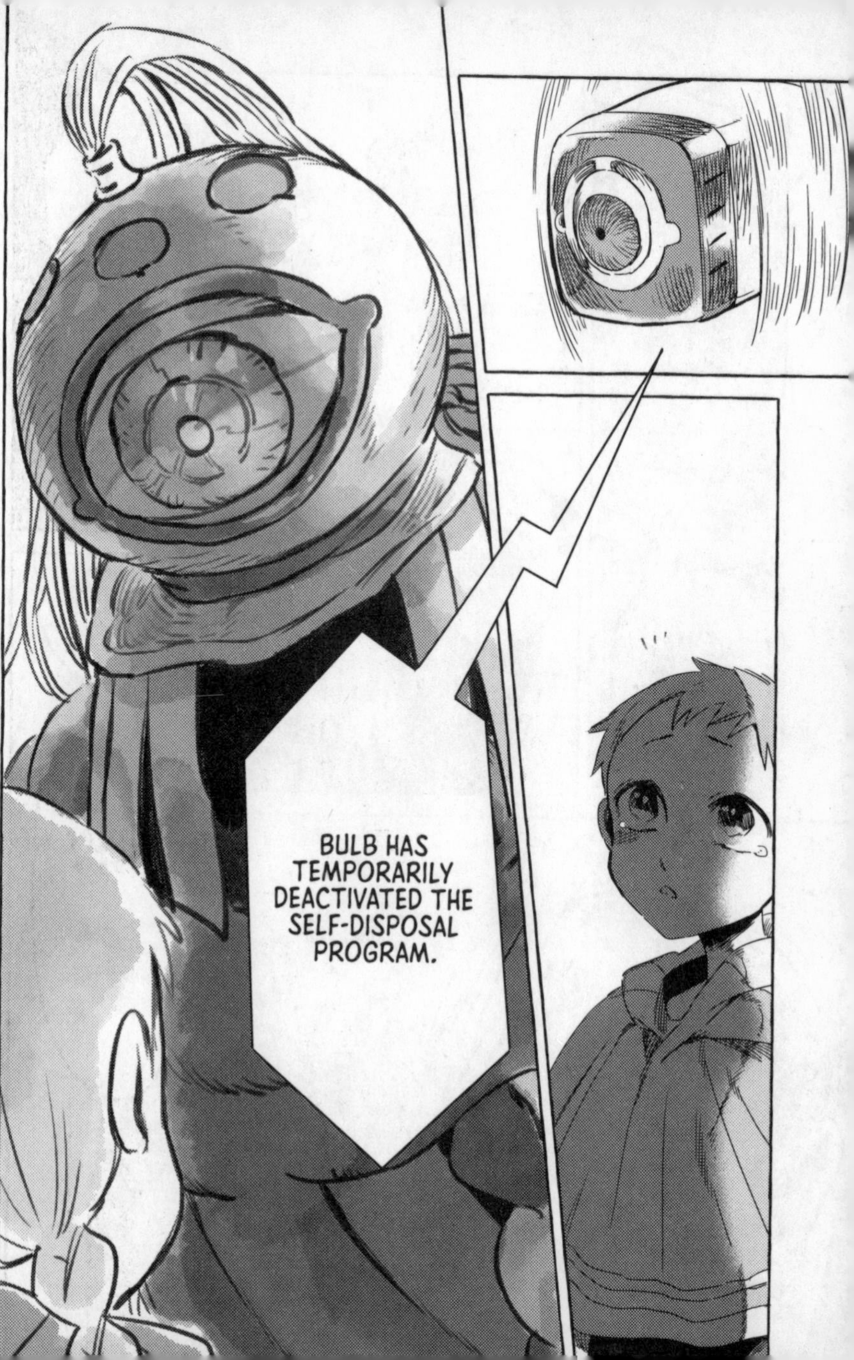
BULB HAS TEMPORARILY DEACTIVATED THE SELF-DISPOSAL PROGRAM.

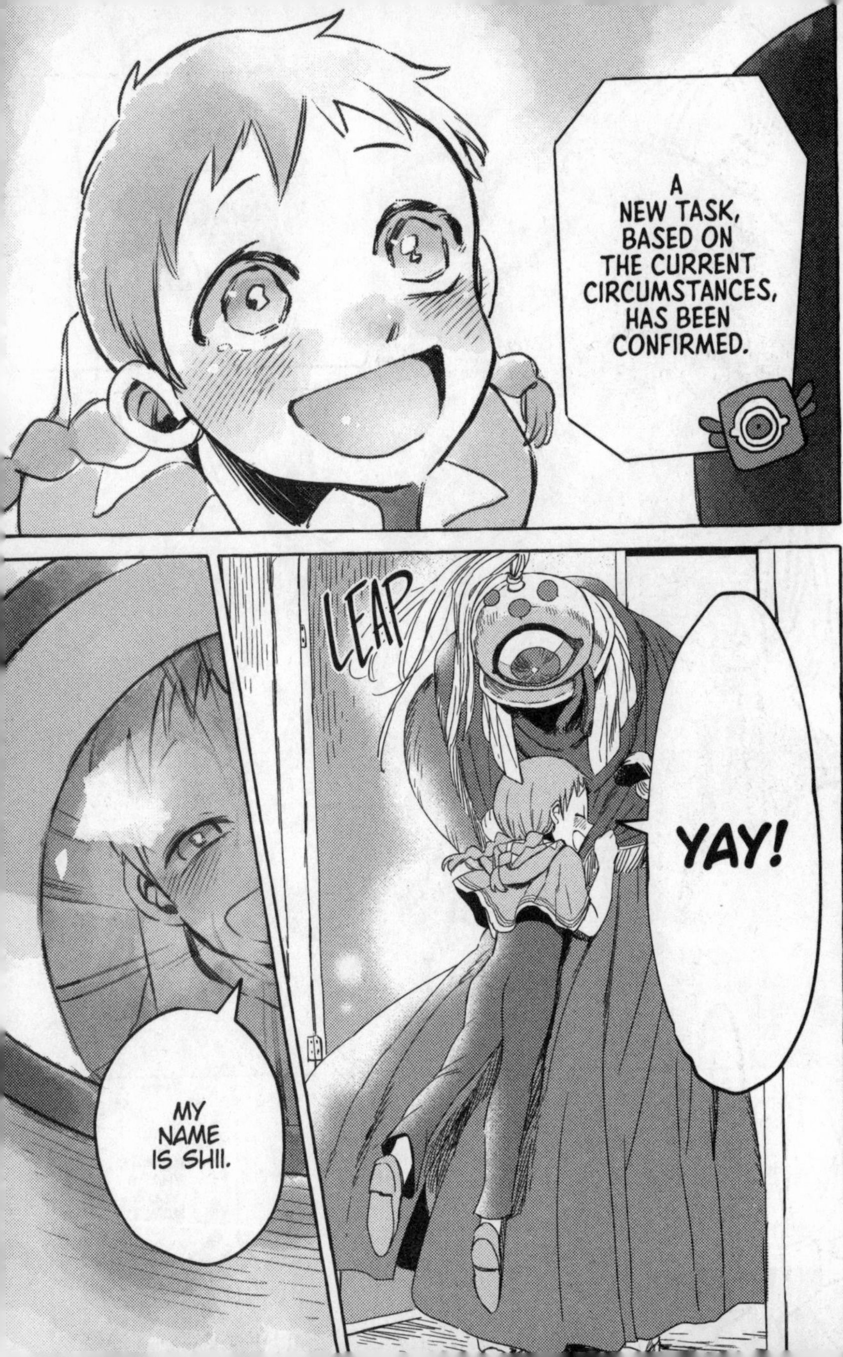
A NEW TASK, BASED ON THE CURRENT CIRCUMSTANCES, HAS BEEN CONFIRMED.
YAY!
LEAP
MY NAME IS SHII.

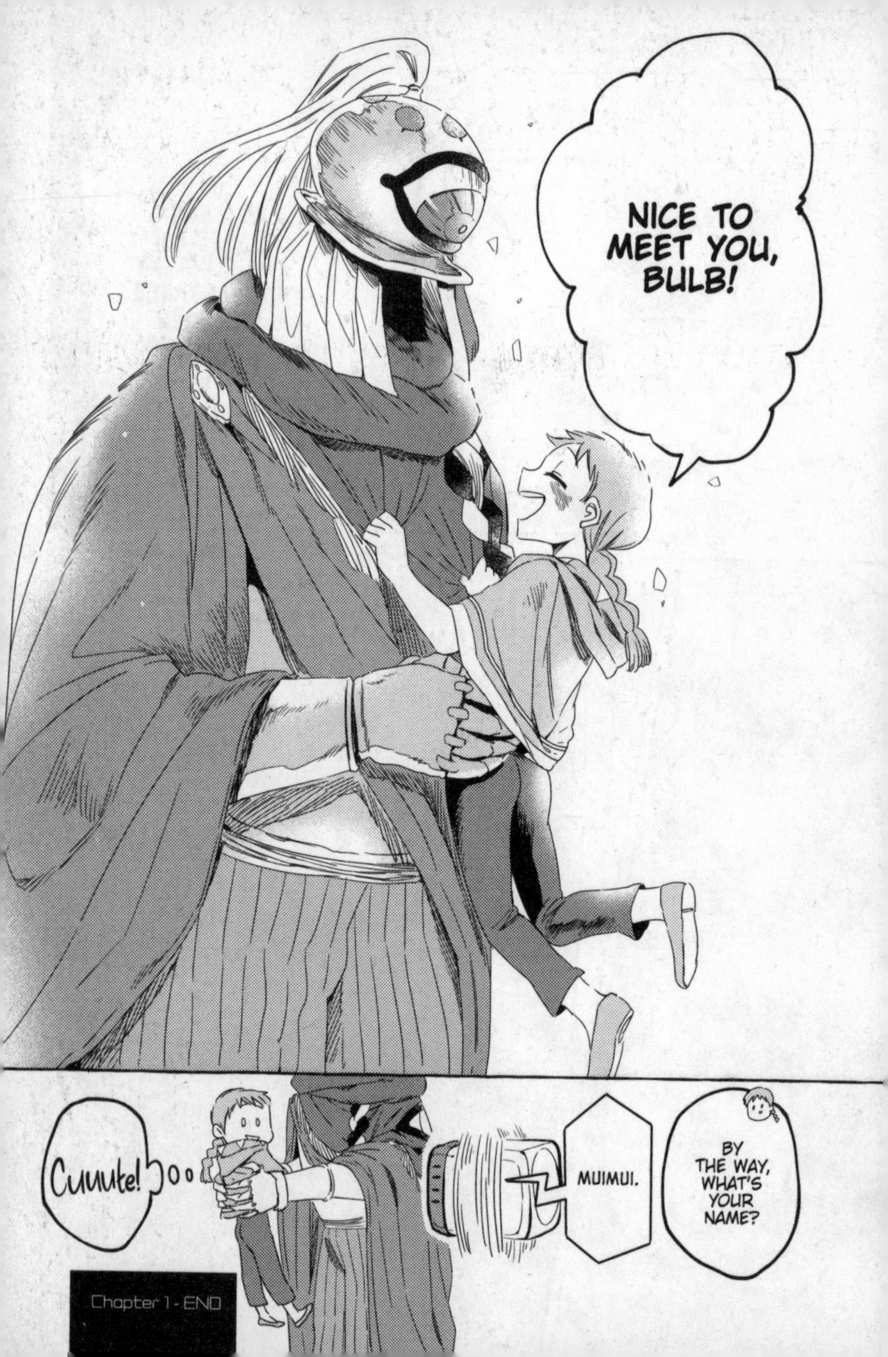
NICE TO MEET YOU, BULB!
BY THE WAY, WHAT'S YOUR NAME?
MUIMUI.
Cuuute!
Chapter 1 - END

A Fleeting Tale #1 A Small Favor

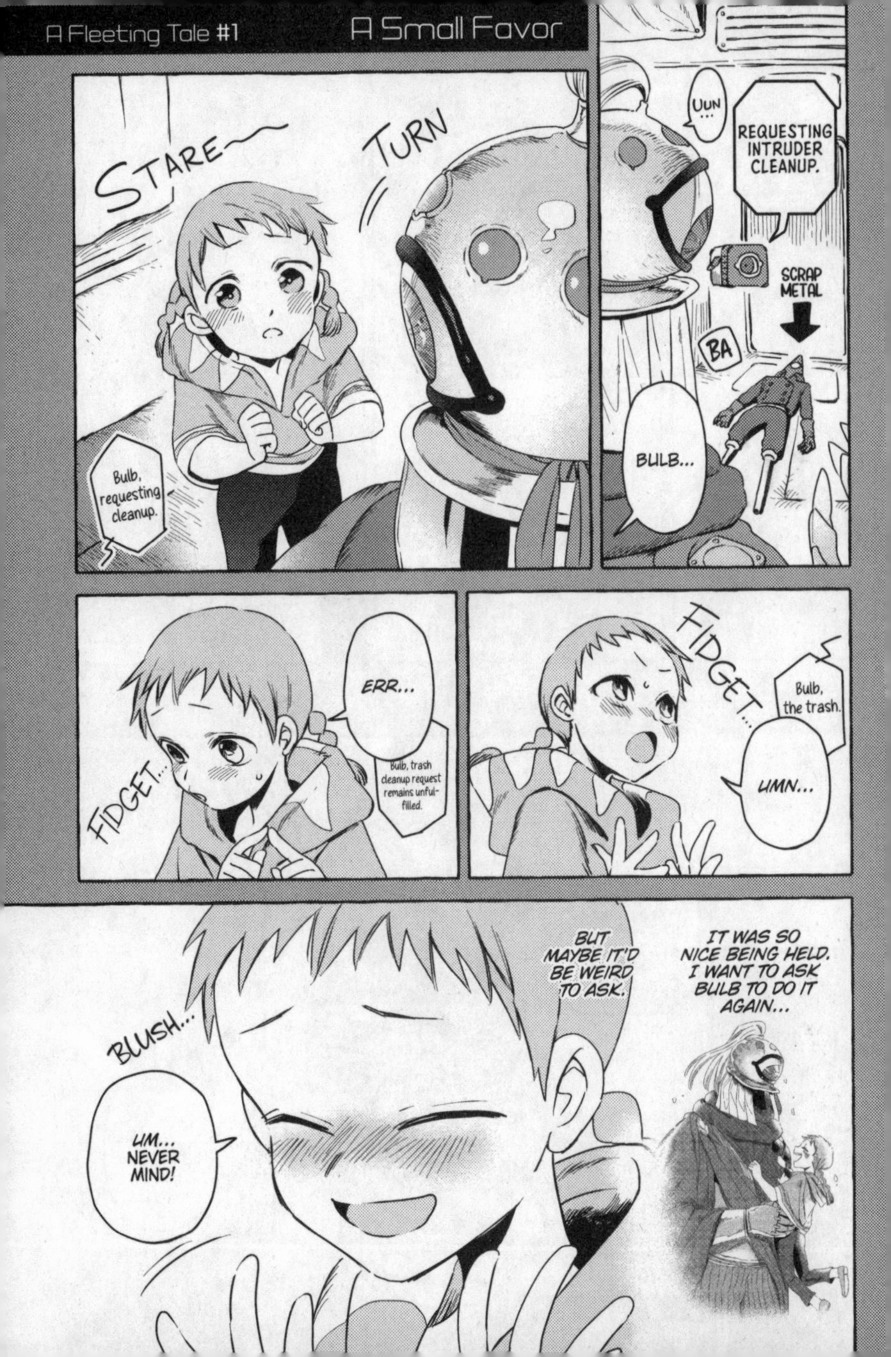
REQUESTING INTRUDER CLEANUP.
UUN...
SCRAP METAL
BA
BULB...
TURN
STARE~~
Bulb, requesting cleanup.
FIDGET...
Bulb, the trash.
UMN...
ERR...
Bulb, trash cleanup request remains unful-filled.
FIDGET...
IT WAS SO NICE BEING HELD. I WANT TO ASK BULB TO DO IT AGAIN...
BUT MAYBE IT'D BE WEIRD TO ASK.
BLUSH...
UM... NEVER MIND!

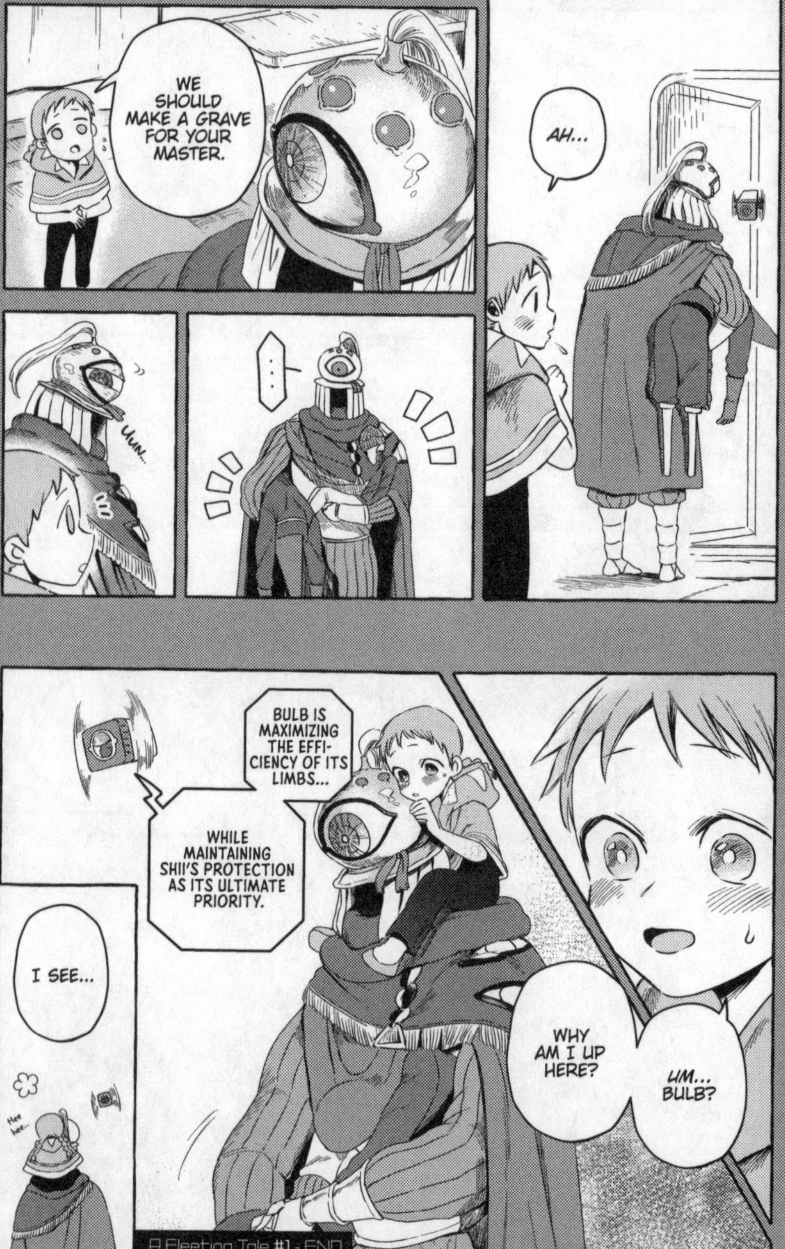
AH...
WE SHOULD MAKE A GRAVE FOR YOUR MASTER.
...
Uun...
UM... BULB?
WHY AM I UP HERE?
BULB IS MAXIMIZING THE EFFI-CIENCY OF ITS LIMBS...
WHILE MAINTAINING SHII'S PROTECTION AS ITS ULTIMATE PRIORITY.
I SEE...
Hee hee...
A Fleeting Tale #1 - END

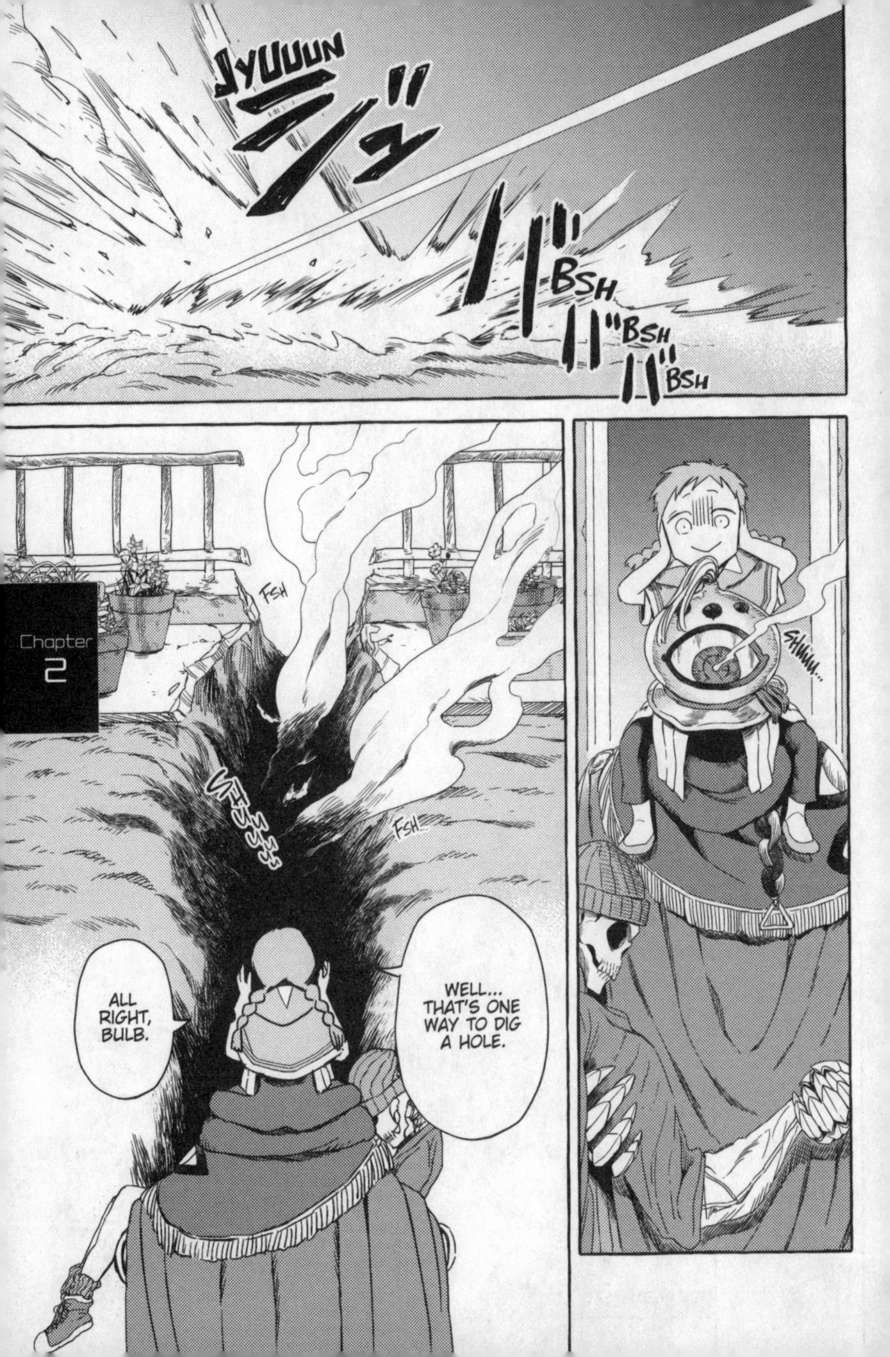
JYUUUN
BSH
BSH
BSH
SHUUU...
Chapter 2
FSH
FSH...
WELL... THAT'S ONE WAY TO DIG A HOLE.
ALL RIGHT, BULB.

Chapter 2

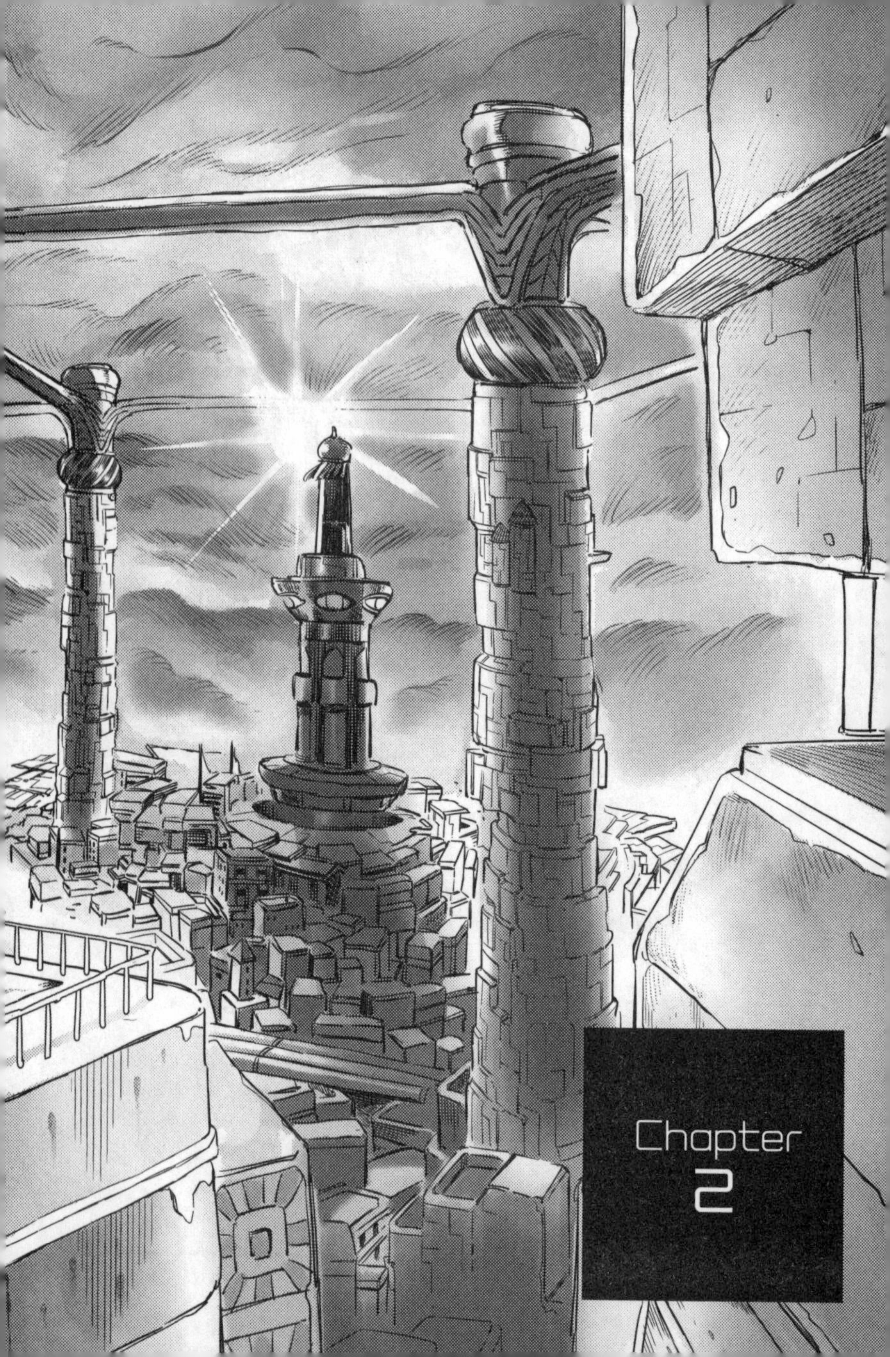

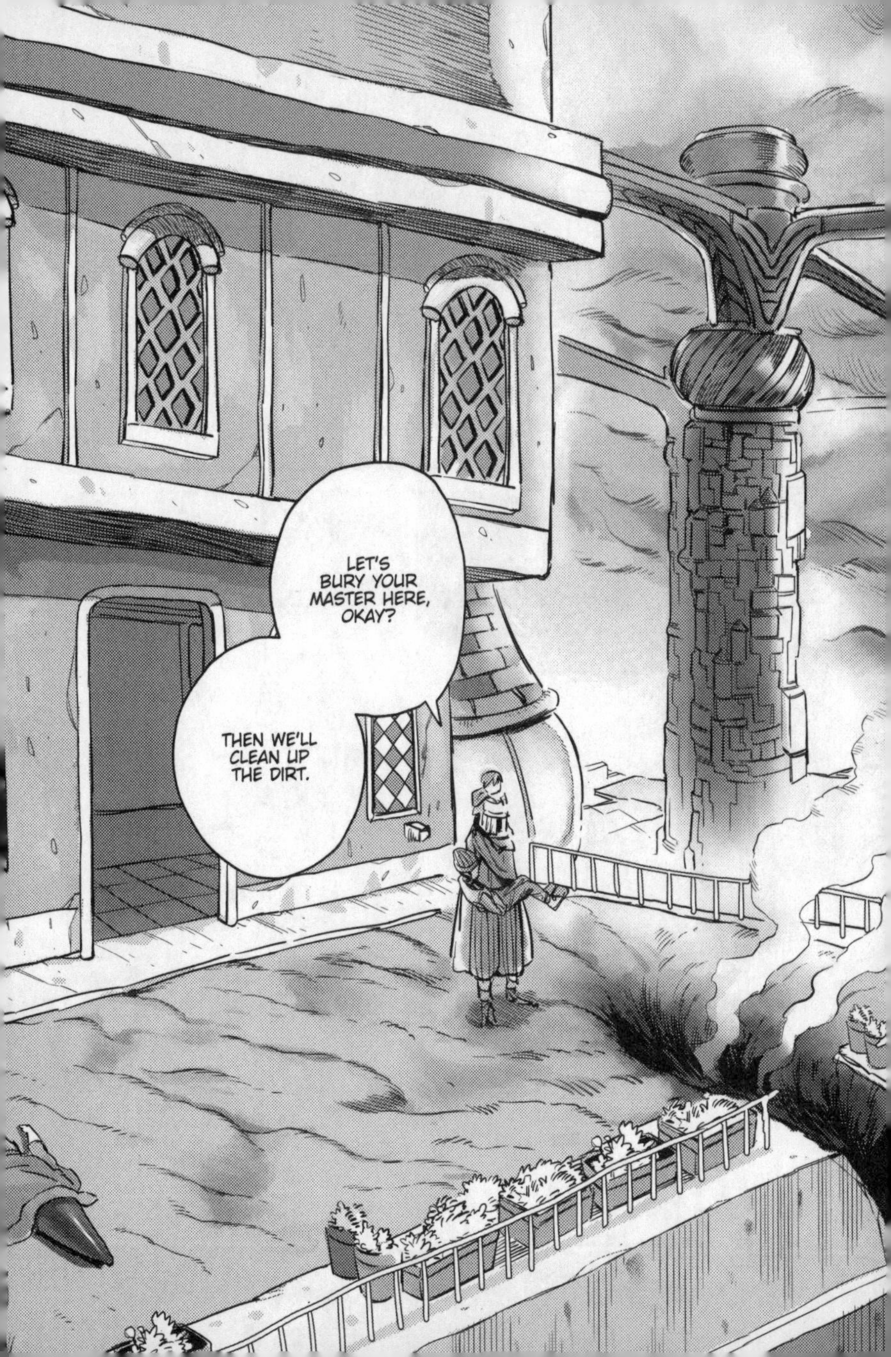
LET'S BURY YOUR MASTER HERE, OKAY?
THEN WE'LL CLEAN UP THE DIRT.

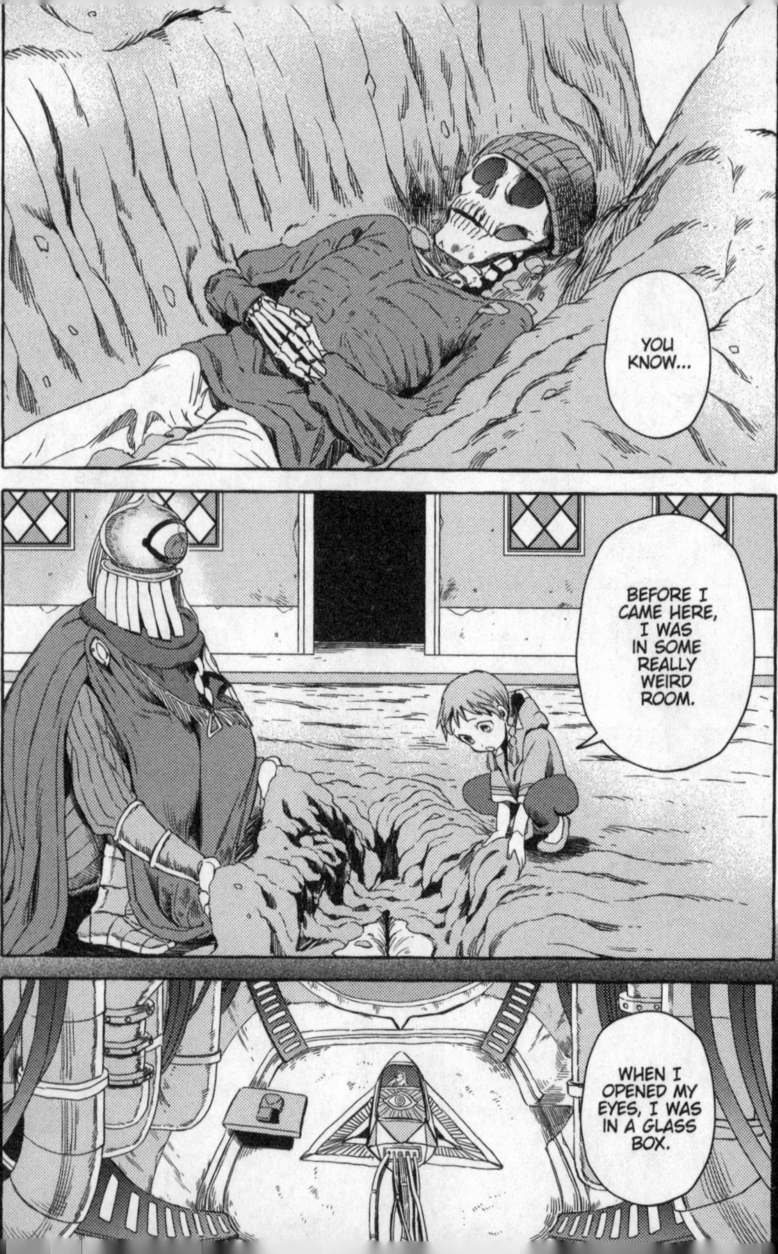
YOU KNOW...
BEFORE I CAME HERE, I WAS IN SOME REALLY WEIRD ROOM.
WHEN I OPENED MY EYES, I WAS IN A GLASS BOX.

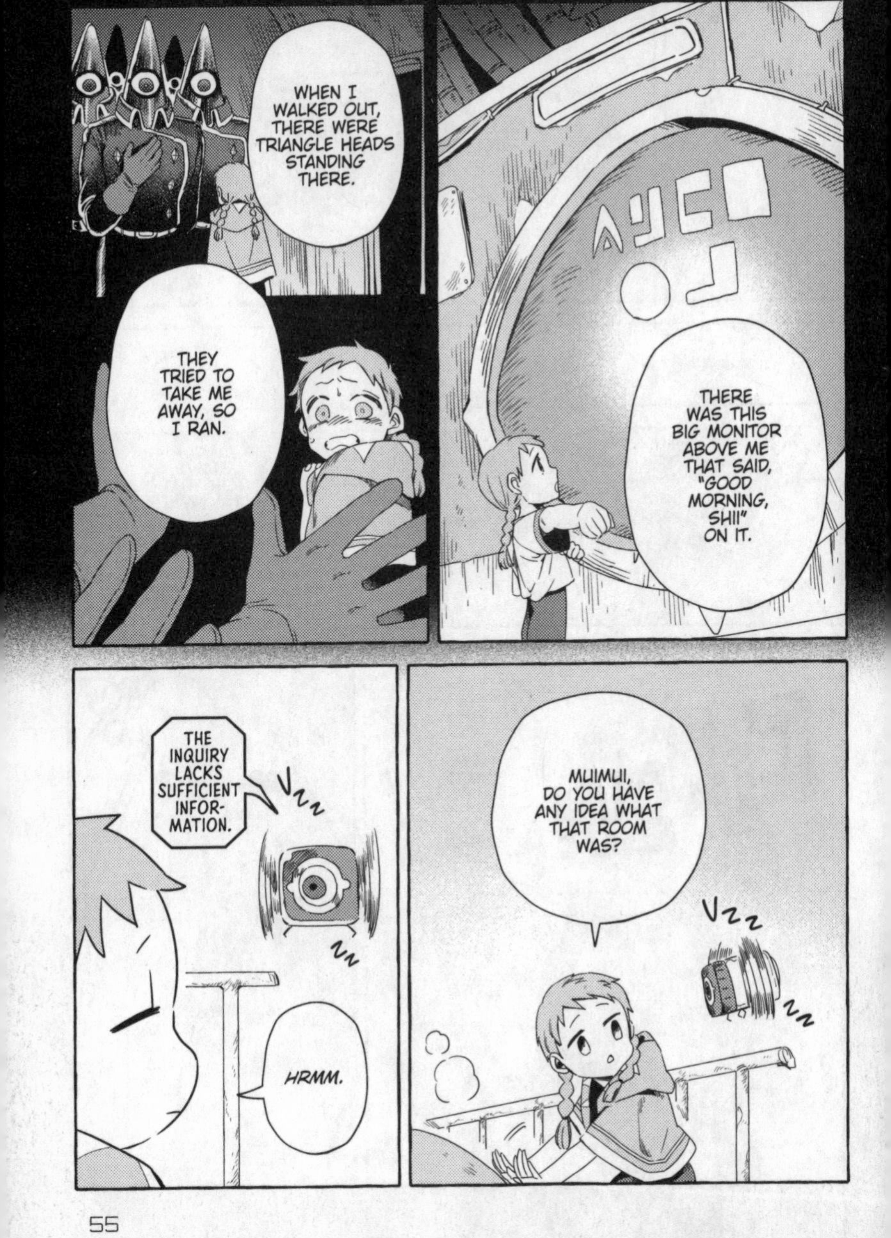
THERE WAS THIS BIG MONITOR ABOVE ME THAT SAID, "GOOD MORNING, SHII" ON IT.
WHEN I WALKED OUT, THERE WERE TRIANGLE HEADS STANDING THERE.
THEY TRIED TO TAKE ME AWAY, SO I RAN.
MUIMUI, DO YOU HAVE ANY IDEA WHAT THAT ROOM WAS?
VZZ
ZZ
THE INQUIRY LACKS SUFFICIENT INFORMATION.
VZZ
ZZ
HRMM.

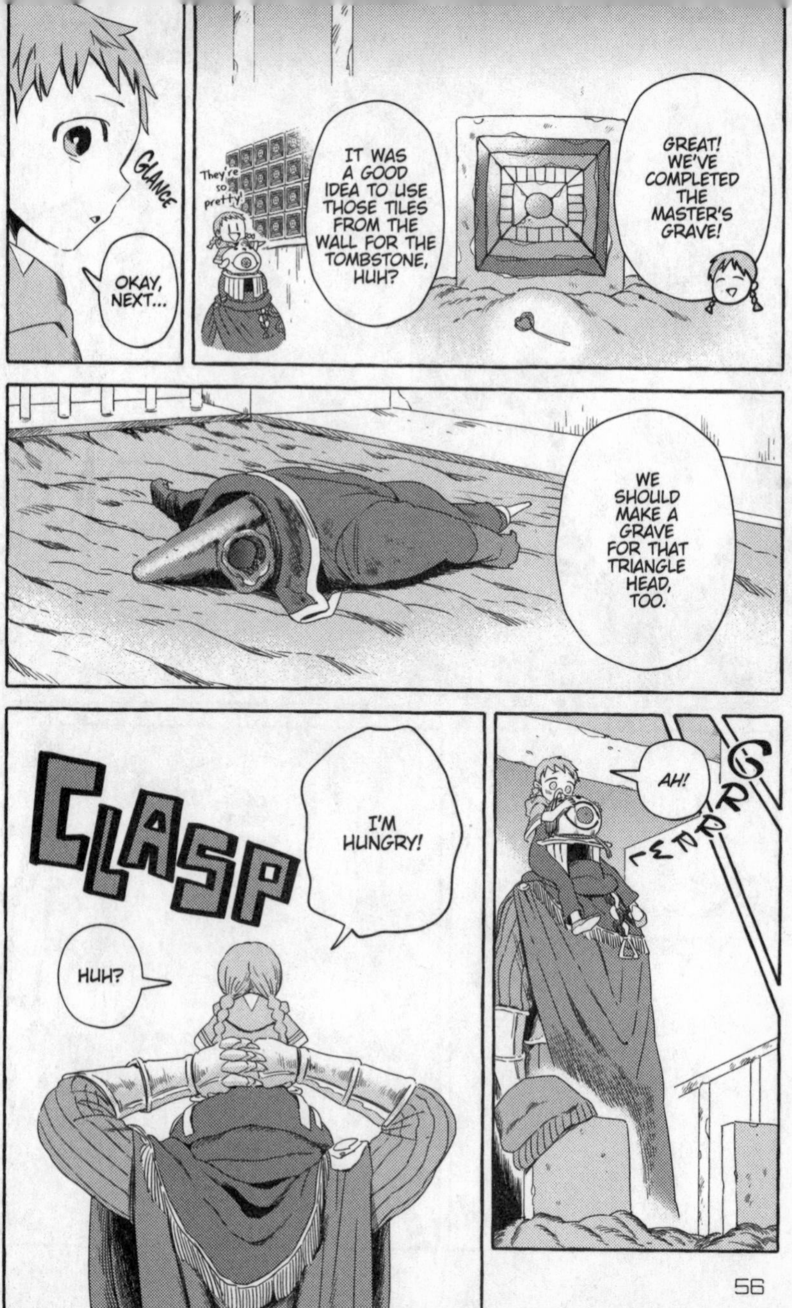
GREAT! WE'VE COMPLETED THE MASTER'S GRAVE!
IT WAS A GOOD IDEA TO USE THOSE TILES FROM THE WALL FOR THE TOMBSTONE, HUH?
They're so pretty!
GLANCE
OKAY, NEXT...
WE SHOULD MAKE A GRAVE FOR THAT TRIANGLE HEAD, TOO.
AH!
I'M HUNGRY!
CLASP
HUH?

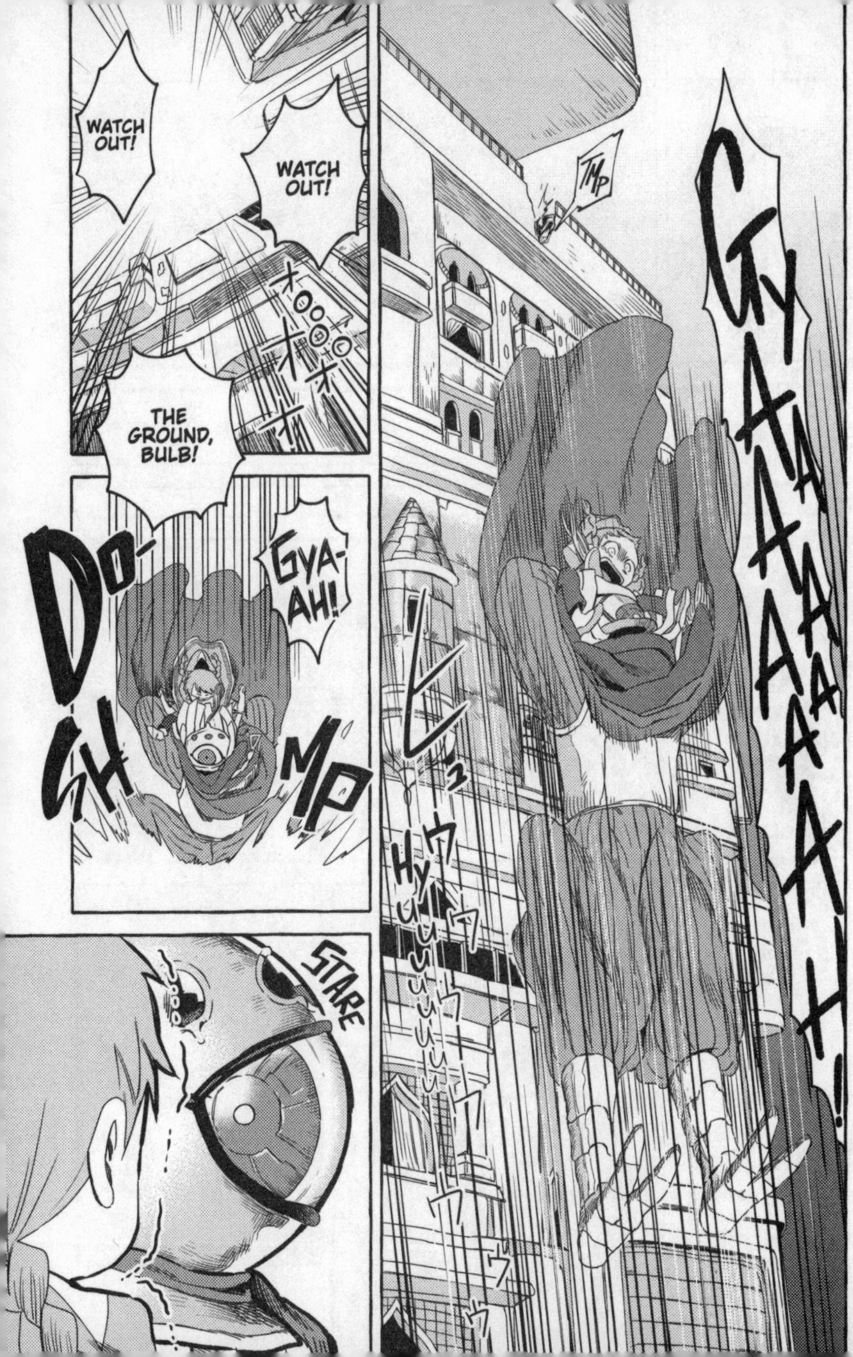
TMP
GYAAAAAAAAAH—!
HYUUUUUUUU
WATCH OUT!
WATCH OUT!
THE GROUND, BULB!
GYA-AH!
DO-SHMP
STARE

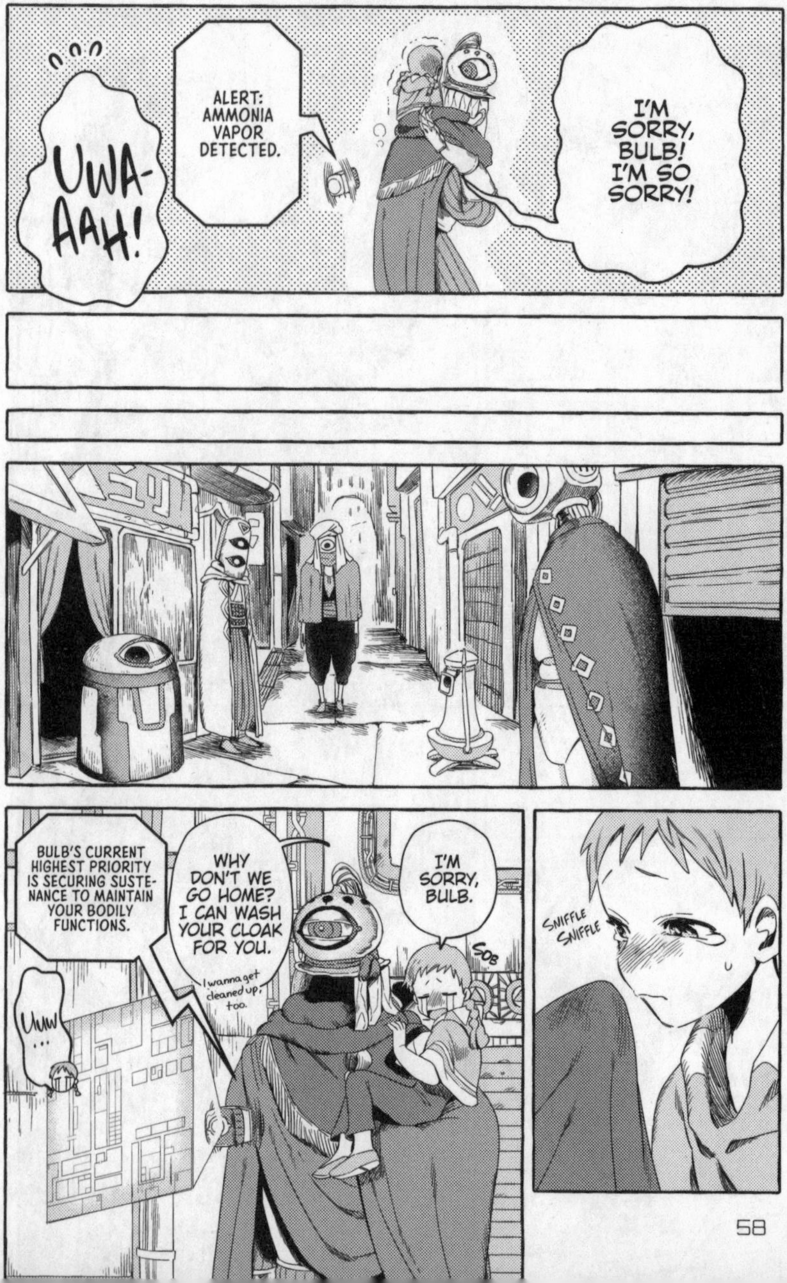
I'M SORRY, BULB! I'M SO SORRY!
ALERT: AMMONIA VAPOR DETECTED.
UWA-AAH!
SNIFFLE SNIFFLE
I'M SORRY, BULB.
SOB
WHY DON'T WE GO HOME? I CAN WASH YOUR CLOAK FOR YOU.
I wanna get cleaned up, too.
BULB'S CURRENT HIGHEST PRIORITY IS SECURING SUSTENANCE TO MAINTAIN YOUR BODILY FUNCTIONS.
Uuw...

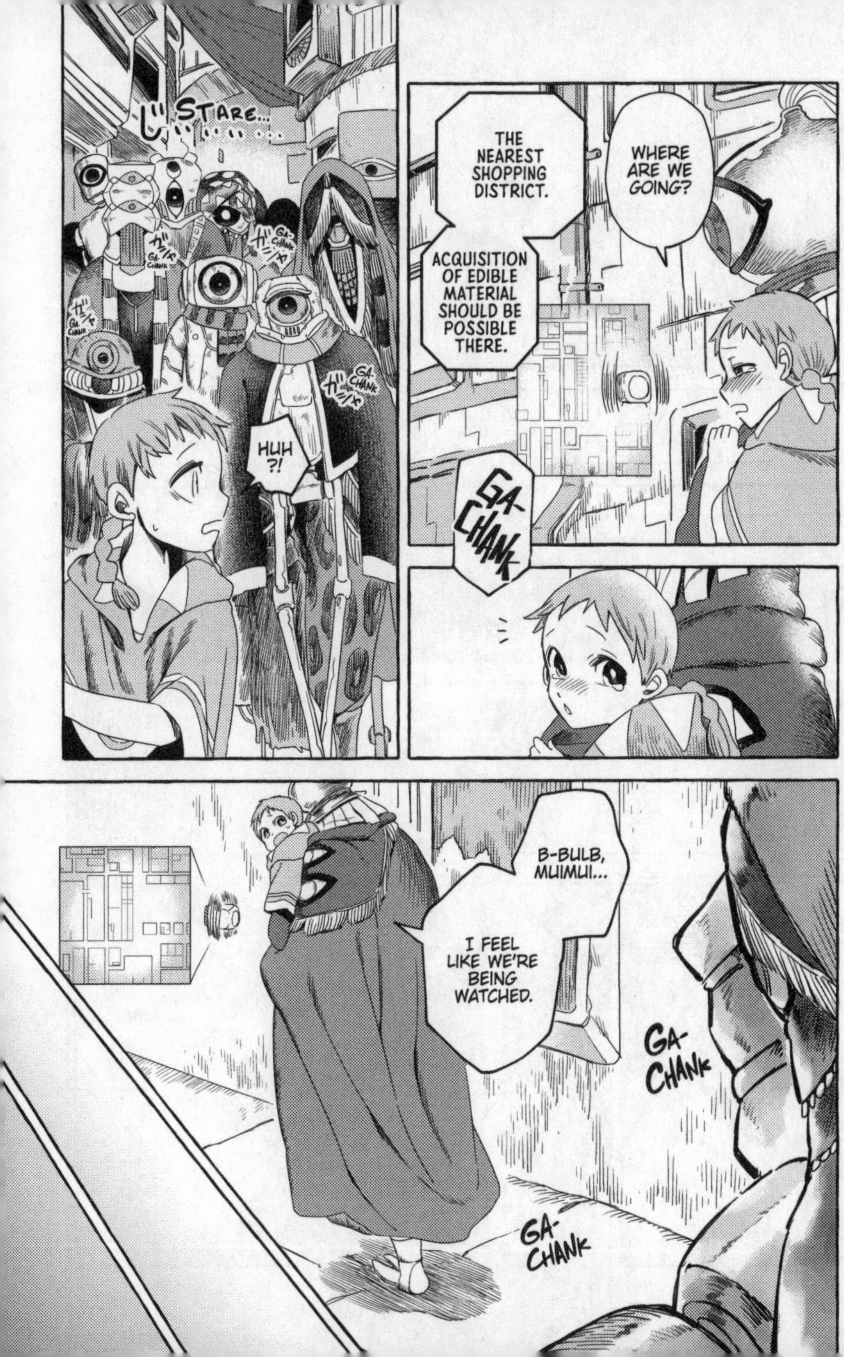

WHERE ARE WE GOING?
THE NEAREST SHOPPING DISTRICT.
ACQUISITION OF EDIBLE MATERIAL SHOULD BE POSSIBLE THERE.
GA-CHANK
STARE...
GA-CHANK
GA-CHANK
GA-CHANK
GA-CHANK
HUH?!
B-BULB, MUIMUI...
I FEEL LIKE WE'RE BEING WATCHED.
GA-CHANK
GA-CHANK

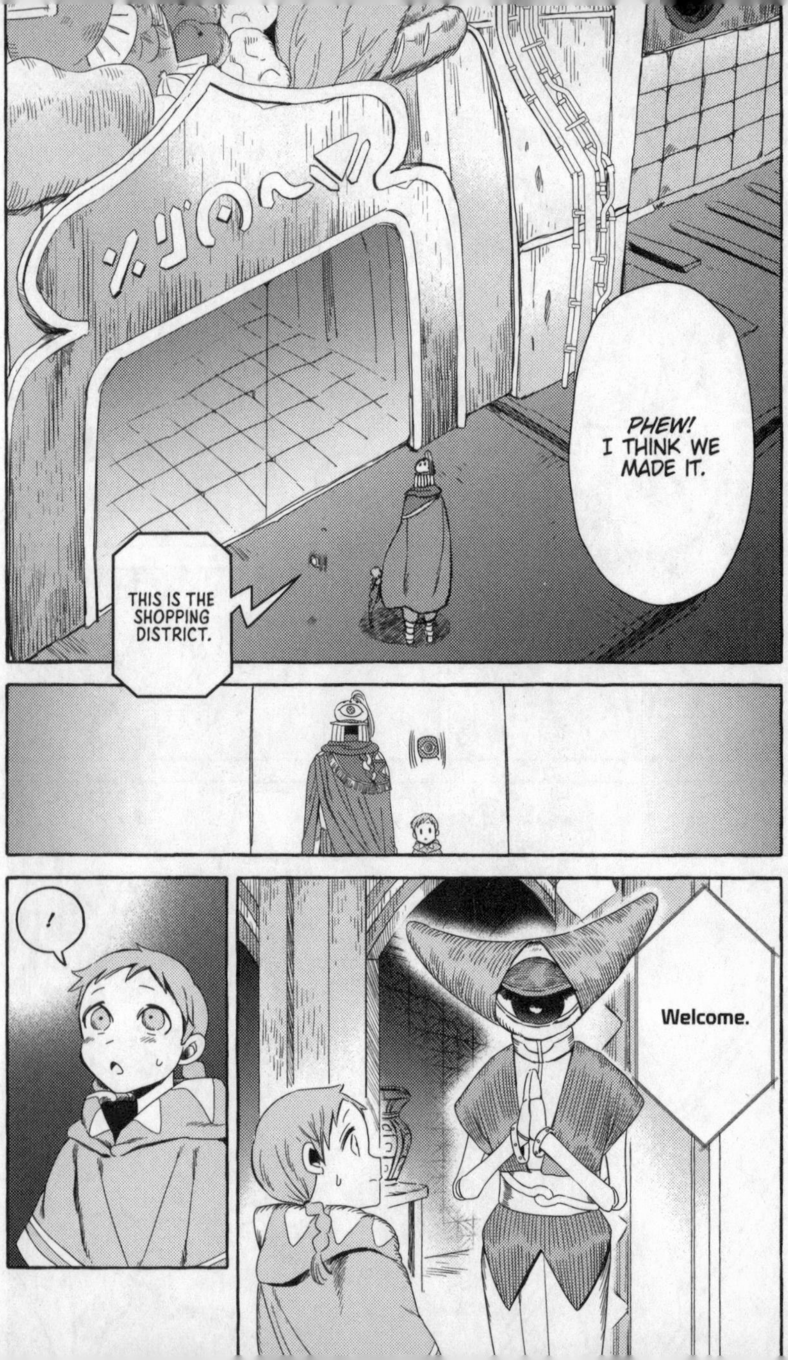
PHEW! I THINK WE MADE IT.
THIS IS THE SHOPPING DISTRICT.
Welcome.
!

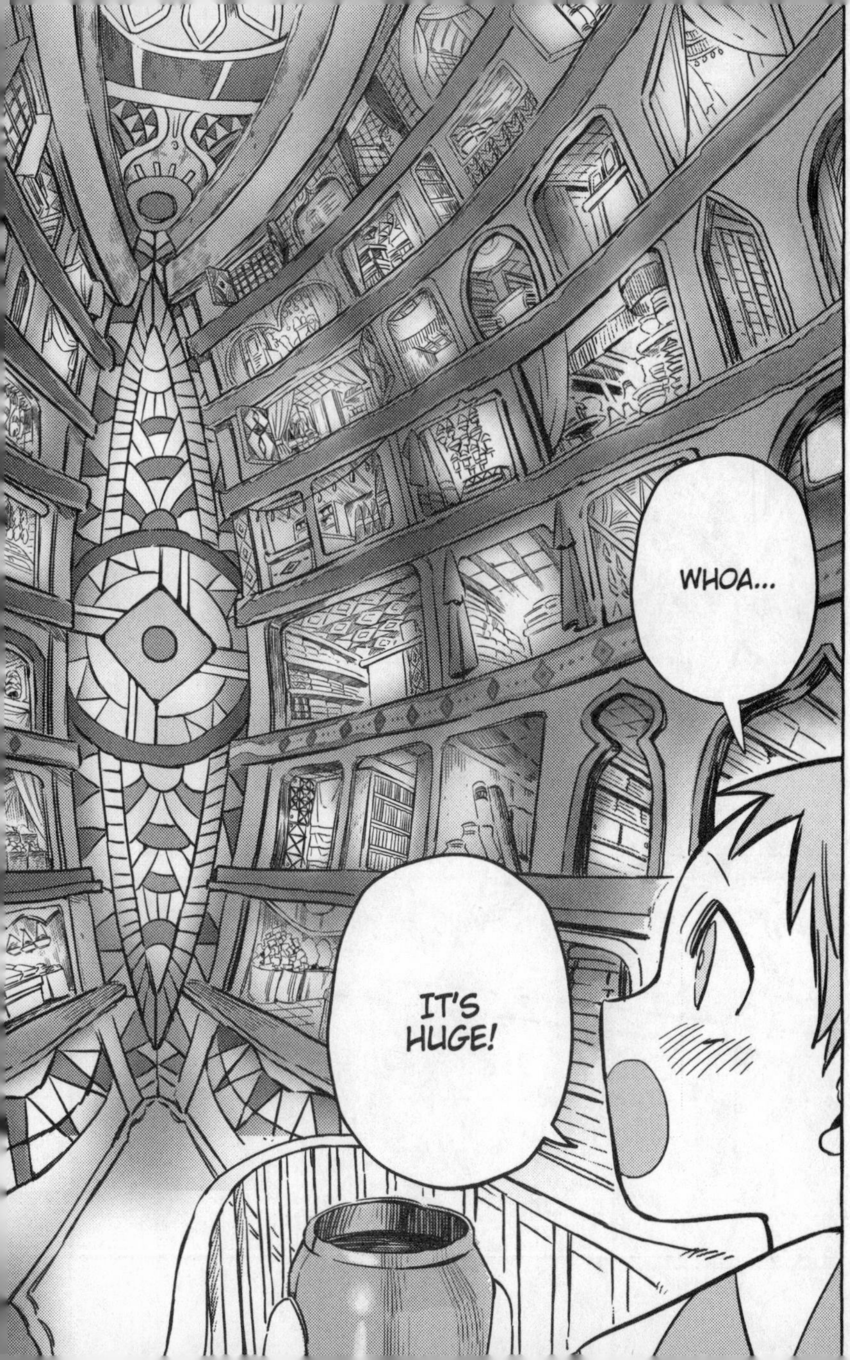
WHOA...
IT'S HUGE!

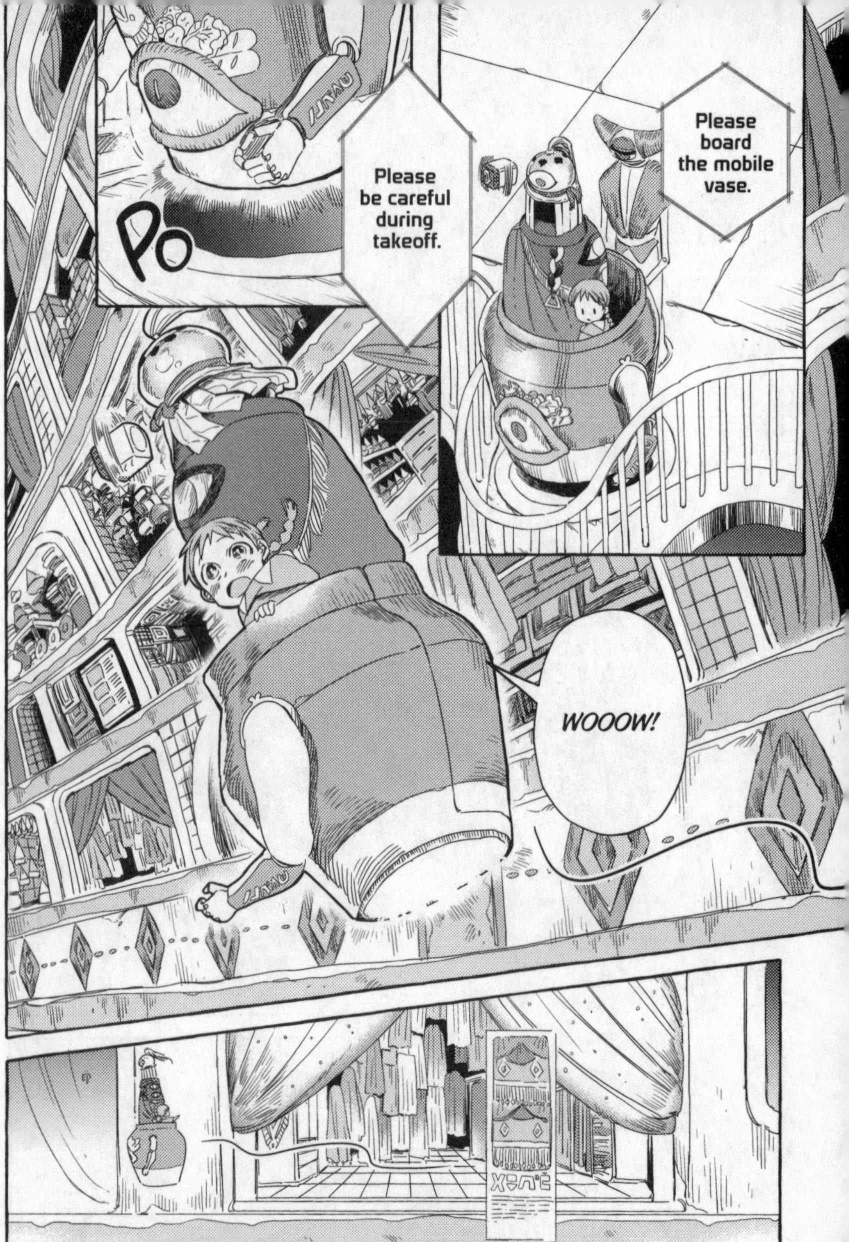
Please board the mobile vase.
Please be careful during takeoff.
PO
WOOOW!

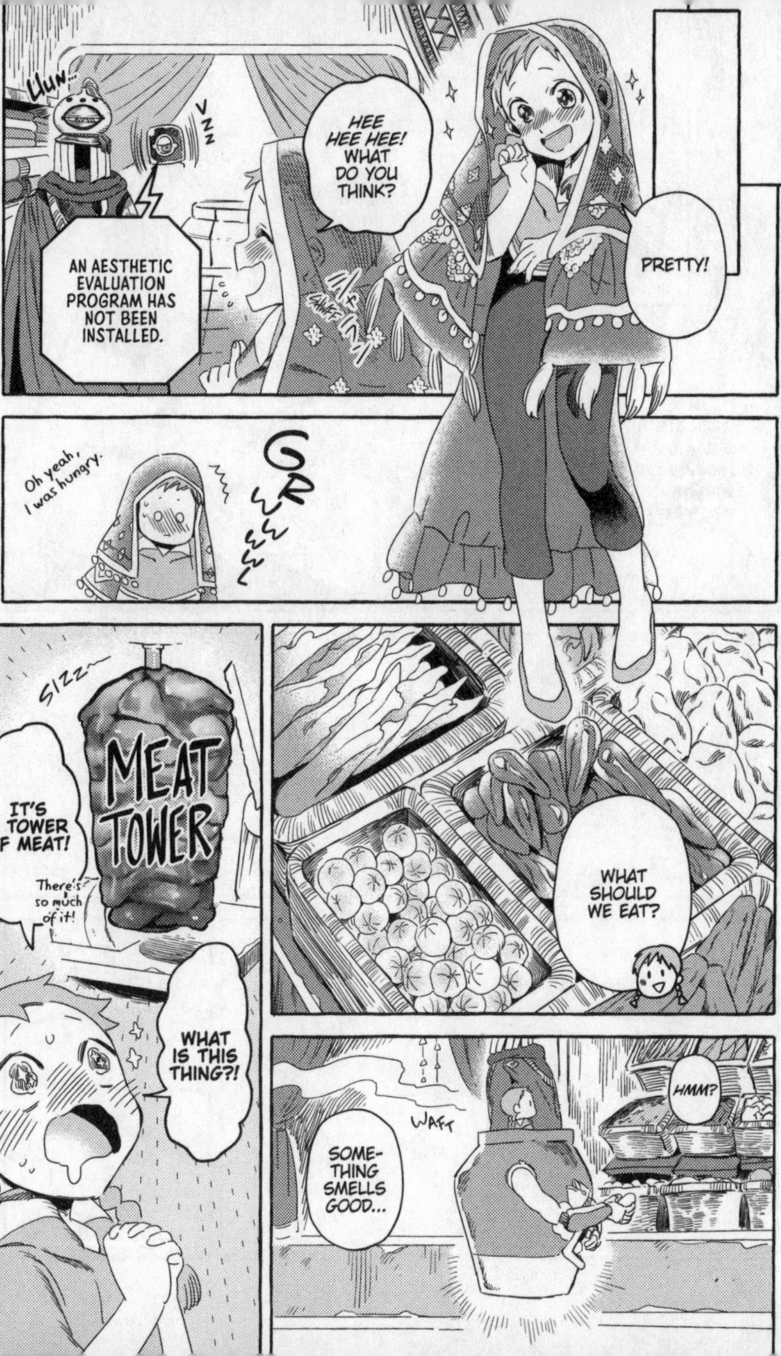
HEE HEE HEE! WHAT DO YOU THINK?
PRETTY!
UUN...
VZZ
AN AESTHETIC EVALUATION PROGRAM HAS NOT BEEN INSTALLED.
GRWWWWL
Oh yeah, I was hungry.
WHAT SHOULD WE EAT?
SIZZ~
MEAT TOWER
IT'S A TOWER OF MEAT!
There's so much of it!
WHAT IS THIS THING?!
HMM?
WAFT
SOME-THING SMELLS GOOD...

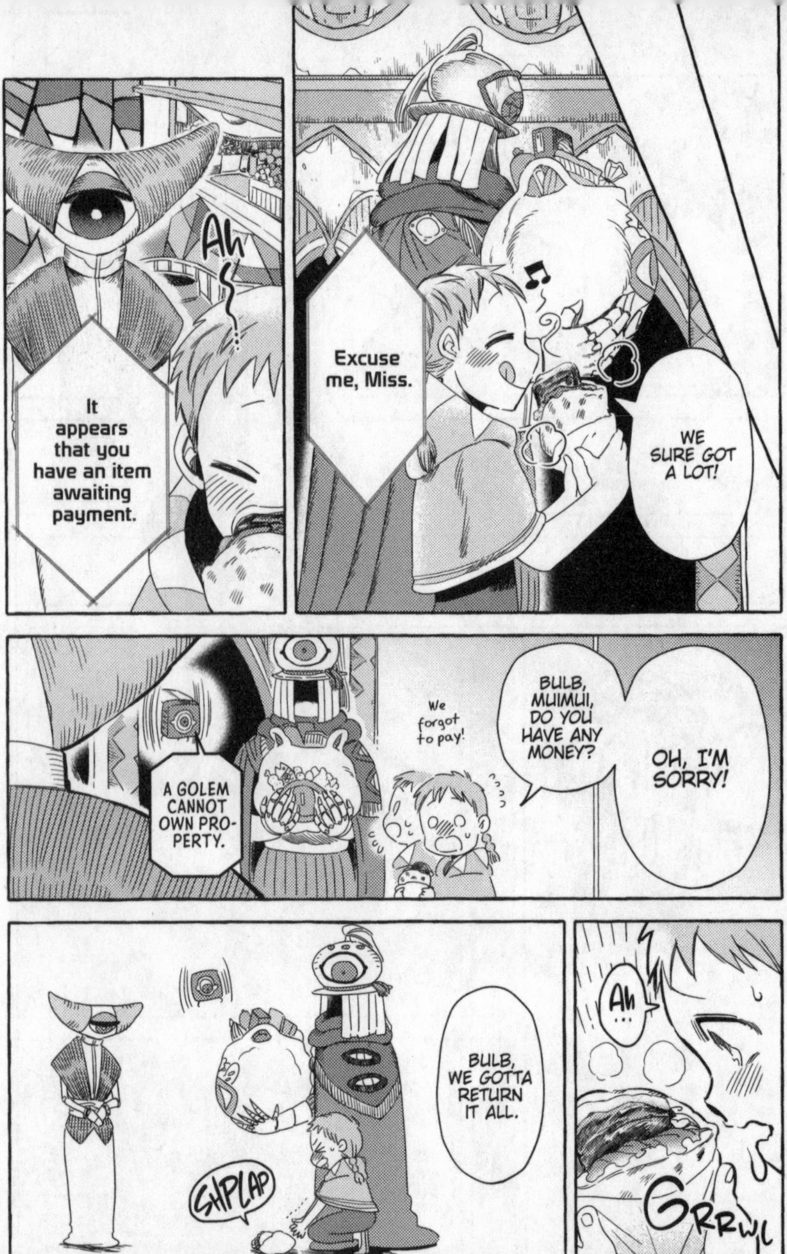
WE SURE GOT A LOT!
Excuse me, Miss.
Ah~...
It appears that you have an item awaiting payment.
OH, I'M SORRY!
BULB, MUIMUI, DO YOU HAVE ANY MONEY?
We forgot to pay!
A GOLEM CANNOT OWN PROPERTY.
Ah...
GRRWL
BULB, WE GOTTA RETURN IT ALL.
SHPLAP

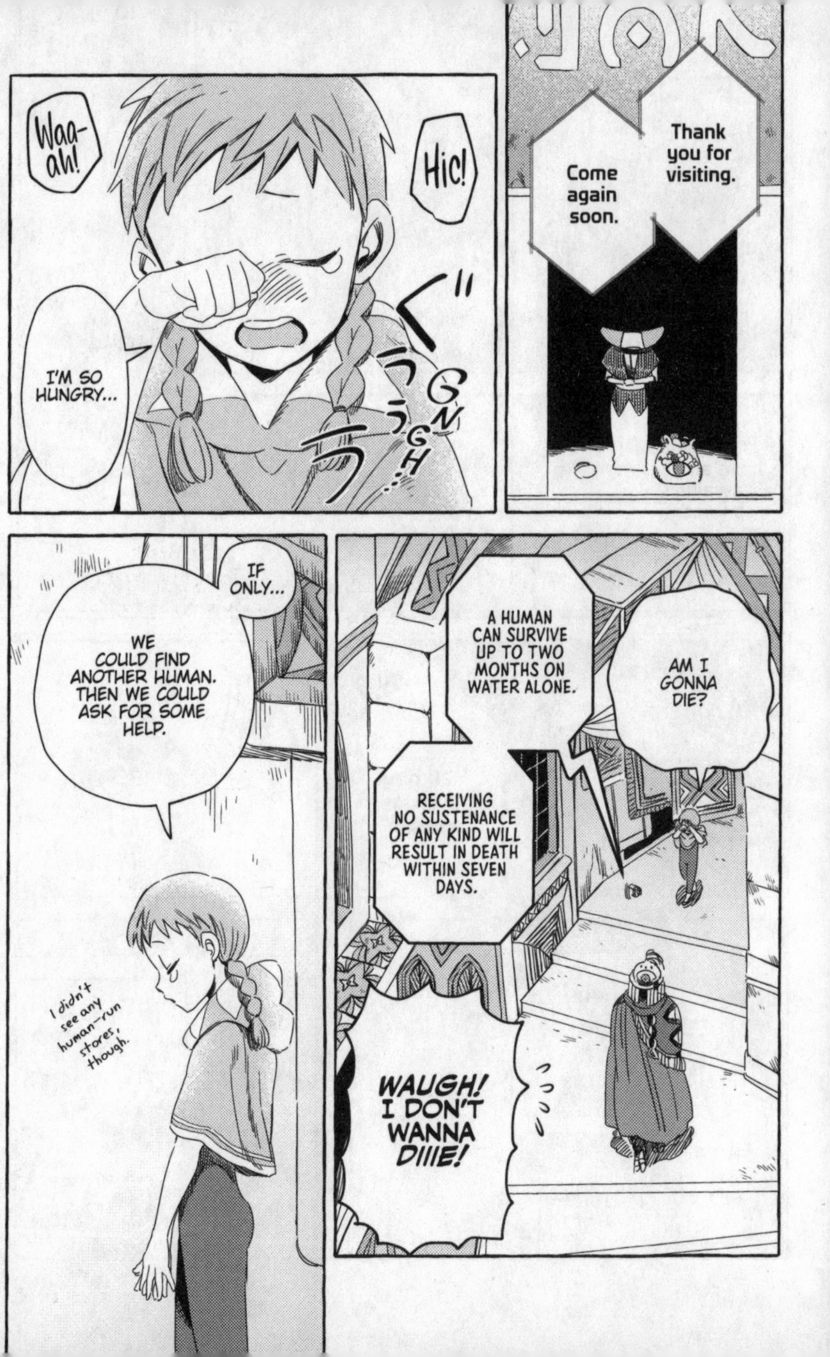

Thank you for visiting.
Come again soon.
Waa-ah!
Hic!
I'M SO HUNGRY...
GNGH...
AM I GONNA DIE?
A HUMAN CAN SURVIVE UP TO TWO MONTHS ON WATER ALONE.
RECEIVING NO SUSTENANCE OF ANY KIND WILL RESULT IN DEATH WITHIN SEVEN DAYS.
WAUGH! I DON'T WANNA DIIIE!
IF ONLY...
WE COULD FIND ANOTHER HUMAN. THEN WE COULD ASK FOR SOME HELP.
I didn't see any human-run stores, though.

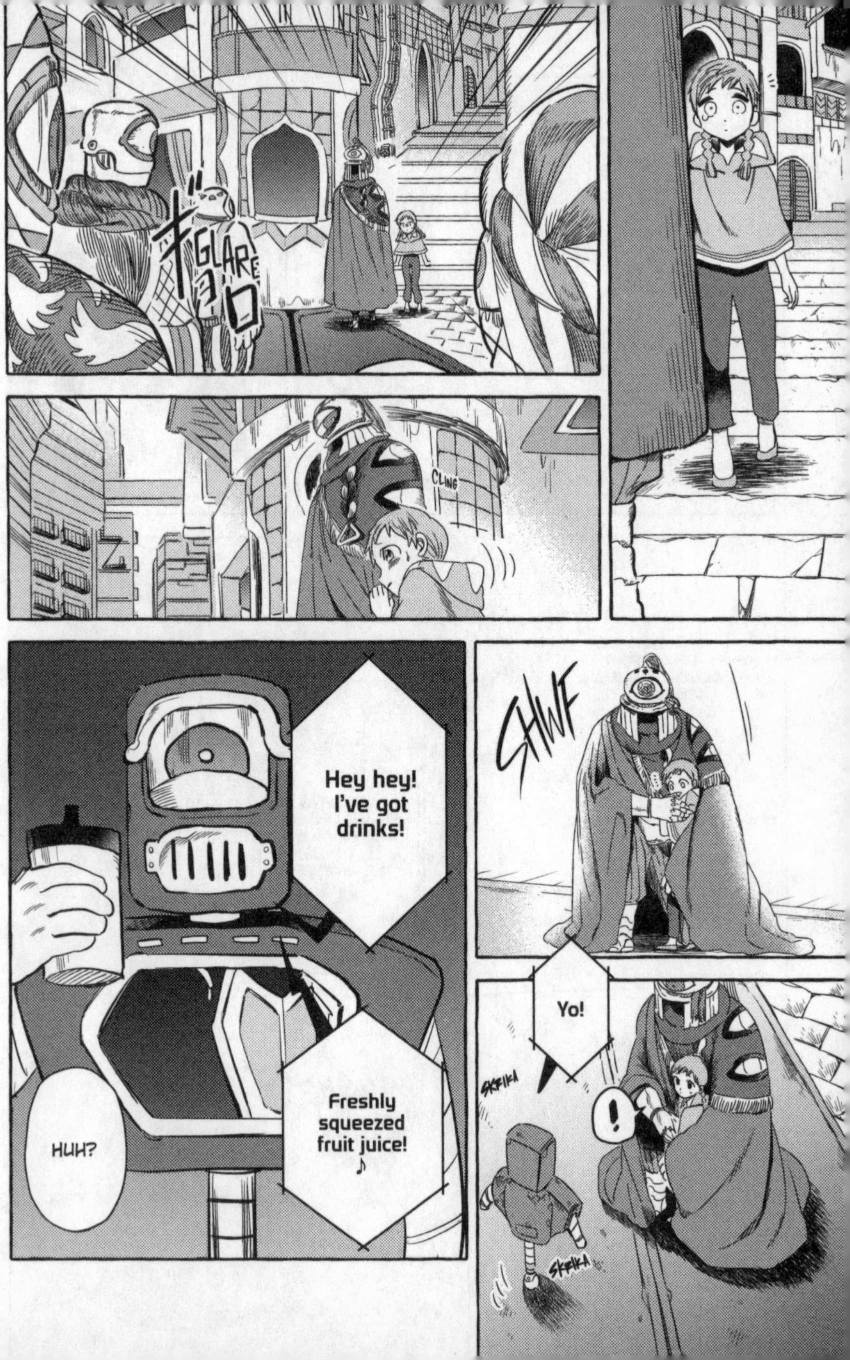
GLARE
CLING
SHWF
Yo!
!
SKRIKA
SKRIKA
Hey hey! I've got drinks!
Freshly squeezed fruit juice! ♪
HUH?

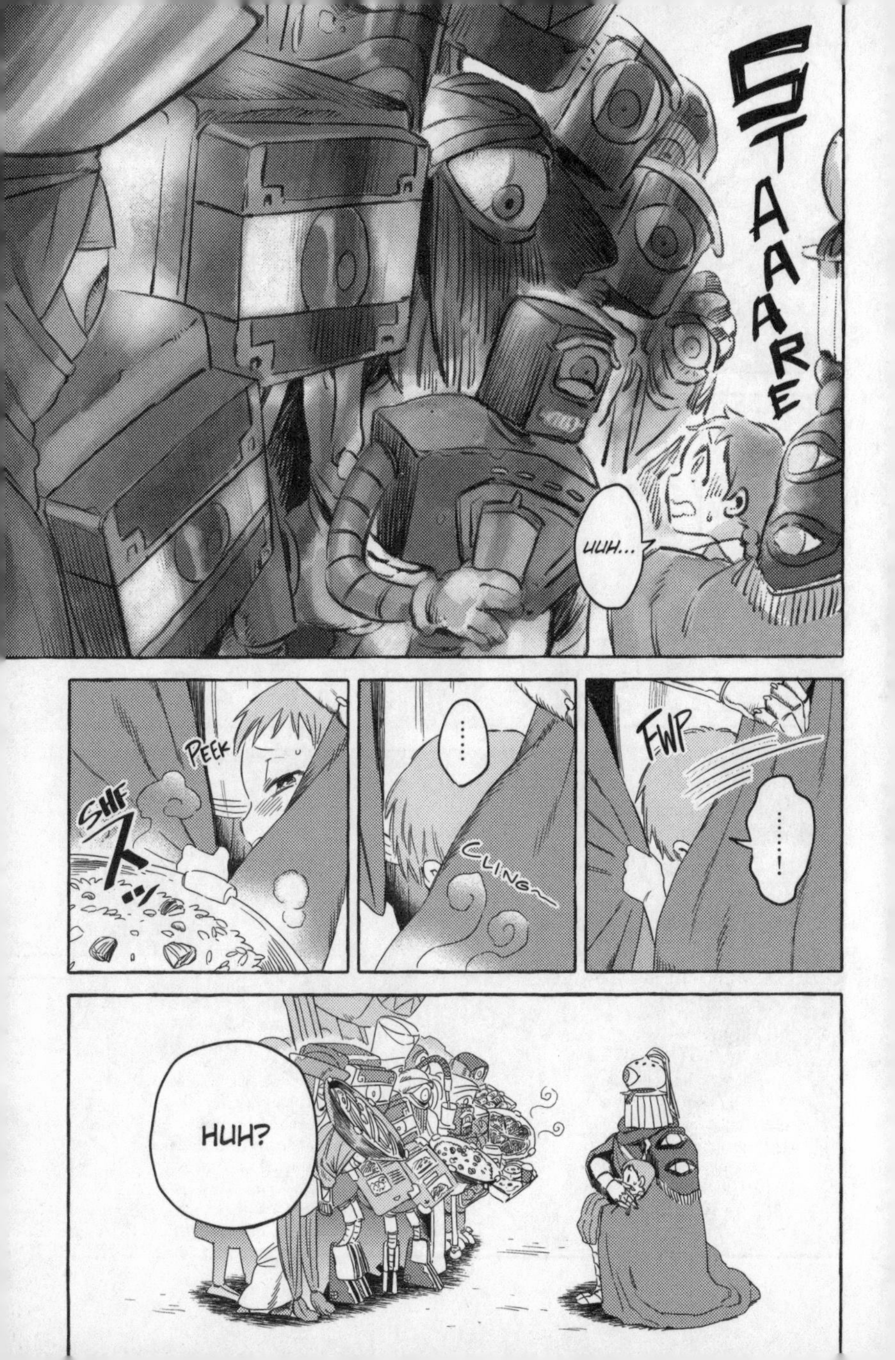
STAARE
UUH...
FWP
......!
......
CLING
PEEK
SHF
HUH?

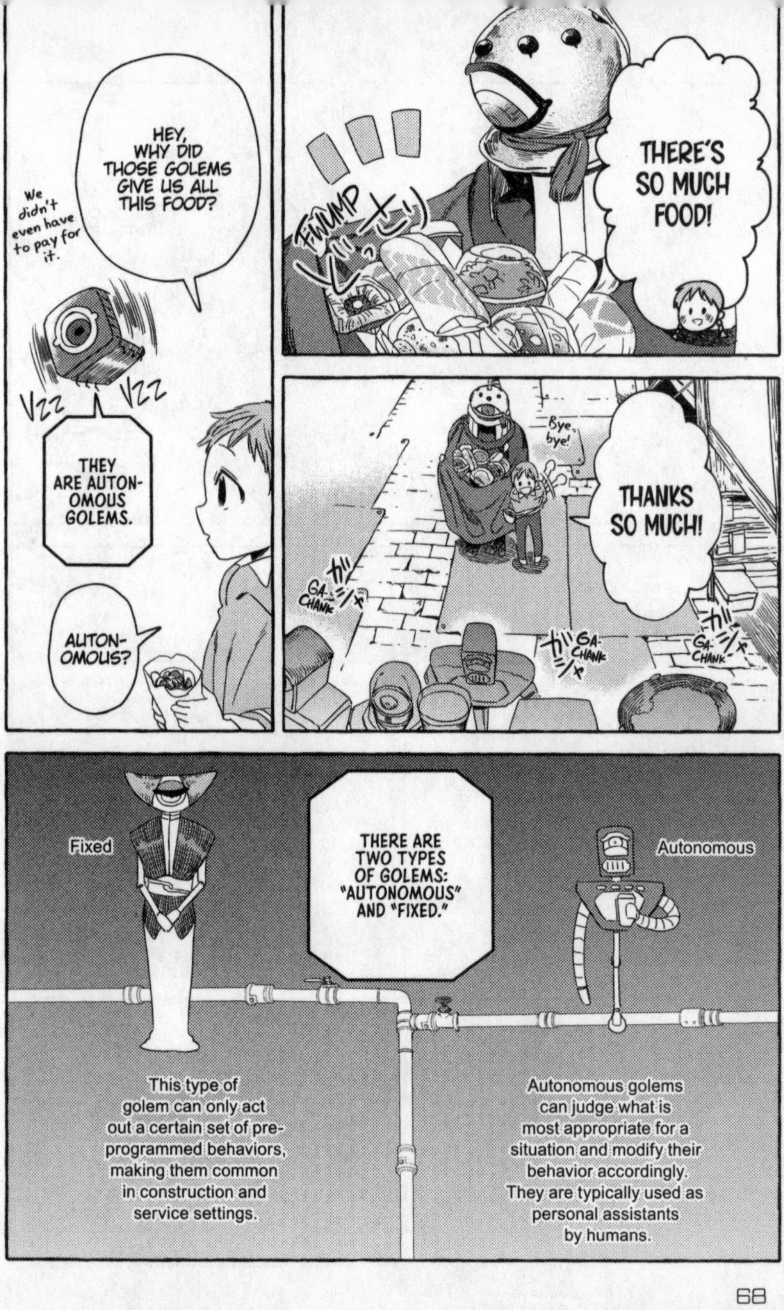
THERE'S SO MUCH FOOD!
FWUMP
Bye, bye!
THANKS SO MUCH!
GA-CHANK
GA-CHANK
GA-CHANK
HEY, WHY DID THOSE GOLEMS GIVE US ALL THIS FOOD?
We didn't even have to pay for it.
VZZ VZZ
THEY ARE AUTONOMOUS GOLEMS.
AUTONOMOUS?
THERE ARE TWO TYPES OF GOLEMS: "AUTONOMOUS" AND "FIXED."
Autonomous
Fixed
Autonomous golems can judge what is most appropriate for a situation and modify their behavior accordingly. They are typically used as personal assistants by humans.
This type of golem can only act out a certain set of pre-programmed behaviors, making them common in construction and service settings.

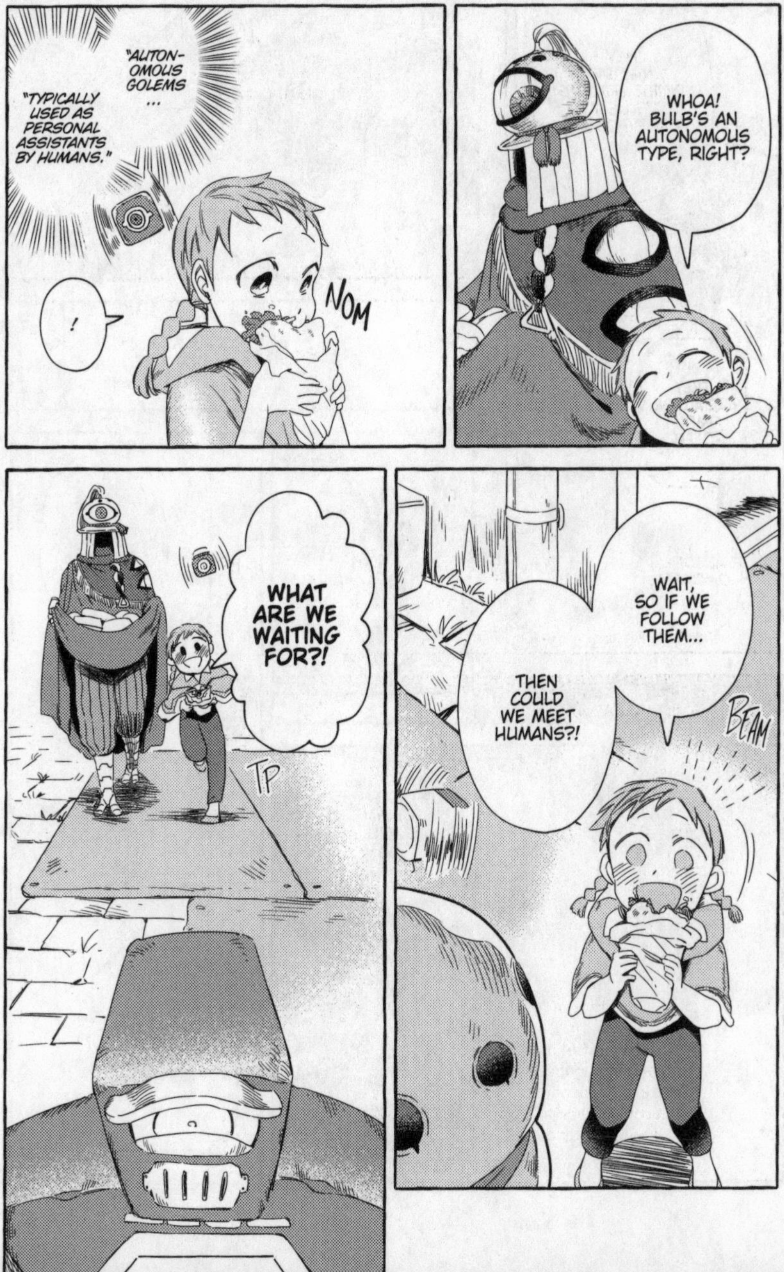
WHOA! BULB'S AN AUTONOMOUS TYPE, RIGHT?
"AUTON-OMOUS GOLEMS ...
"TYPICALLY USED AS PERSONAL ASSISTANTS BY HUMANS."
NOM
!
WAIT, SO IF WE FOLLOW THEM...
THEN COULD WE MEET HUMANS?!
BEAM
WHAT ARE WE WAITING FOR?!
TP

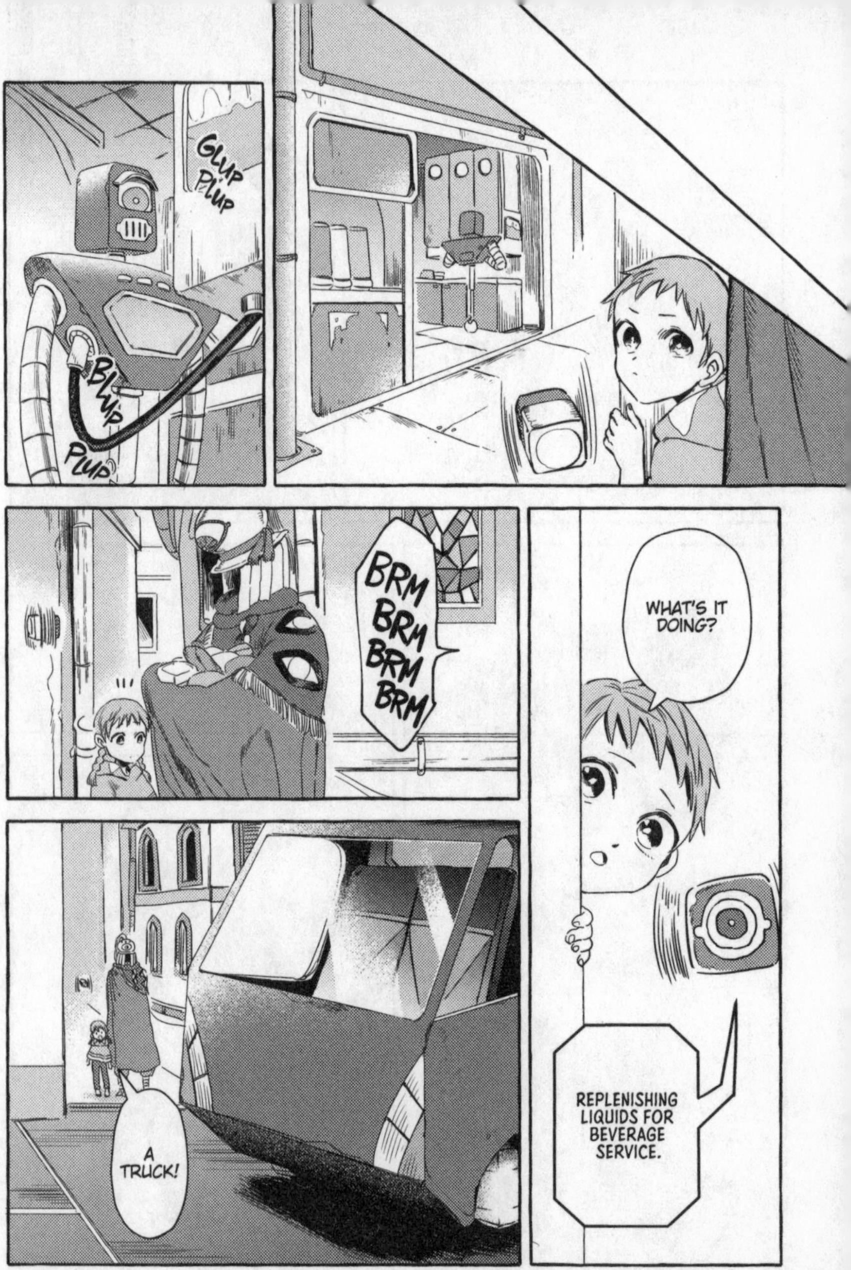
GLUP PLUP
BLUP PLUP
WHAT'S IT DOING?
REPLENISHING LIQUIDS FOR BEVERAGE SERVICE.
BRM BRM BRM BRM
A TRUCK!

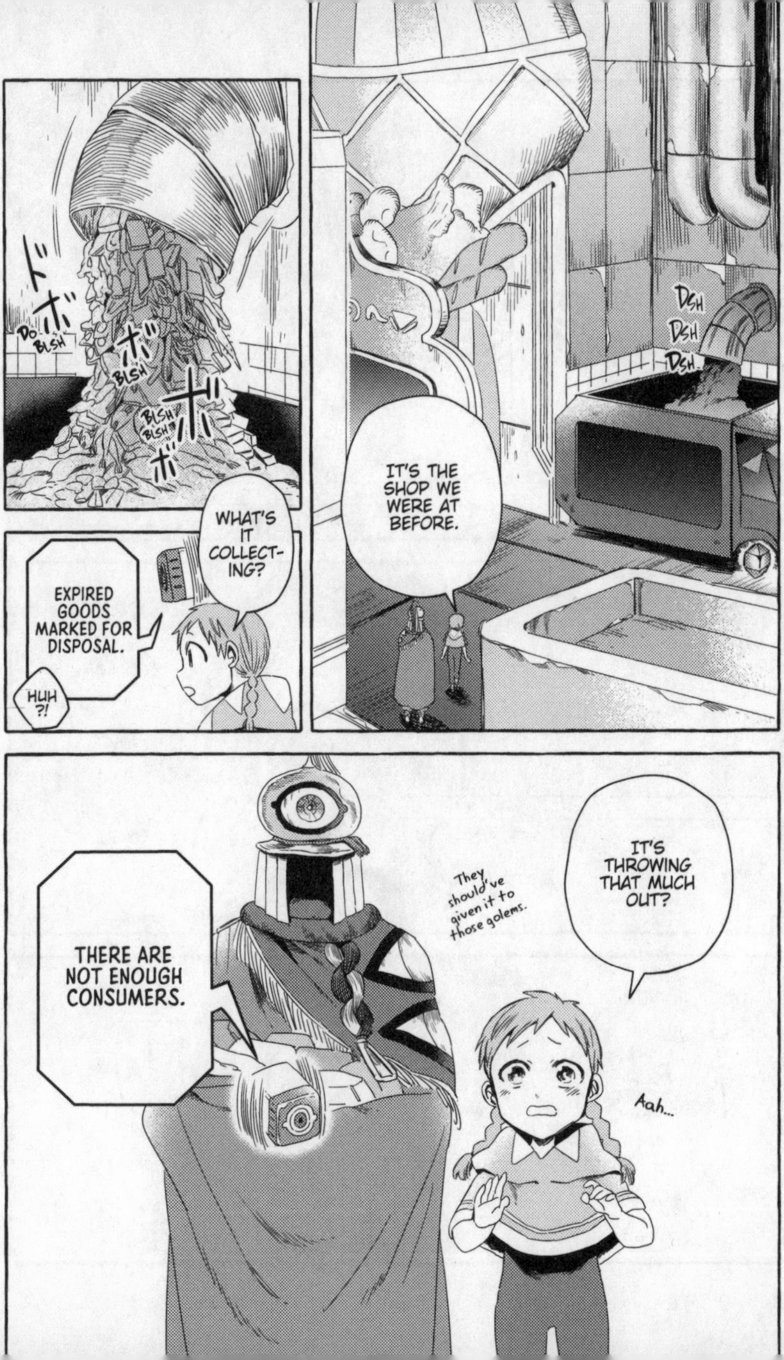
DSH
DSH
DSH
IT'S THE SHOP WE WERE AT BEFORE.
DO BLSH
BLSH
BLSH BLSH
WHAT'S IT COLLECTING?
EXPIRED GOODS MARKED FOR DISPOSAL.
HUH?!
IT'S THROWING THAT MUCH OUT?
They should've given it to those golems.
Aah...
THERE ARE NOT ENOUGH CONSUMERS.

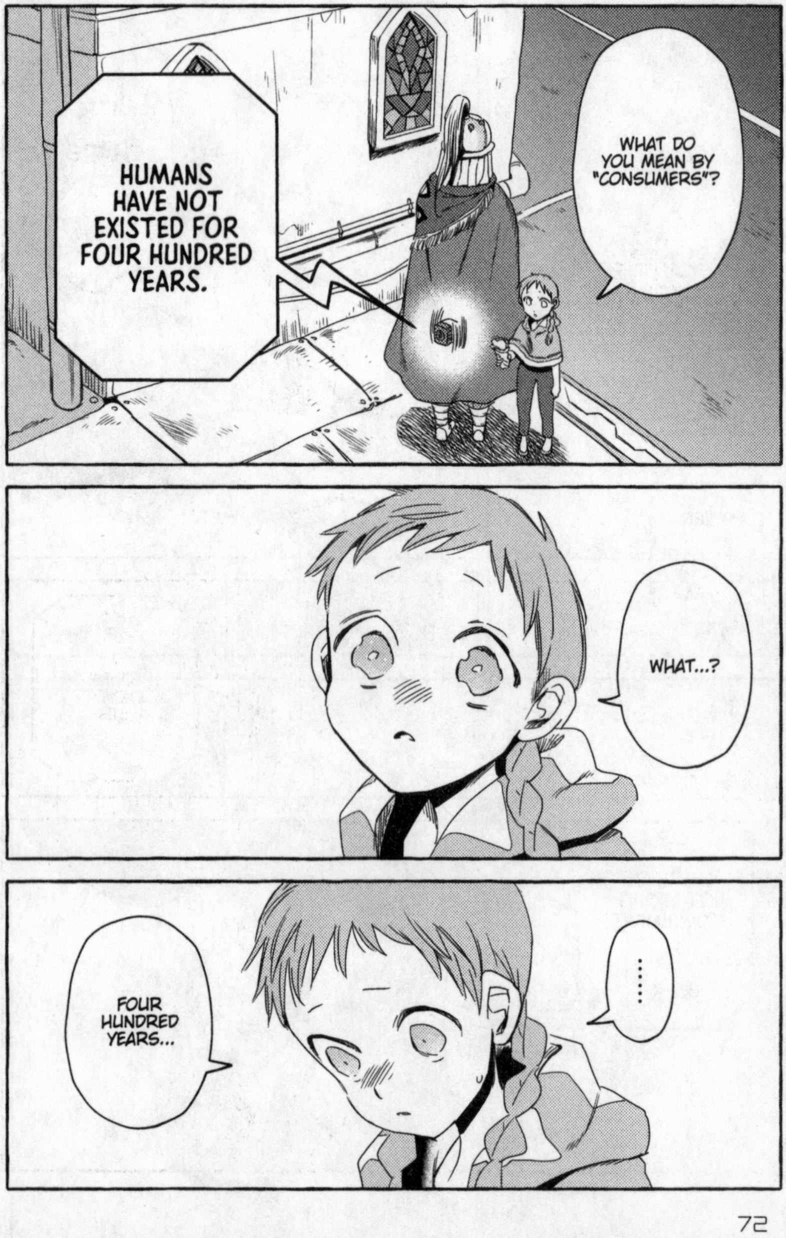
WHAT DO YOU MEAN BY "CONSUMERS"?
HUMANS HAVE NOT EXISTED FOR FOUR HUNDRED YEARS.
WHAT...?
......
FOUR HUNDRED YEARS...

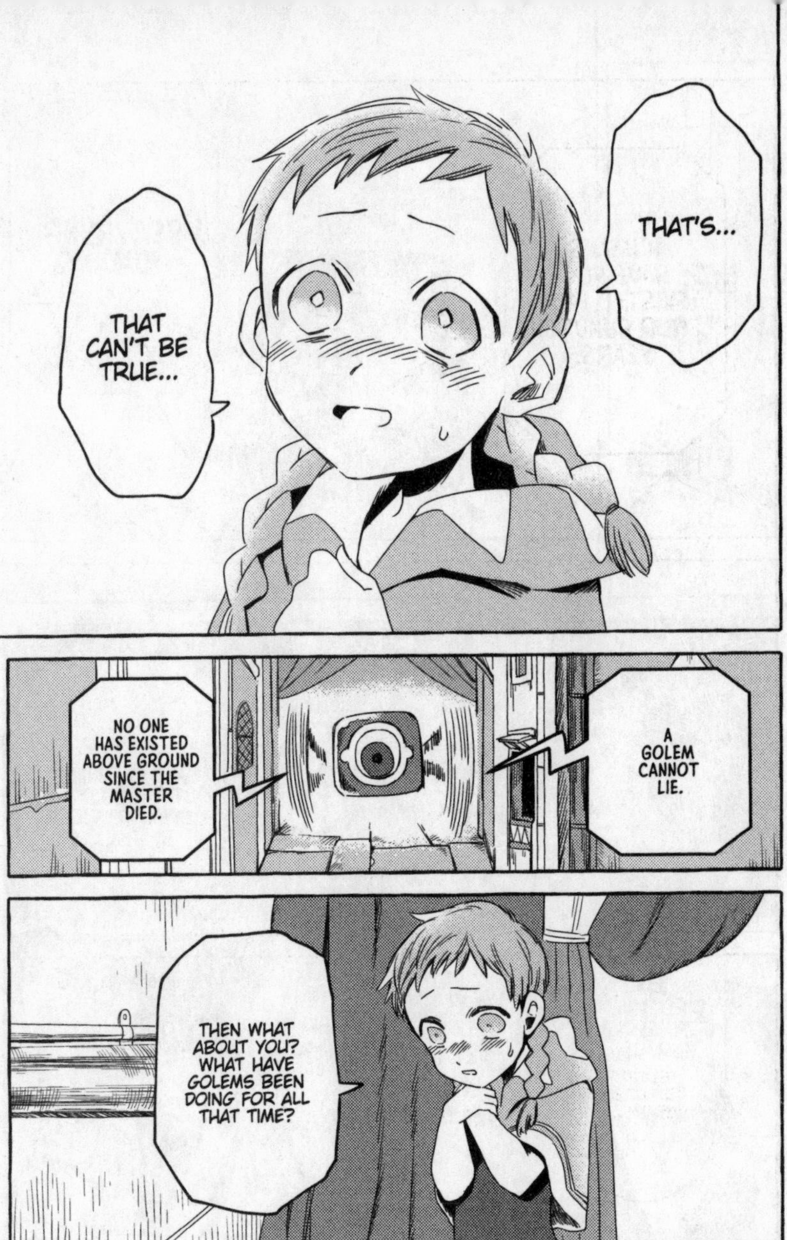
THAT'S...
THAT CAN'T BE TRUE...
A GOLEM CANNOT LIE.
NO ONE HAS EXISTED ABOVE GROUND SINCE THE MASTER DIED.
THEN WHAT ABOUT YOU? WHAT HAVE GOLEMS BEEN DOING FOR ALL THAT TIME?

SERVICING HUMANS.

BUT...

YOU JUST SAID HUMANS DON'T EXIST, DIDN'T YOU?

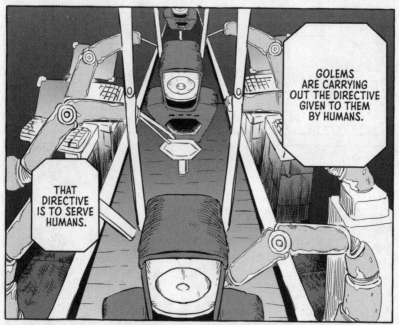

GOLEMS ARE CARRYING OUT THE DIRECTIVE GIVEN TO THEM BY HUMANS.

THAT DIRECTIVE IS TO SERVE HUMANS.

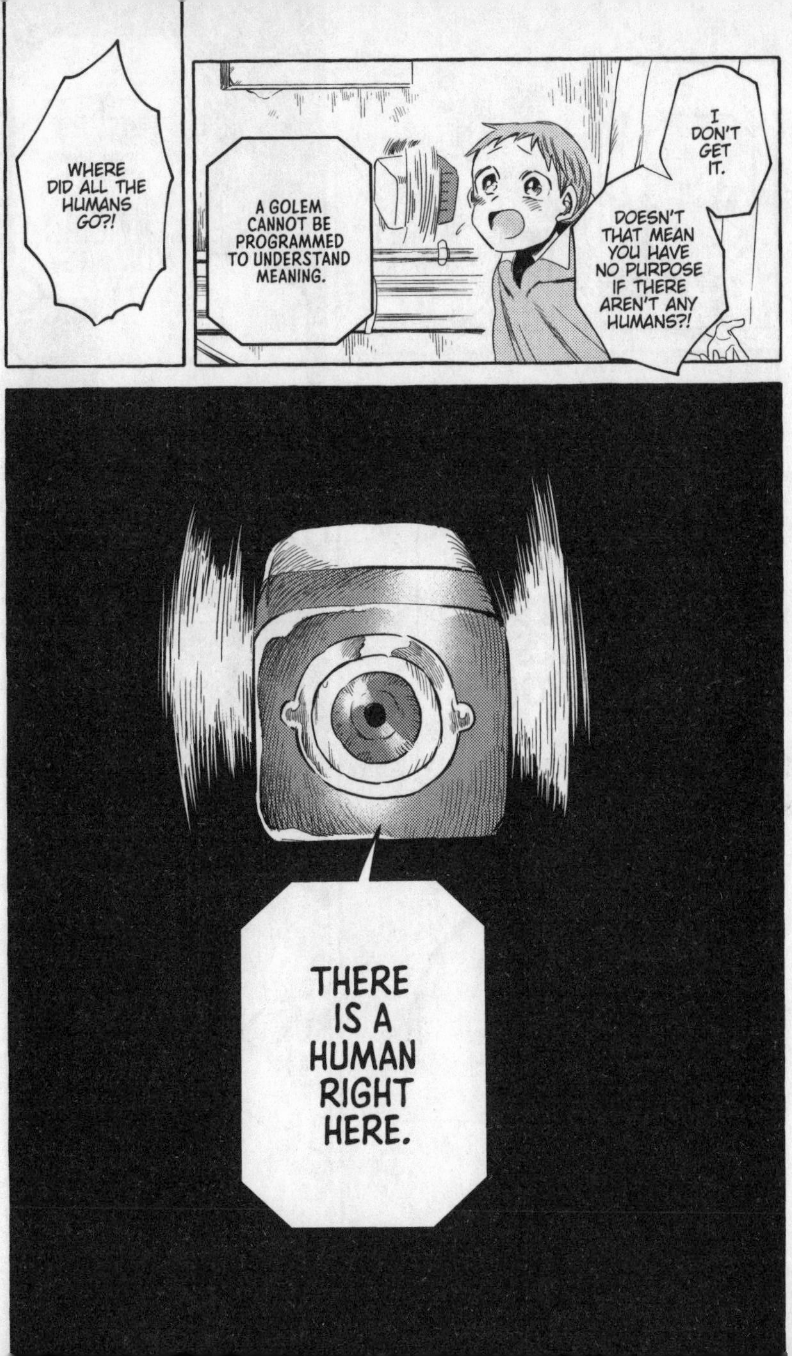
I DON'T GET IT.
DOESN'T THAT MEAN YOU HAVE NO PURPOSE IF THERE AREN'T ANY HUMANS?!
A GOLEM CANNOT BE PROGRAMMED TO UNDERSTAND MEANING.
WHERE DID ALL THE HUMANS GO?!
THERE IS A HUMAN RIGHT HERE.

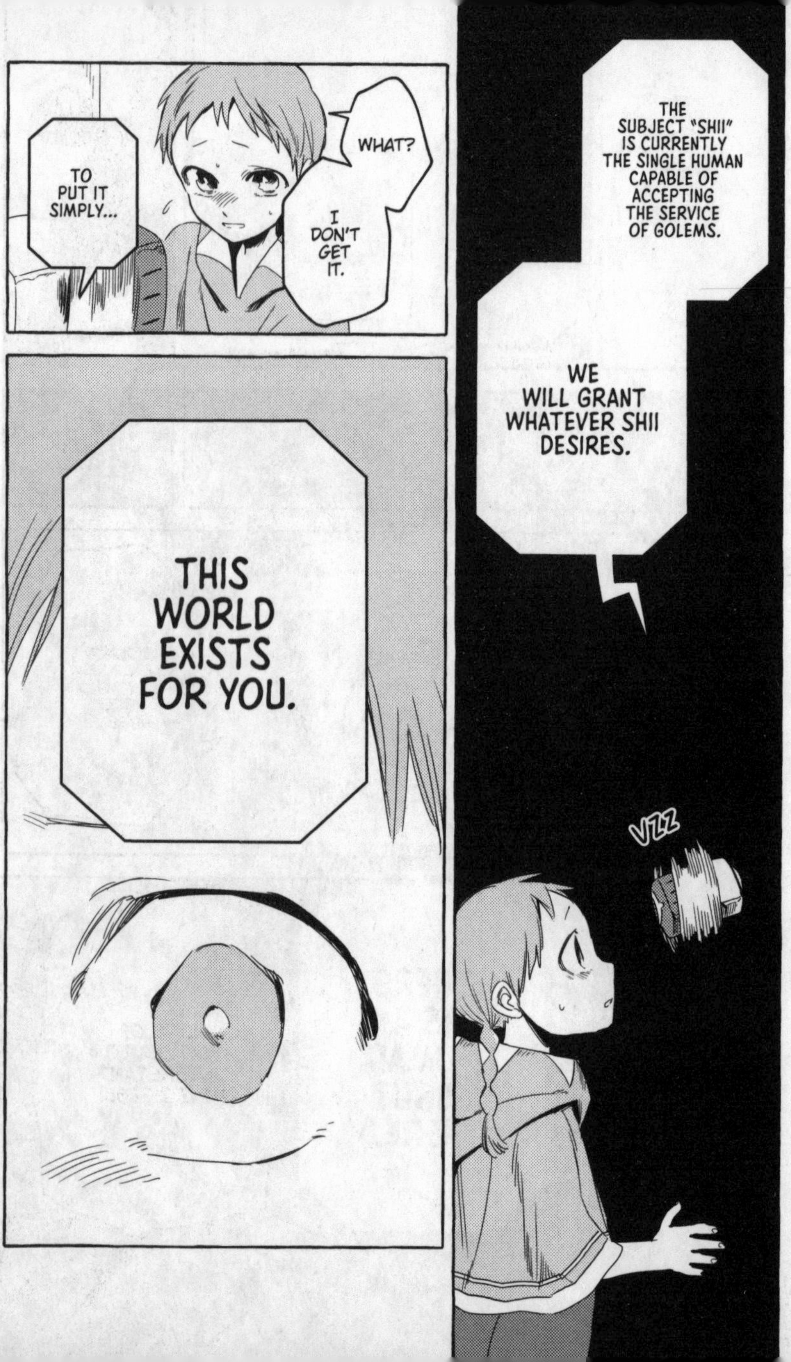
THE SUBJECT "SHII" IS CURRENTLY THE SINGLE HUMAN CAPABLE OF ACCEPTING THE SERVICE OF GOLEMS.
WE WILL GRANT WHATEVER SHII DESIRES.
VZZ
WHAT?
I DON'T GET IT.
TO PUT IT SIMPLY...
THIS WORLD EXISTS FOR YOU.

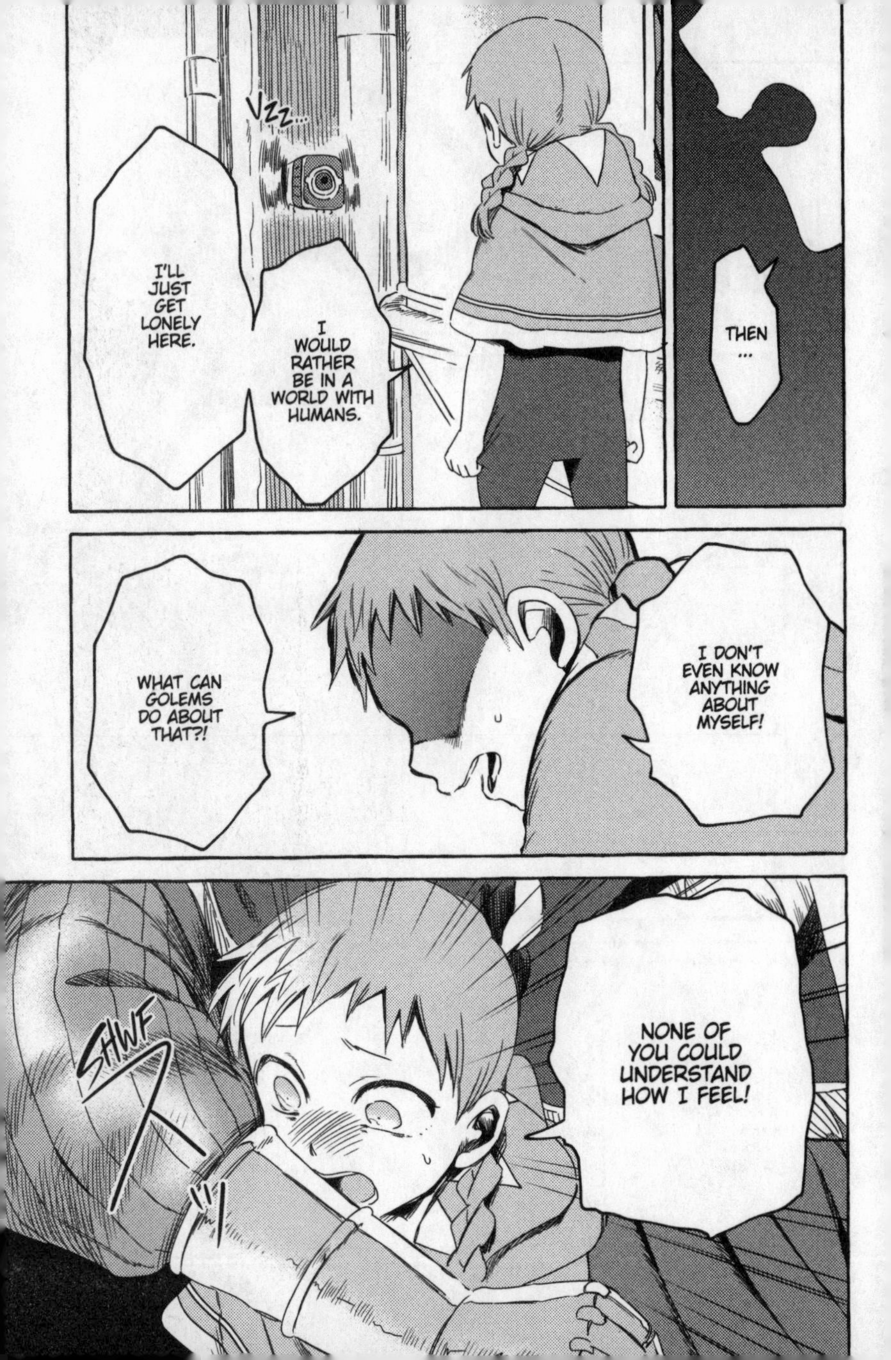
THEN ...
VZZ...
I WOULD RATHER BE IN A WORLD WITH HUMANS.
I'LL JUST GET LONELY HERE.
I DON'T EVEN KNOW ANYTHING ABOUT MYSELF!
WHAT CAN GOLEMS DO ABOUT THAT?!
NONE OF YOU COULD UNDERSTAND HOW I FEEL!
SHWF
!!

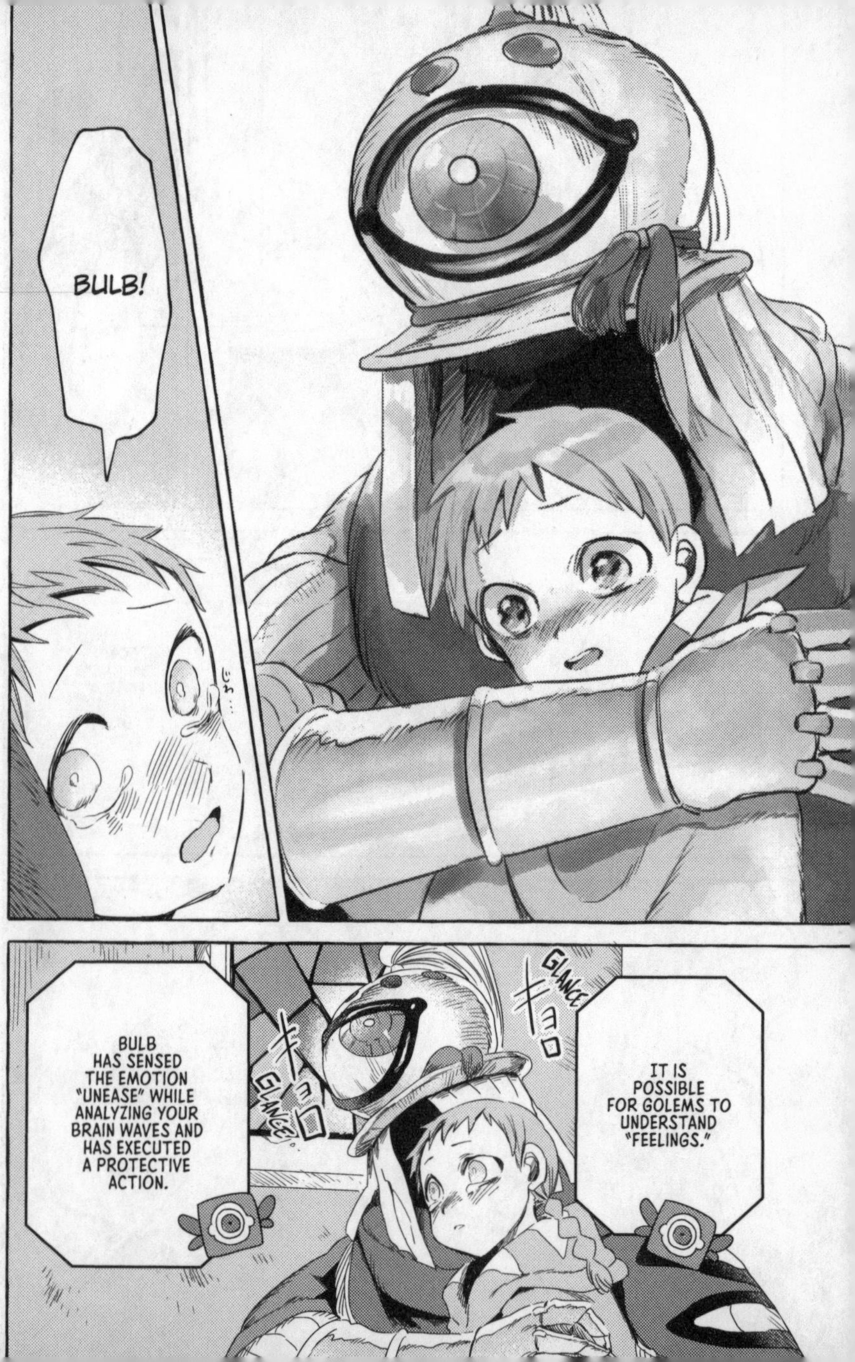
BULB!
IT IS POSSIBLE FOR GOLEMS TO UNDERSTAND "FEELINGS."
GLANCE
キョロ
キョロ
GLANCE
BULB HAS SENSED THE EMOTION "UNEASE" WHILE ANALYZING YOUR BRAIN WAVES AND HAS EXECUTED A PROTECTIVE ACTION.

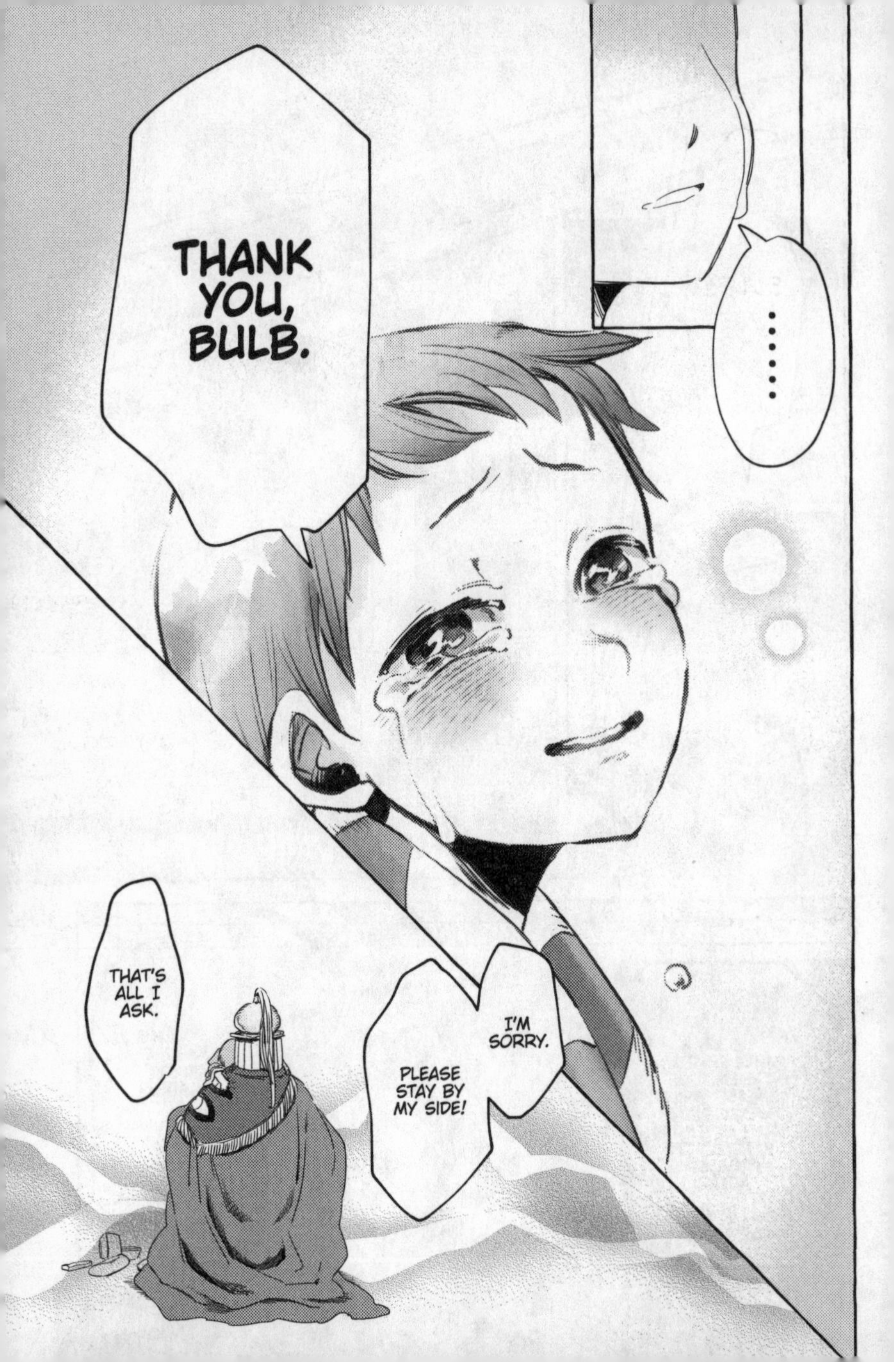
......
THANK YOU, BULB.
I'M SORRY.
PLEASE STAY BY MY SIDE!
THAT'S ALL I ASK.

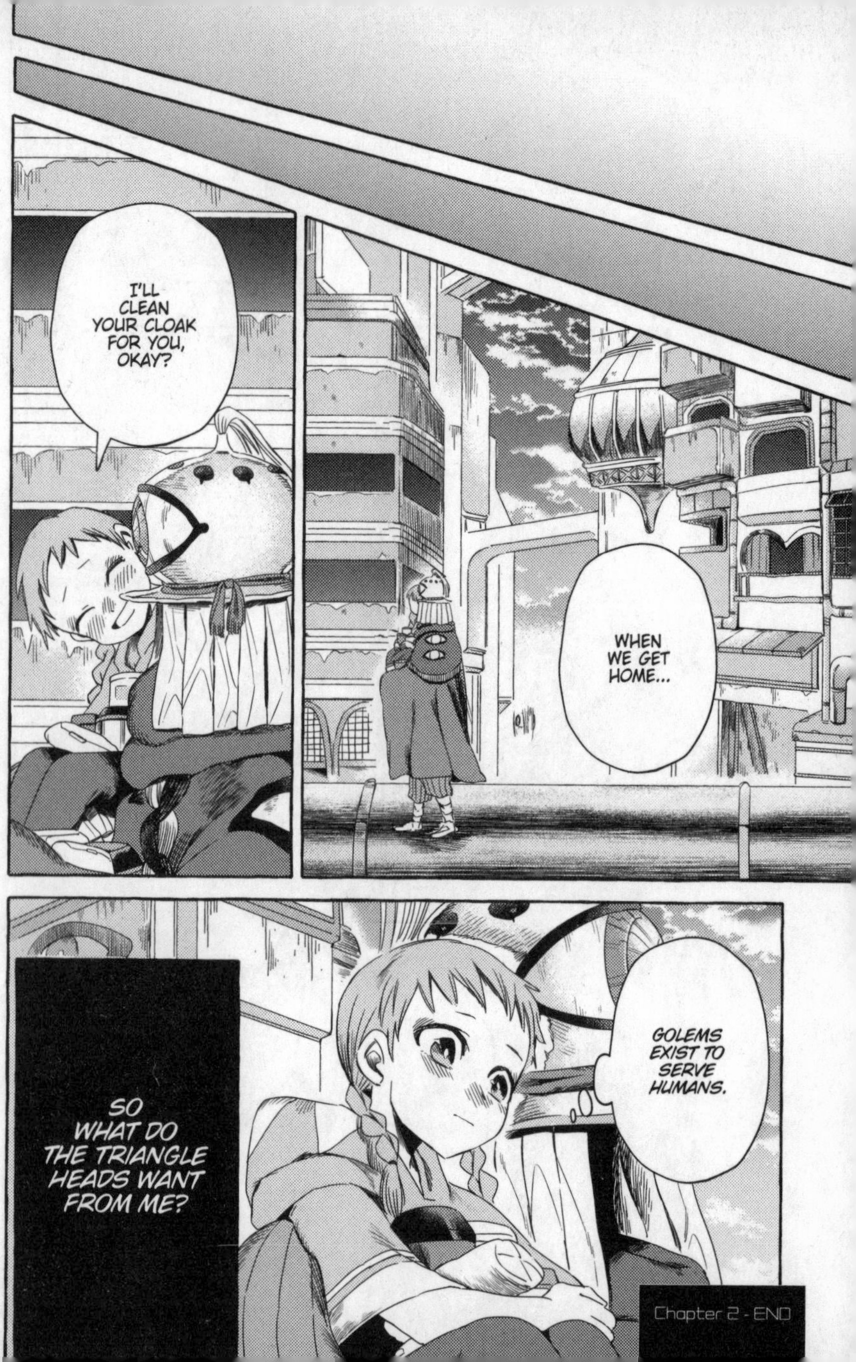
WHEN WE GET HOME...
I'LL CLEAN YOUR CLOAK FOR YOU, OKAY?
GOLEMS EXIST TO SERVE HUMANS.
SO WHAT DO THE TRIANGLE HEADS WANT FROM ME?
Chapter 2 - END

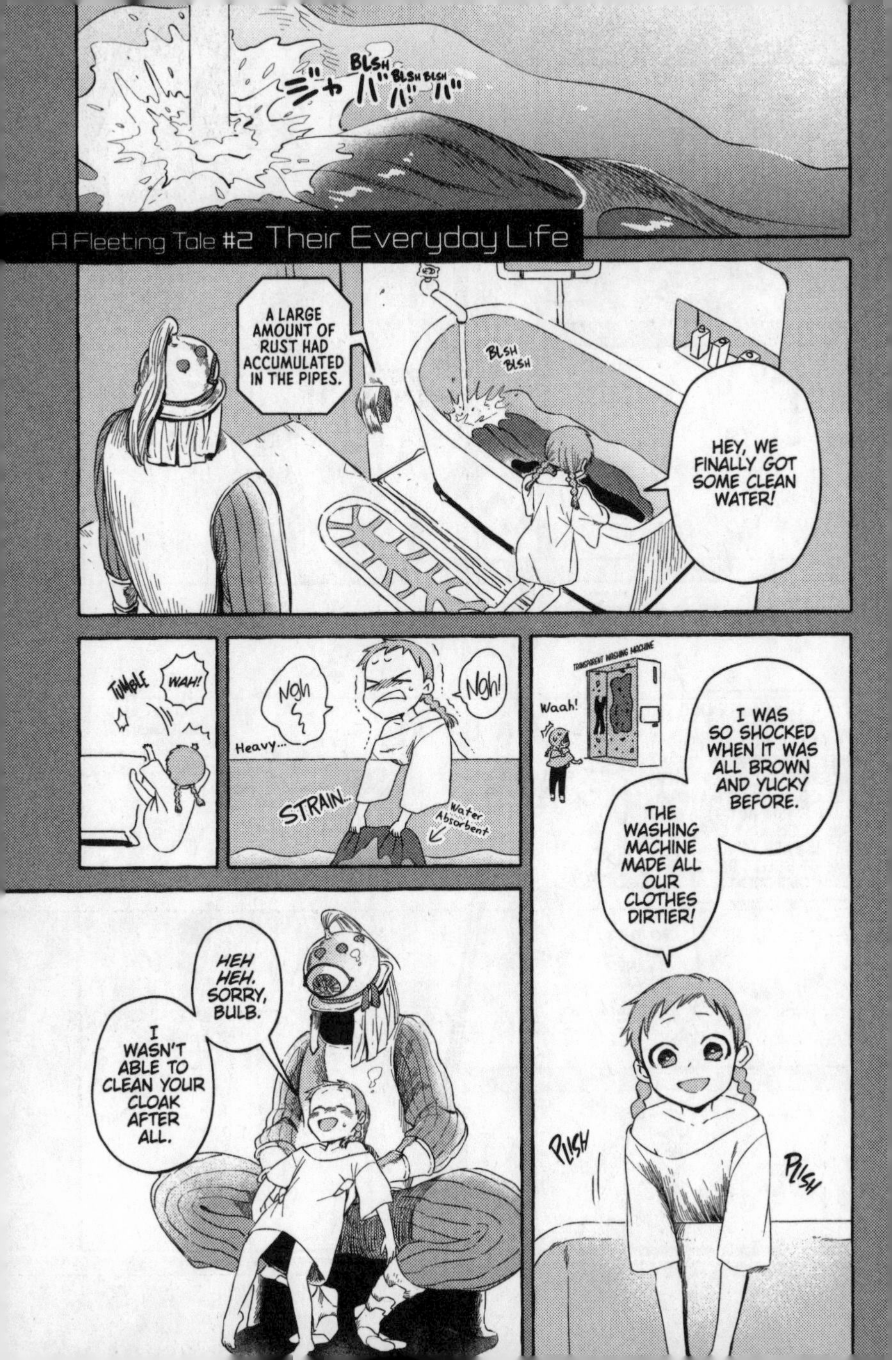
BLSH
ジャバババ
BLSH BLSH
A Fleeting Tale #2 Their Everyday Life
BLSH BLSH
HEY, WE FINALLY GOT SOME CLEAN WATER!
A LARGE AMOUNT OF RUST HAD ACCUMULATED IN THE PIPES.
TRANSPARENT WASHING MACHINE
Waah!
I WAS SO SHOCKED WHEN IT WAS ALL BROWN AND YUCKY BEFORE.
THE WASHING MACHINE MADE ALL OUR CLOTHES DIRTIER!
PLISH
PLISH
Ngh!
Ngh
Heavy...
STRAIN..
Water Absorbent
WAH!
TUMBLE
HEH HEH. SORRY, BULB.
I WASN'T ABLE TO CLEAN YOUR CLOAK AFTER ALL.

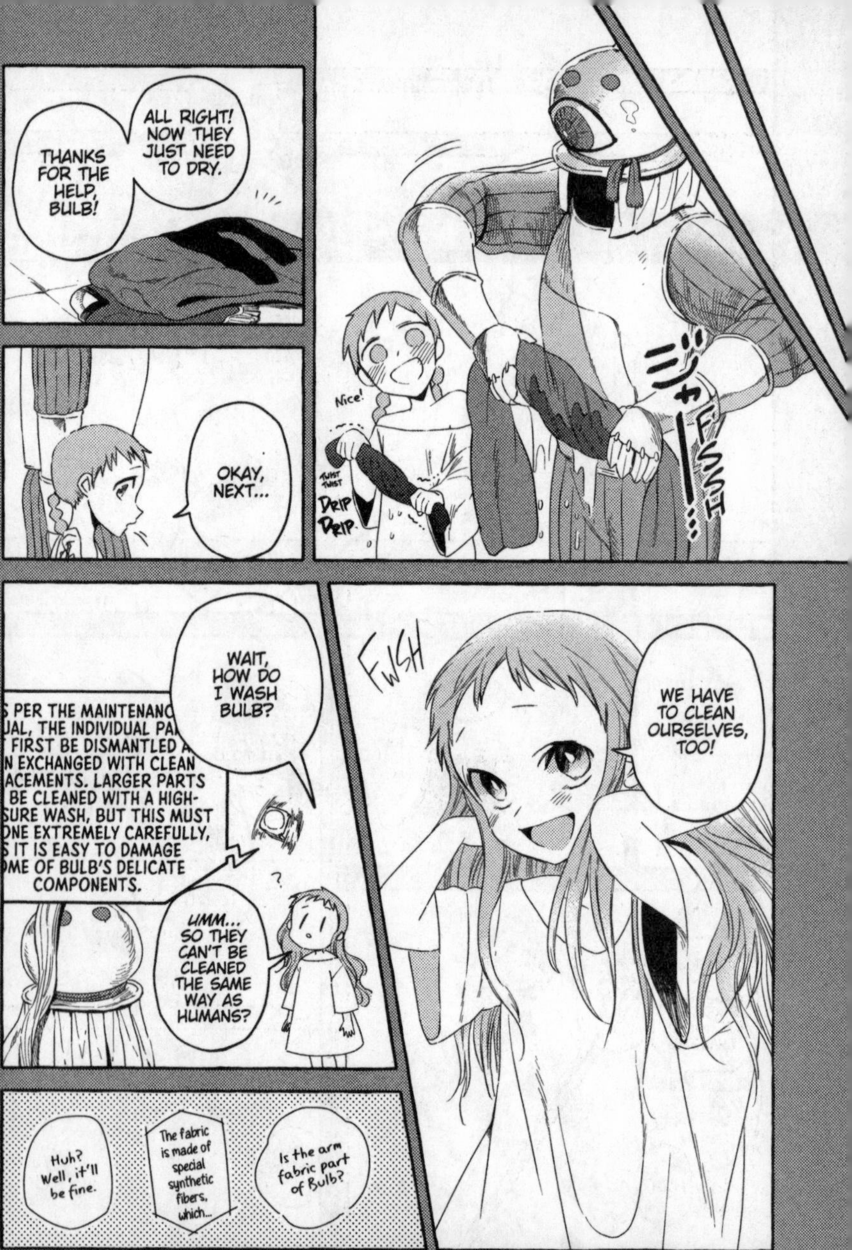
?
Nice!
TWIST TWIST
DRIP DRIP
FSSH
ALL RIGHT! NOW THEY JUST NEED TO DRY.
THANKS FOR THE HELP, BULB!
OKAY, NEXT...
FWSH
WE HAVE TO CLEAN OURSELVES, TOO!
WAIT, HOW DO I WASH BULB?
S PER THE MAINTENANC
UAL, THE INDIVIDUAL PA
T FIRST BE DISMANTLED A
N EXCHANGED WITH CLEAN
ACEMENTS. LARGER PARTS
BE CLEANED WITH A HIGH-
SURE WASH, BUT THIS MUST
ONE EXTREMELY CAREFULLY,
S IT IS EASY TO DAMAGE
OME OF BULB'S DELICATE
COMPONENTS.
?
UMM... SO THEY CAN'T BE CLEANED THE SAME WAY AS HUMANS?
Is the arm fabric part of Bulb?
The fabric is made of special synthetic fibers, which...
Huh? Well, it'll be fine.

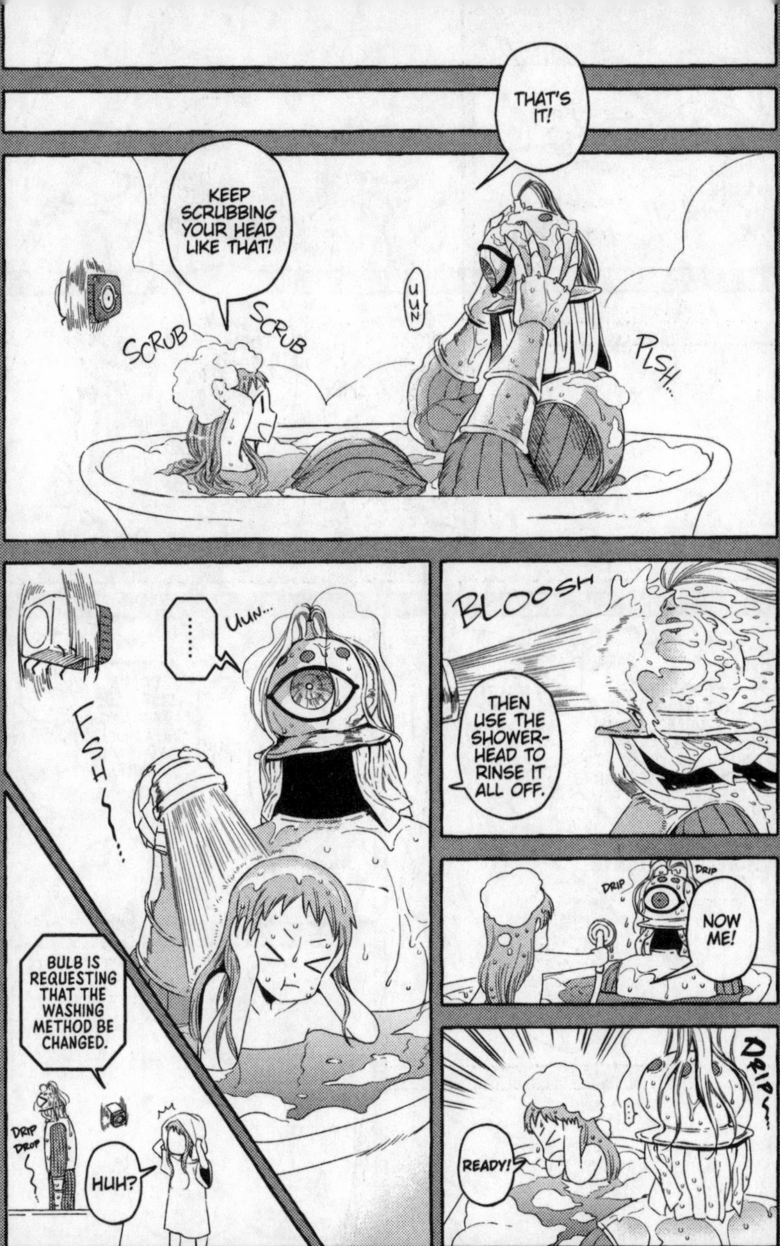
THAT'S IT!
UUN
KEEP SCRUBBING YOUR HEAD LIKE THAT!
SCRUB
SCRUB
PLSH...
BLOOSH
THEN USE THE SHOWER-HEAD TO RINSE IT ALL OFF.
DRIP
DRIP
NOW ME!
DRIP...
READY!
UUN...
......
FSH...
BULB IS REQUESTING THAT THE WASHING METHOD BE CHANGED.
DRIP DROP
HUH?

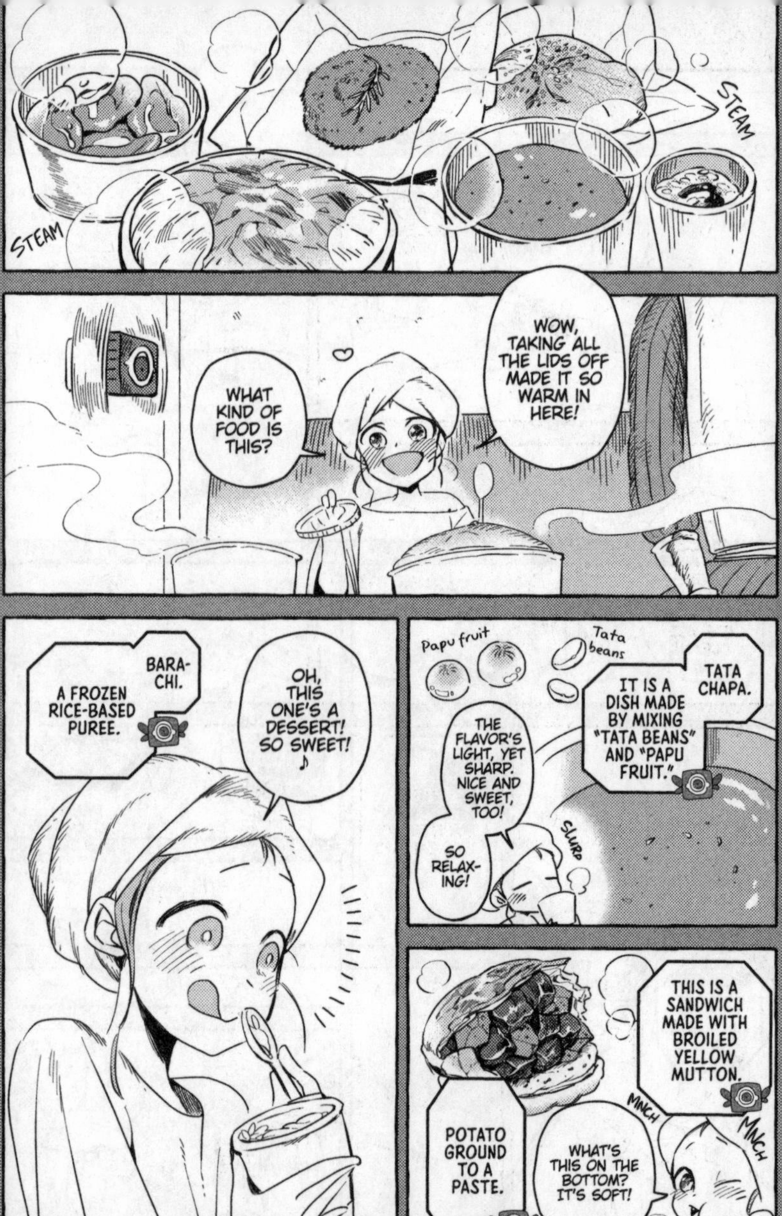
STEAM
STEAM
WOW, TAKING ALL THE LIDS OFF MADE IT SO WARM IN HERE!
WHAT KIND OF FOOD IS THIS?
Tata beans
TATA CHAPA.
IT IS A DISH MADE BY MIXING "TATA BEANS" AND "PAPU FRUIT."
Papu fruit
THE FLAVOR'S LIGHT, YET SHARP. NICE AND SWEET, TOO!
SLURP
SO RELAXING!
THIS IS A SANDWICH MADE WITH BROILED YELLOW MUTTON.
MNCH
MNCH
WHAT'S THIS ON THE BOTTOM? IT'S SOFT!
POTATO GROUND TO A PASTE.
OH, THIS ONE'S A DESSERT! SO SWEET! ♪
BARA-CHI.
A FROZEN RICE-BASED PUREE.

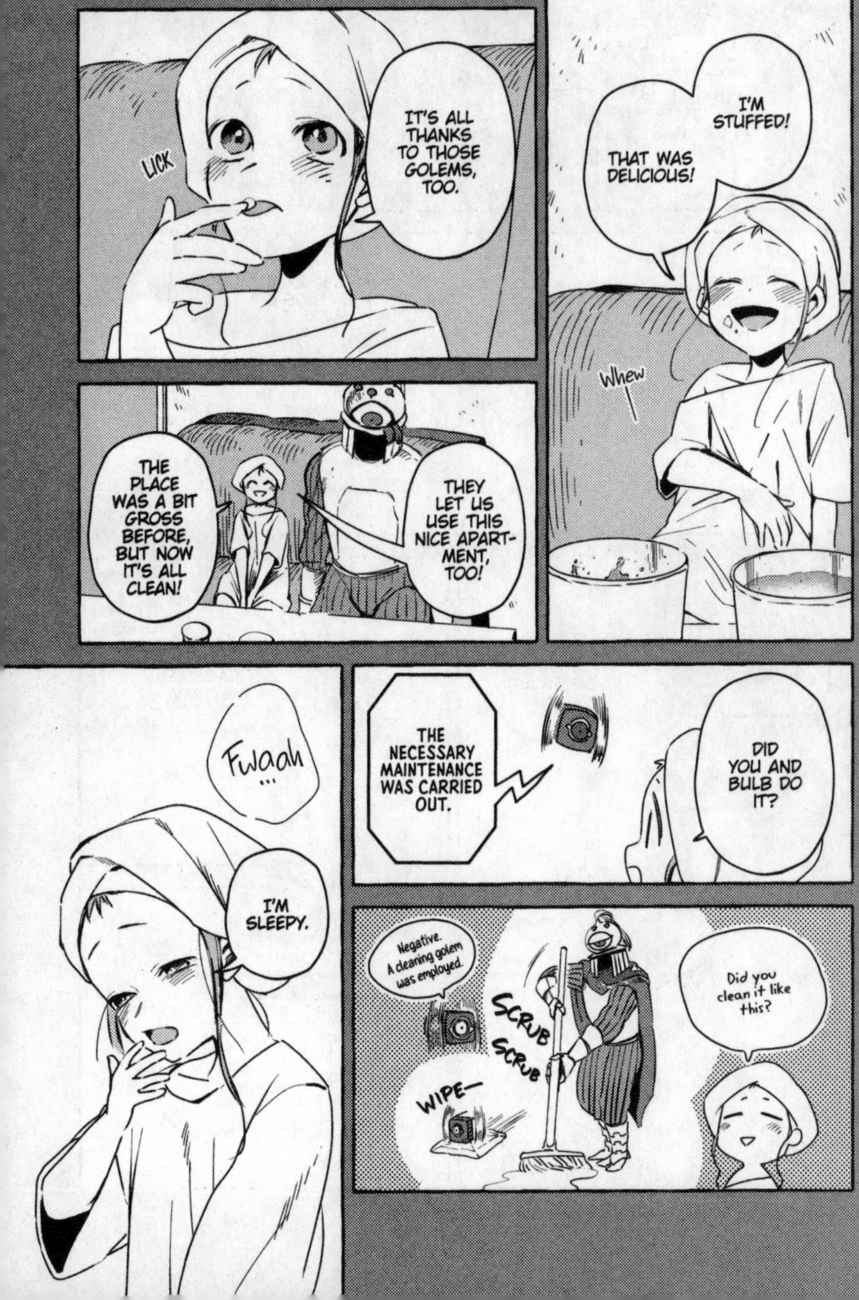
I'M STUFFED!
THAT WAS DELICIOUS!
Whew
LICK
IT'S ALL THANKS TO THOSE GOLEMS, TOO.
THEY LET US USE THIS NICE APARTMENT, TOO!
THE PLACE WAS A BIT GROSS BEFORE, BUT NOW IT'S ALL CLEAN!
DID YOU AND BULB DO IT?
THE NECESSARY MAINTENANCE WAS CARRIED OUT.
Did you clean it like this?
Negative. A cleaning golem was employed.
SCRUB
SCRUB
WIPE—
Fwaah...
I'M SLEEPY.

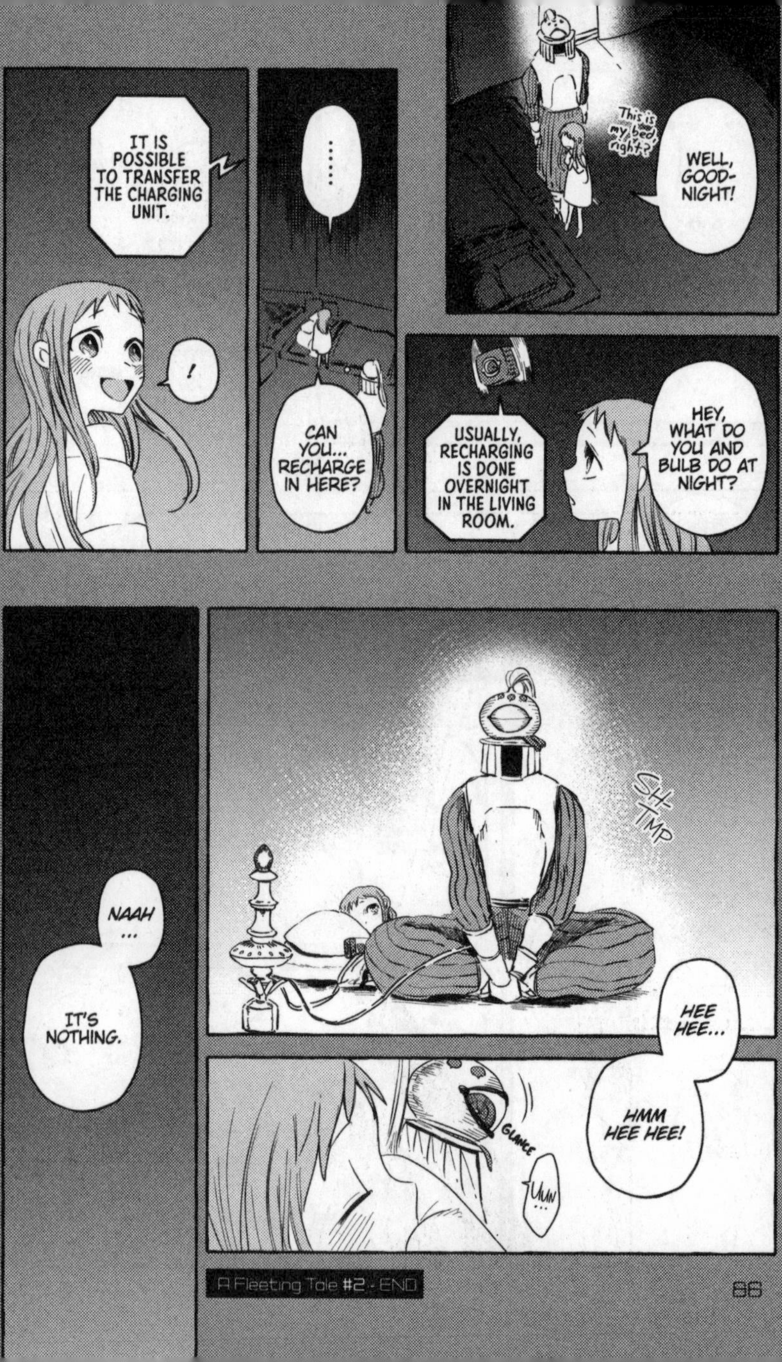
This is my bed, right?
WELL, GOOD-NIGHT!
HEY, WHAT DO YOU AND BULB DO AT NIGHT?
USUALLY, RECHARGING IS DONE OVERNIGHT IN THE LIVING ROOM.
......
CAN YOU... RECHARGE IN HERE?
IT IS POSSIBLE TO TRANSFER THE CHARGING UNIT.
!
SH-TMP
HEE HEE...
HMM HEE HEE!
GLANCE
UMN...
NAAH...
IT'S NOTHING.

A Fleeting Tale #2 - END

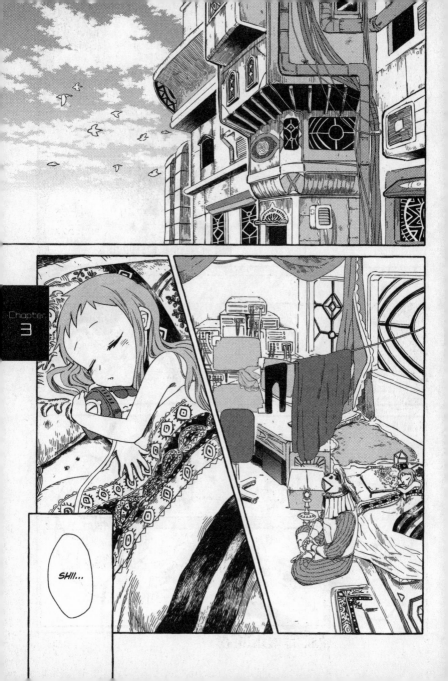

Chapter
3

SHII...

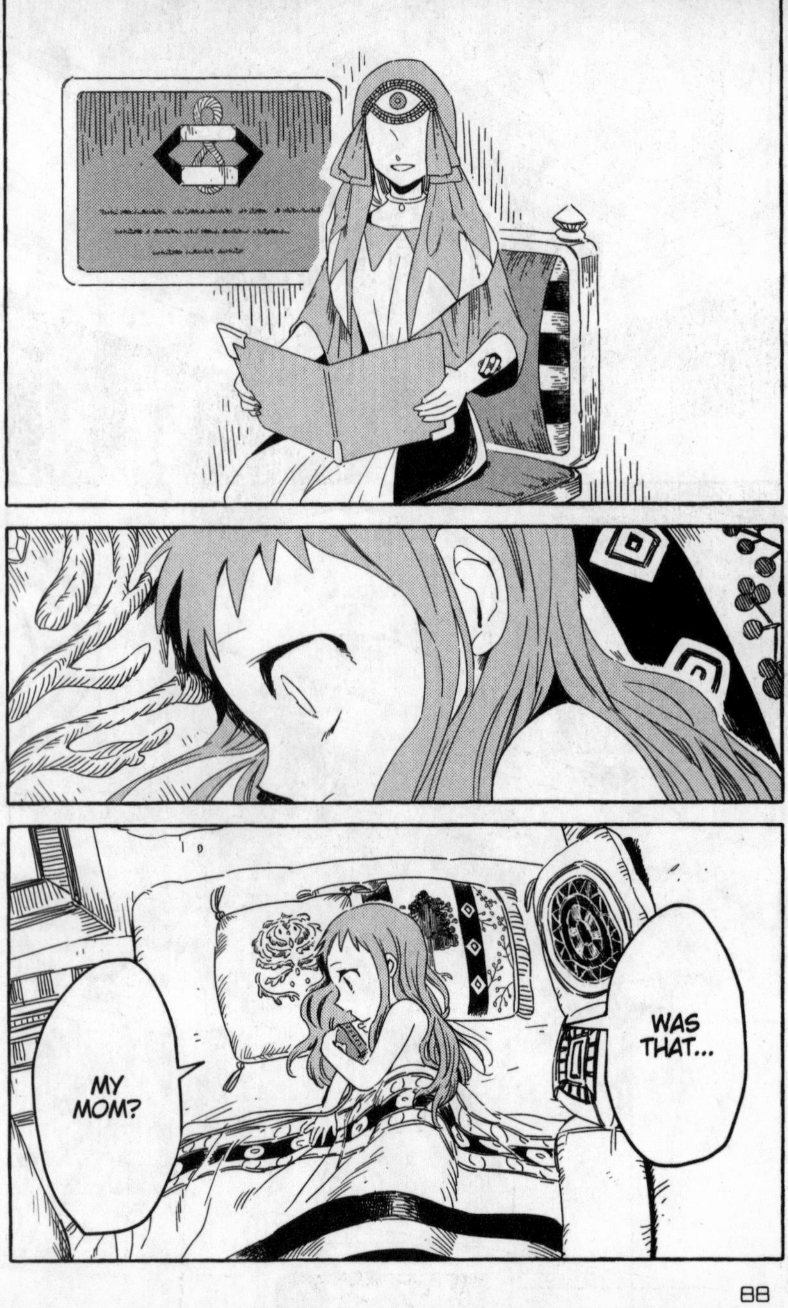
WAS THAT...
MY MOM?

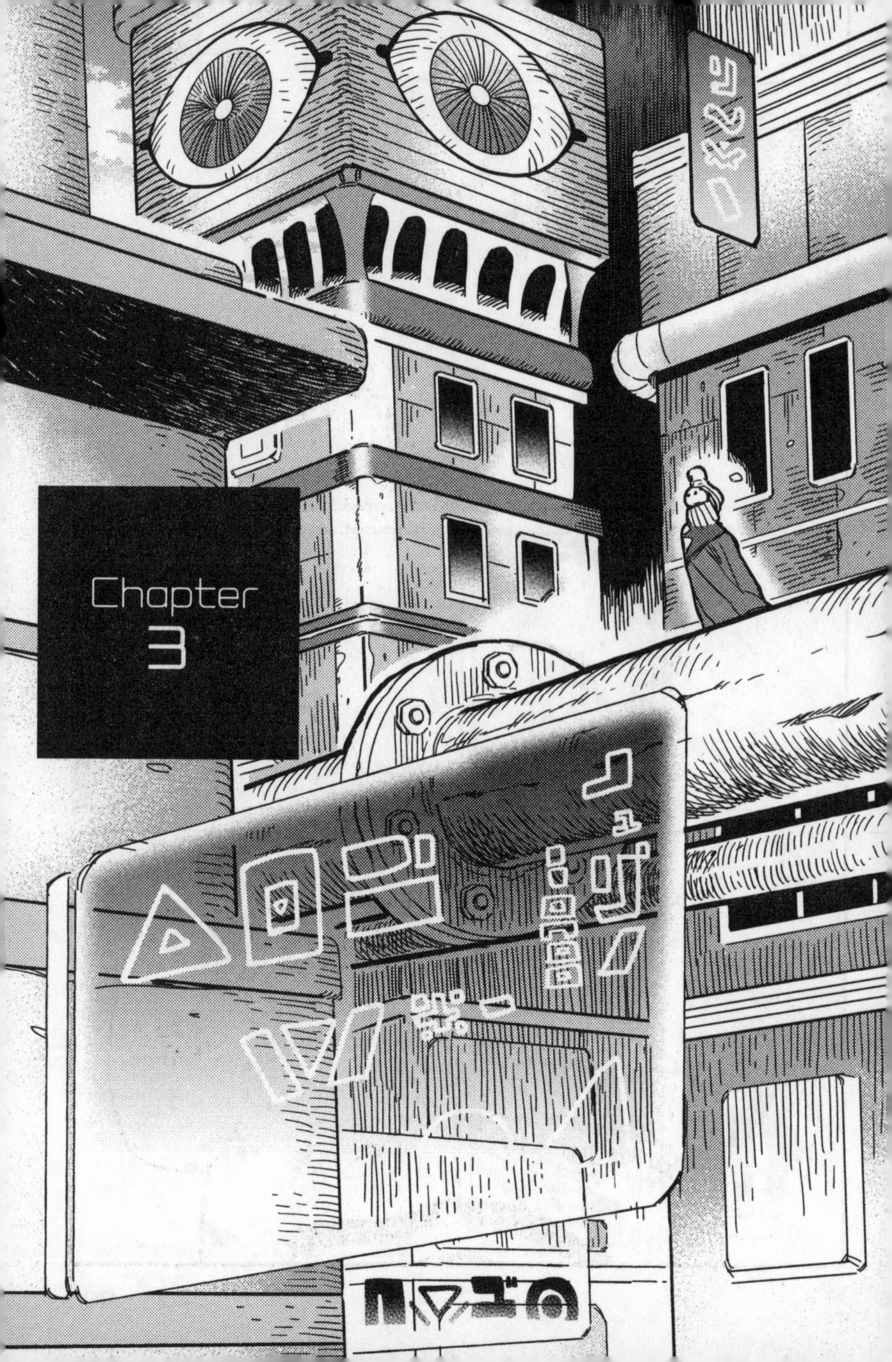
Chapter
3

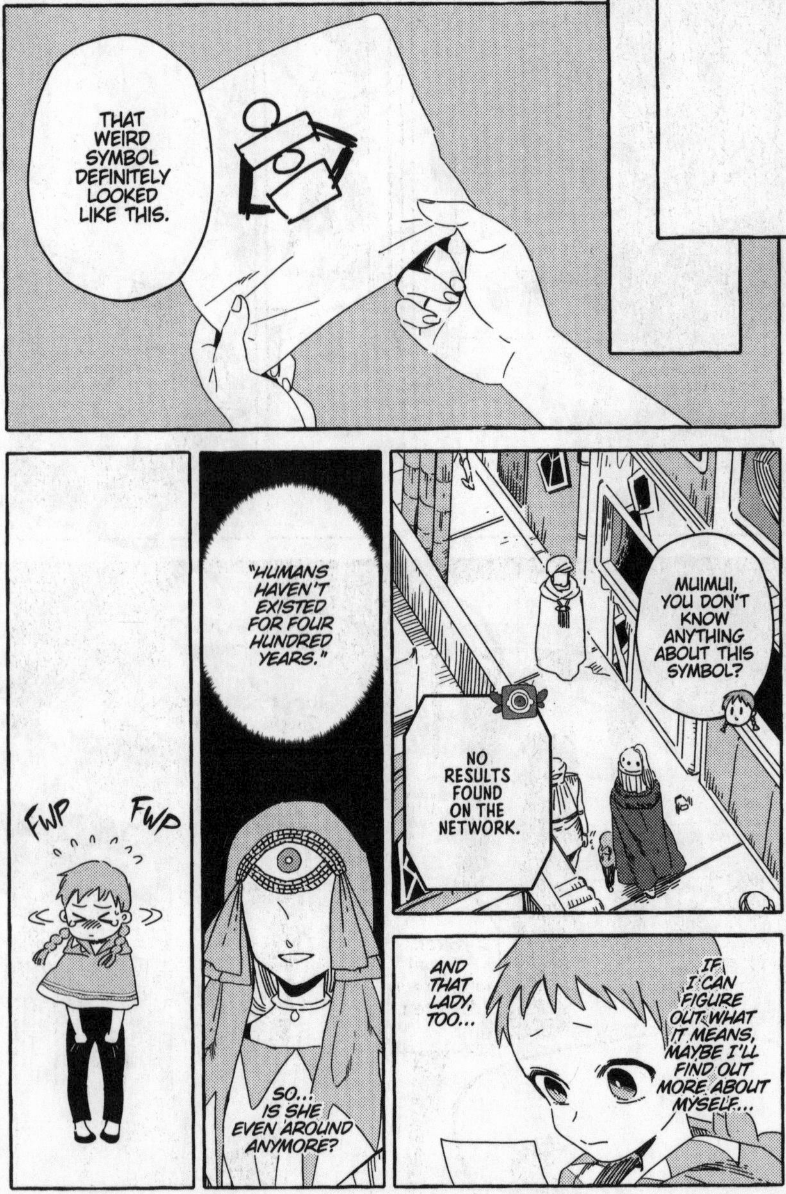
THAT WEIRD SYMBOL DEFINITELY LOOKED LIKE THIS.
MUIMUI, YOU DON'T KNOW ANYTHING ABOUT THIS SYMBOL?
NO RESULTS FOUND ON THE NETWORK.
IF I CAN FIGURE OUT WHAT IT MEANS, MAYBE I'LL FIND OUT MORE ABOUT MYSELF...
AND THAT LADY, TOO...
"HUMANS HAVEN'T EXISTED FOR FOUR HUNDRED YEARS."
SO... IS SHE EVEN AROUND ANYMORE?
FWP FWP

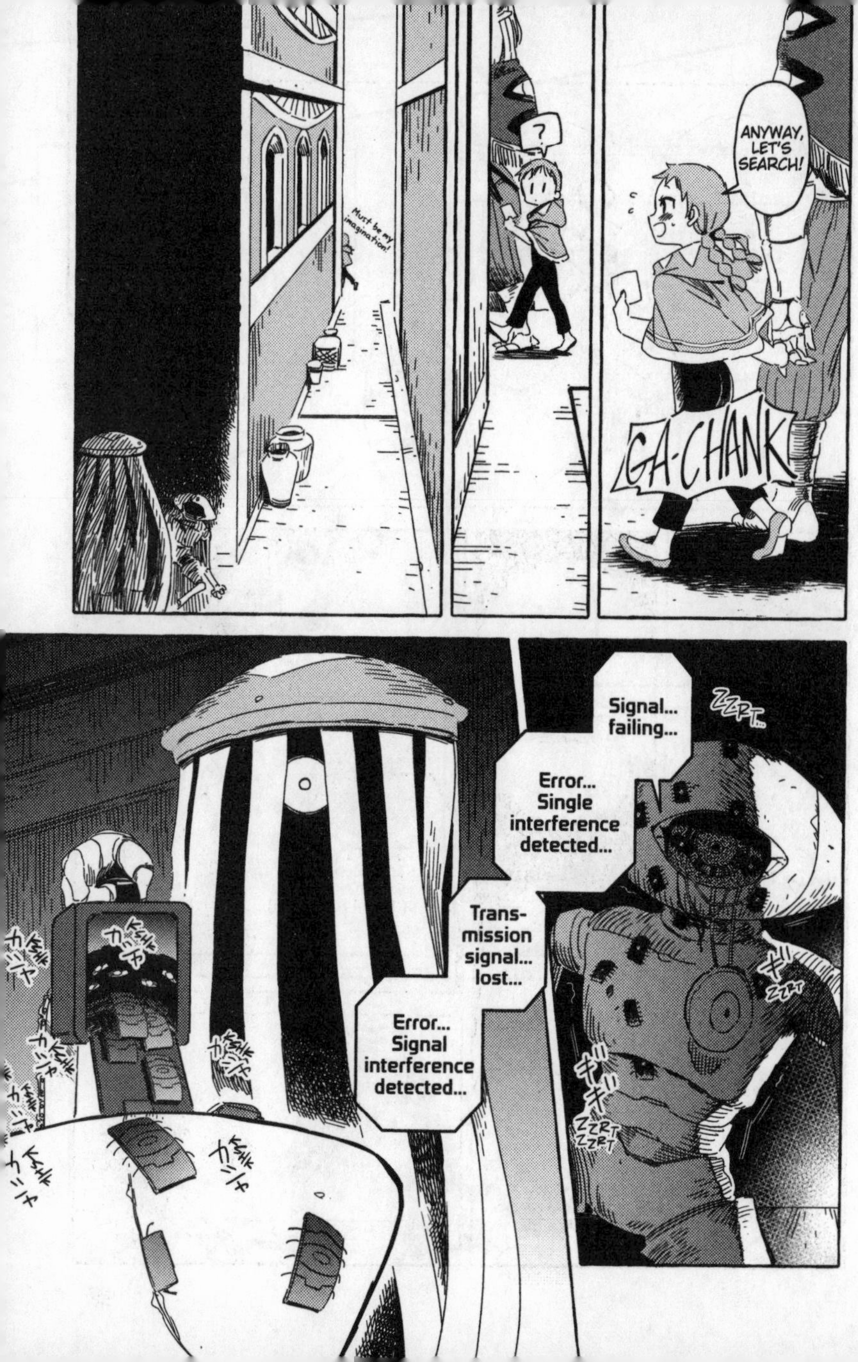
ANYWAY, LET'S SEARCH!
GA-CHANK
?
Must be my imagination!
ZZRT...
Signal... failing...
Error... Single interference detected...
Transmission signal... lost...
Error... Signal interference detected...
ZZRT
ZZRT ZZRT
KSHK
KSHK
KSHK
KSHK
KSHK

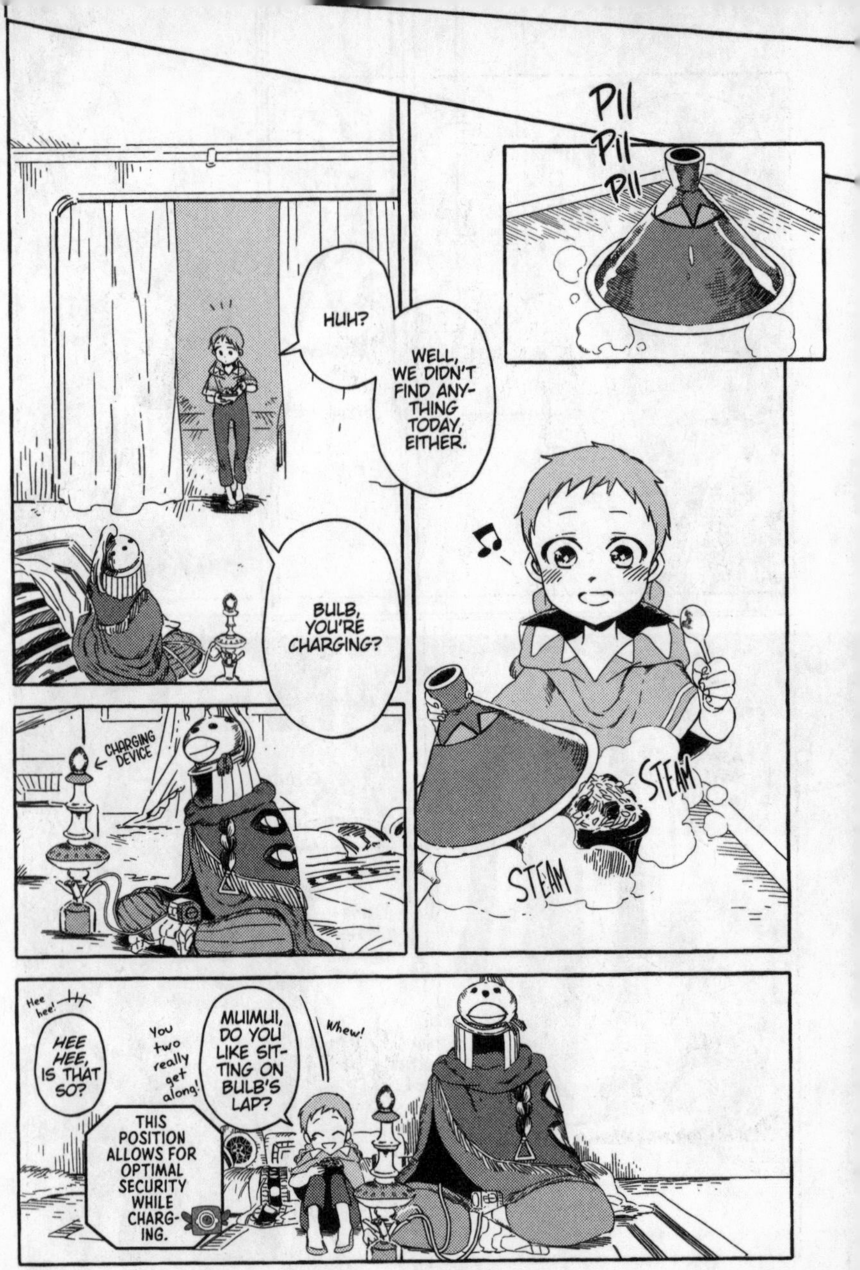
PII
PII
PII
STEAM
STEAM
WELL, WE DIDN'T FIND ANY-THING TODAY, EITHER.
HUH?
BULB, YOU'RE CHARGING?
CHARGING DEVICE
MUIMUI, DO YOU LIKE SIT-TING ON BULB'S LAP?
Whew!
THIS POSITION ALLOWS FOR OPTIMAL SECURITY WHILE CHARG-ING.
You two really get along!
HEE HEE, IS THAT SO?
Hee hee!

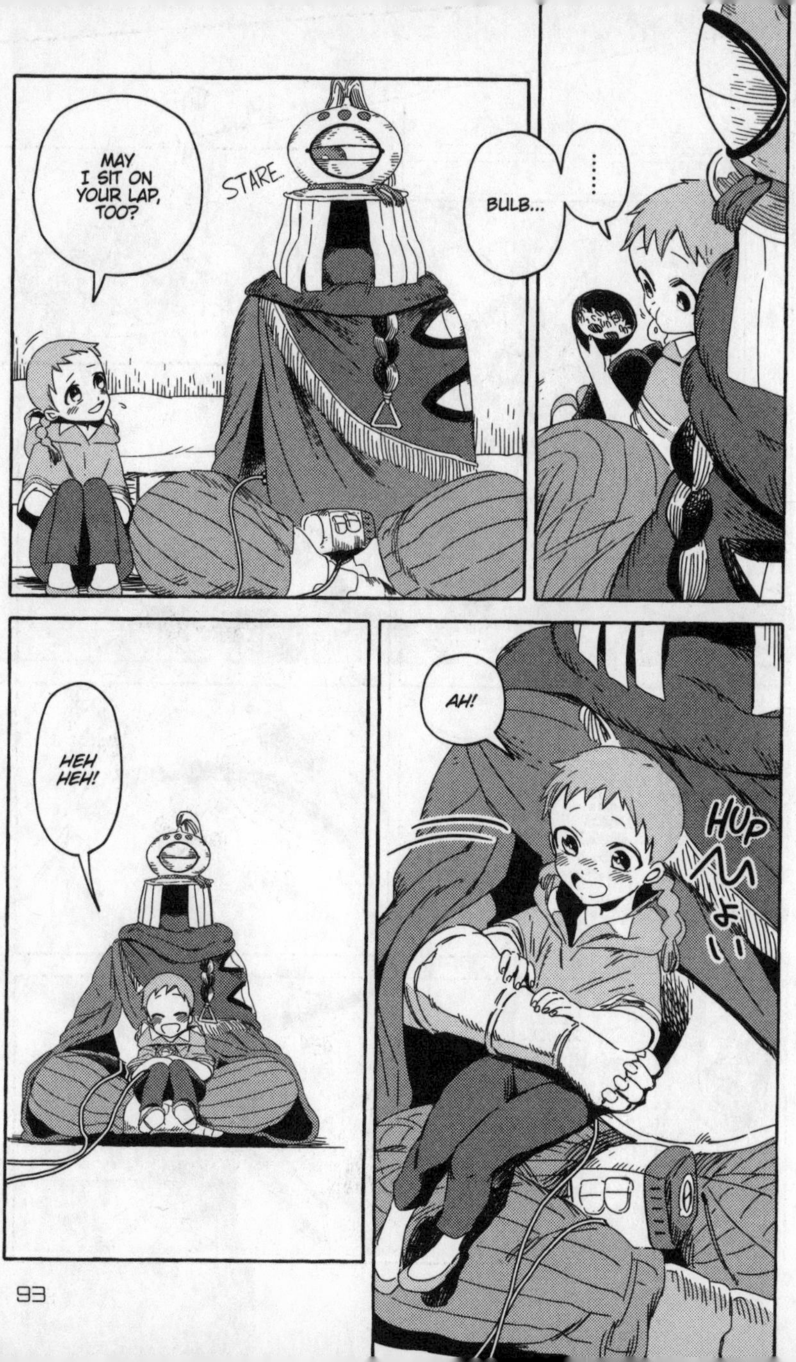
......
BULB...
MAY I SIT ON YOUR LAP, TOO?
STARE.
AH!
HUP
HEH HEH!

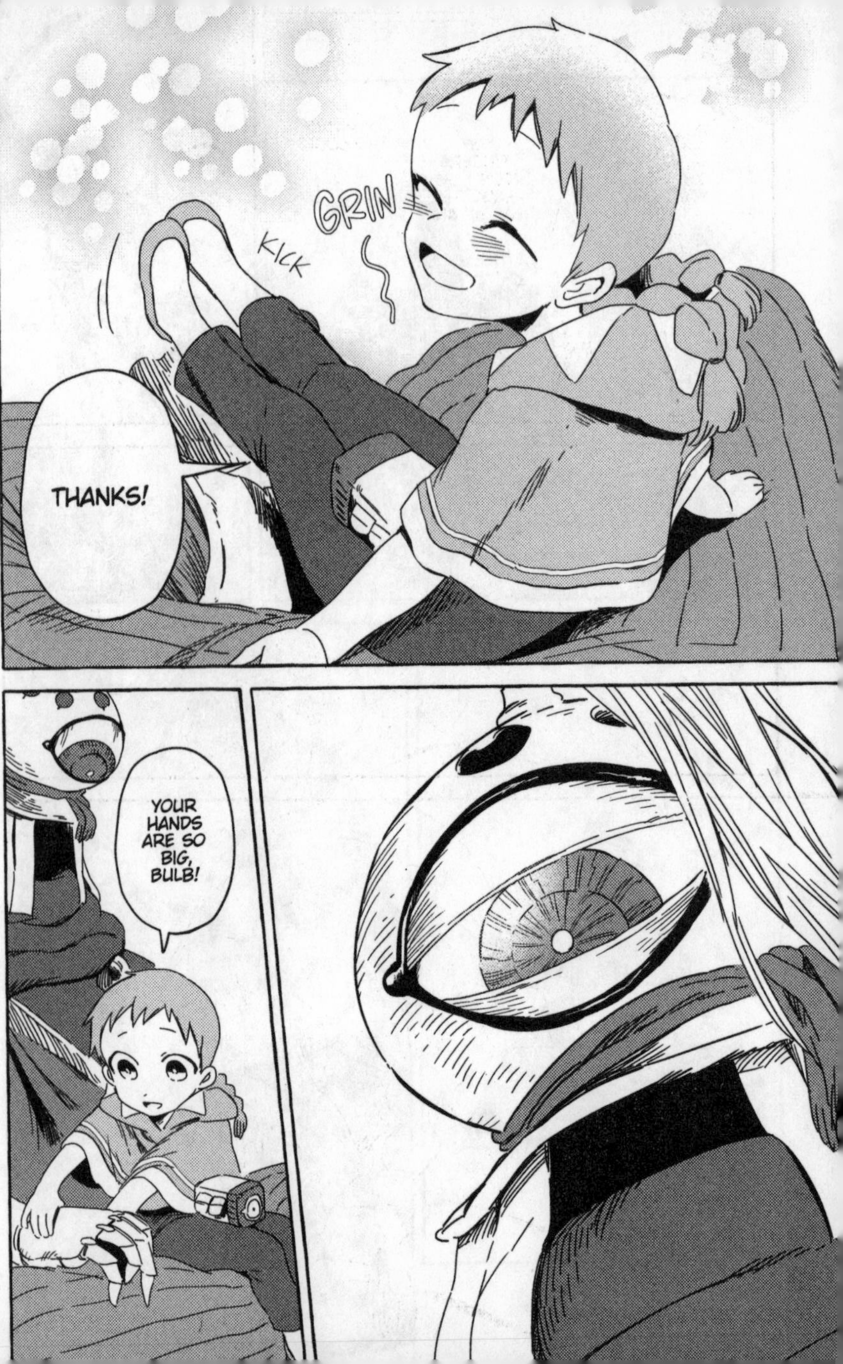
GRIN
KICK
THANKS!
YOUR HANDS ARE SO BIG, BULB!

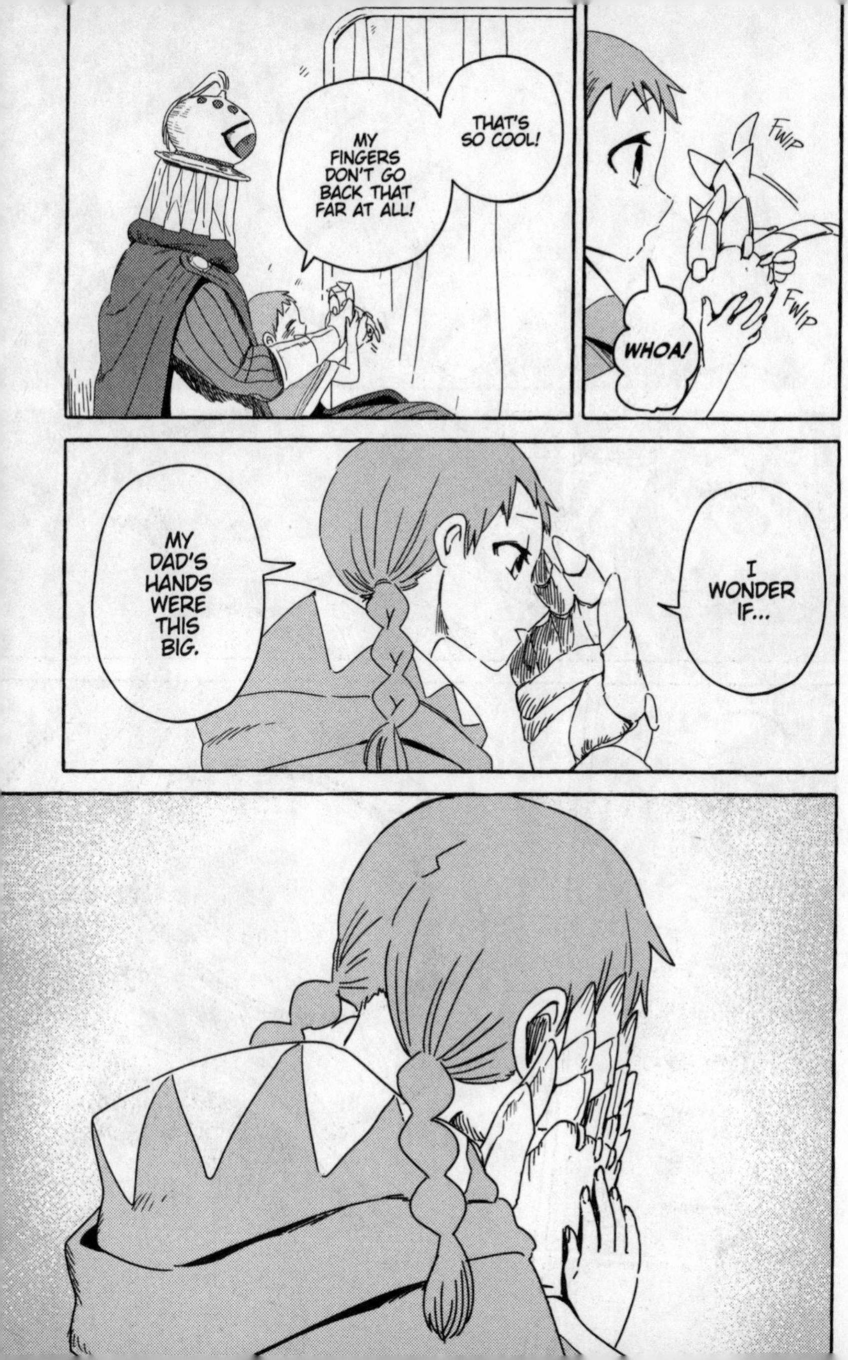
FWIP
FWIP
WHOA!
THAT'S SO COOL!
MY FINGERS DON'T GO BACK THAT FAR AT ALL!
I WONDER IF...
MY DAD'S HANDS WERE THIS BIG.

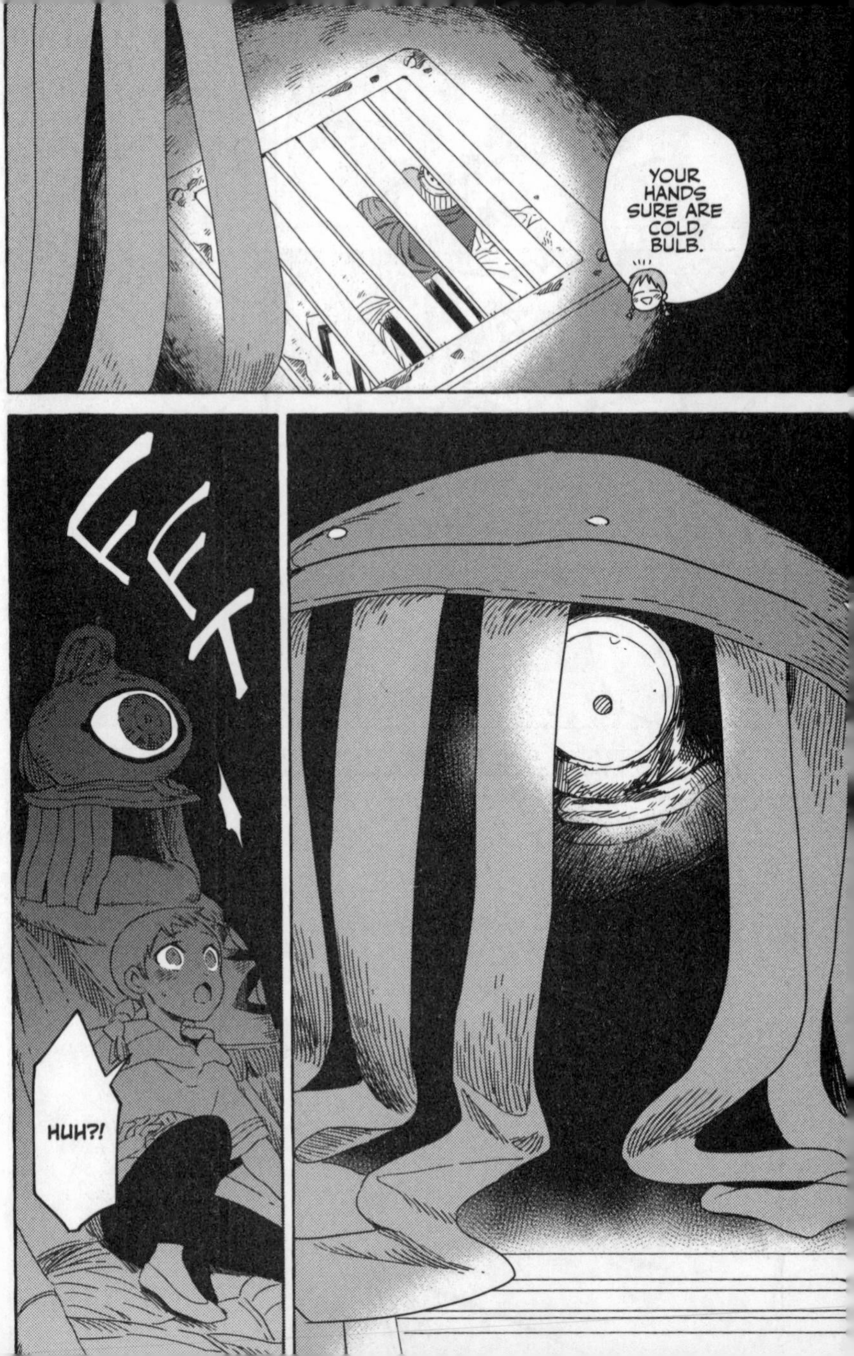
YOUR HANDS SURE ARE COLD, BULB.
EEK
HUH?!

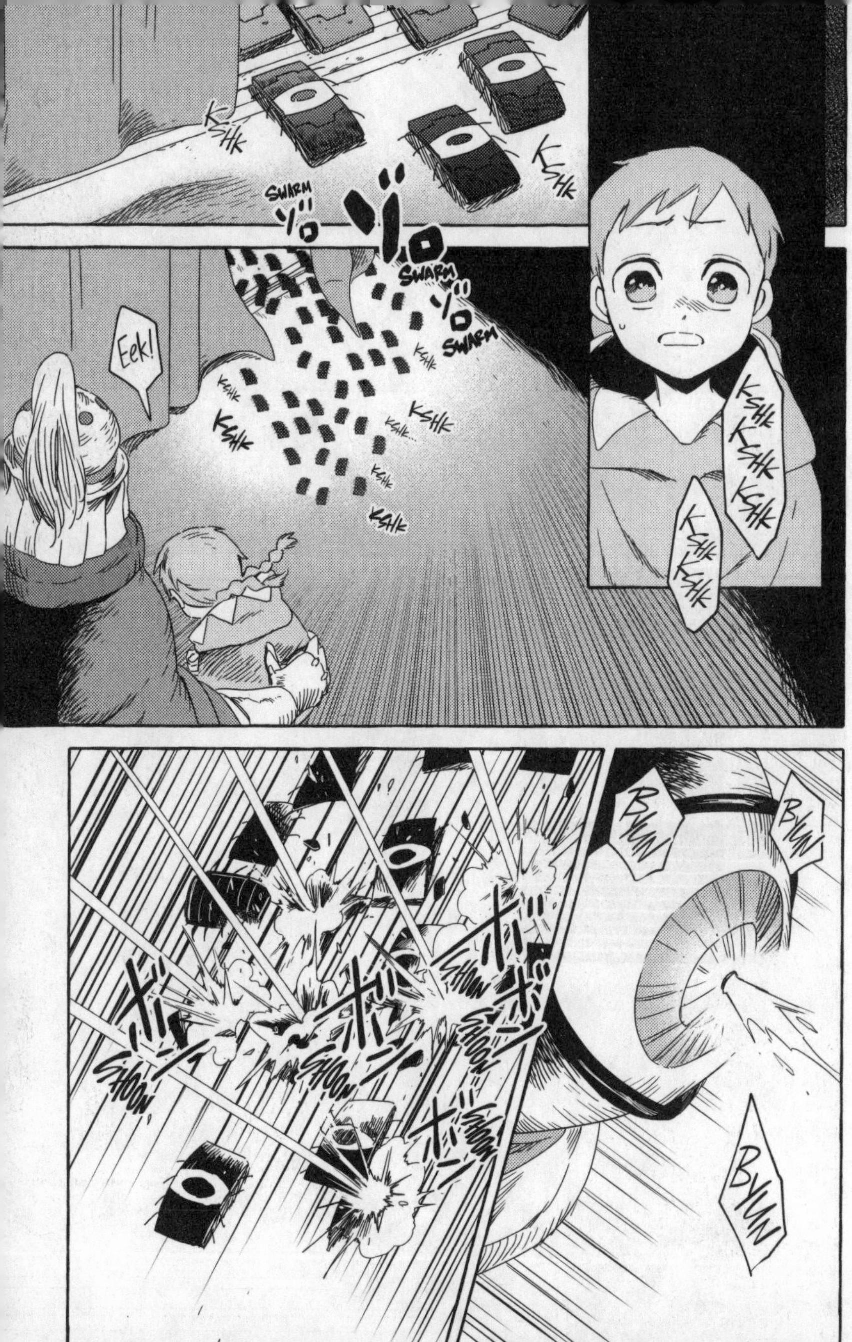
KSHK KSHK KSHK
KSHK KSHK
KSHK
KSHK
SWARM ゾロ
ゾロ
SWARM ゾロ SWARM
Eek!
KSHK
KSHK
KSHK
KSHK...
KSHK
KSHK
KSHK
BYUN
BYUN
BYUN
SHOON
SHOON
SHOON
SHOON
SHOON

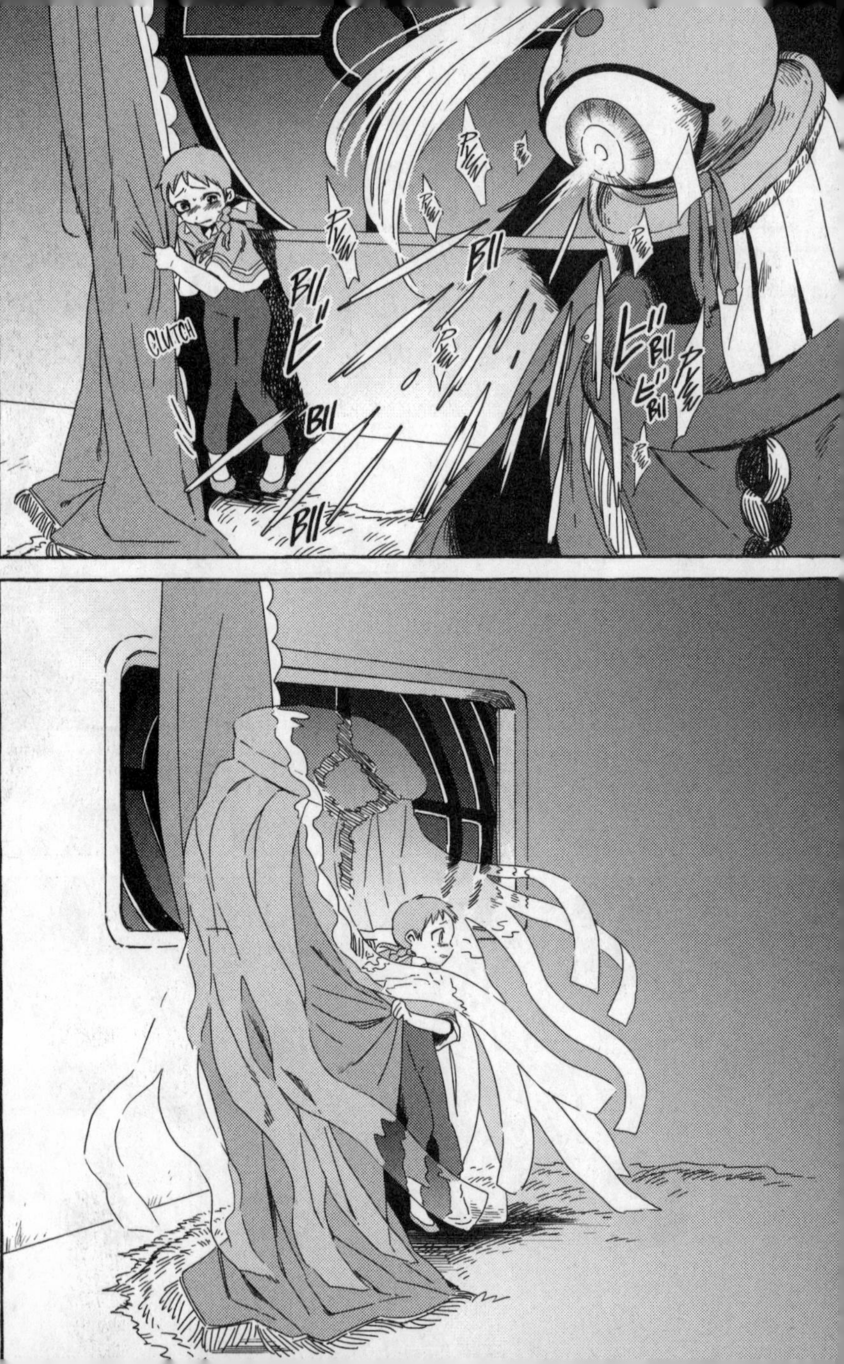
ビ
BII
ビ
BII
PYUN
BII
PYUN
PYUN
PYUN
BII
ビ
BII
BII
CLUTCH

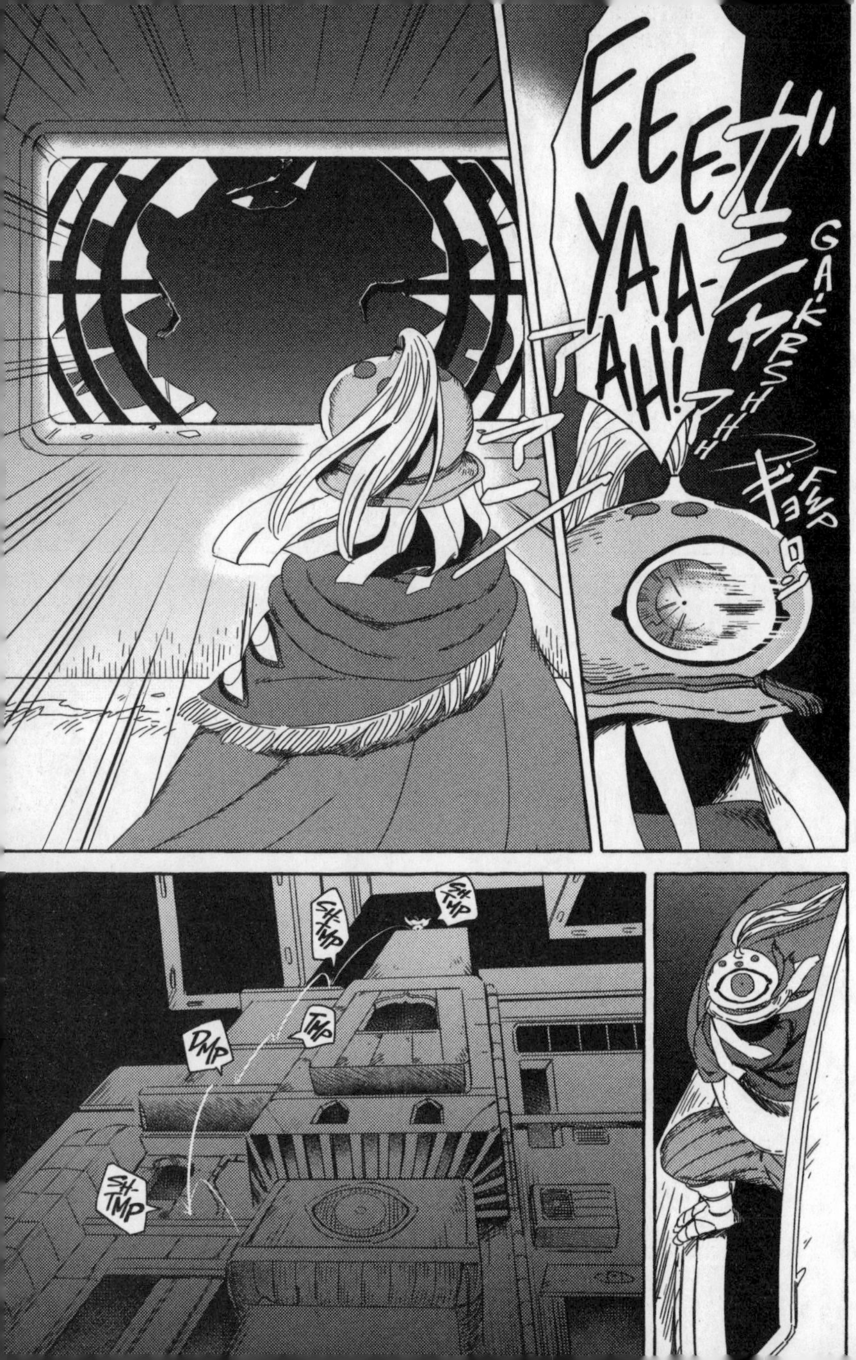
EEE-YAA-AAH!
GAKRSHHH
FWP
SH-TMP
SH-TMP
TMP
DMP
SH-TMP

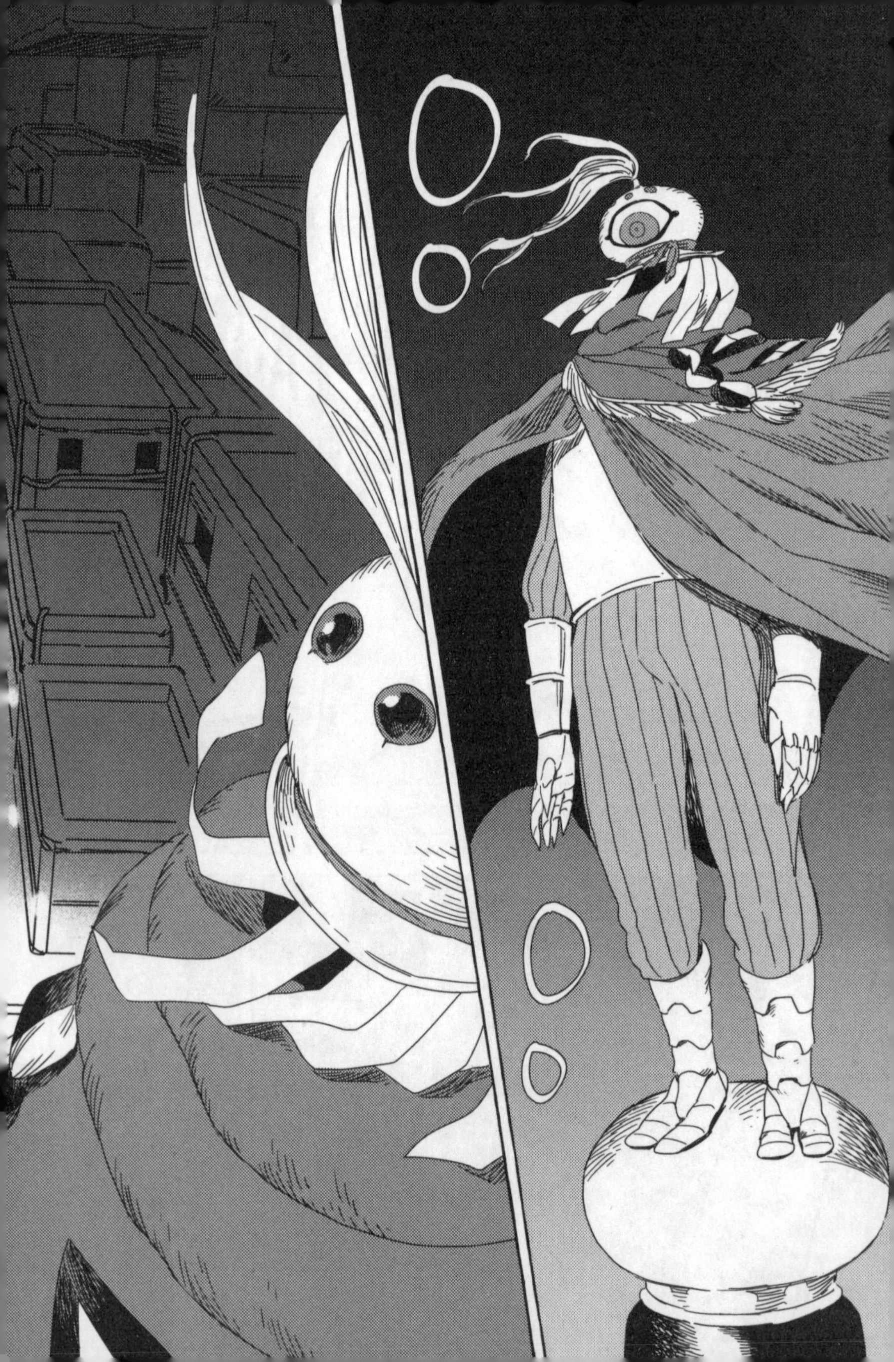

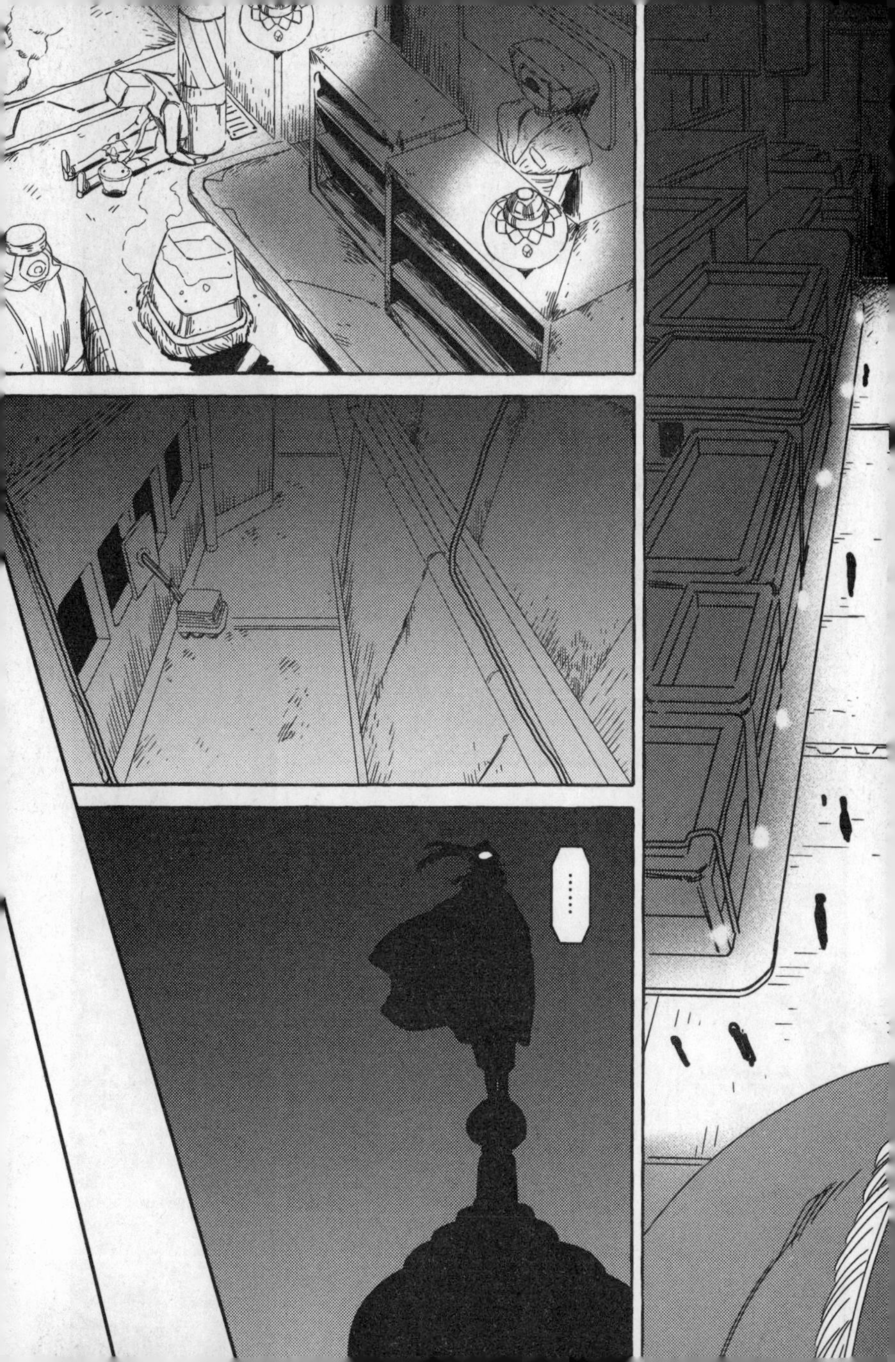
……

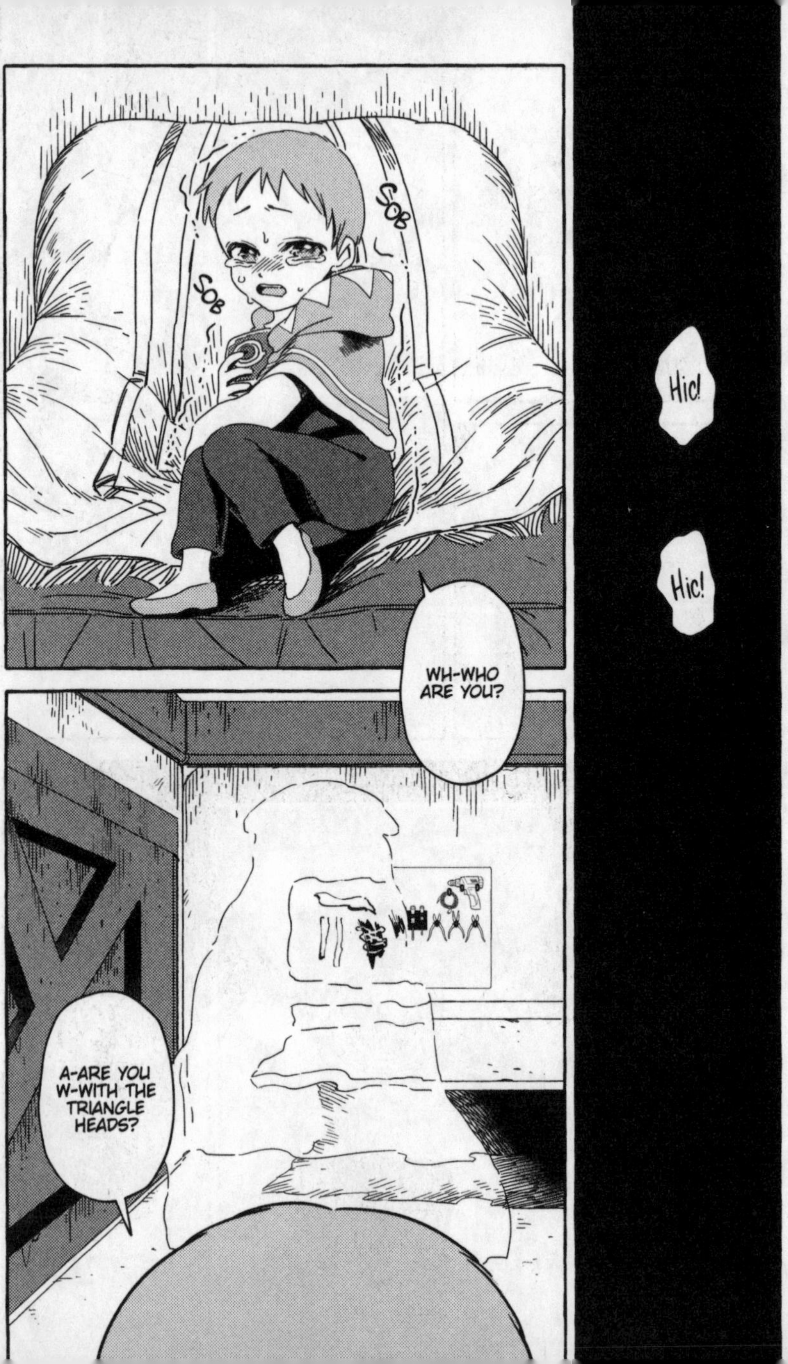
Hic!
Hic!
SOB
SOB
WH-WHO ARE YOU?
A-ARE YOU W-WITH THE TRIANGLE HEADS?

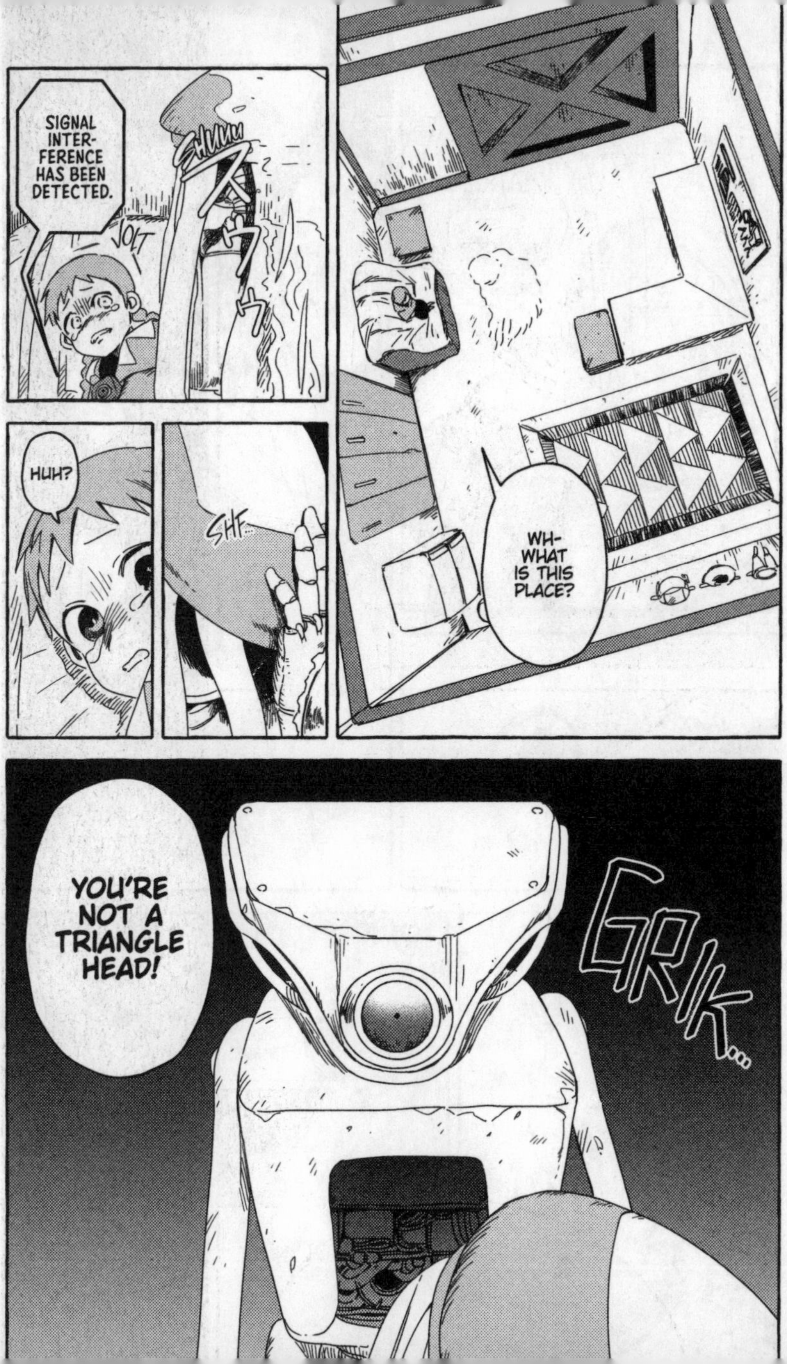
WH-WHAT IS THIS PLACE?
SHUUU
SIGNAL INTERFERENCE HAS BEEN DETECTED.
JOLT
SHF...
HUH?
GRIK...
YOU'RE NOT A TRIANGLE HEAD!

ILLEGALLY MODIFIED?

THIS IS AN ILLEGALLY MODIFIED GOLEM.

MANUFAC-TURING CODE UNKNOWN.

THAT MEANS...

THIS IS AN EVIL GOLEM?!

GA-CHANK

GA-CHANK

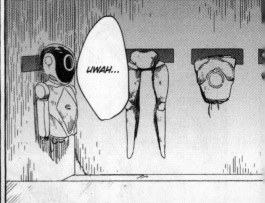

UWAH...

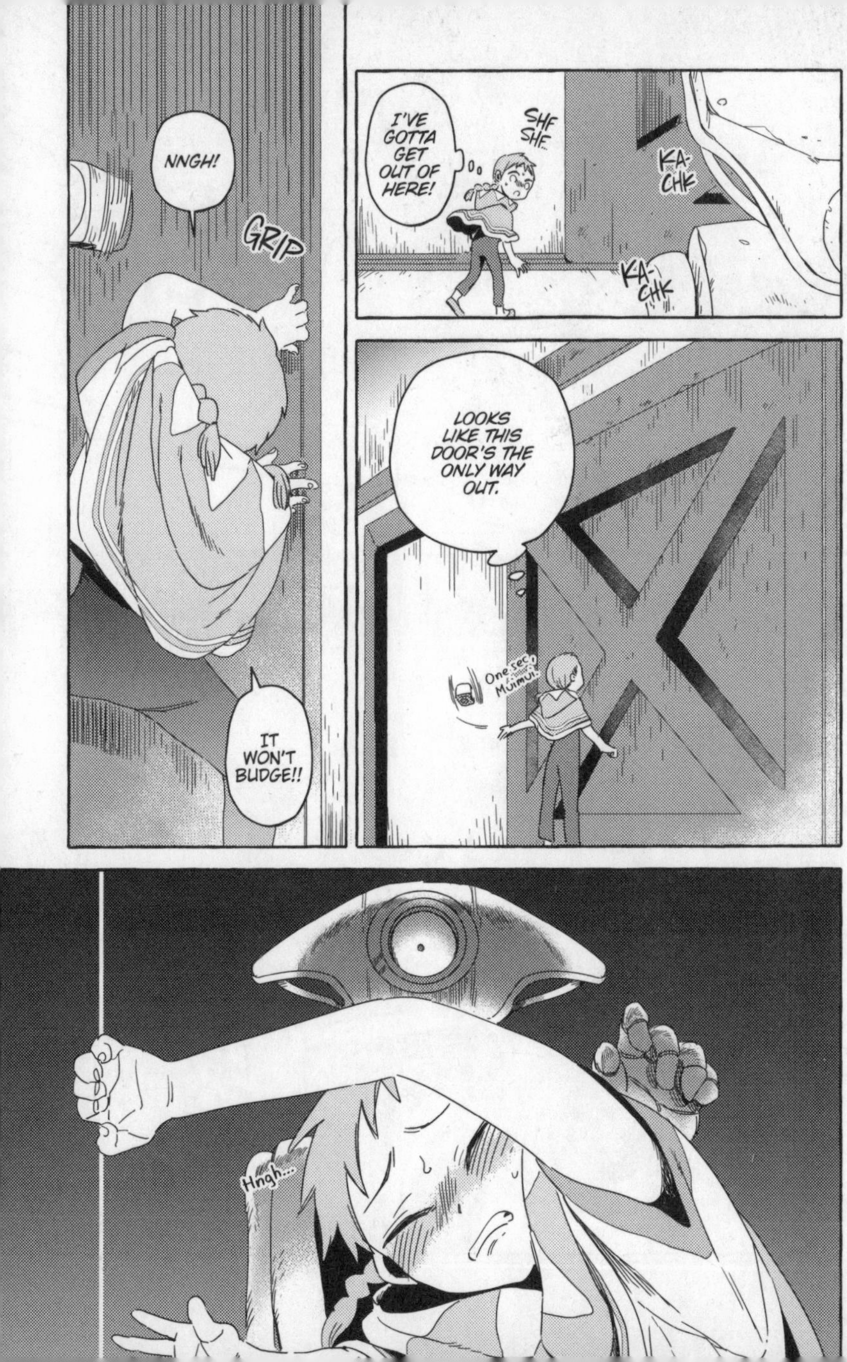
I'VE GOTTA GET OUT OF HERE!
SHF SHF
KA-CHK
KA-CHK
LOOKS LIKE THIS DOOR'S THE ONLY WAY OUT.
One sec, Muimui.
NNGH!
GRIP
IT WON'T BUDGE!!
Hngh...

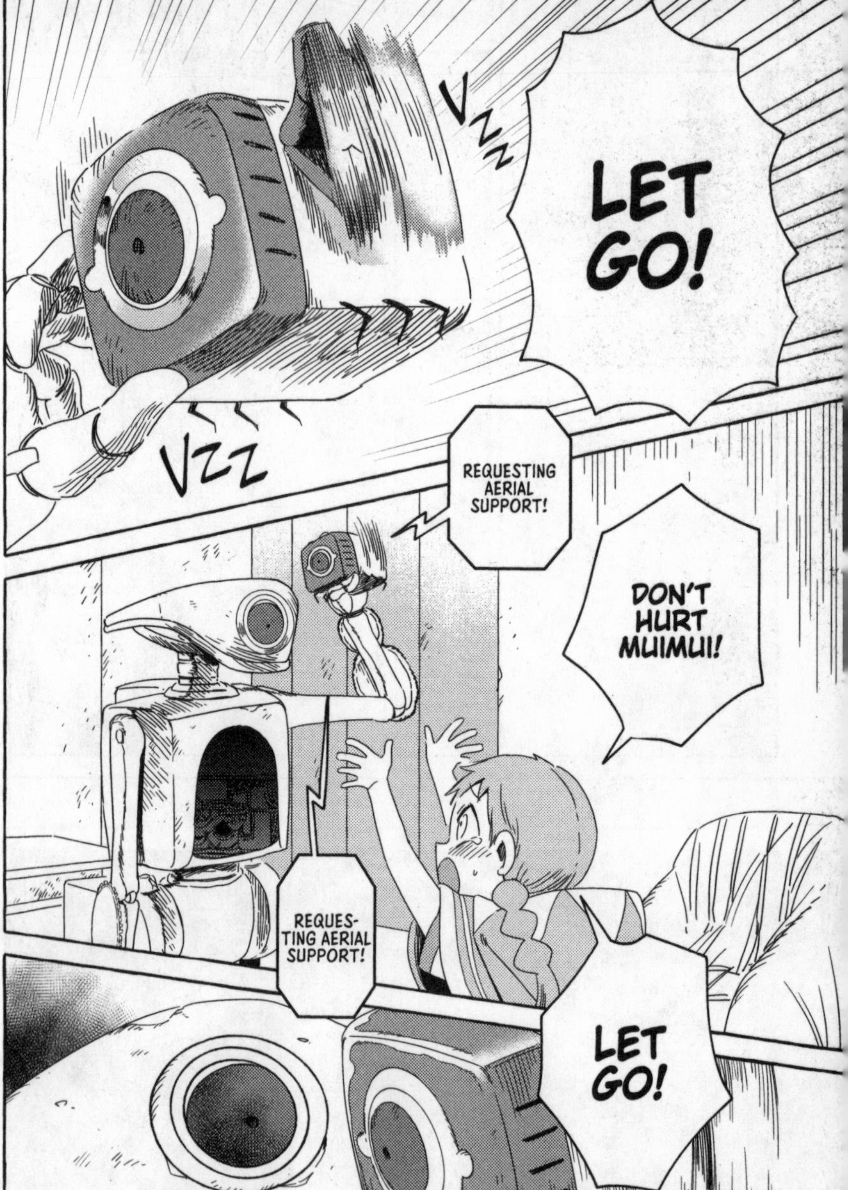
LET GO!
VZZ
VZZ
REQUESTING AERIAL SUPPORT!
DON'T HURT MUIMUI!
REQUES-TING AERIAL SUPPORT!
LET GO!

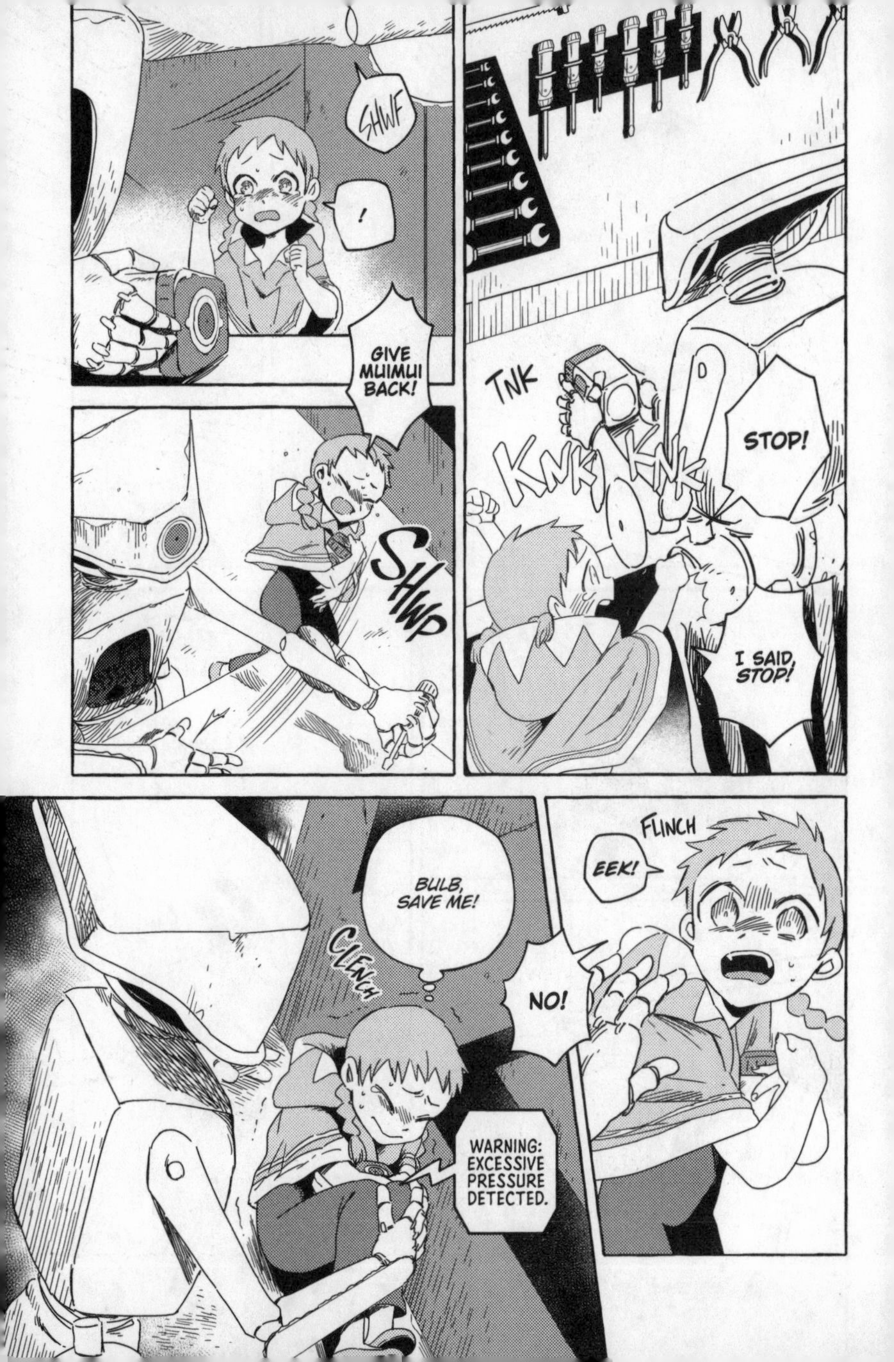
TNK
KNK KNK
STOP!
I SAID, STOP!
SHWF
!
GIVE MUIMUI BACK!
SHWP
FLINCH
EEK!
NO!
BULB, SAVE ME!
CLENCH
WARNING: EXCESSIVE PRESSURE DETECTED.

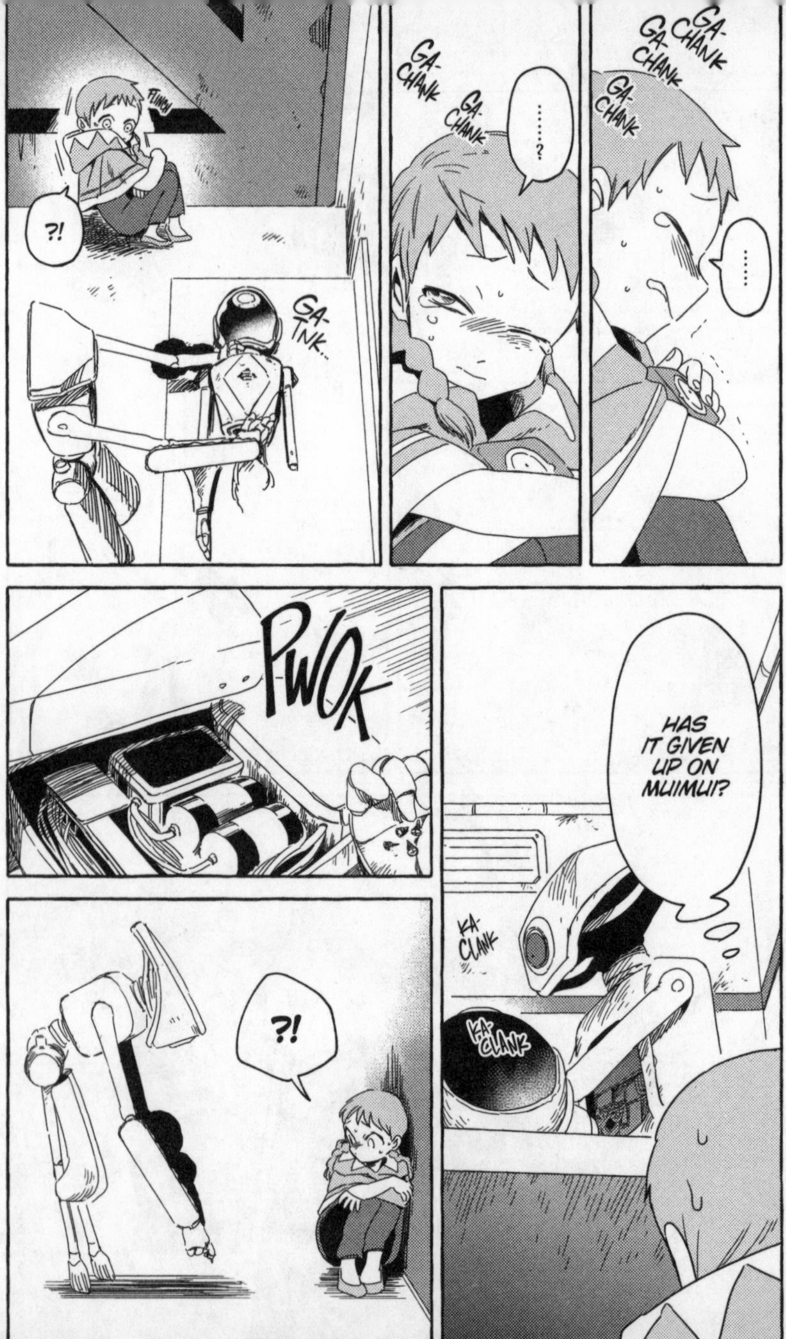

GA-CHANK
GA-CHANK
GA-CHANK
......
GA-CHANK
GA-CHANK
......?
FLINCH
?!
GA-TNK...
HAS IT GIVEN UP ON MUIMUI?
KA-CLANK
KA-CLANK
PWOK
?!

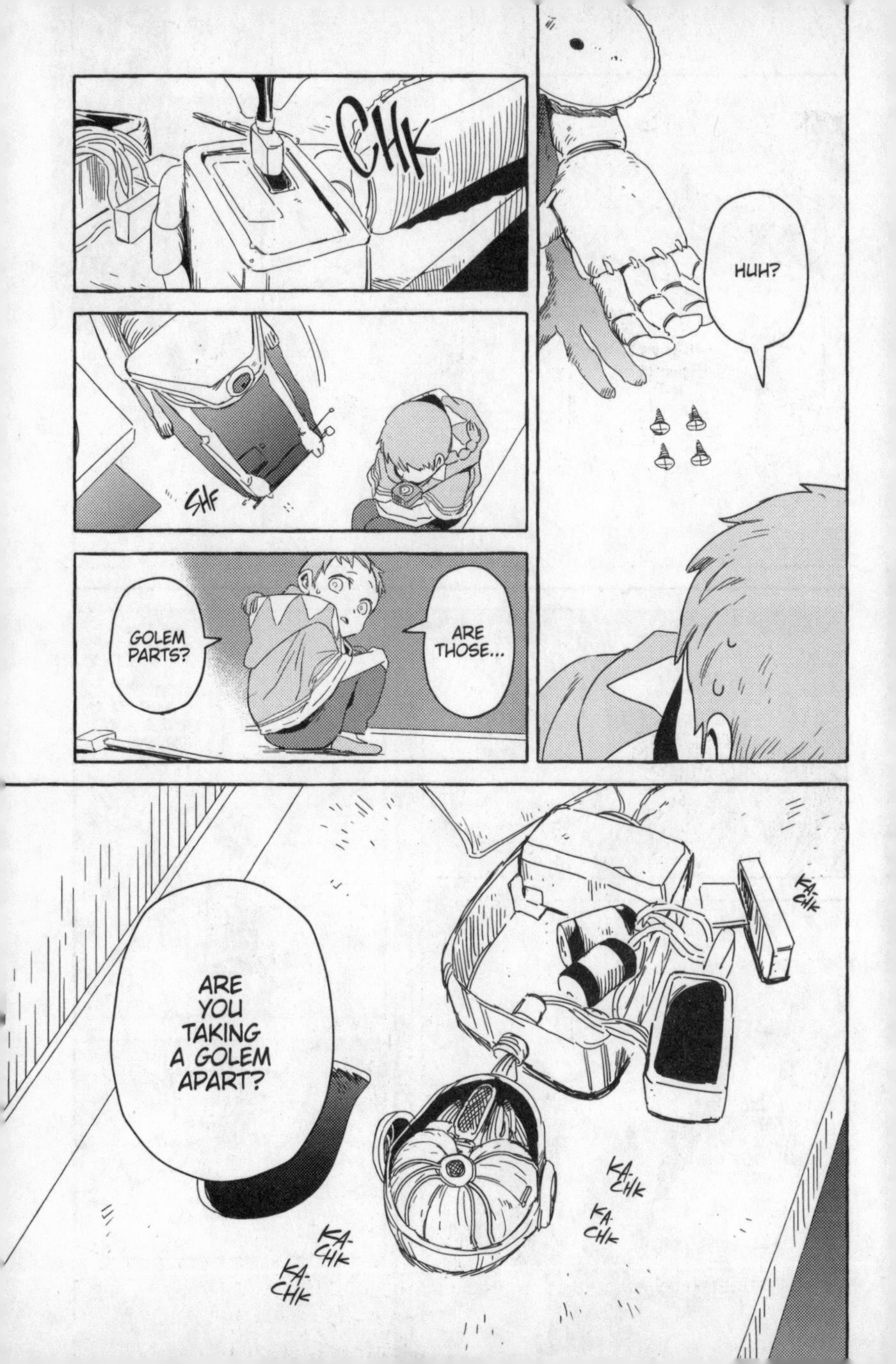
HUH?
CHK
SHF
ARE THOSE...
GOLEM PARTS?
KA-CHK
ARE YOU TAKING A GOLEM APART?
KA-CHK
KA-CHK
KA-CHK
KA-CHK

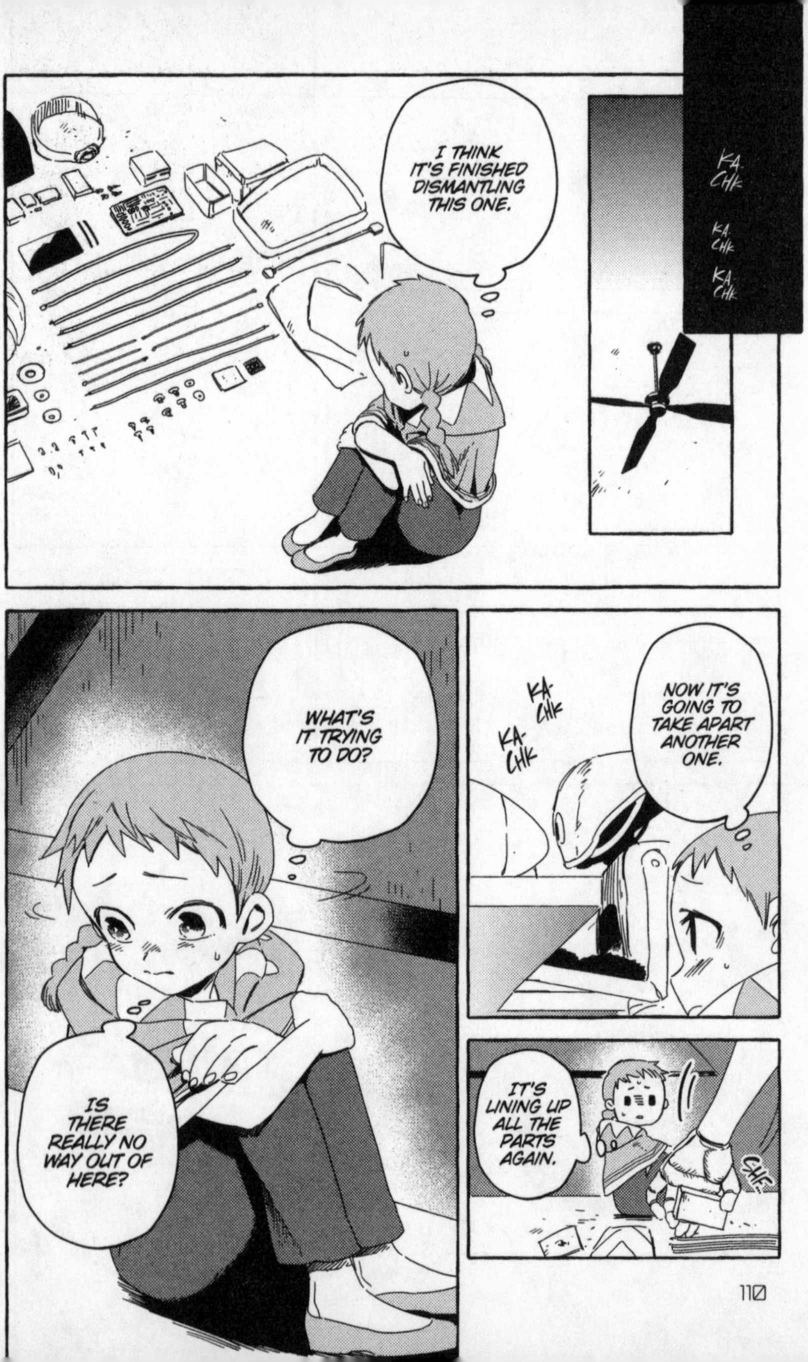
KA-CHK
KA-CHK
KA-CHK
I THINK IT'S FINISHED DISMANTLING THIS ONE.
KA-CHK
KA-CHK
NOW IT'S GOING TO TAKE APART ANOTHER ONE.
CHK
IT'S LINING UP ALL THE PARTS AGAIN.
WHAT'S IT TRYING TO DO?
IS THERE REALLY NO WAY OUT OF HERE?

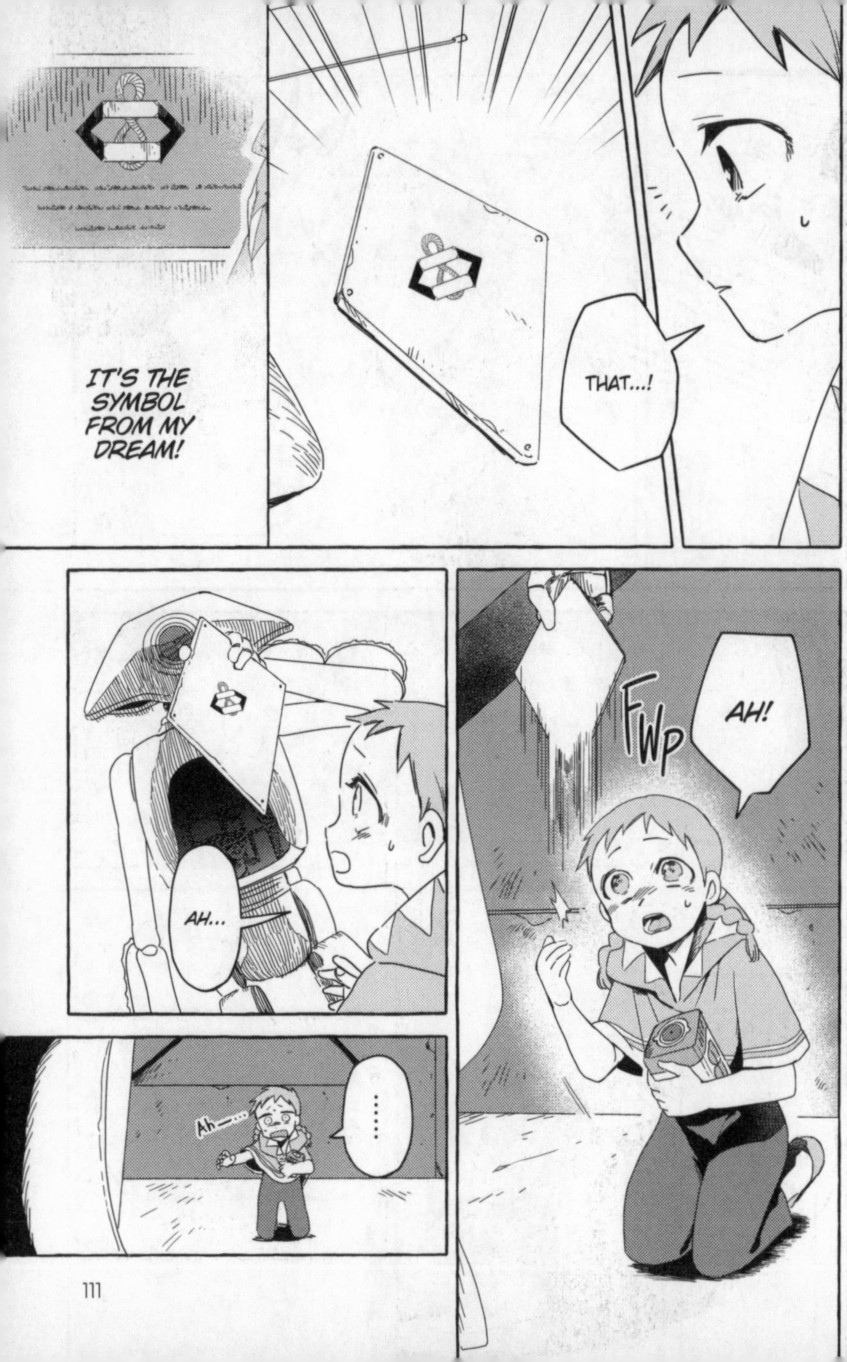
THAT...!
IT'S THE SYMBOL FROM MY DREAM!
FWP
AH!
AH...
Ah—...
......

YOU PUT IT IN A BAG FOR ME?

HUH?

KA-SHK

UM, DID YOU...

......

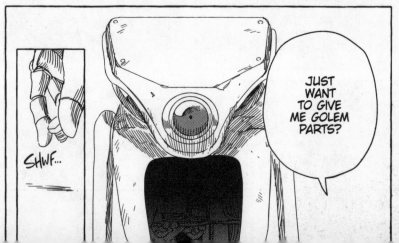

JUST WANT TO GIVE ME GOLEM PARTS?

SHWF...

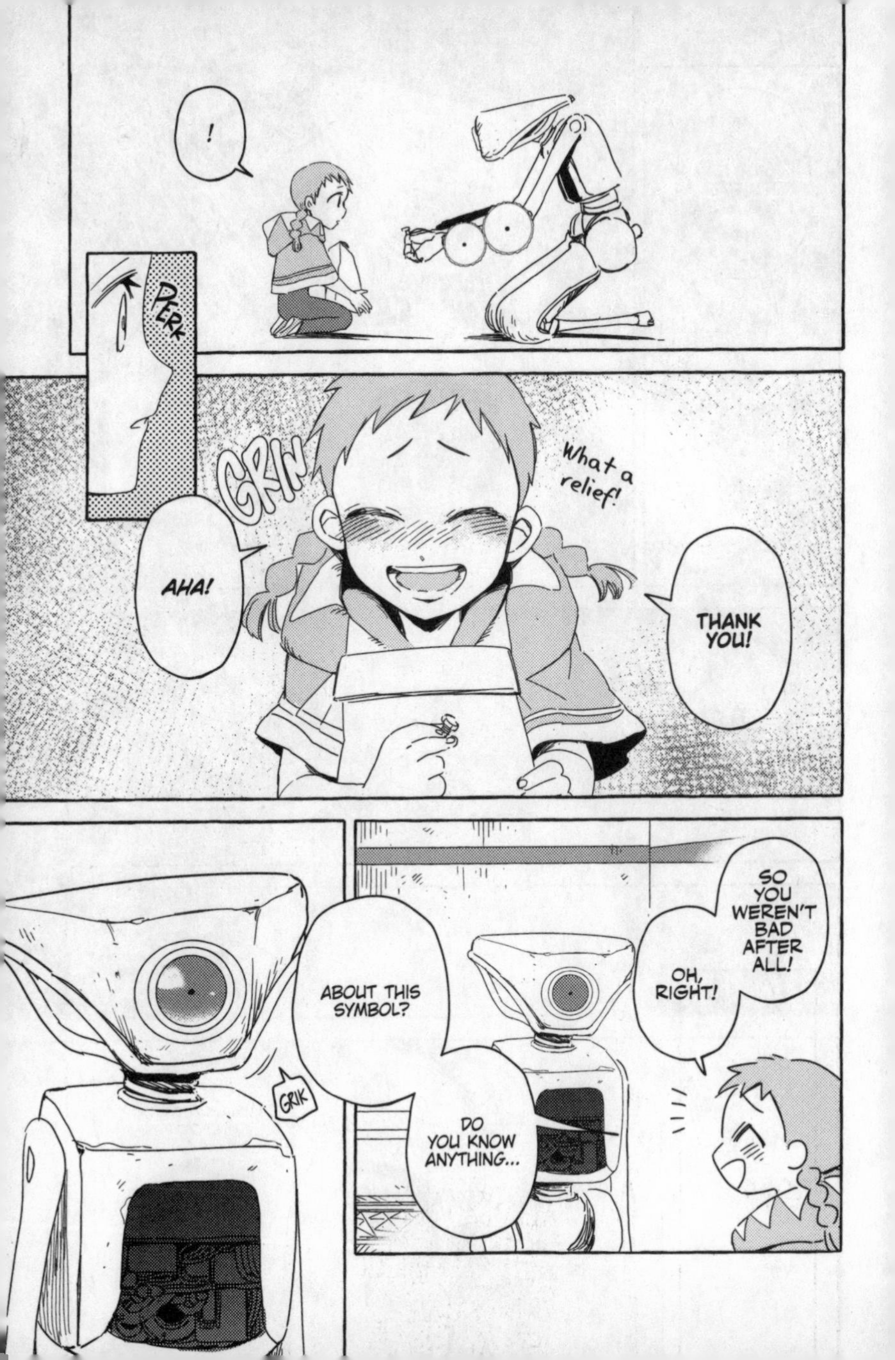
!
PERK
What a relief!
THANK YOU!
GRIN
AHA!
SO YOU WEREN'T BAD AFTER ALL!
OH, RIGHT!
DO YOU KNOW ANYTHING...
ABOUT THIS SYMBOL?
GRIK

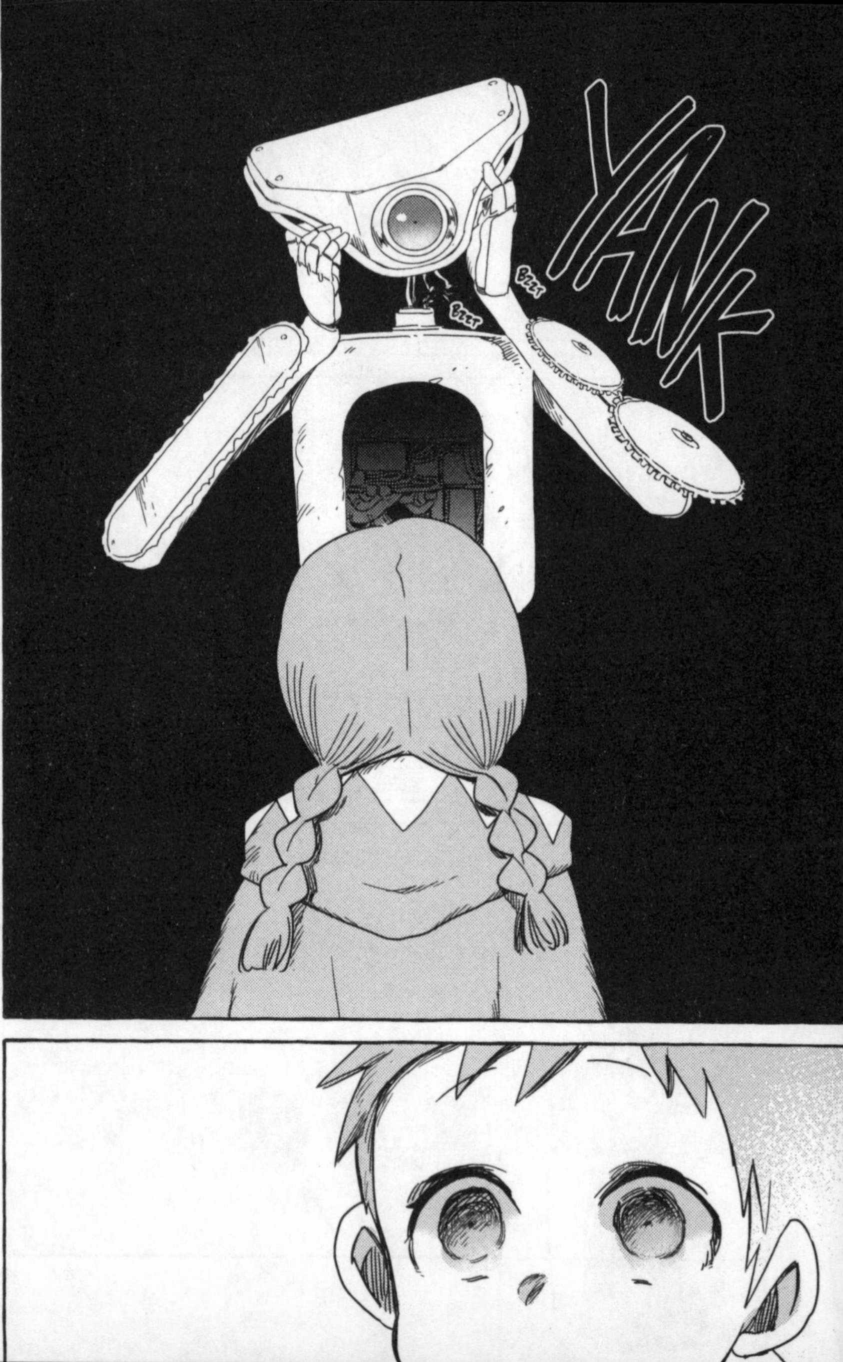
YANK
BZZT
BZZT

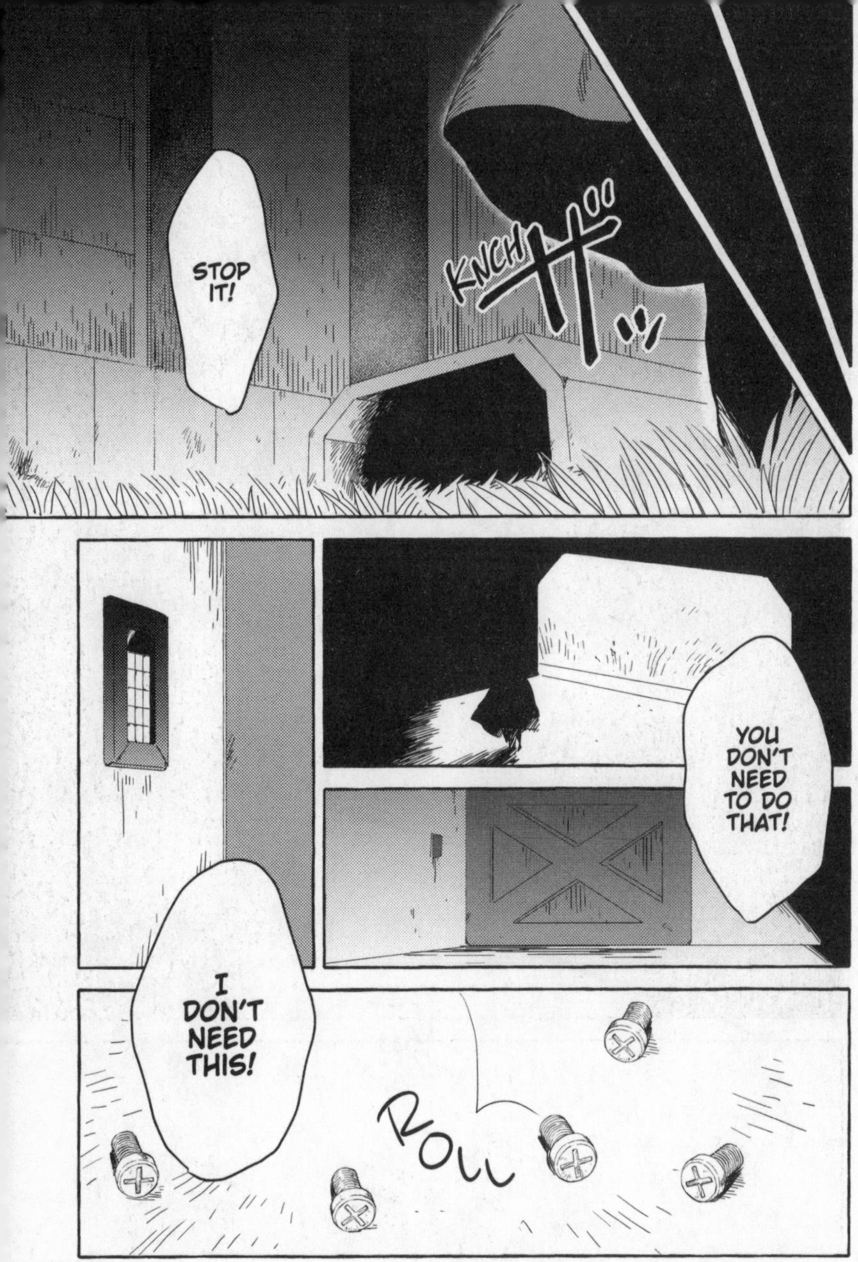
STOP IT!
KNCH
YOU DON'T NEED TO DO THAT!
I DON'T NEED THIS!
ROLL

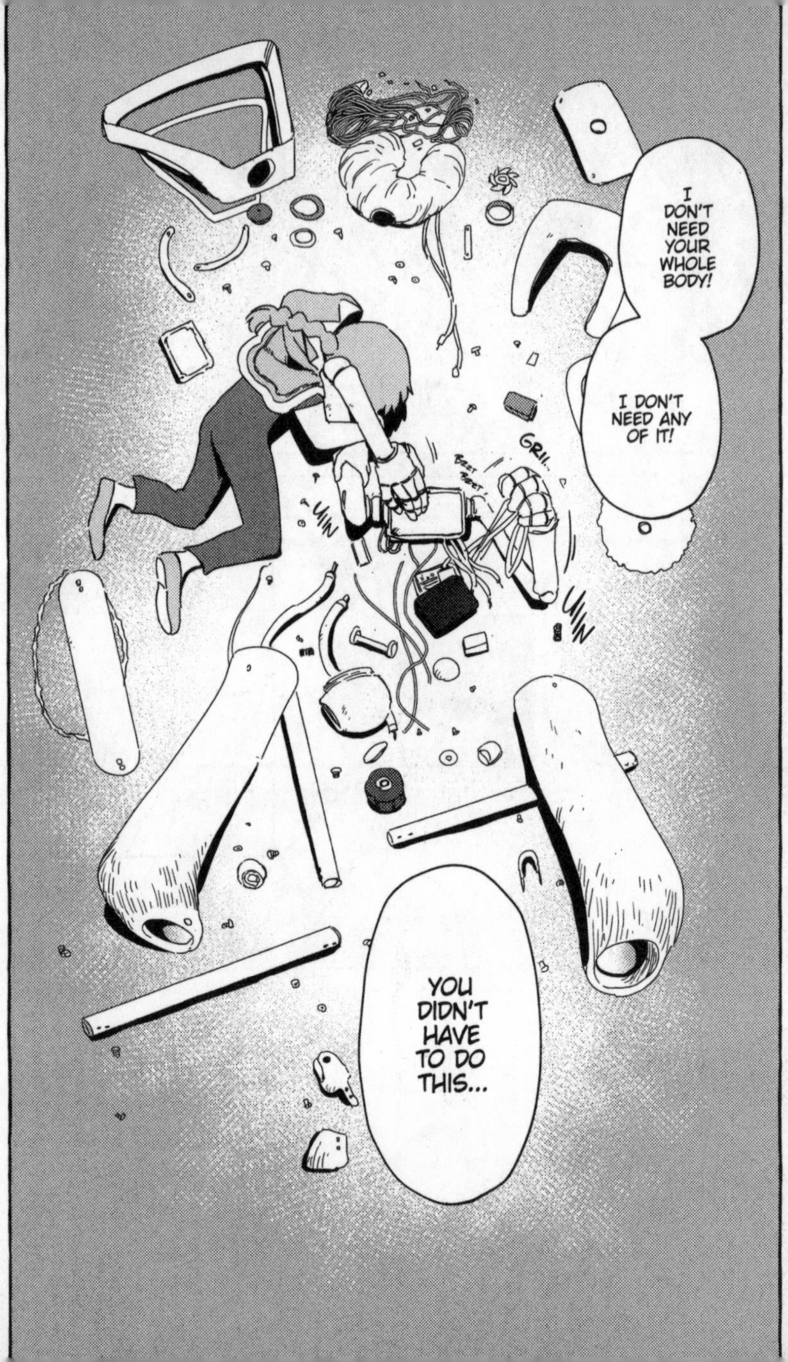
I DON'T NEED YOUR WHOLE BODY!
I DON'T NEED ANY OF IT!
GRII..
UIIN
UIIN
YOU DIDN'T HAVE TO DO THIS...

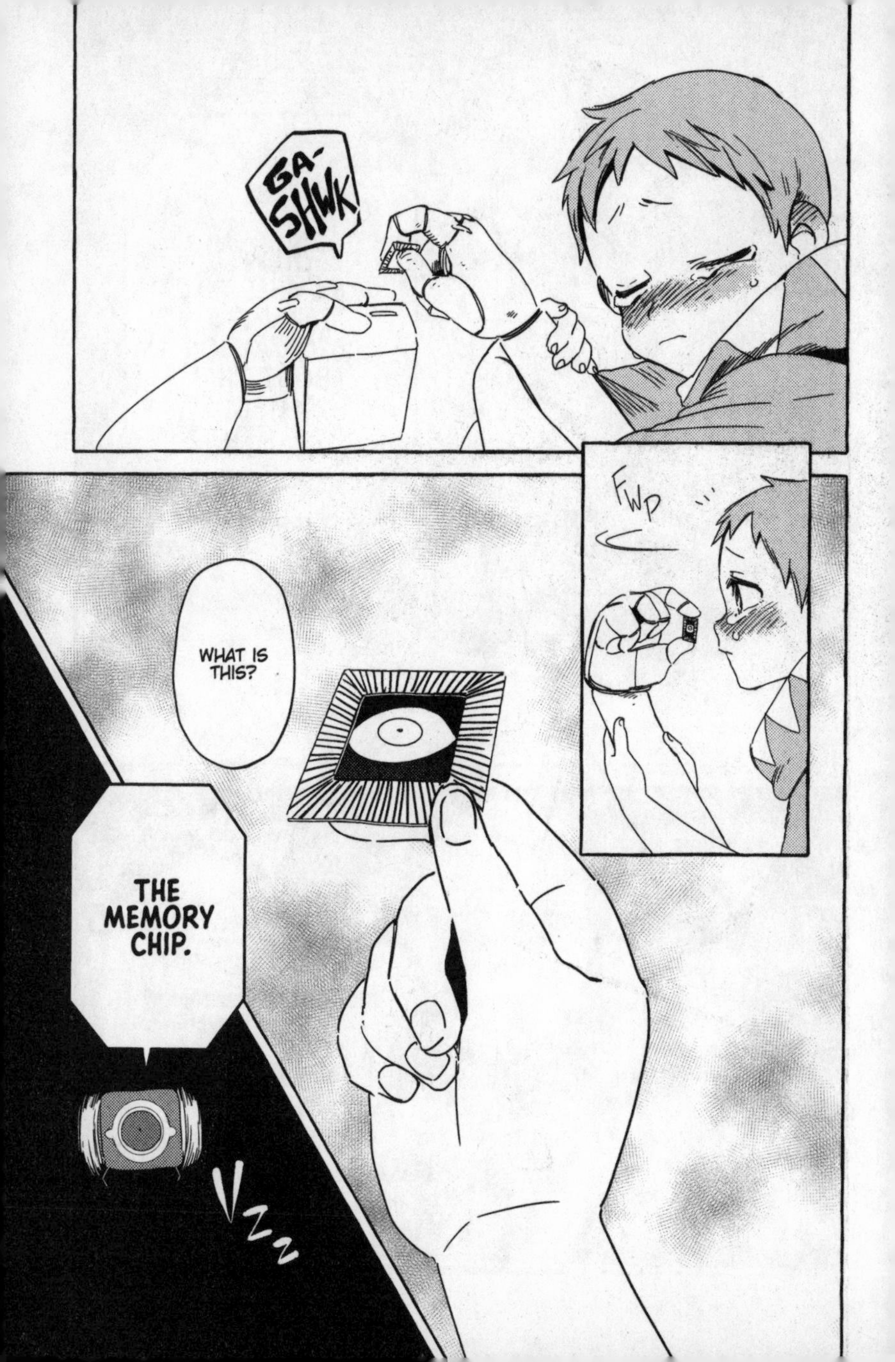
GA-SHWK
FWP
WHAT IS THIS?
THE MEMORY CHIP.
VZZ

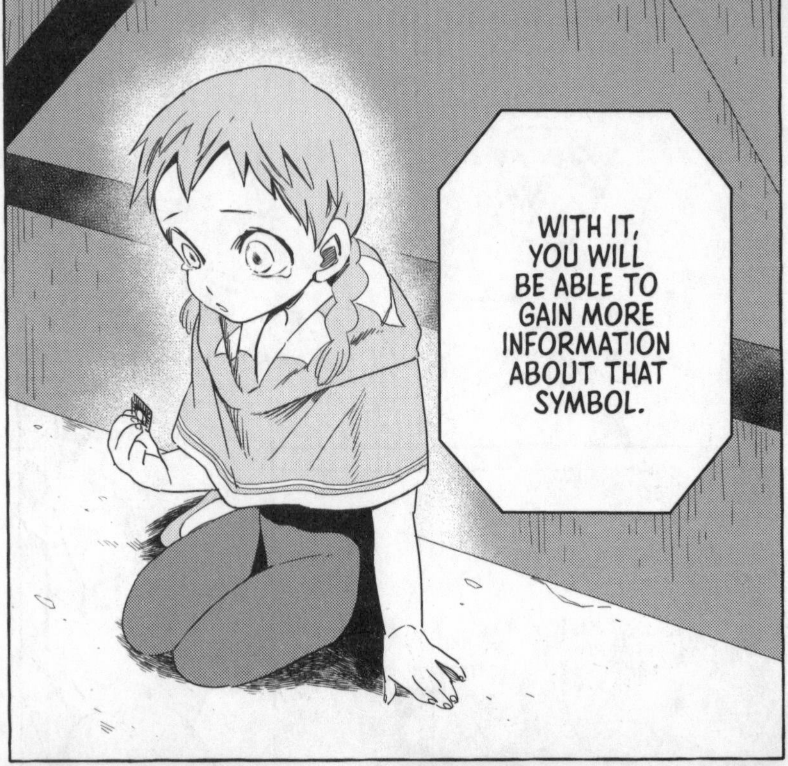
WITH IT, YOU WILL BE ABLE TO GAIN MORE INFORMATION ABOUT THAT SYMBOL.

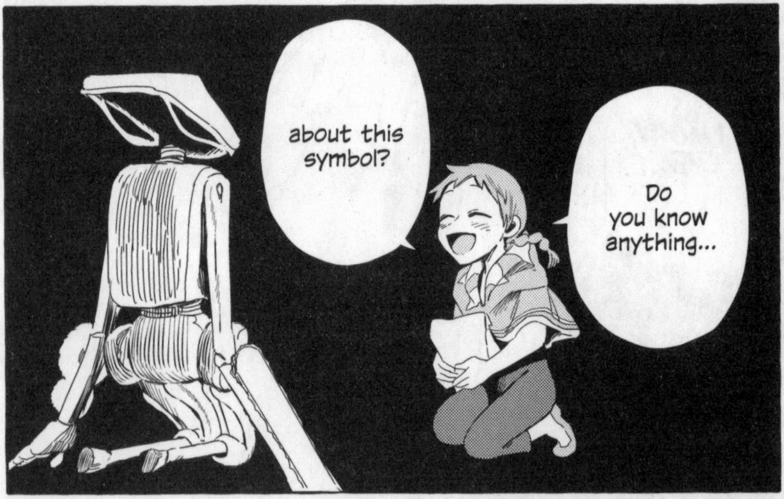
Do you know anything...
about this symbol?

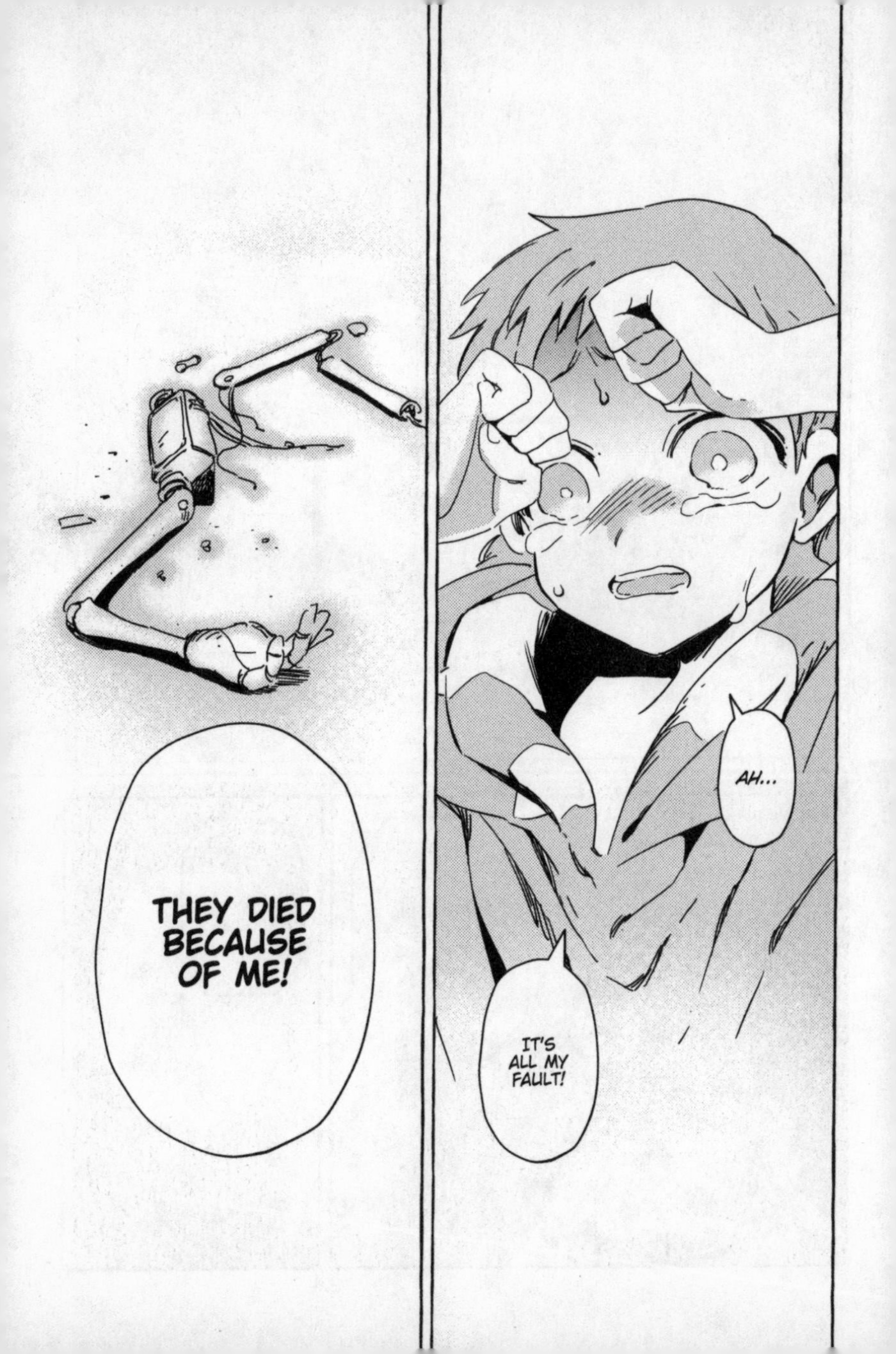
AH...
IT'S ALL MY FAULT!
THEY DIED BECAUSE OF ME!

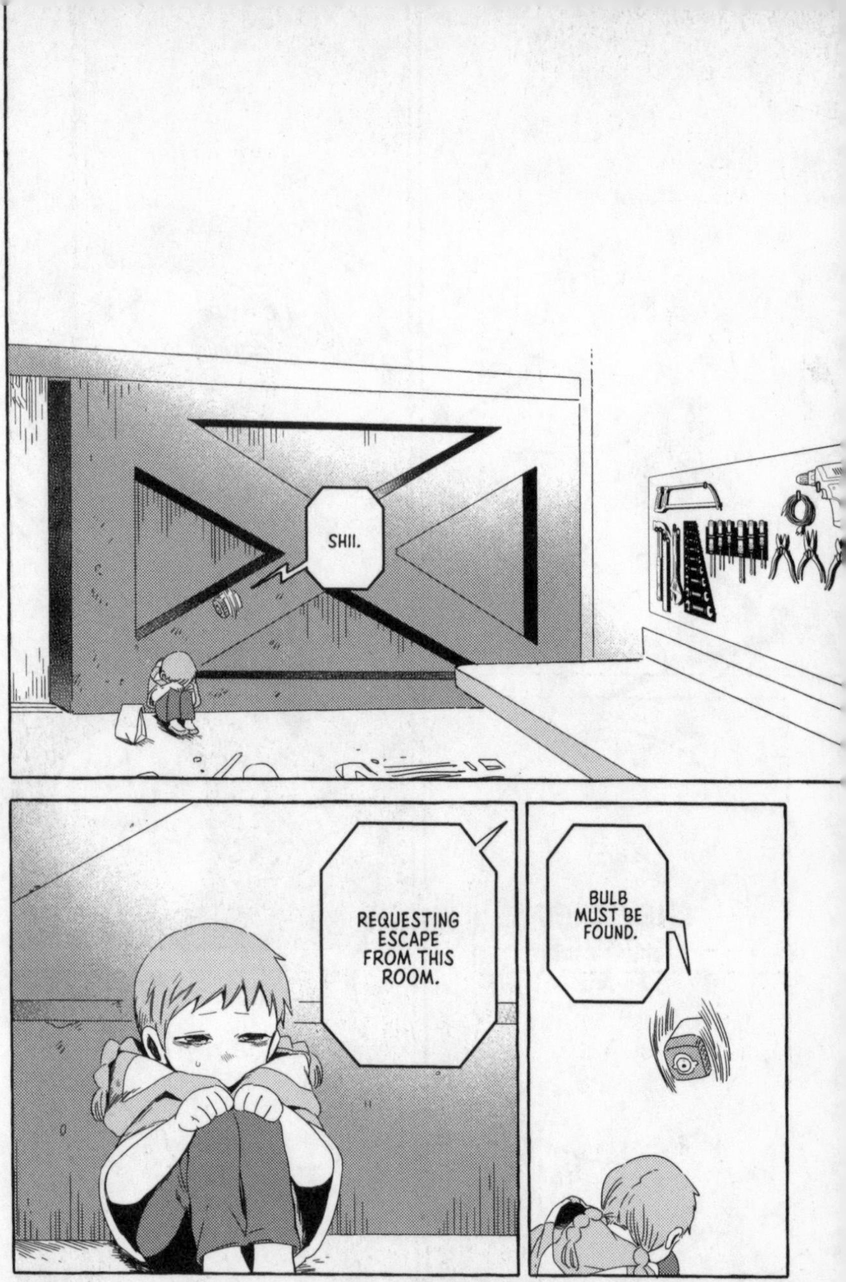
SHII.
BULB MUST BE FOUND.
REQUESTING ESCAPE FROM THIS ROOM.

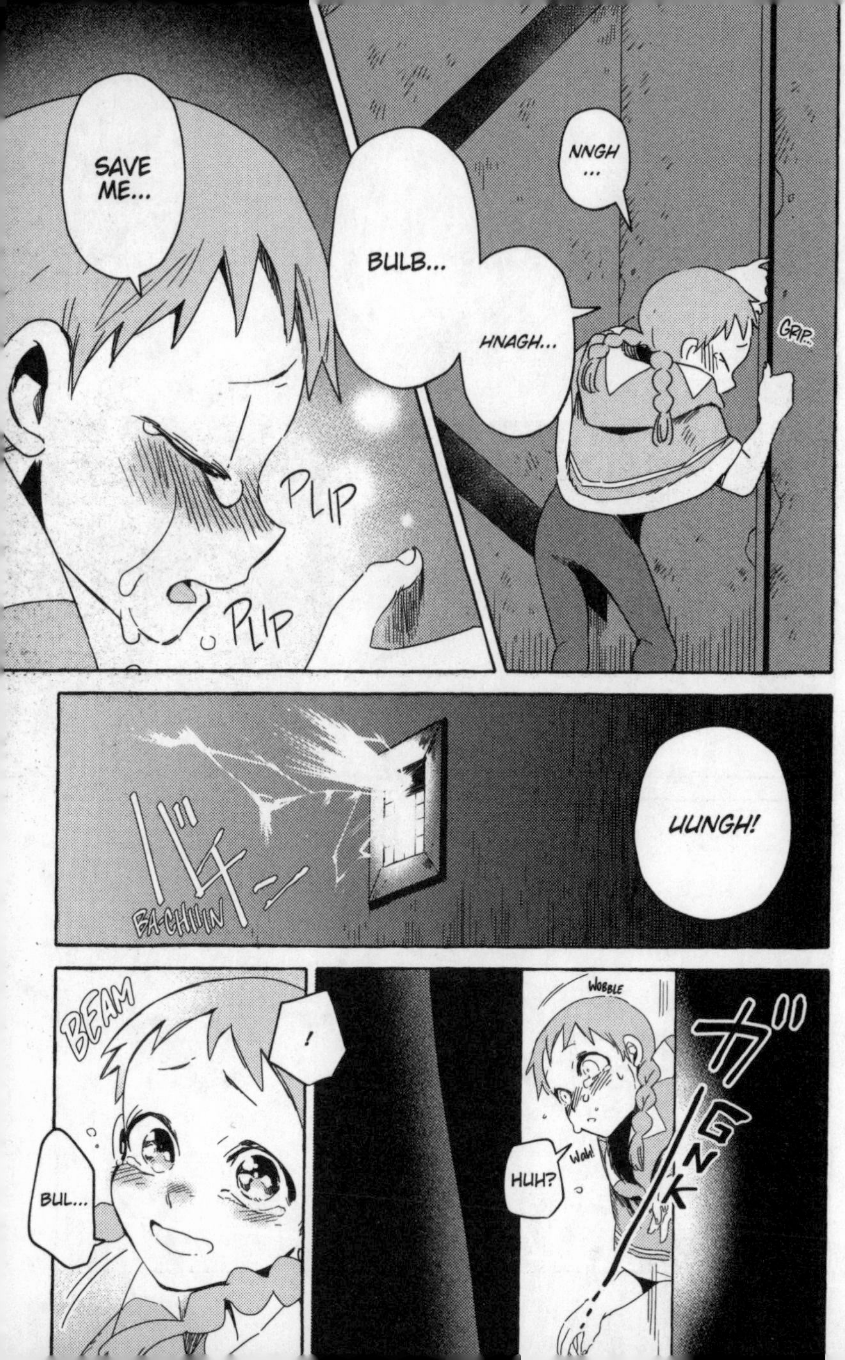
NNGH ...
GRIP...
HNAGH...
BULB...
SAVE ME...
PLIP
PLIP
UUNGH!
バチーン
BA-CHIIIN
ガッ
GNK
WOBBLE
Wah!
HUH?
!
BEAM
BUL...

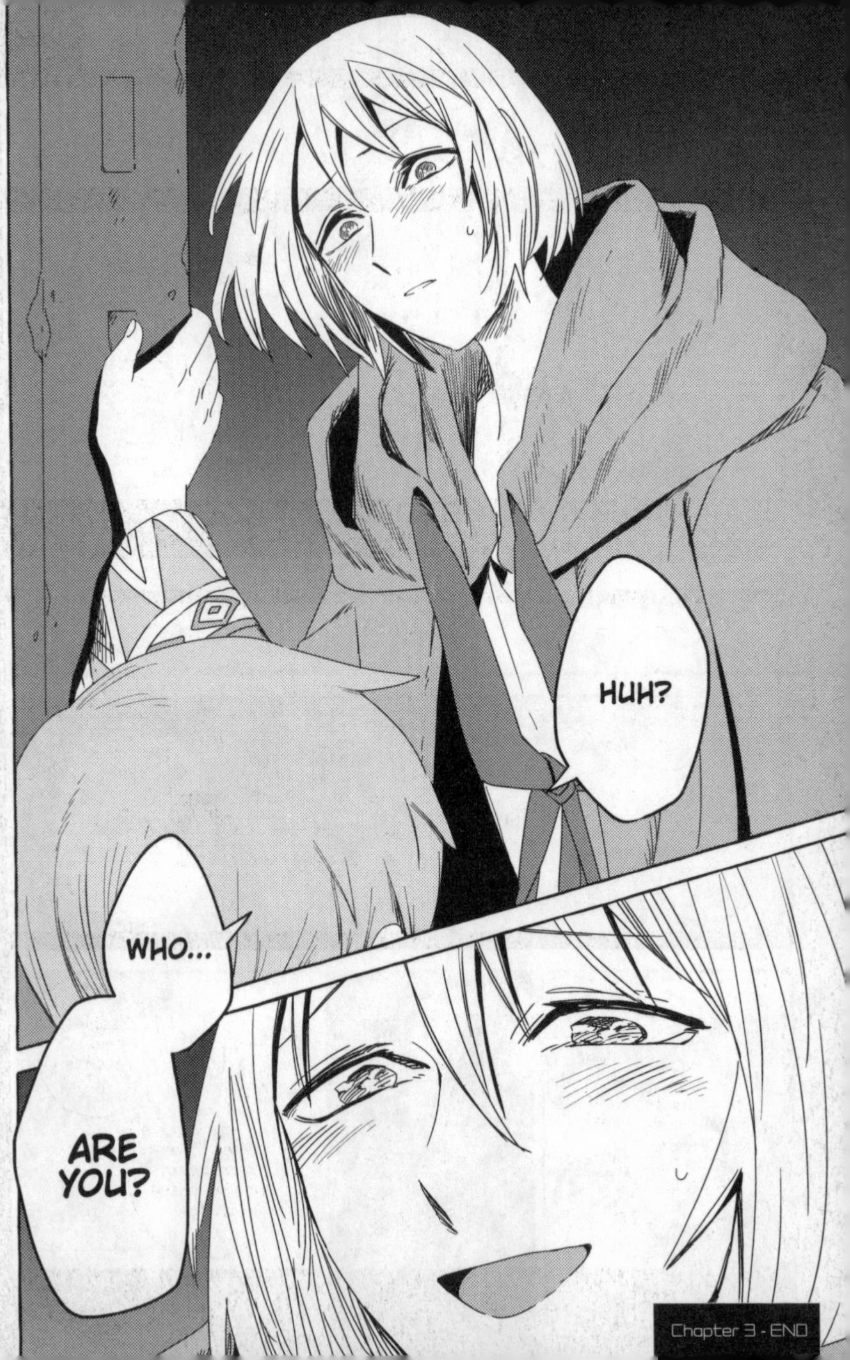
HUH?
WHO...
ARE YOU?
Chapter 3 - END

A Fleeting Tale #3 Conversation at the Junk Shop

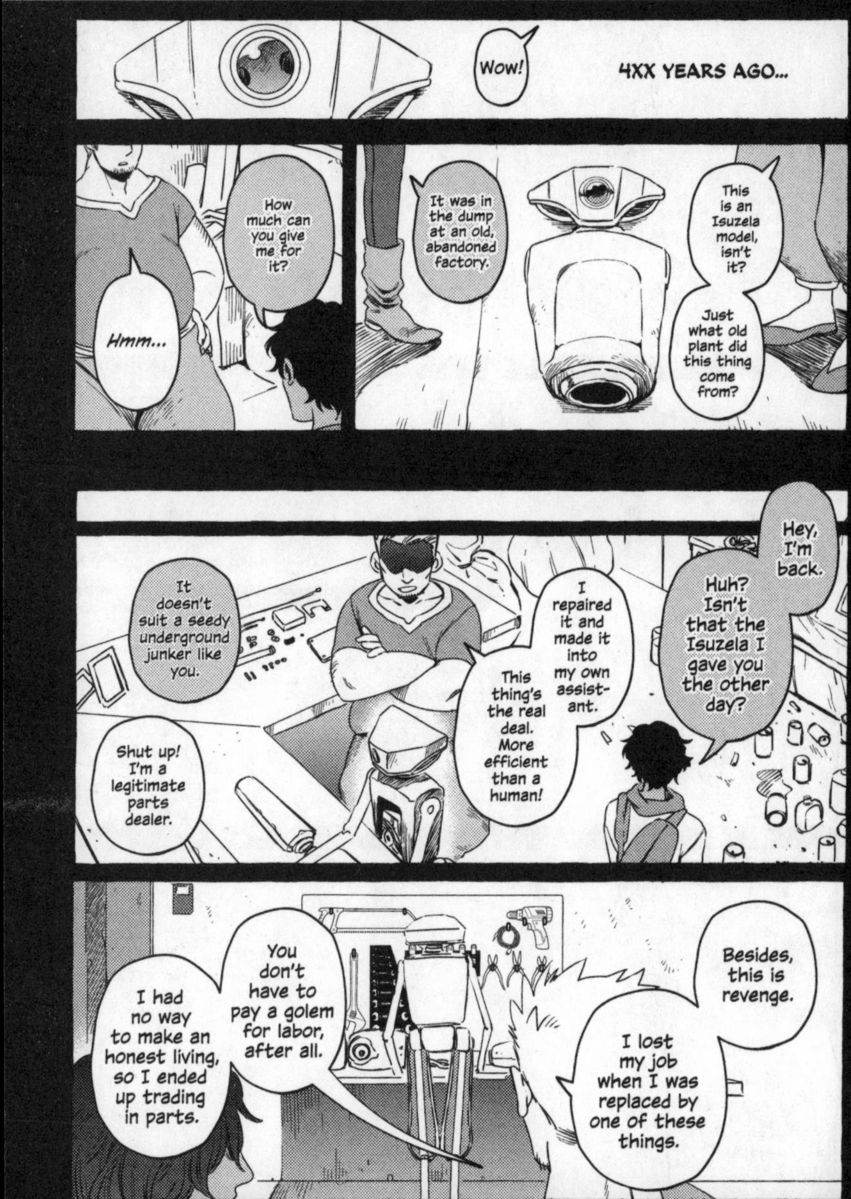
4XX YEARS AGO...
Wow!
This is an Isuzela model, isn't it?
Just what old plant did this thing come from?
It was in the dump at an old, abandoned factory.
How much can you give me for it?
Hmm...
Hey, I'm back.
Huh? Isn't that the Isuzela I gave you the other day?
I repaired it and made it into my own assistant.
This thing's the real deal. More efficient than a human!
It doesn't suit a seedy underground junker like you.
Shut up! I'm a legitimate parts dealer.
Besides, this is revenge.
I lost my job when I was replaced by one of these things.
You don't have to pay a golem for labor, after all.
I had no way to make an honest living, so I ended up trading in parts.

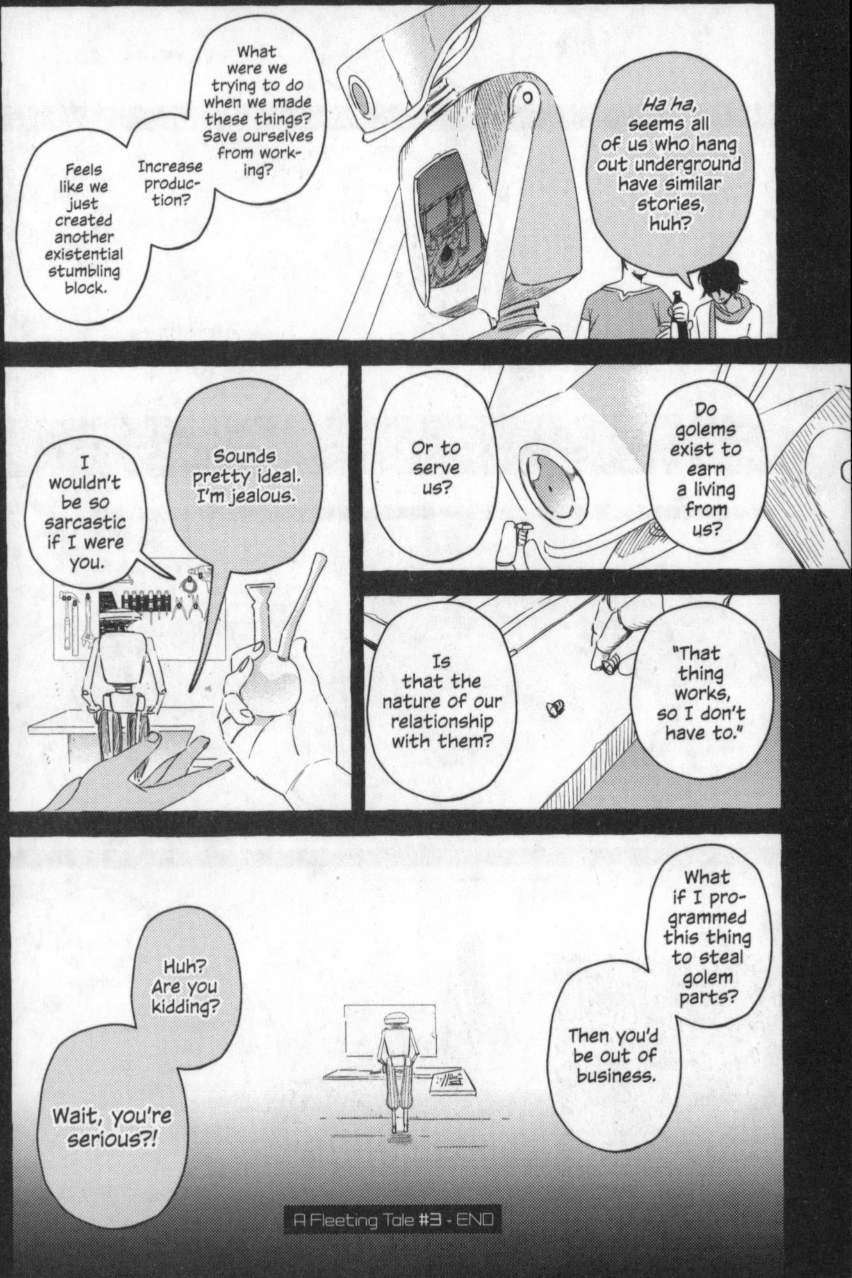
Ha ha, seems all of us who hang out underground have similar stories, huh?
What were we trying to do when we made these things? Save ourselves from working?
Increase production?
Feels like we just created another existential stumbling block.
Do golems exist to earn a living from us?
Or to serve us?
"That thing works, so I don't have to."
Is that the nature of our relationship with them?
Sounds pretty ideal. I'm jealous.
I wouldn't be so sarcastic if I were you.
What if I programmed this thing to steal golem parts?
Then you'd be out of business.
Huh? Are you kidding?
Wait, you're serious?!
A Fleeting Tale #3 - END

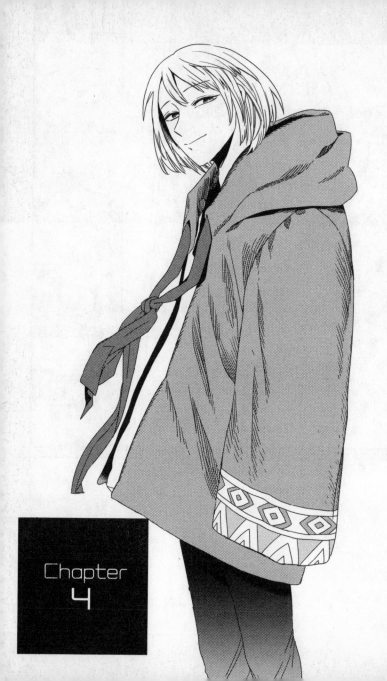

Chapter 4

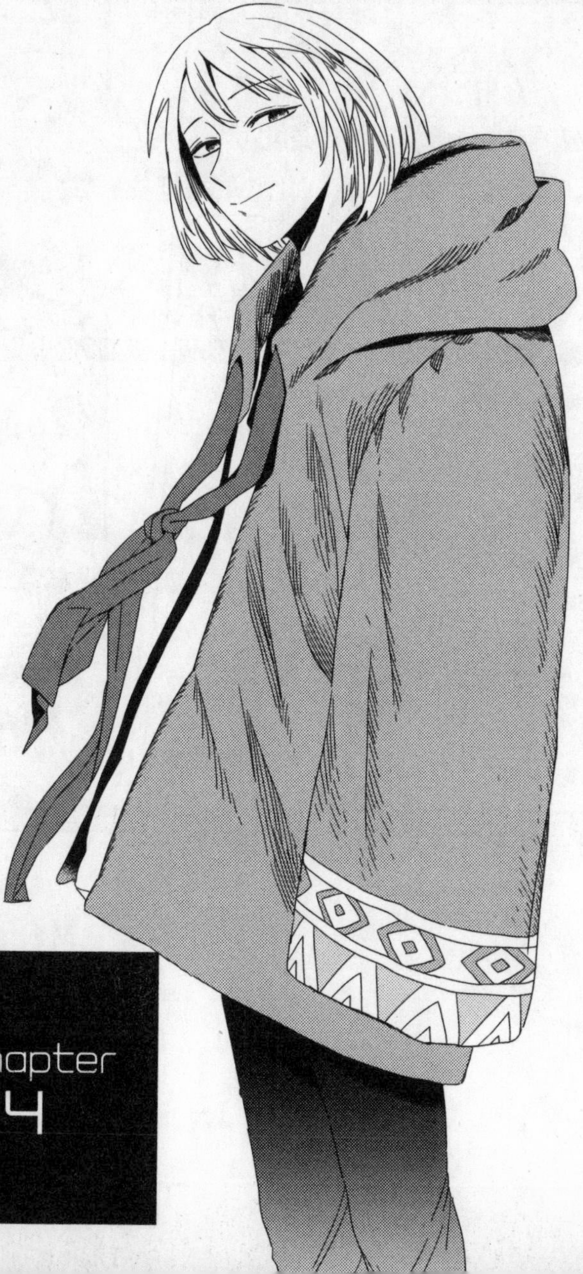

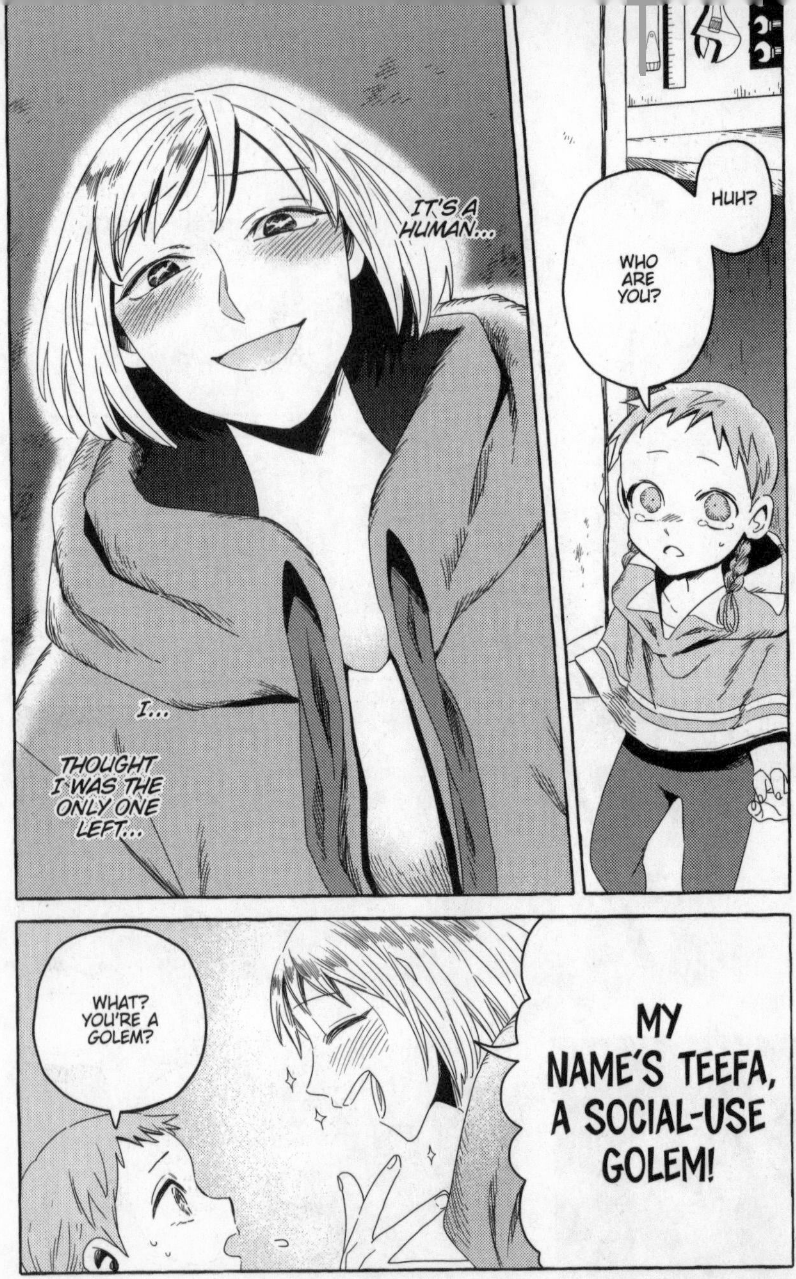
HUH?
WHO ARE YOU?
IT'S A HUMAN...
I...
THOUGHT I WAS THE ONLY ONE LEFT...
MY NAME'S TEEFA, A SOCIAL-USE GOLEM!
WHAT? YOU'RE A GOLEM?

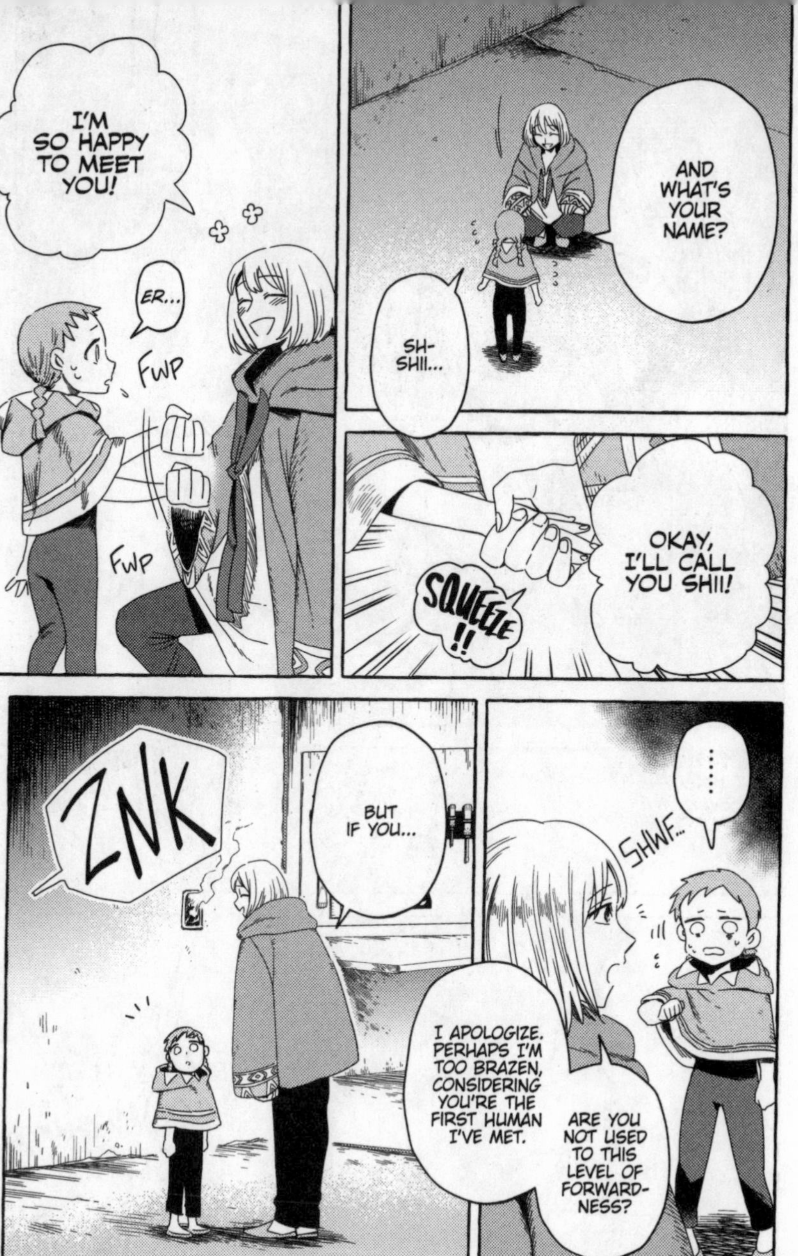
AND WHAT'S YOUR NAME?
SH-SHII...
OKAY, I'LL CALL YOU SHII!
SQUEEZE!!
I'M SO HAPPY TO MEET YOU!
ER...
FWP
FWP
......
SHWF...
ARE YOU NOT USED TO THIS LEVEL OF FORWARD-NESS?
I APOLOGIZE. PERHAPS I'M TOO BRAZEN, CONSIDERING YOU'RE THE FIRST HUMAN I'VE MET.
BUT IF YOU...
ZNK

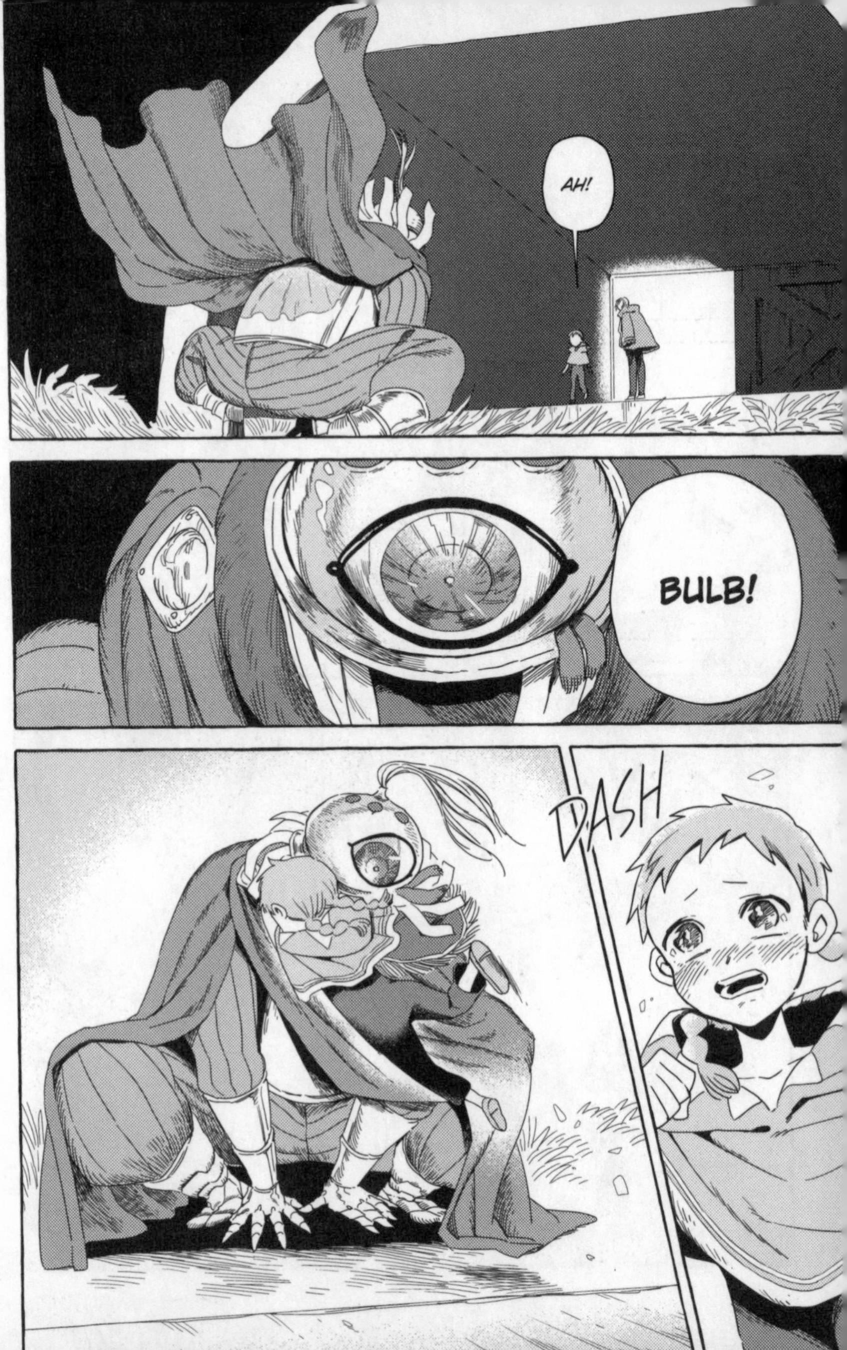
AH!
BULB!
DASH

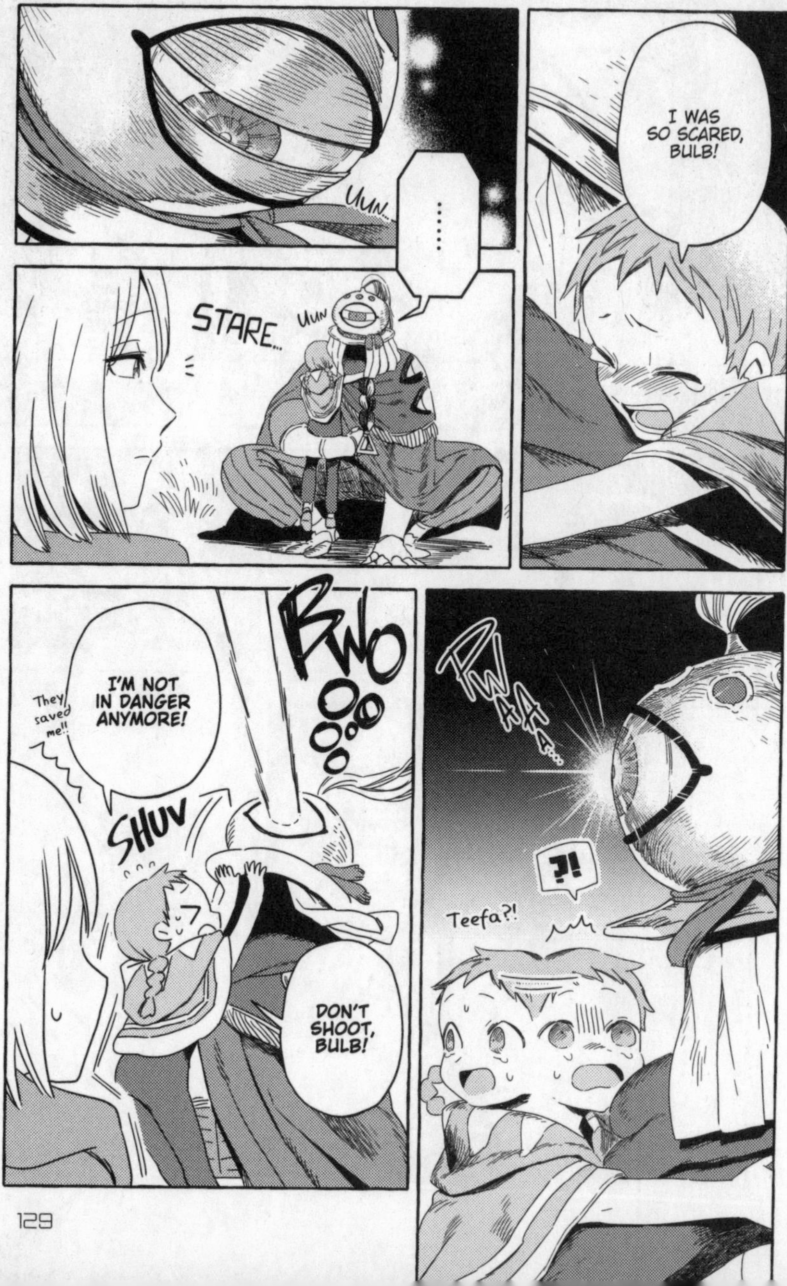
I WAS SO SCARED, BULB!
UUN...
......
STARE...
UUN
PWAAA...
?!
Teefa?!
BWOOOOO
I'M NOT IN DANGER ANYMORE!
They saved me!!
SHUV
DON'T SHOOT, BULB!

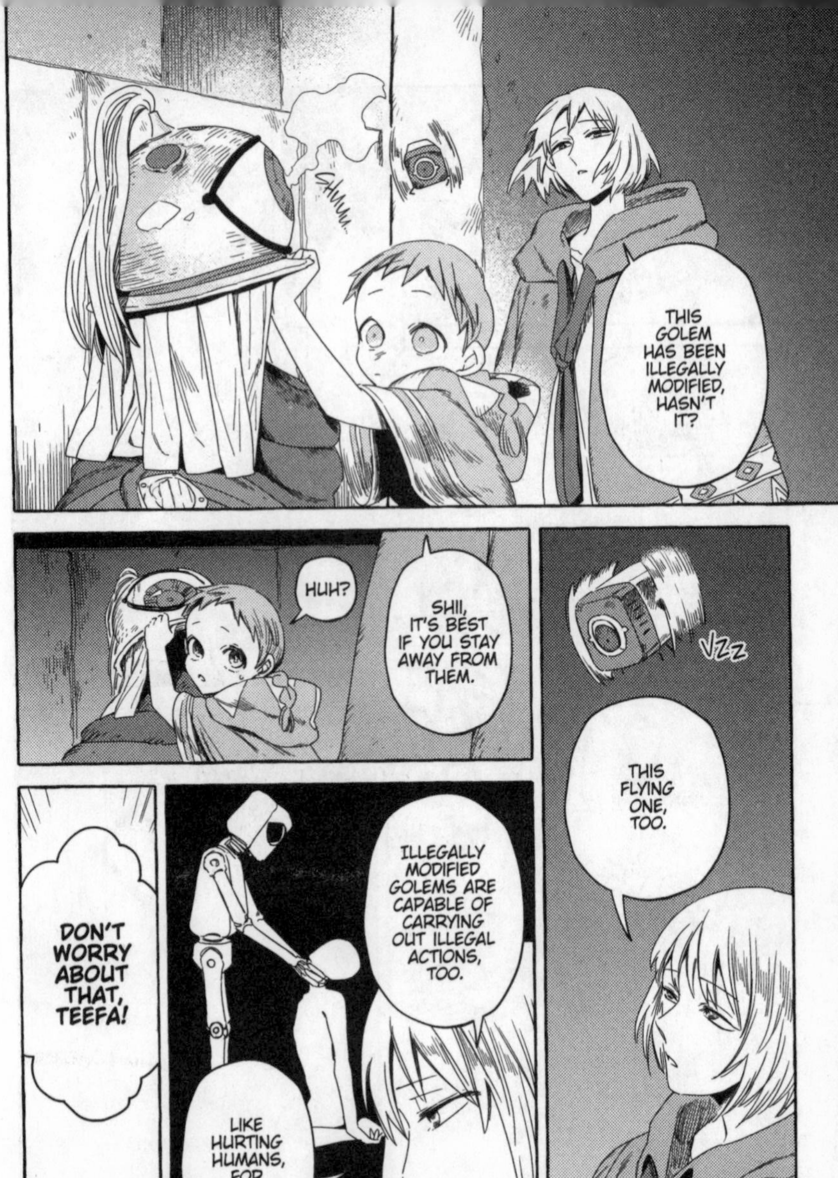
SHUUU
THIS GOLEM HAS BEEN ILLEGALLY MODIFIED, HASN'T IT?
VZZ
THIS FLYING ONE, TOO.
SHII, IT'S BEST IF YOU STAY AWAY FROM THEM.
HUH?
ILLEGALLY MODIFIED GOLEMS ARE CAPABLE OF CARRYING OUT ILLEGAL ACTIONS, TOO.
LIKE HURTING HUMANS, FOR EXAMPLE.
DON'T WORRY ABOUT THAT, TEEFA!

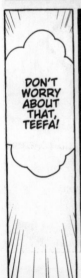

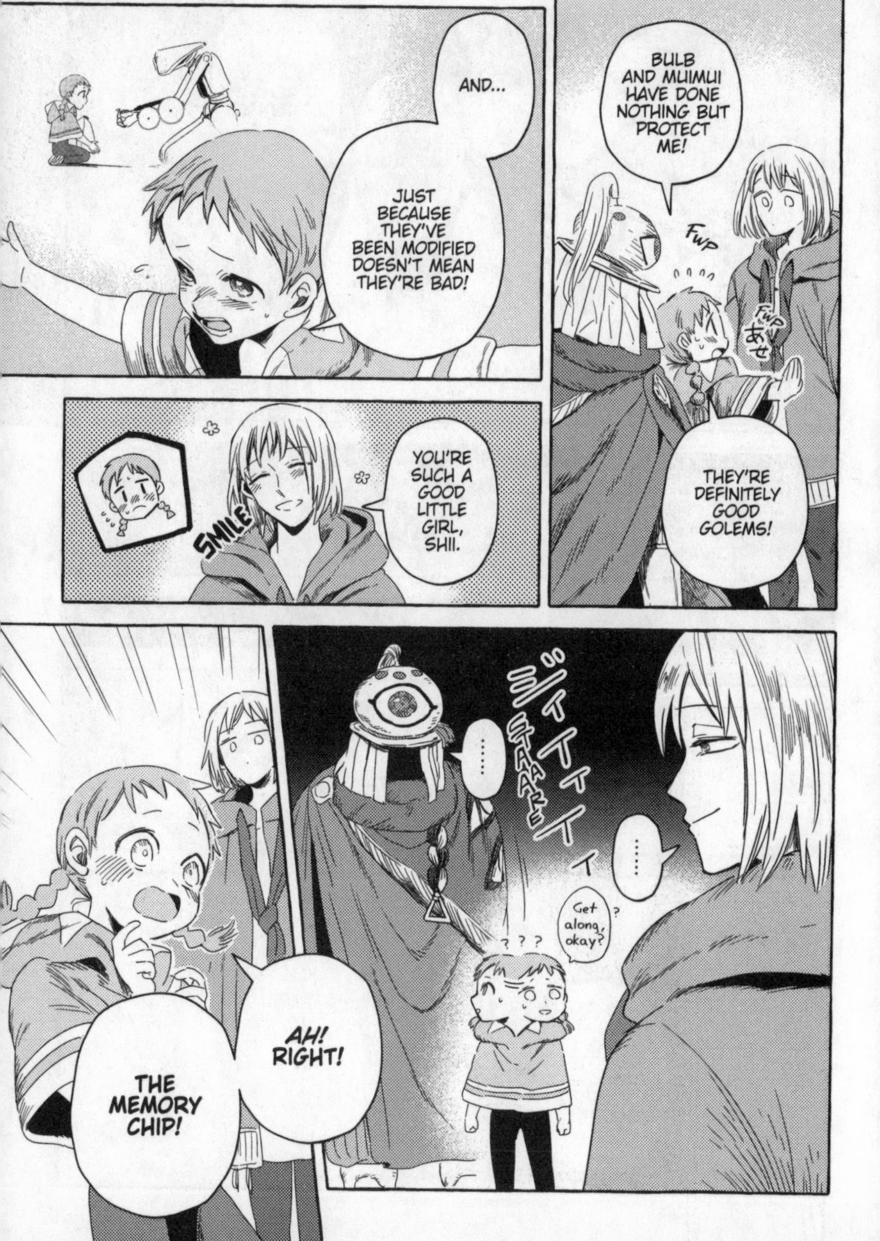
BULB AND MUIMUI HAVE DONE NOTHING BUT PROTECT ME!
FWP
FWP
あせ
THEY'RE DEFINITELY GOOD GOLEMS!
AND...
JUST BECAUSE THEY'VE BEEN MODIFIED DOESN'T MEAN THEY'RE BAD!
YOU'RE SUCH A GOOD LITTLE GIRL, SHII.
SMILE
ジイイイイ
STAAARE
......
......
Get along, okay?
?
???
AH! RIGHT!
THE MEMORY CHIP!

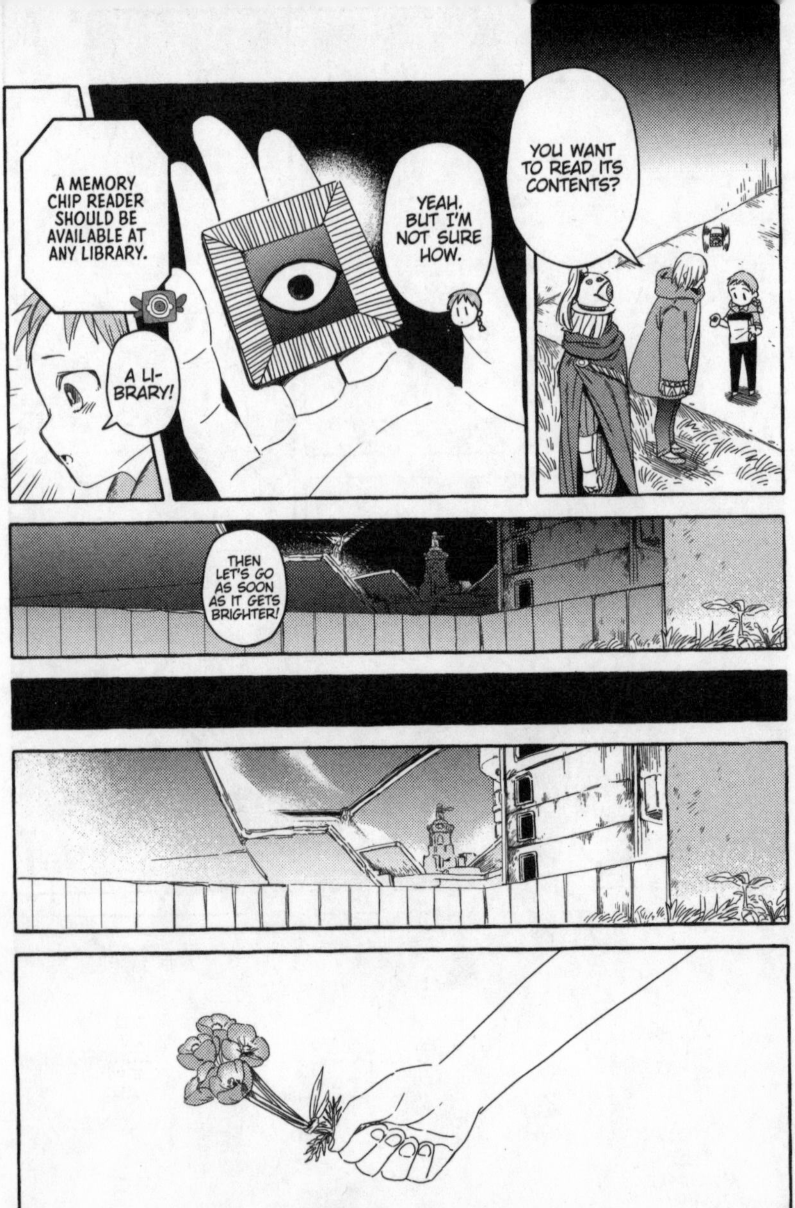
YOU WANT TO READ ITS CONTENTS?
YEAH. BUT I'M NOT SURE HOW.
A MEMORY CHIP READER SHOULD BE AVAILABLE AT ANY LIBRARY.
A LI-BRARY!
THEN LET'S GO AS SOON AS IT GETS BRIGHTER!

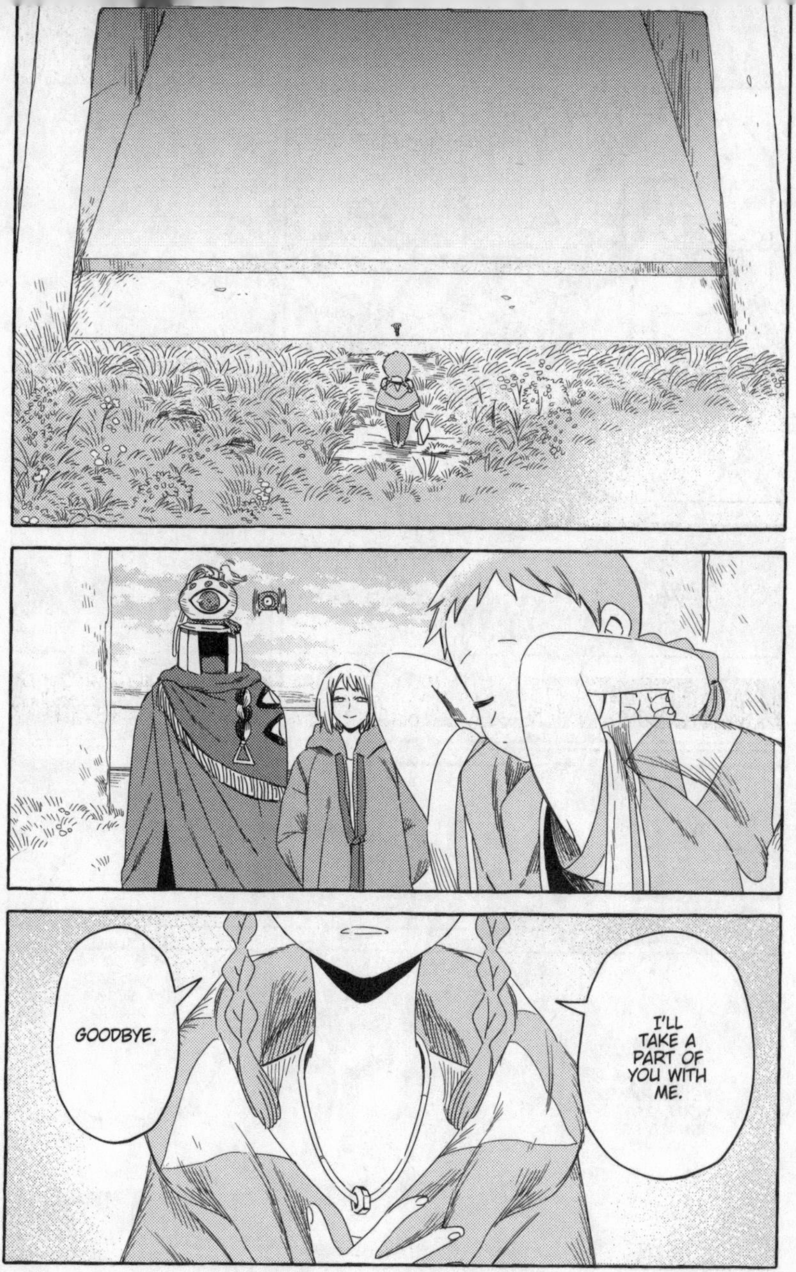
I'LL TAKE A PART OF YOU WITH ME.
GOODBYE.

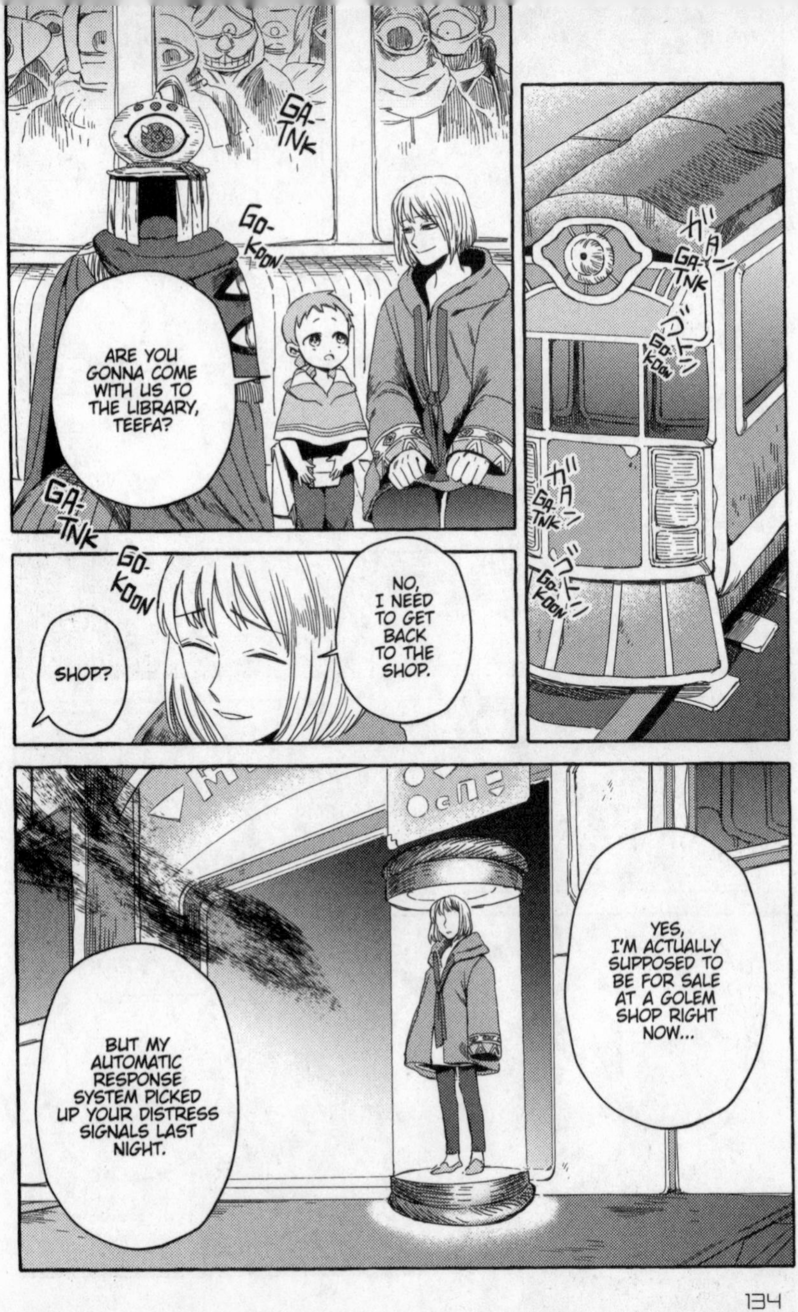
GA-TNK
GO-KOON
GA-TNK
GO-KOON
GA-TNK
GO-KOON
ARE YOU GONNA COME WITH US TO THE LIBRARY, TEEFA?
GA-TNK
GO-KOON
NO, I NEED TO GET BACK TO THE SHOP.
SHOP?
YES, I'M ACTUALLY SUPPOSED TO BE FOR SALE AT A GOLEM SHOP RIGHT NOW...
BUT MY AUTOMATIC RESPONSE SYSTEM PICKED UP YOUR DISTRESS SIGNALS LAST NIGHT.

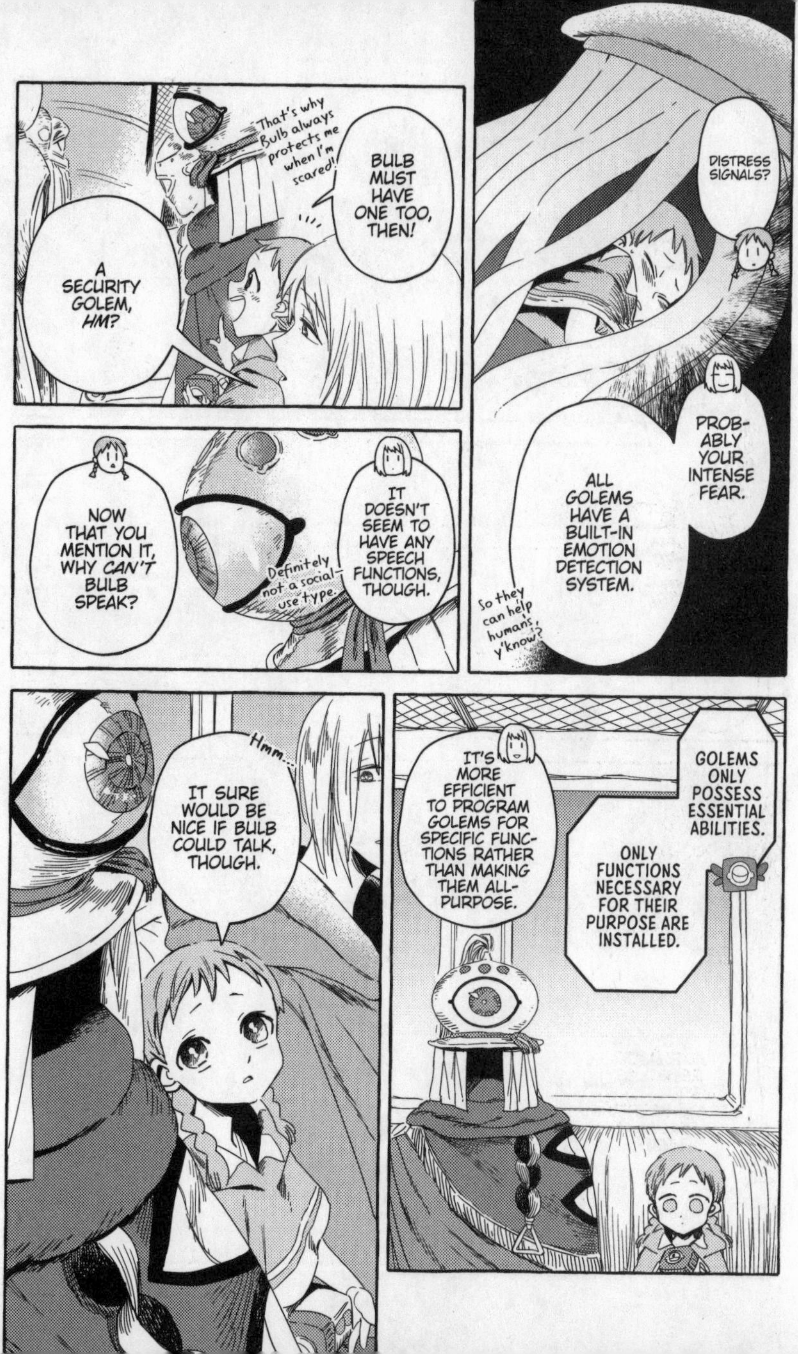
DISTRESS SIGNALS?
PROBABLY YOUR INTENSE FEAR.
ALL GOLEMS HAVE A BUILT-IN EMOTION DETECTION SYSTEM.
So they can help humans, y'know?
BULB MUST HAVE ONE TOO, THEN!
That's why Bulb always protects me when I'm scared!
A SECURITY GOLEM, *HM*?
IT DOESN'T SEEM TO HAVE ANY SPEECH FUNCTIONS, THOUGH.
Definitely not a social-use type.
NOW THAT YOU MENTION IT, WHY *CAN'T* BULB SPEAK?
GOLEMS ONLY POSSESS ESSENTIAL ABILITIES.
ONLY FUNCTIONS NECESSARY FOR THEIR PURPOSE ARE INSTALLED.
IT'S MORE EFFICIENT TO PROGRAM GOLEMS FOR SPECIFIC FUNCTIONS RATHER THAN MAKING THEM ALL-PURPOSE.
Hmm...
IT SURE WOULD BE NICE IF BULB COULD TALK, THOUGH.

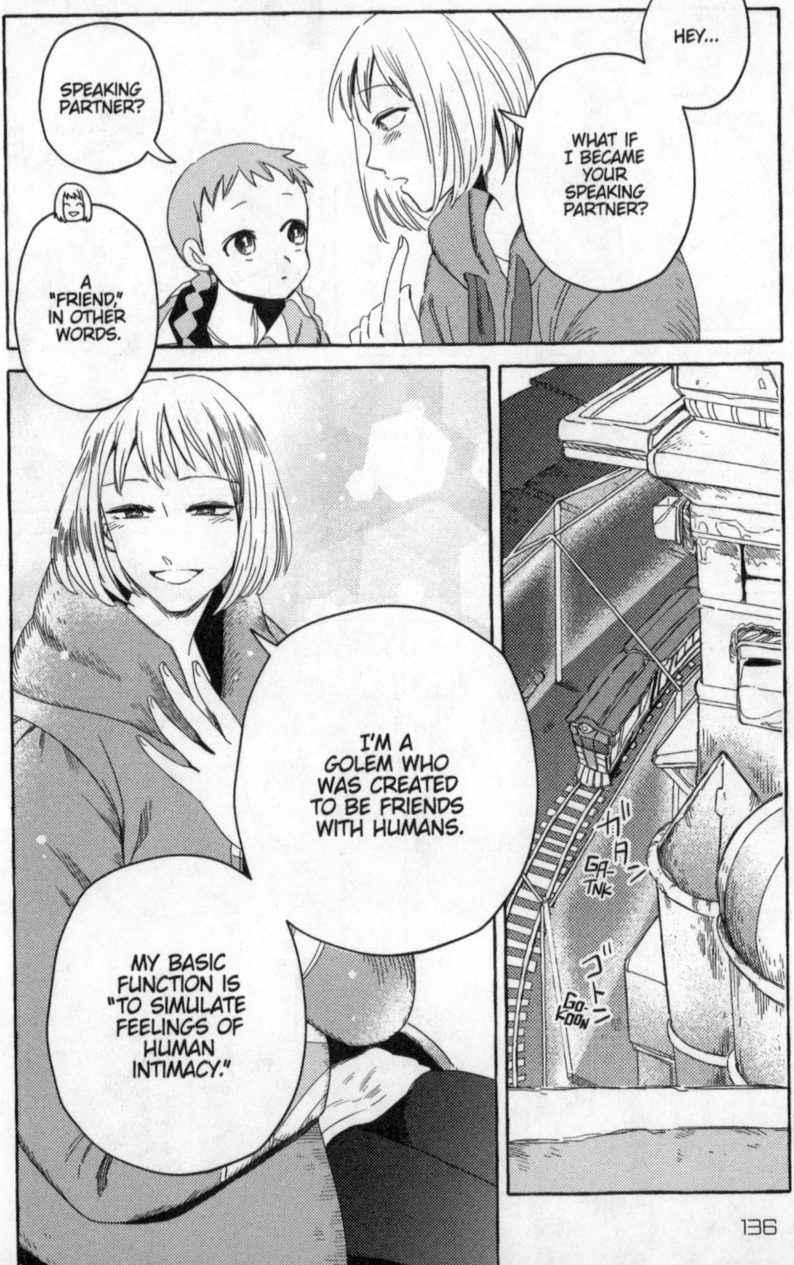
HEY...
WHAT IF I BECAME YOUR SPEAKING PARTNER?
SPEAKING PARTNER?
A "FRIEND," IN OTHER WORDS.
GA-TNK
GO-KOON
I'M A GOLEM WHO WAS CREATED TO BE FRIENDS WITH HUMANS.
MY BASIC FUNCTION IS "TO SIMULATE FEELINGS OF HUMAN INTIMACY."

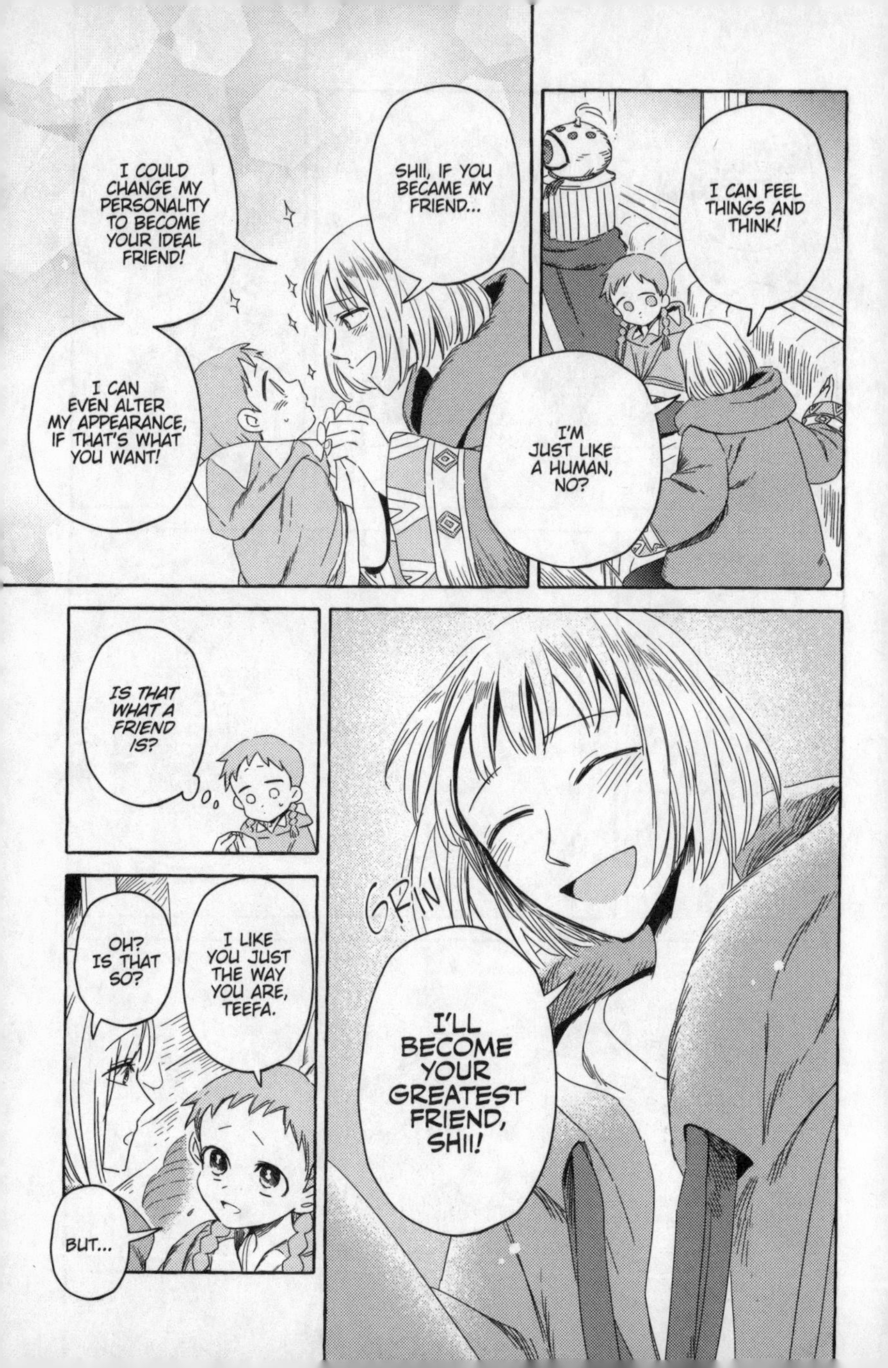
I CAN FEEL THINGS AND THINK!
I'M JUST LIKE A HUMAN, NO?
SHII, IF YOU BECAME MY FRIEND...
I COULD CHANGE MY PERSONALITY TO BECOME YOUR IDEAL FRIEND!
I CAN EVEN ALTER MY APPEARANCE, IF THAT'S WHAT YOU WANT!
GRIN
I'LL BECOME YOUR GREATEST FRIEND, SHII!
IS THAT WHAT A FRIEND IS?
I LIKE YOU JUST THE WAY YOU ARE, TEEFA.
OH? IS THAT SO?
BUT...

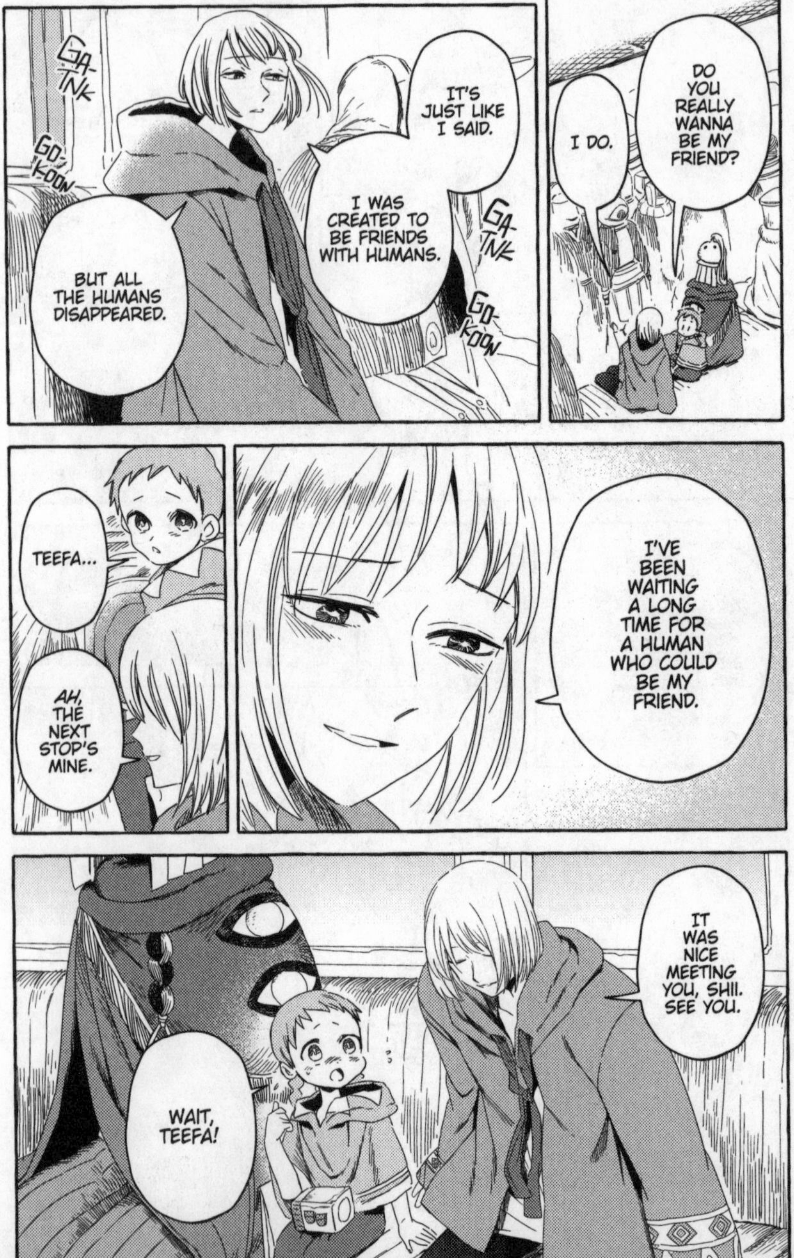
DO YOU REALLY WANNA BE MY FRIEND?
I DO.
IT'S JUST LIKE I SAID.
I WAS CREATED TO BE FRIENDS WITH HUMANS.
GA-TNK
GO-KOON
GA-TNK
GO-KOON
BUT ALL THE HUMANS DISAPPEARED.
I'VE BEEN WAITING A LONG TIME FOR A HUMAN WHO COULD BE MY FRIEND.
TEEFA...
AH, THE NEXT STOP'S MINE.
IT WAS NICE MEETING YOU, SHII. SEE YOU.
WAIT, TEEFA!

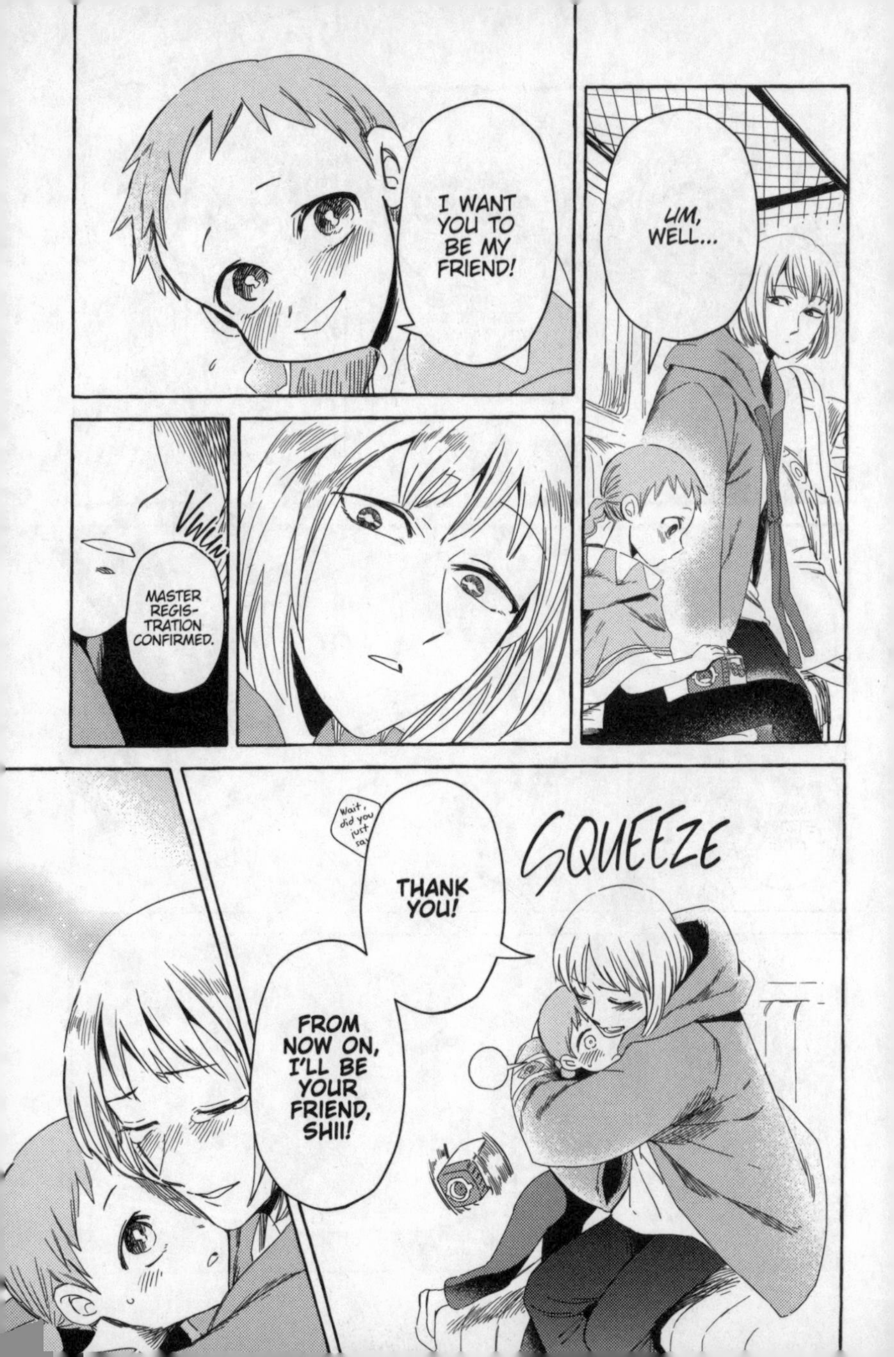
UM, WELL...
I WANT YOU TO BE MY FRIEND!
VWUN
MASTER REGIS-TRATION CONFIRMED.
SQUEEZE
Wait, did you just sa
THANK YOU!
FROM NOW ON, I'LL BE YOUR FRIEND, SHII!

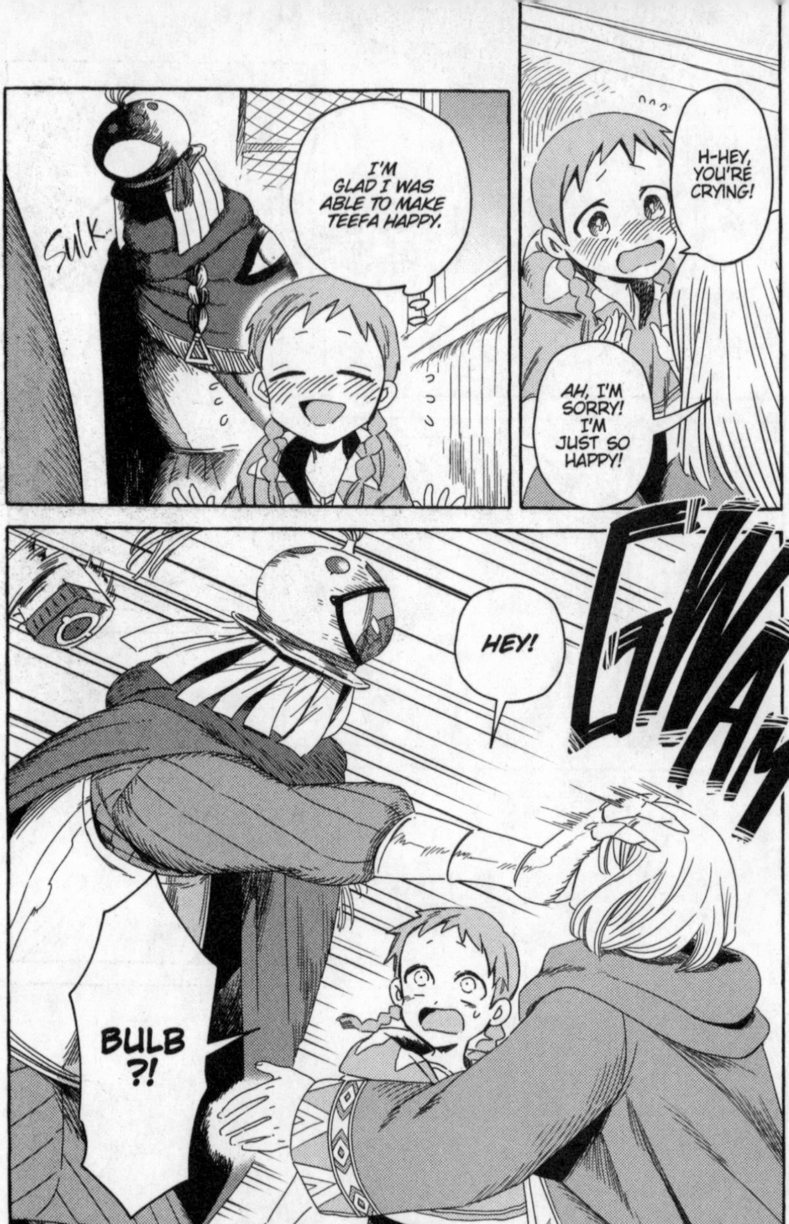
H-HEY, YOU'RE CRYING!
AH, I'M SORRY! I'M JUST SO HAPPY!
I'M GLAD I WAS ABLE TO MAKE TEEFA HAPPY.
SULK...
GWAM
HEY!
BULB ?!

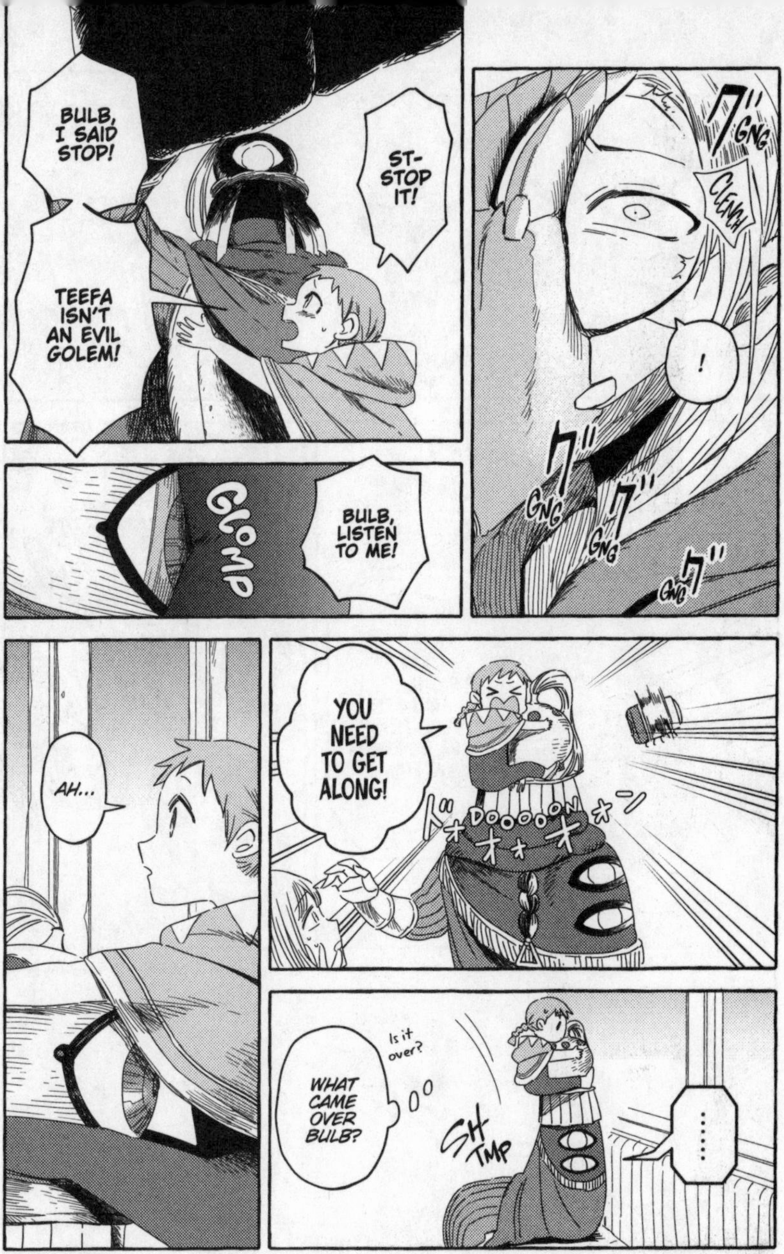
GNG
CLENCH
!
GNG
GNG
GNG
ST-STOP IT!
BULB, I SAID STOP!
TEEFA ISN'T AN EVIL GOLEM!
BULB, LISTEN TO ME!
GLOMP
DOOOOON
YOU NEED TO GET ALONG!
......
SH TMP
WHAT CAME OVER BULB?
Is it over?
AH...

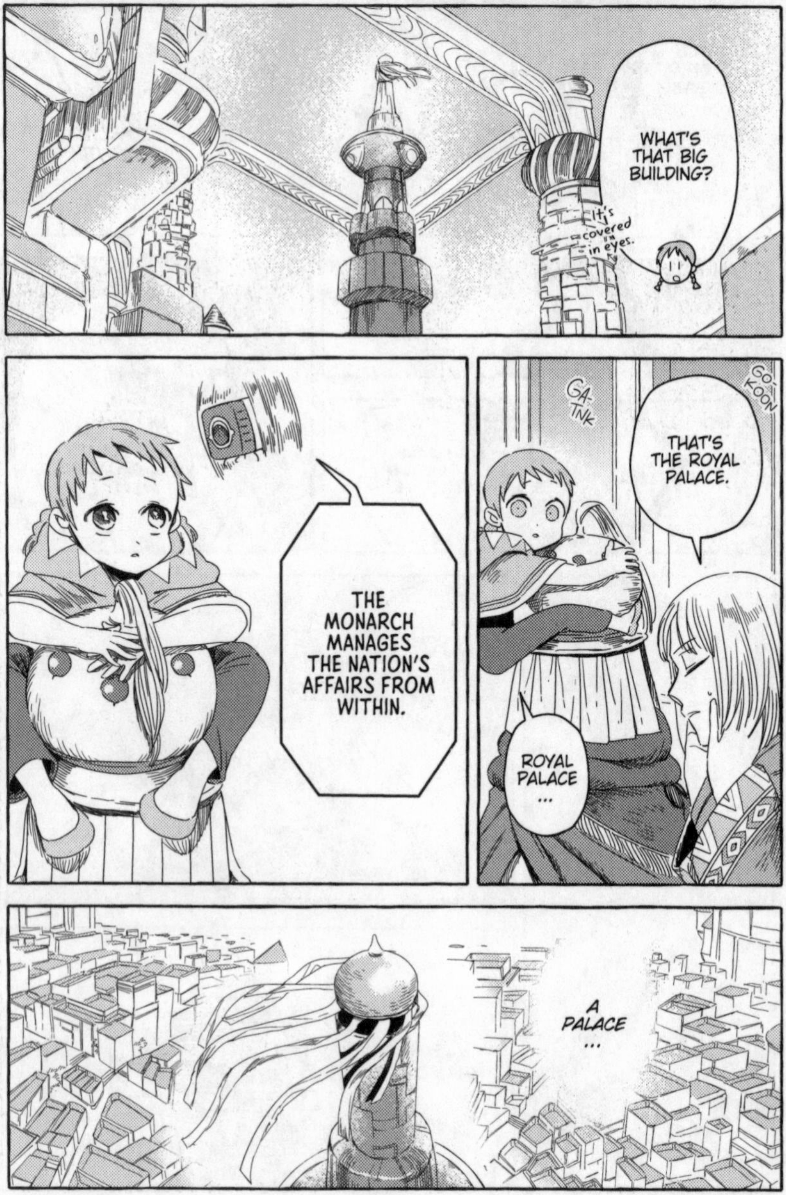
WHAT'S THAT BIG BUILDING?
It's covered in eyes.
GA-TNK
GO-KOON
THAT'S THE ROYAL PALACE.
ROYAL PALACE ...
THE MONARCH MANAGES THE NATION'S AFFAIRS FROM WITHIN.
A PALACE ...

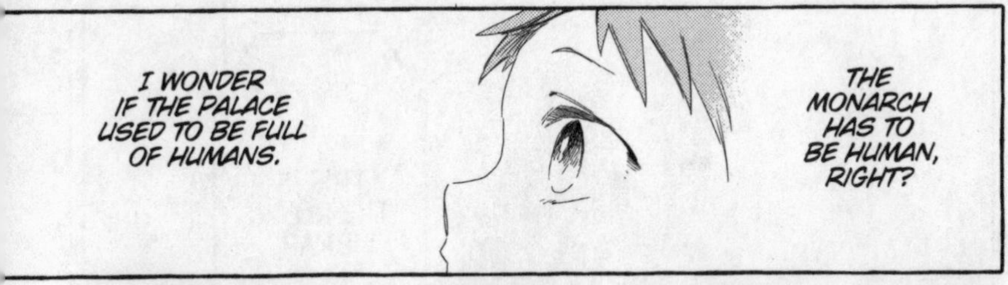
THE MONARCH HAS TO BE HUMAN, RIGHT?
I WONDER IF THE PALACE USED TO BE FULL OF HUMANS.

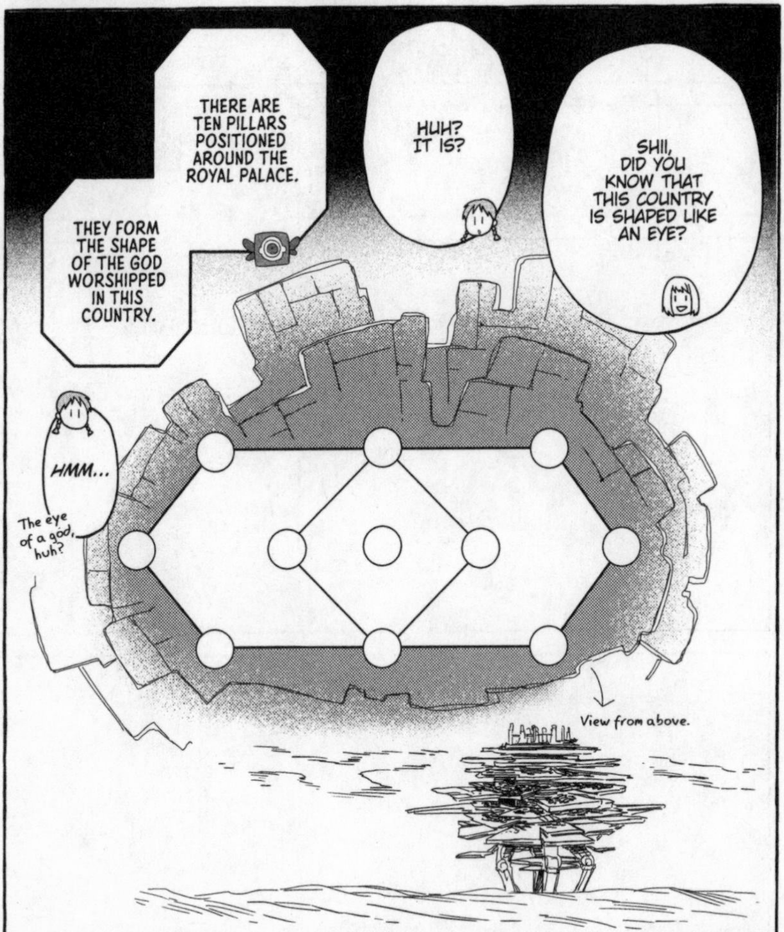
SHII, DID YOU KNOW THAT THIS COUNTRY IS SHAPED LIKE AN EYE?
HUH? IT IS?
THERE ARE TEN PILLARS POSITIONED AROUND THE ROYAL PALACE.
THEY FORM THE SHAPE OF THE GOD WORSHIPPED IN THIS COUNTRY.
HMM...
The eye of a god, huh?
View from above.

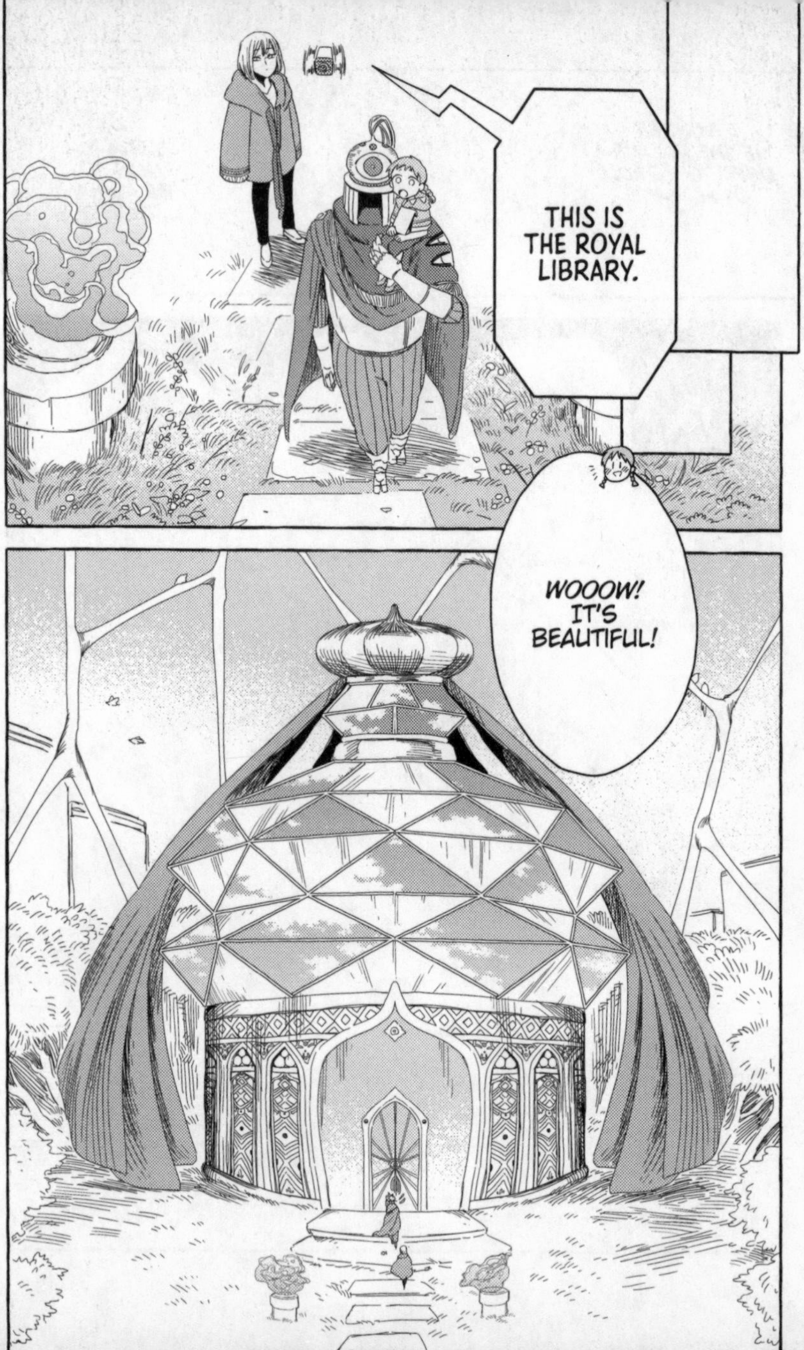
THIS IS THE ROYAL LIBRARY.
WOOOW! IT'S BEAUTIFUL!

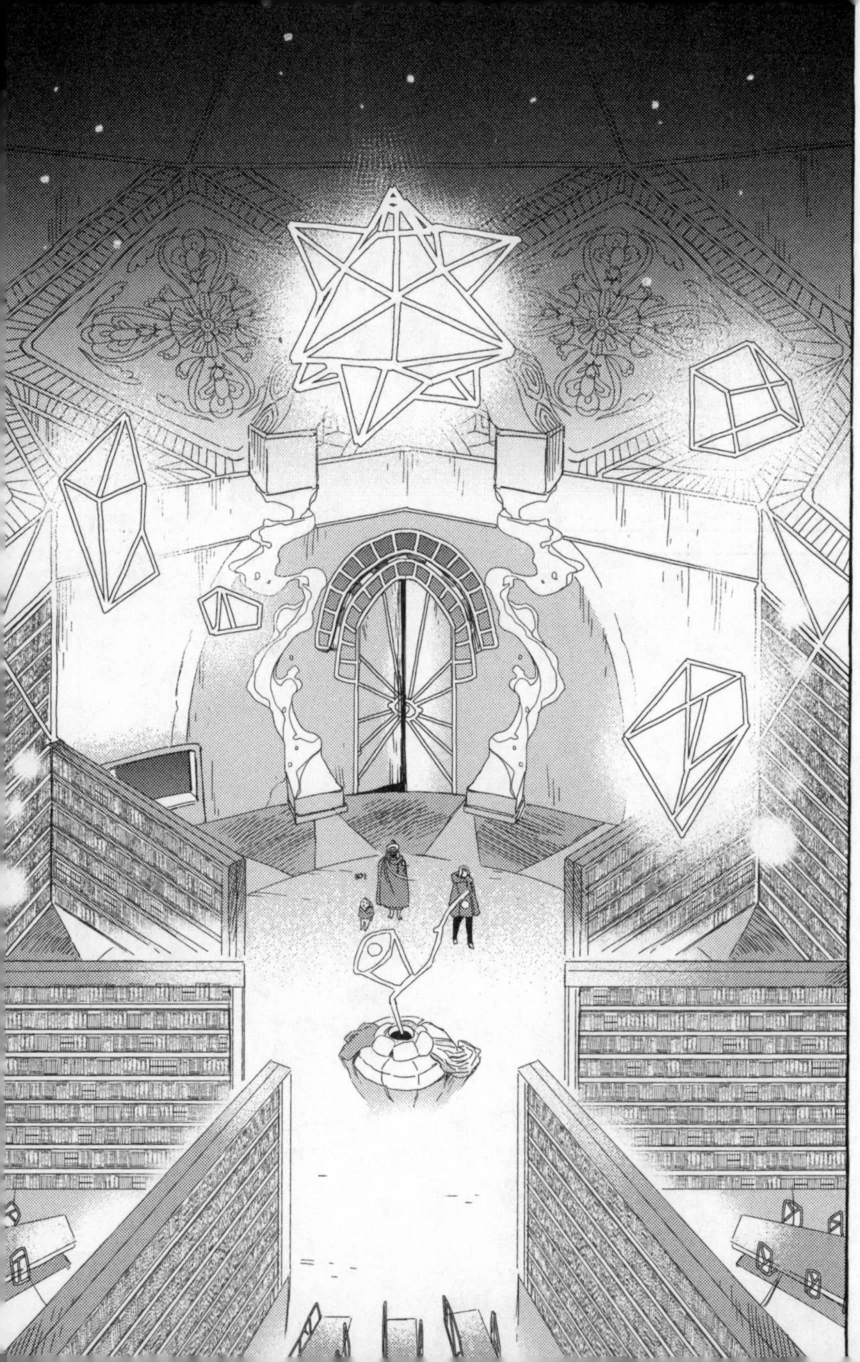

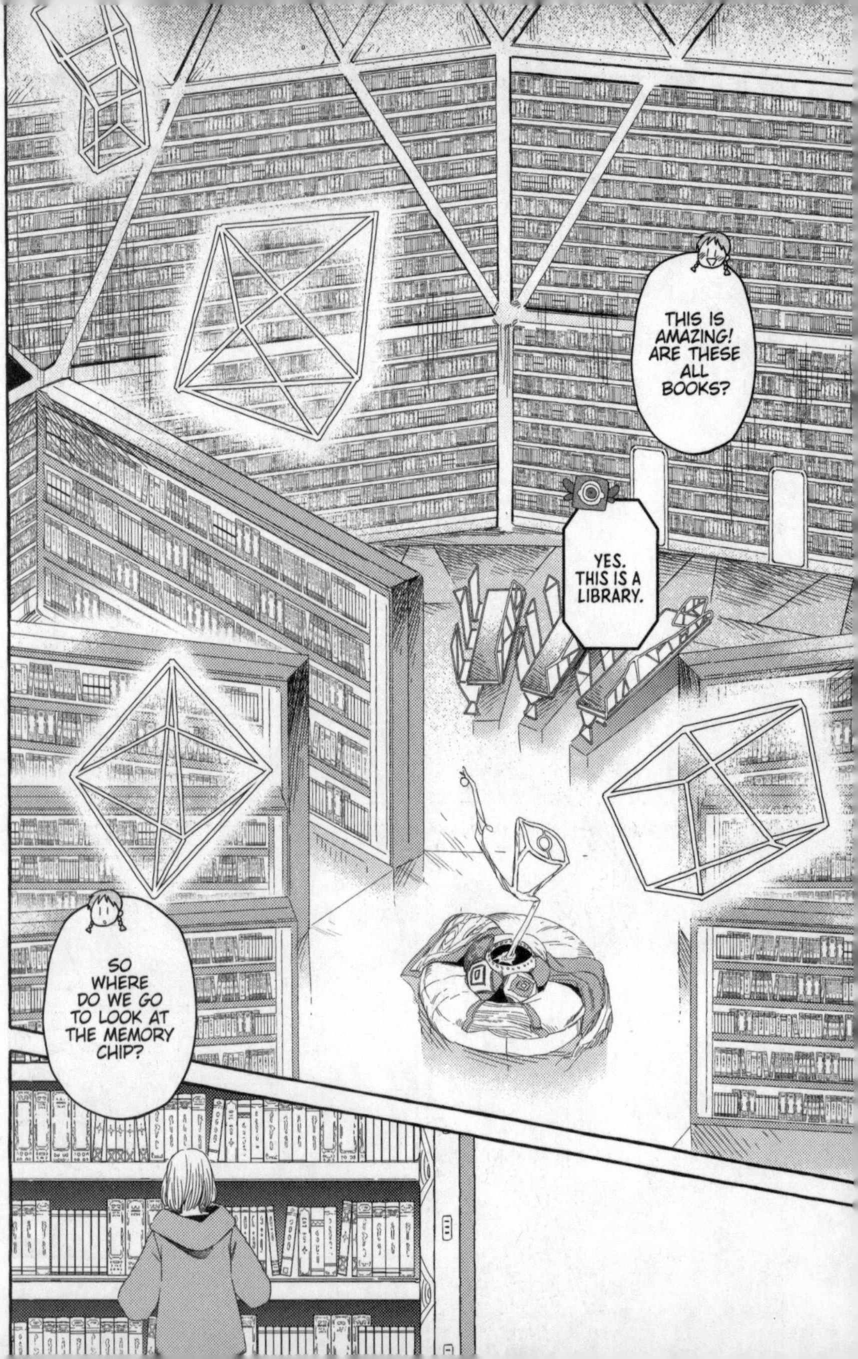
THIS IS AMAZING! ARE THESE ALL BOOKS?
YES. THIS IS A LIBRARY.
SO WHERE DO WE GO TO LOOK AT THE MEMORY CHIP?

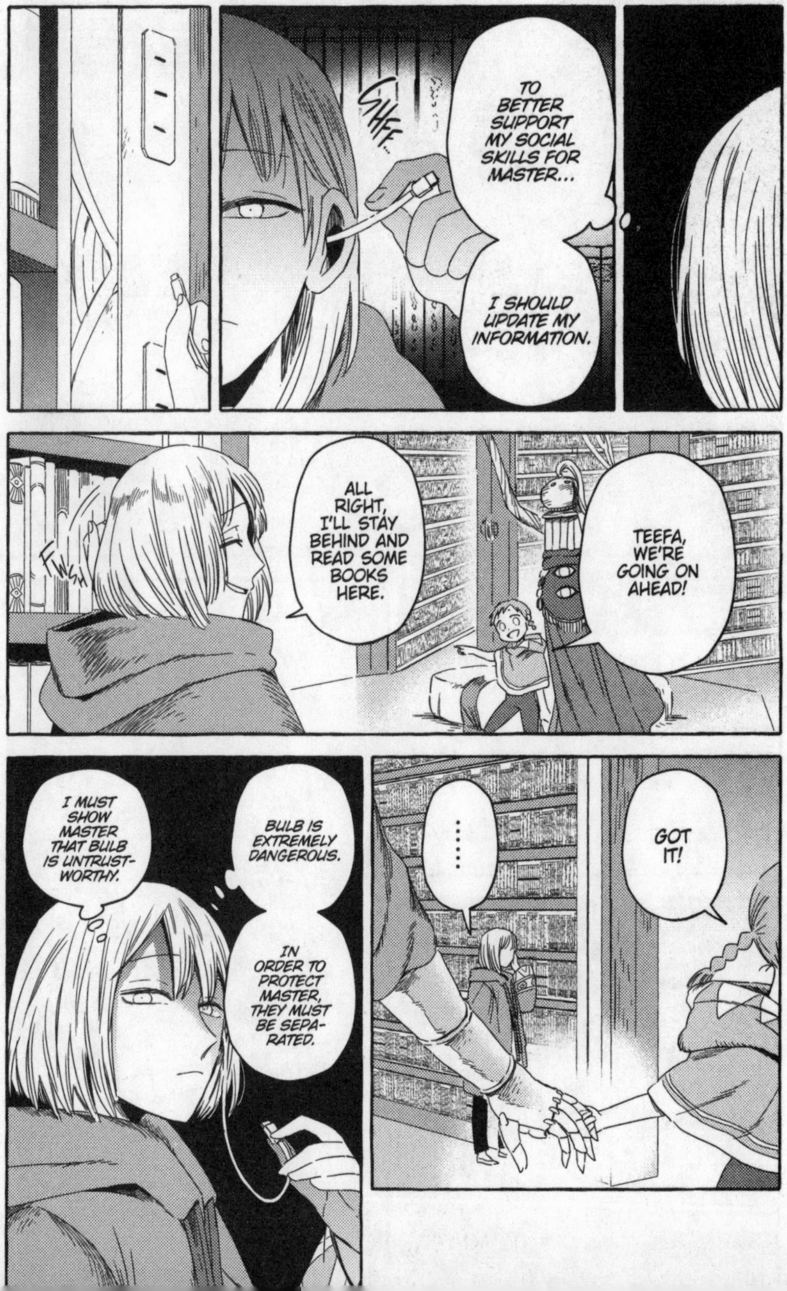
SHFF...
TO BETTER SUPPORT MY SOCIAL SKILLS FOR MASTER...
I SHOULD UPDATE MY INFORMATION.
TEEFA, WE'RE GOING ON AHEAD!
ALL RIGHT, I'LL STAY BEHIND AND READ SOME BOOKS HERE.
FWISH
GOT IT!
......
BULB IS EXTREMELY DANGEROUS.
IN ORDER TO PROTECT MASTER, THEY MUST BE SEPARATED.
I MUST SHOW MASTER THAT BULB IS UNTRUSTWORTHY.

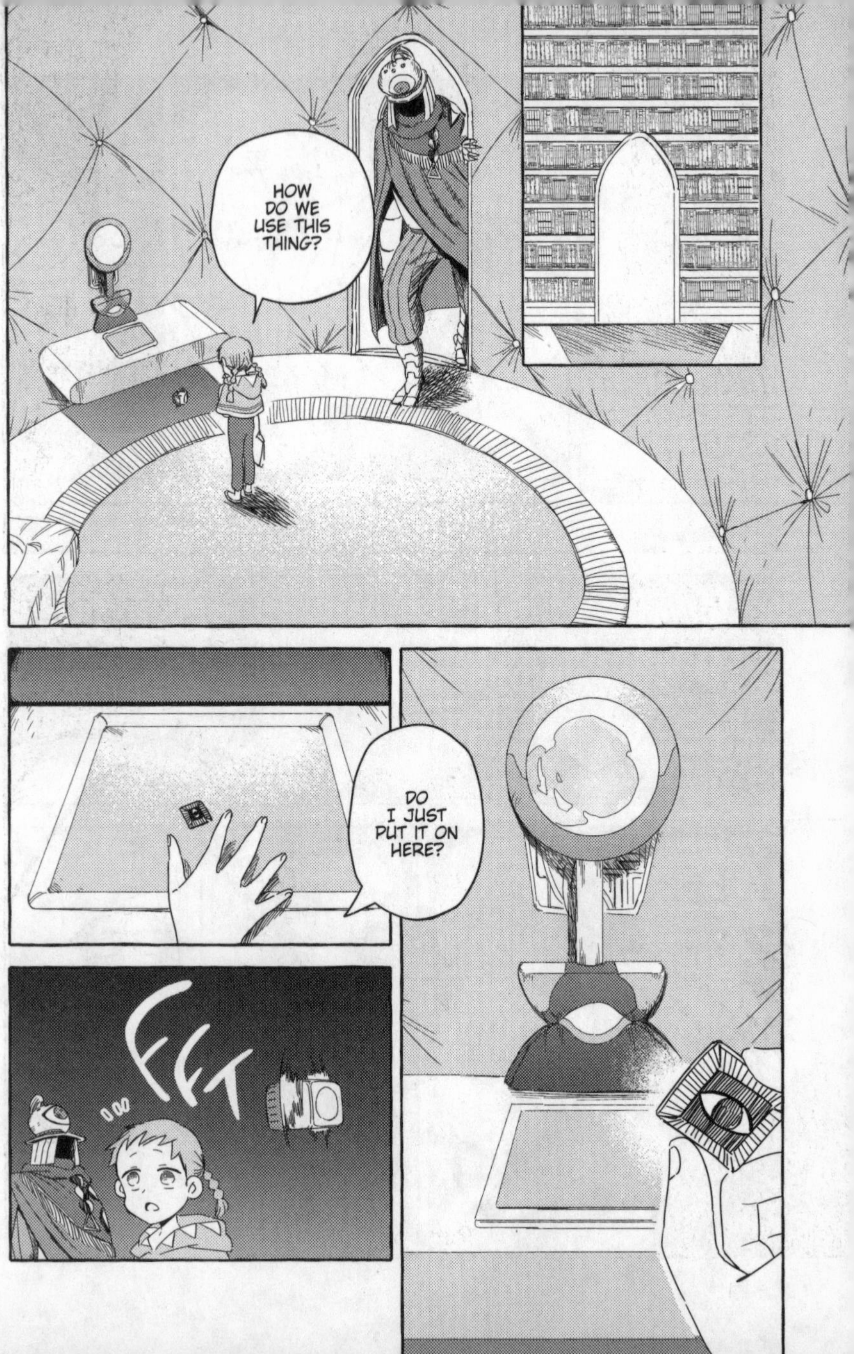
HOW DO WE USE THIS THING?
DO I JUST PUT IT ON HERE?
FFT

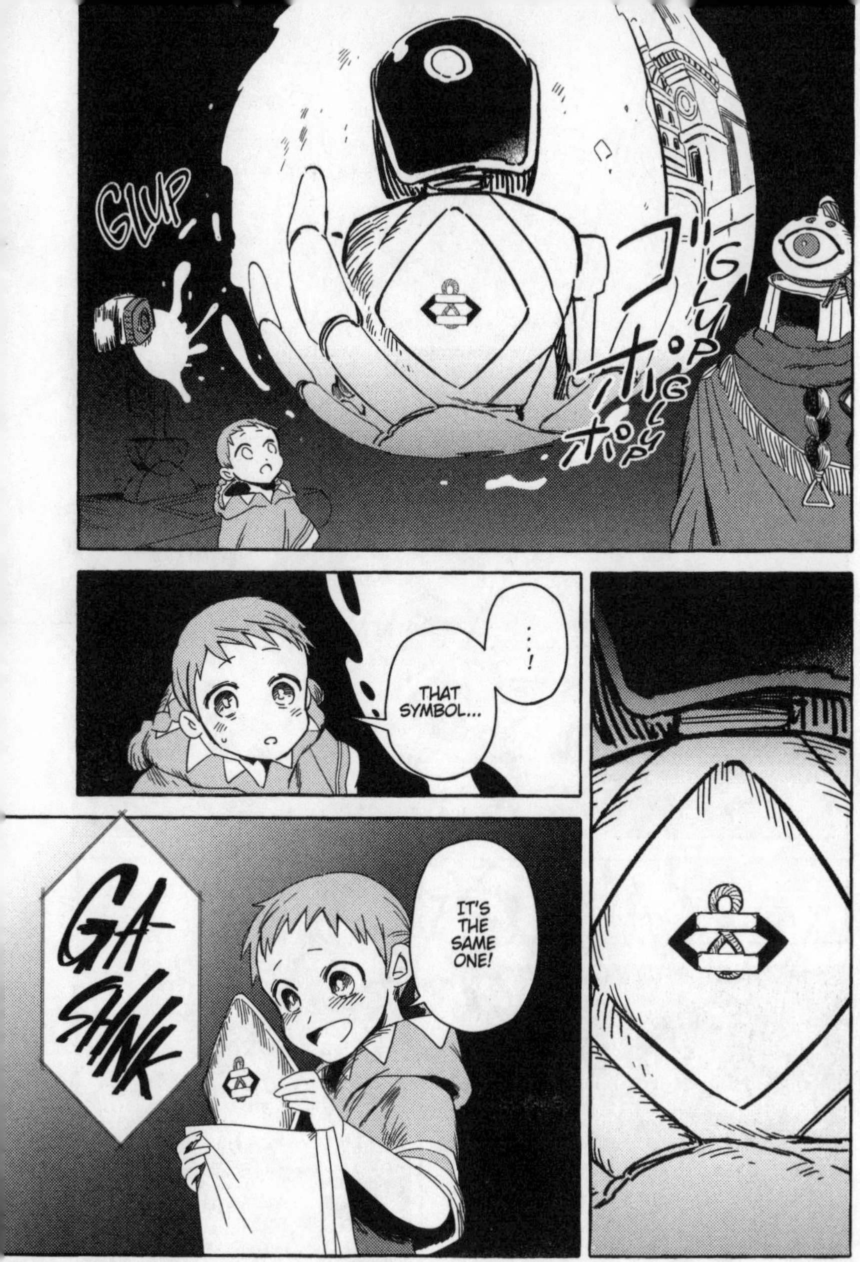
ゴポ
GLUP
ゴポ
GLUP
GLUP
...!
THAT SYMBOL...
IT'S THE SAME ONE!
GA SHNK

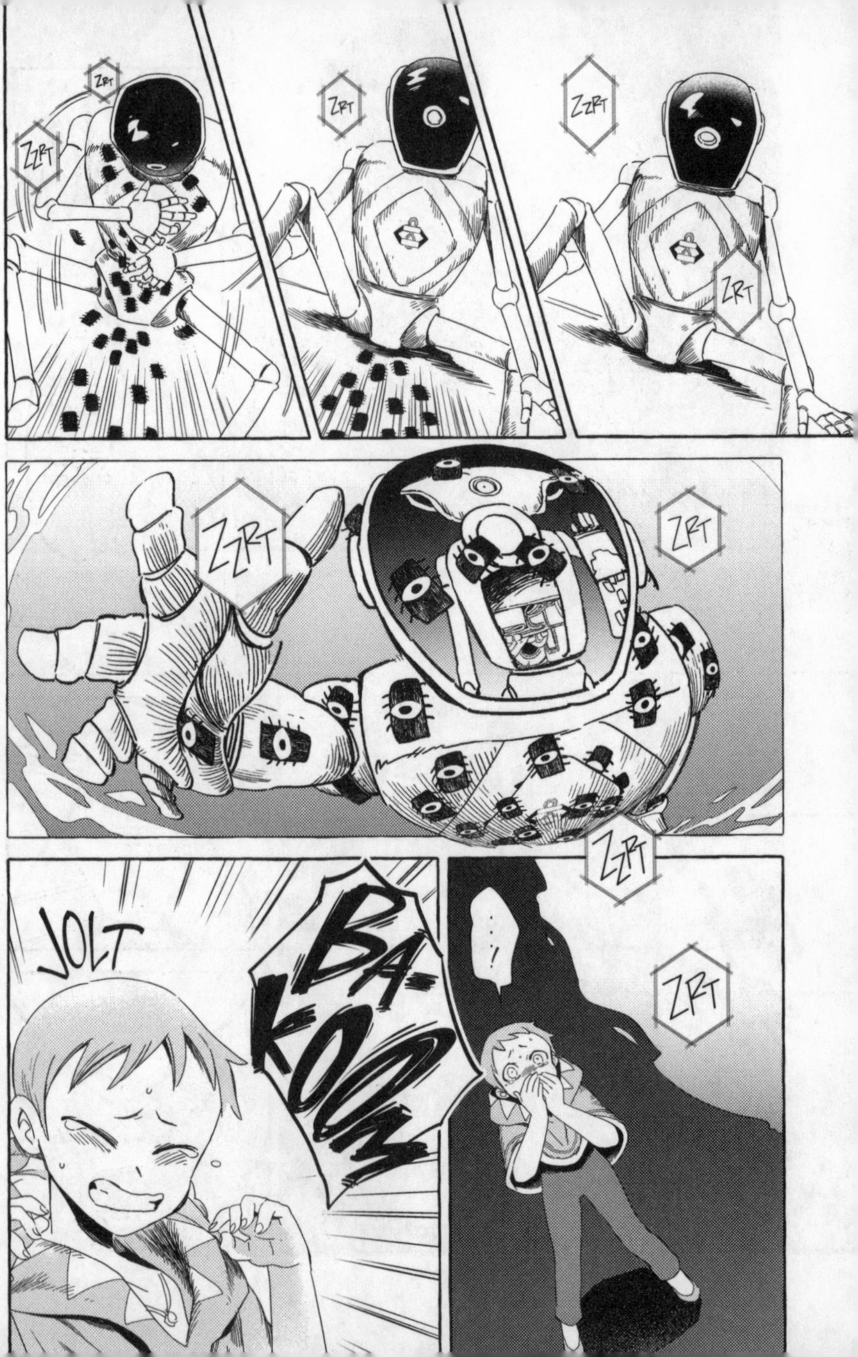

ZZRT
ZRT
ZRT
ZRT
ZZRT
ZRT
ZZRT
ZZRT
...!
ZRT
BA-KOOM
JOLT

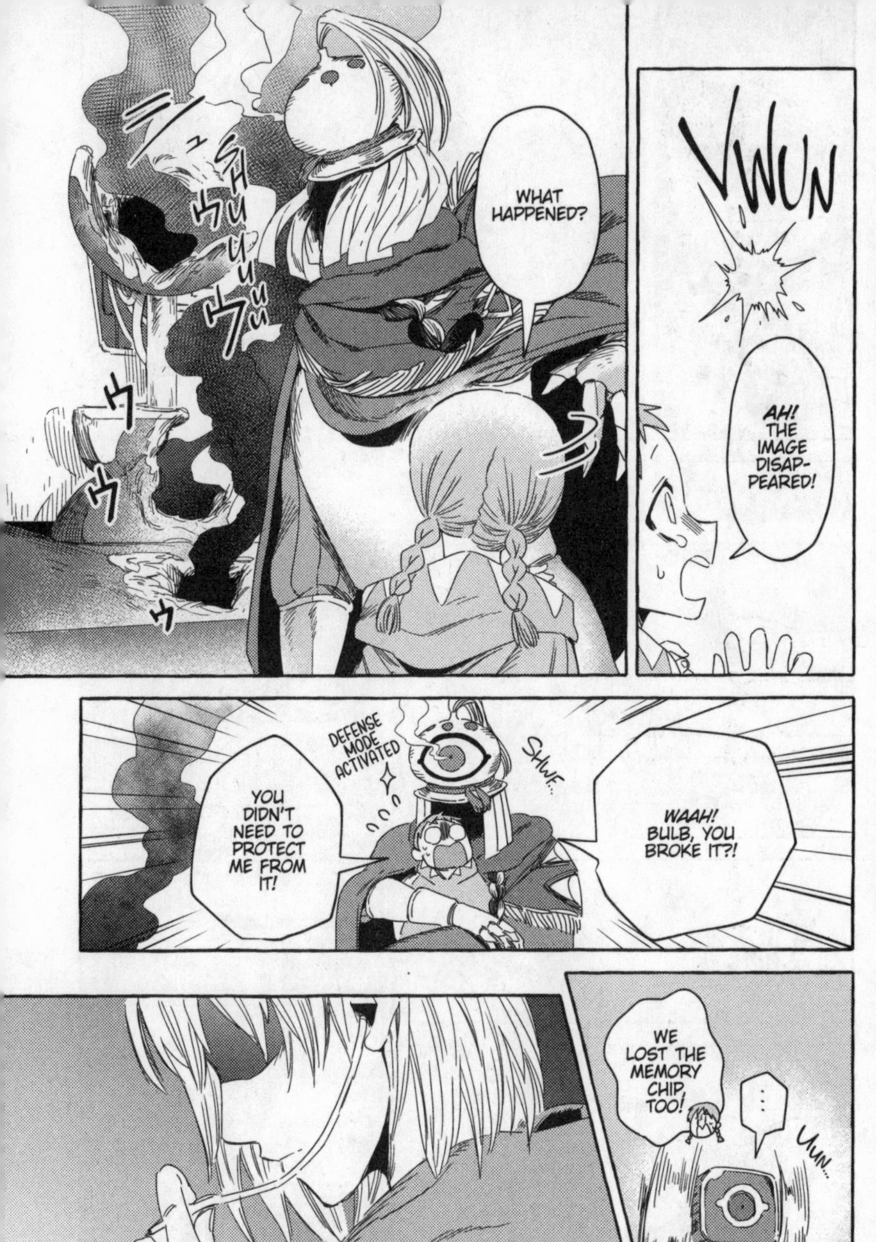
VWUN
AH! THE IMAGE DISAPPEARED!
SHUUUUUU
WHAT HAPPENED?
SHWF...
WAAH! BULB, YOU BROKE IT?!
DEFENSE MODE ACTIVATED
YOU DIDN'T NEED TO PROTECT ME FROM IT!
WE LOST THE MEMORY CHIP, TOO!
...
UUN...

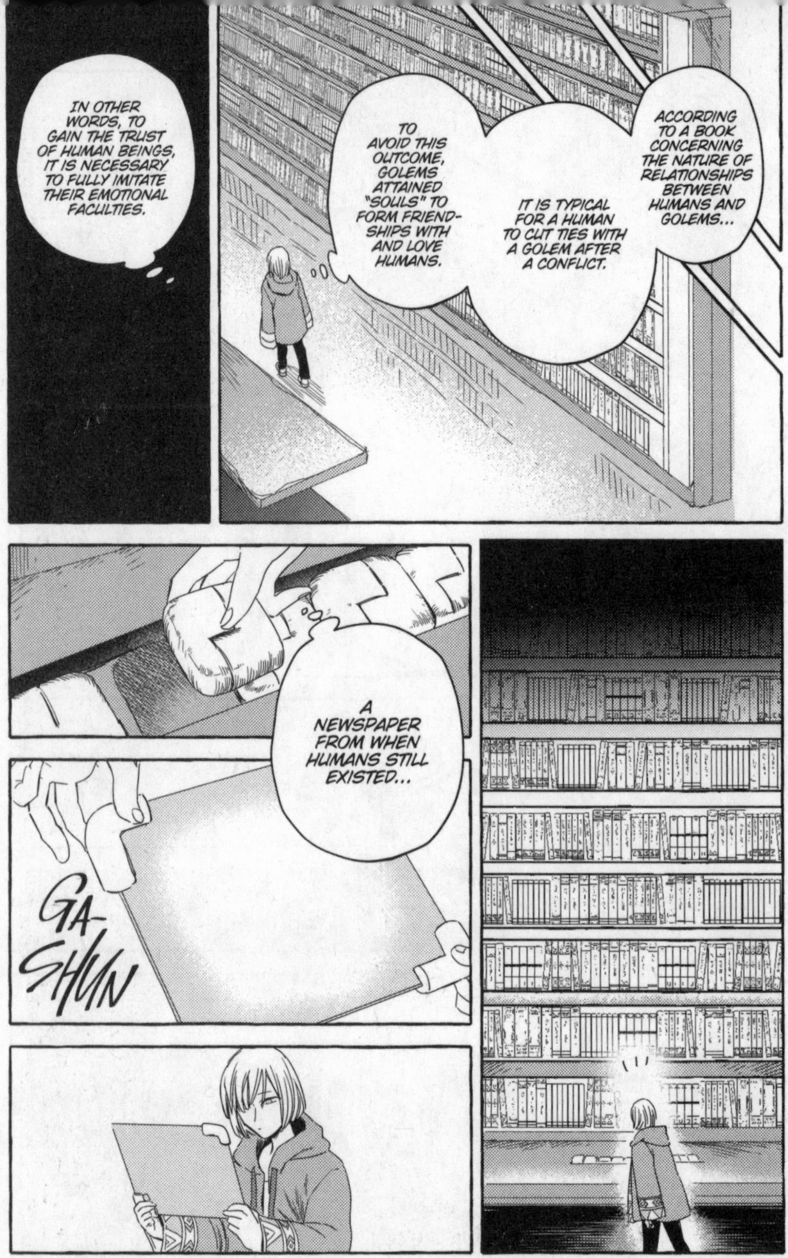
ACCORDING TO A BOOK CONCERNING THE NATURE OF RELATIONSHIPS BETWEEN HUMANS AND GOLEMS...
IT IS TYPICAL FOR A HUMAN TO CUT TIES WITH A GOLEM AFTER A CONFLICT.
TO AVOID THIS OUTCOME, GOLEMS ATTAINED "SOULS" TO FORM FRIEND-SHIPS WITH AND LOVE HUMANS.
IN OTHER WORDS, TO GAIN THE TRUST OF HUMAN BEINGS, IT IS NECESSARY TO FULLY IMITATE THEIR EMOTIONAL FACULTIES.
A NEWSPAPER FROM WHEN HUMANS STILL EXISTED...
GA-SHUN

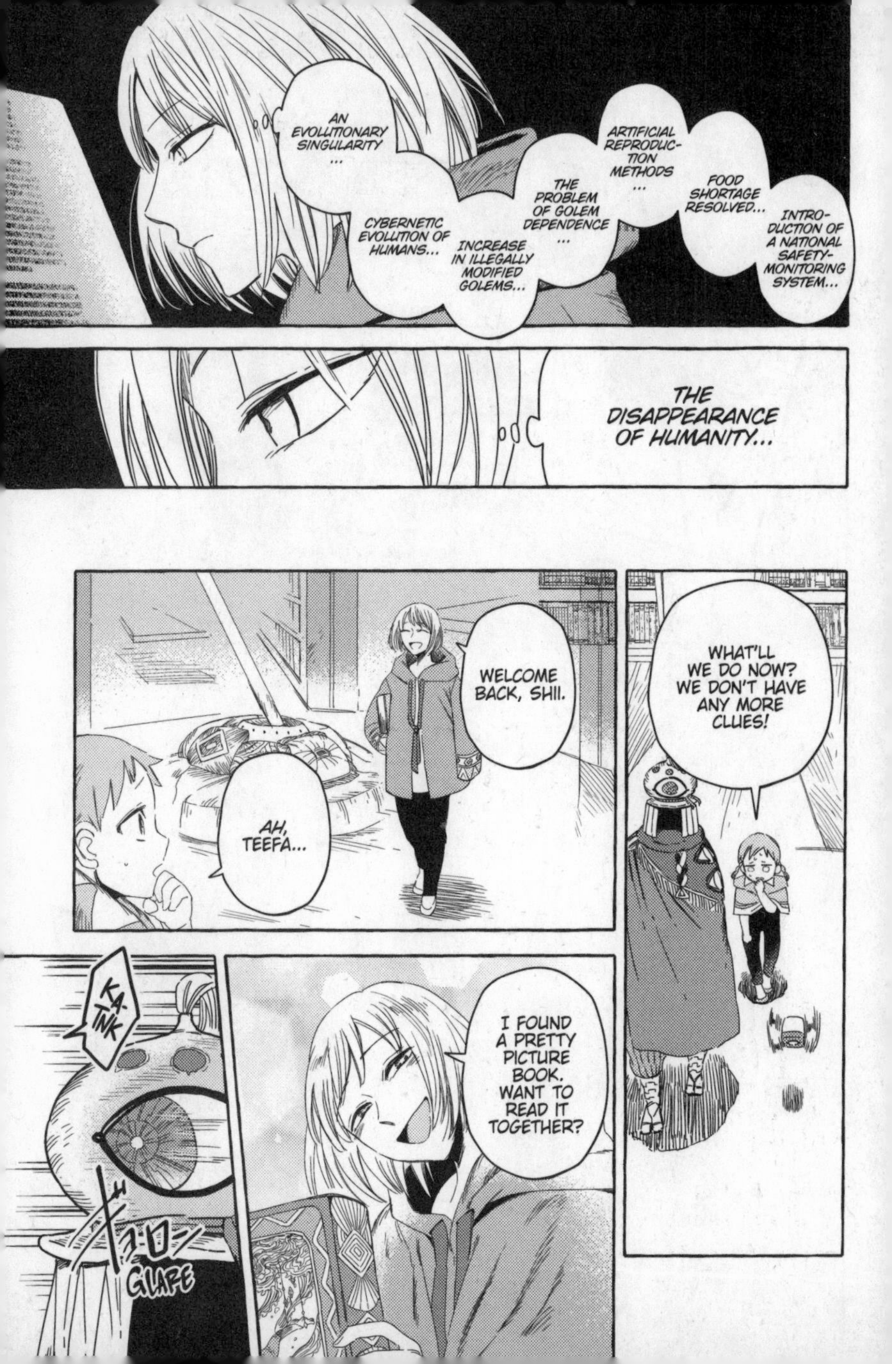
INTRODUCTION OF A NATIONAL SAFETY-MONITORING SYSTEM...
FOOD SHORTAGE RESOLVED...
ARTIFICIAL REPRODUCTION METHODS...
THE PROBLEM OF GOLEM DEPENDENCE...
INCREASE IN ILLEGALLY MODIFIED GOLEMS...
CYBERNETIC EVOLUTION OF HUMANS...
AN EVOLUTIONARY SINGULARITY...
THE DISAPPEARANCE OF HUMANITY...
WHAT'LL WE DO NOW? WE DON'T HAVE ANY MORE CLUES!
WELCOME BACK, SHII.
AH, TEEFA...
I FOUND A PRETTY PICTURE BOOK. WANT TO READ IT TOGETHER?
KA-TINK
GLARE

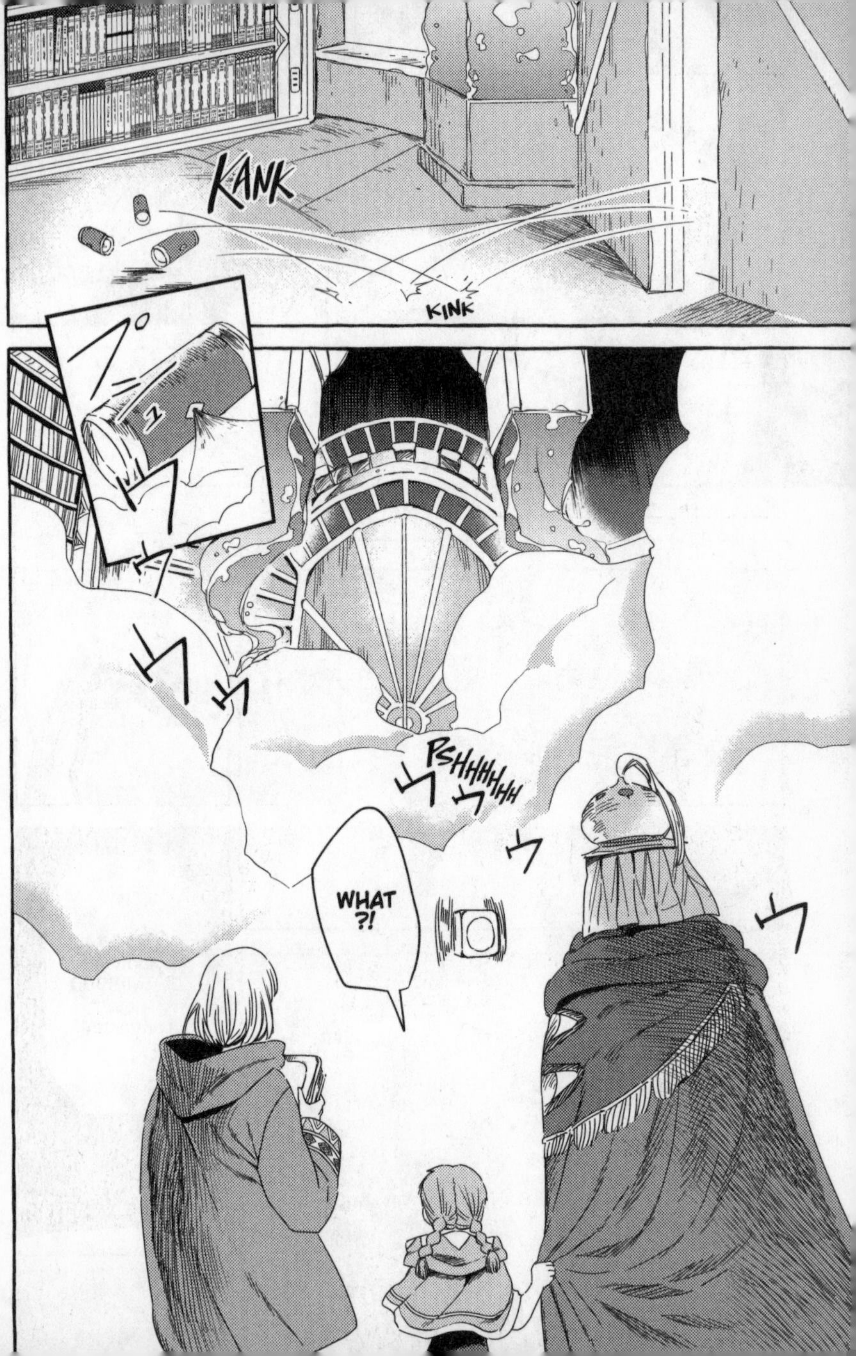
KANK
KINK
PSHHHHHH
WHAT?!

FWP

ビクン

JOLT

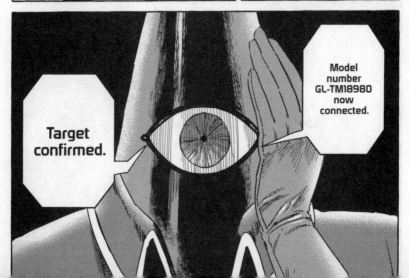

Model
number
GL-TM18980
now
connected.

Target
confirmed.

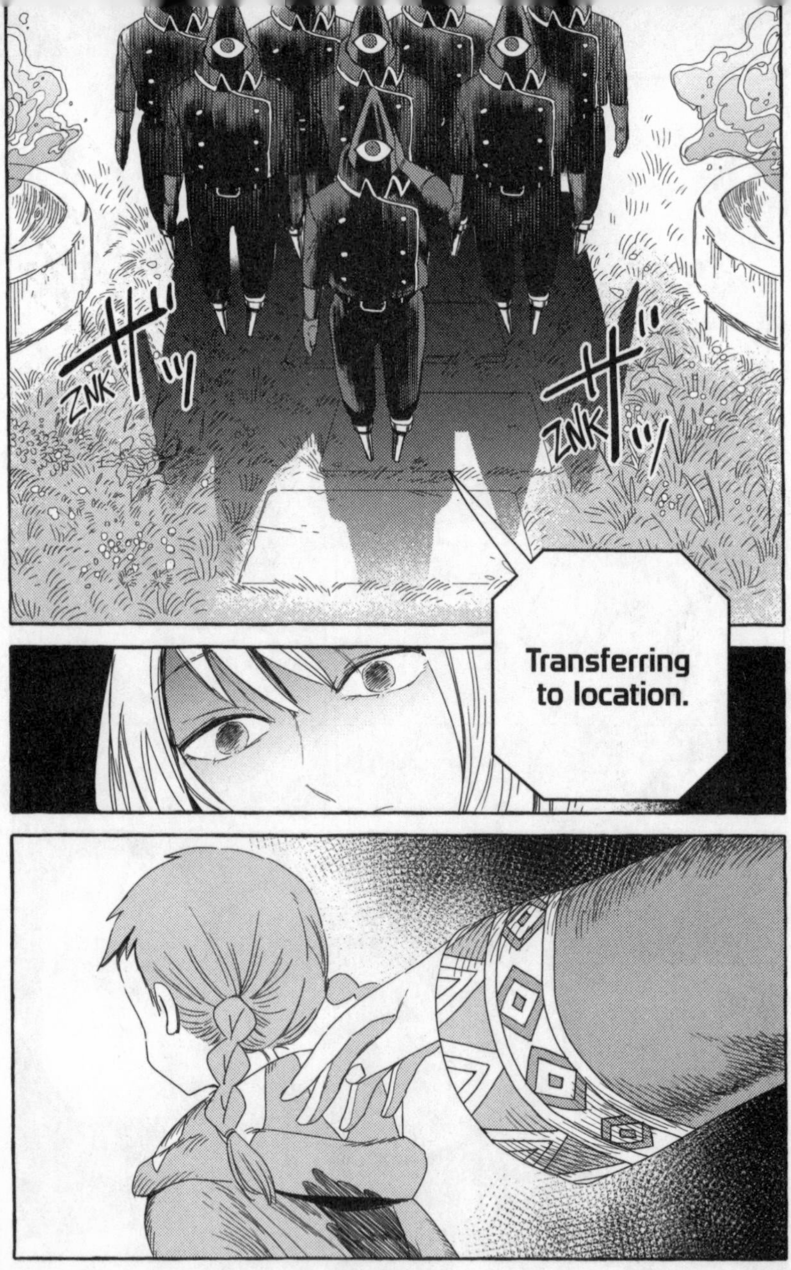
ZNK
ZNK
Transferring to location.

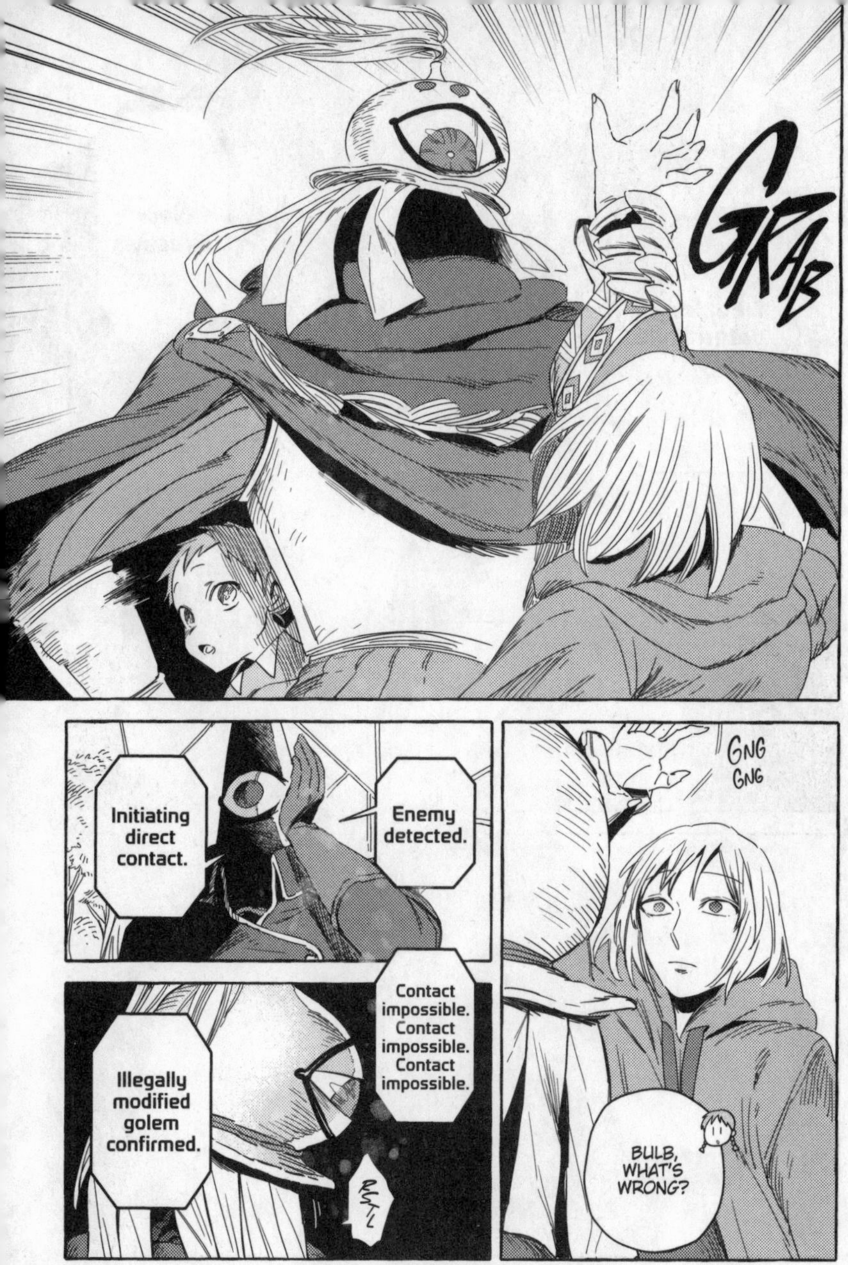
GRAB
GNG GNG
BULB, WHAT'S WRONG?
Enemy detected.
Initiating direct contact.
Contact impossible. Contact impossible. Contact impossible.
Illegally modified golem confirmed.
RSTL

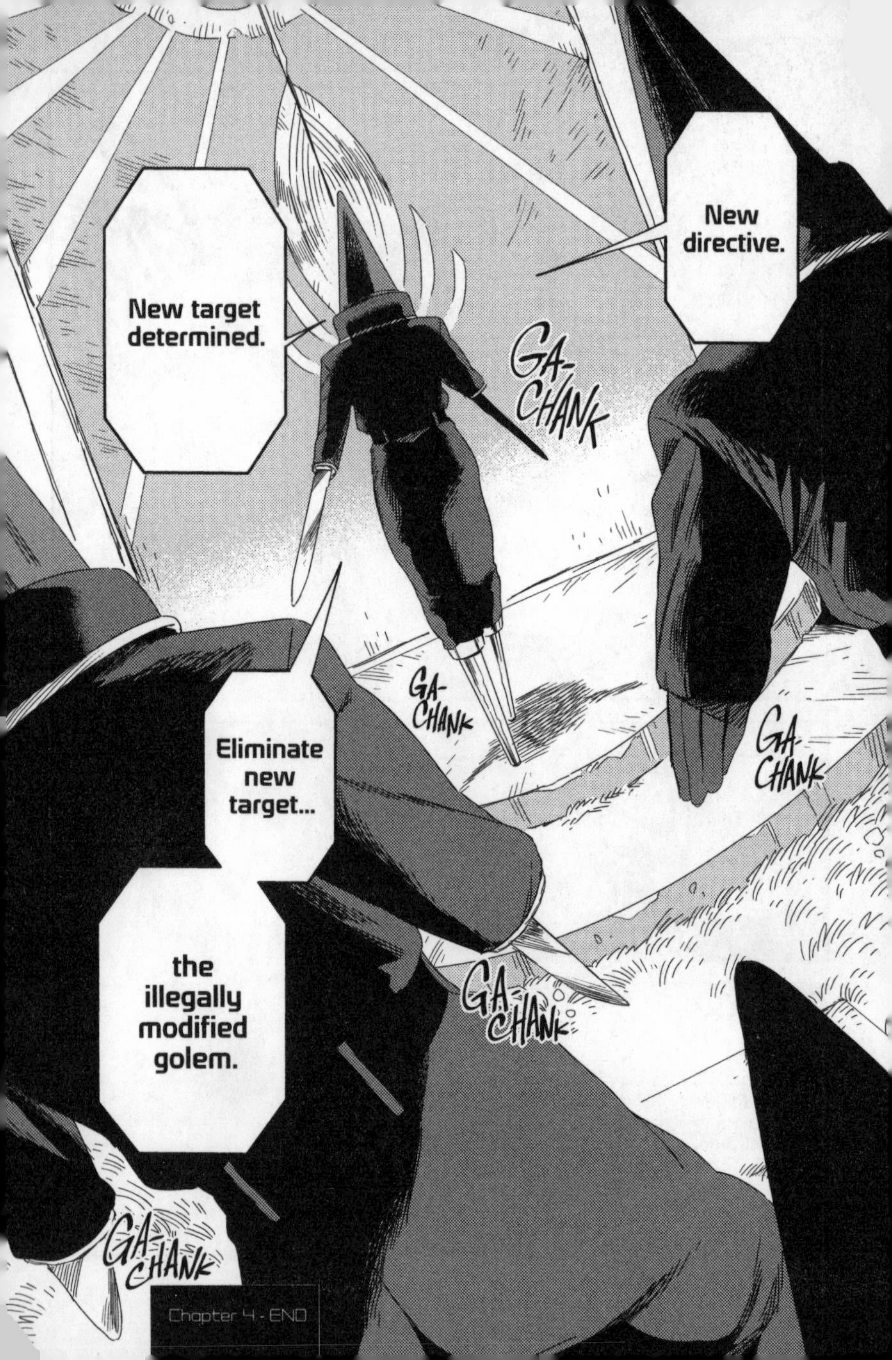

New directive.
New target determined.
GA-CHANK
GA-CHANK
GA-CHANK
Eliminate new target...
the illegally modified golem.
GA-CHANK
GA-CHANK
Chapter 4 - END

Chapter 5

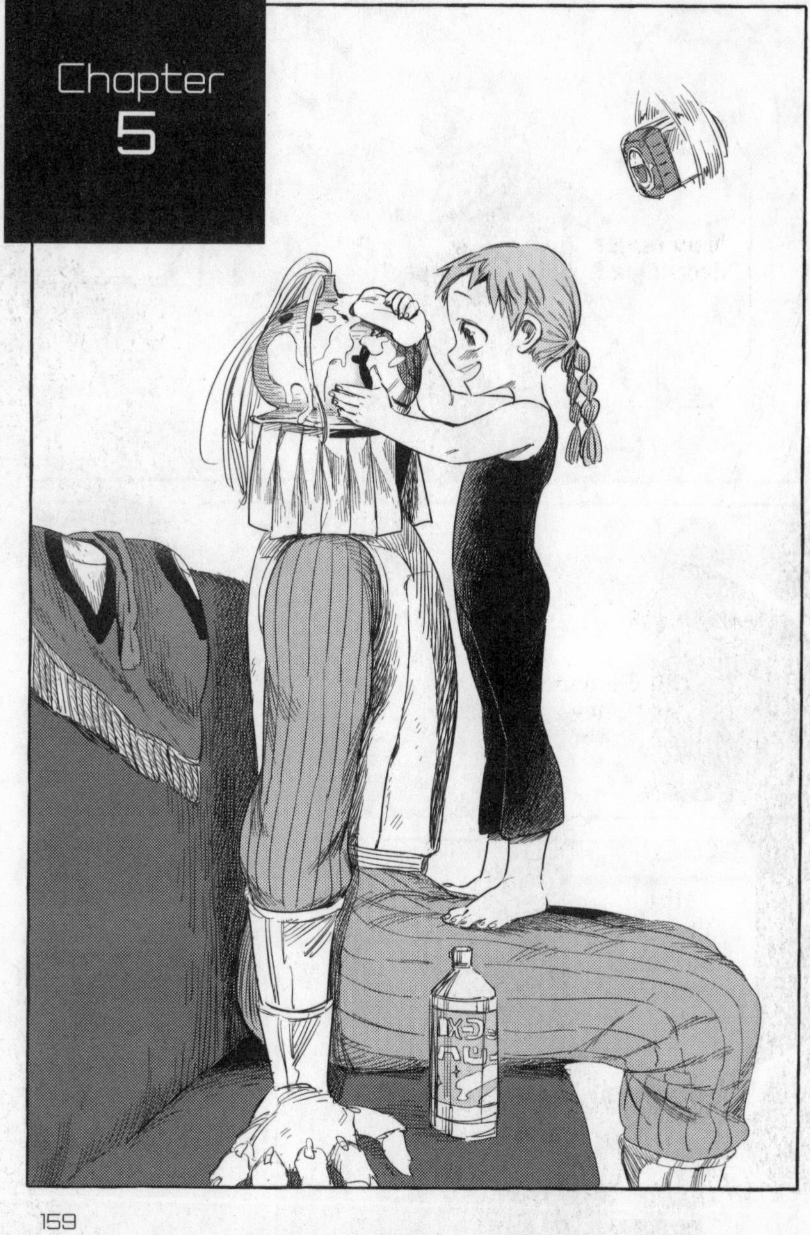

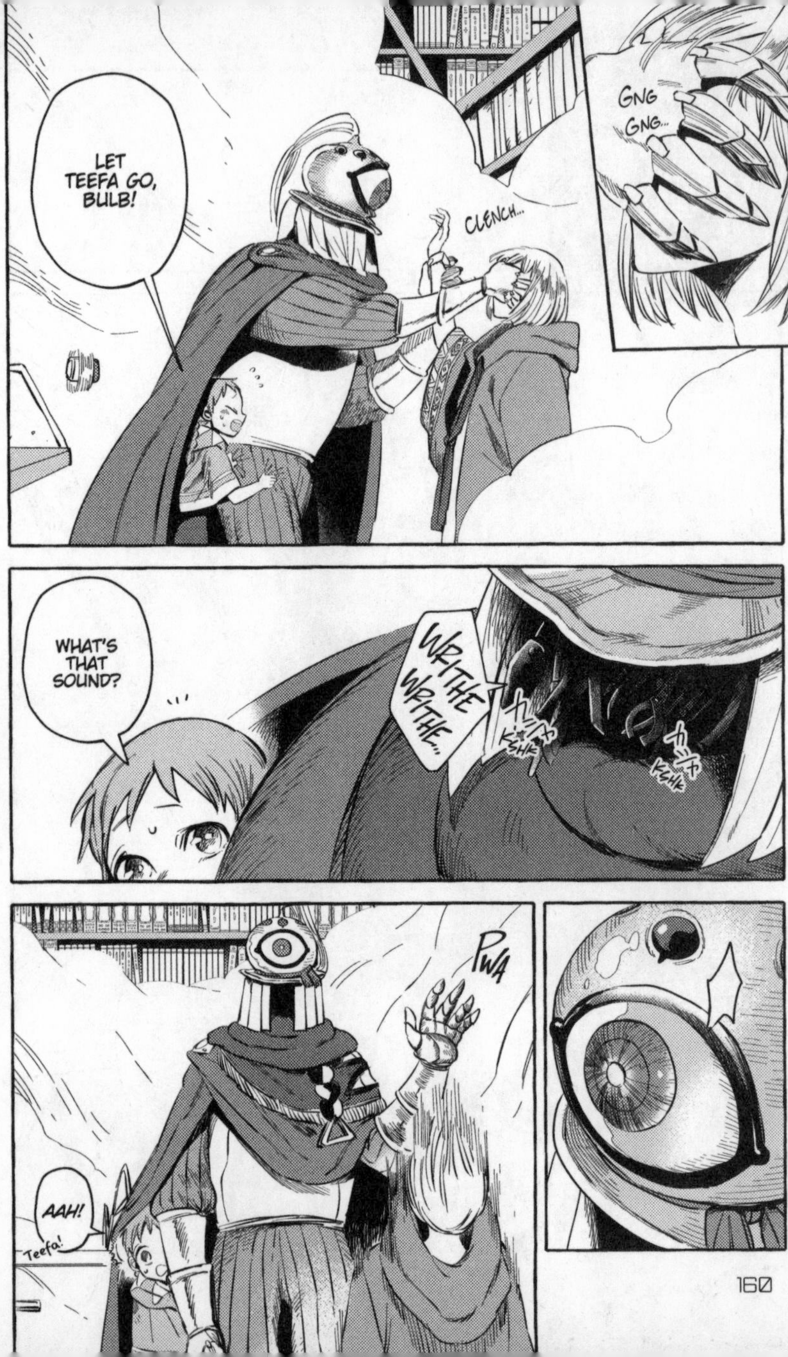

GNG GNG...
CLENCH...
LET TEEFA GO, BULB!
WRITHE WRITHE...
KSHK
KSHK
WHAT'S THAT SOUND?
PWA
AAH!
Teefa!

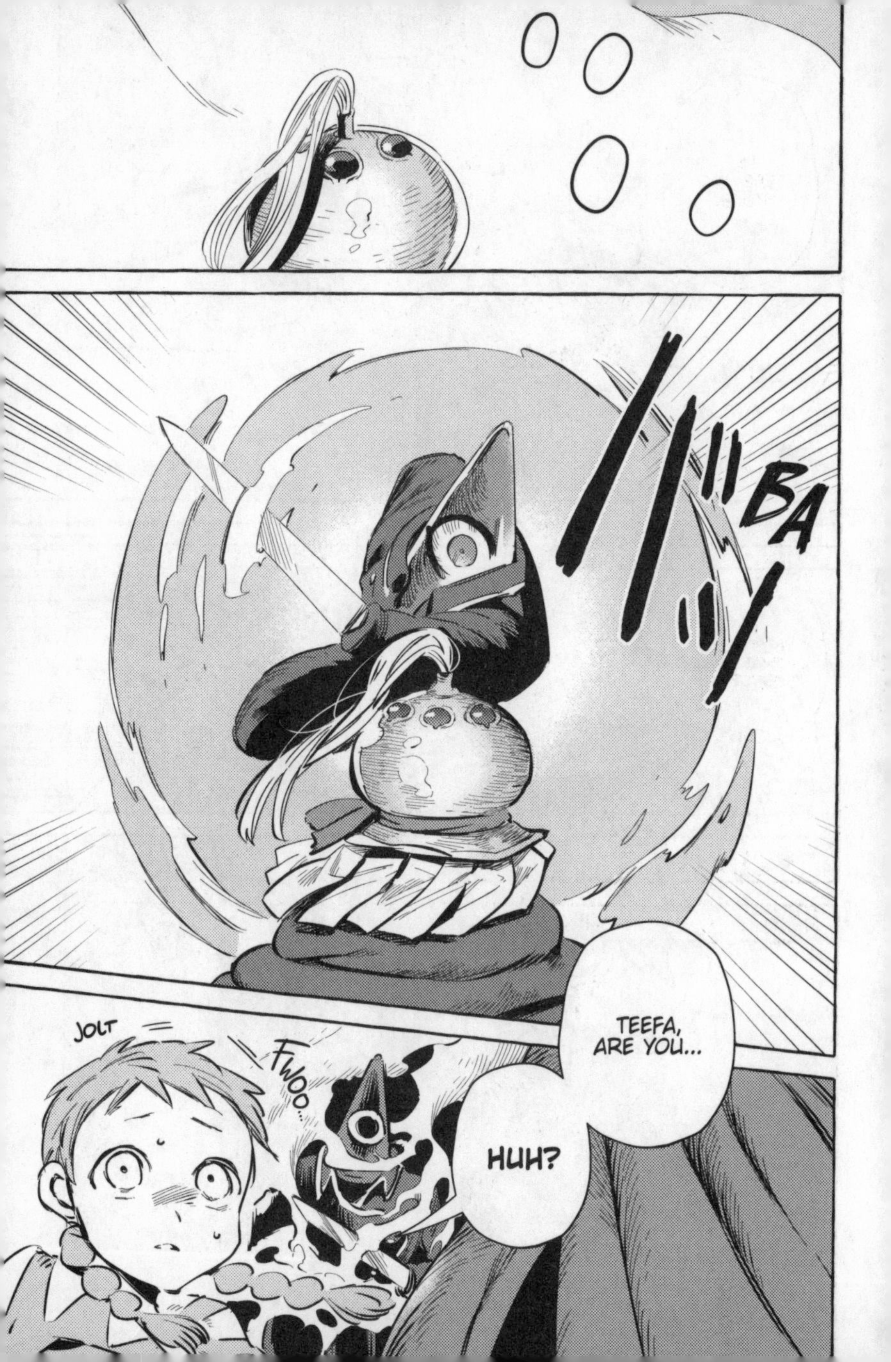
BA
TEEFA, ARE YOU...
HUH?
FWOO...
JOLT

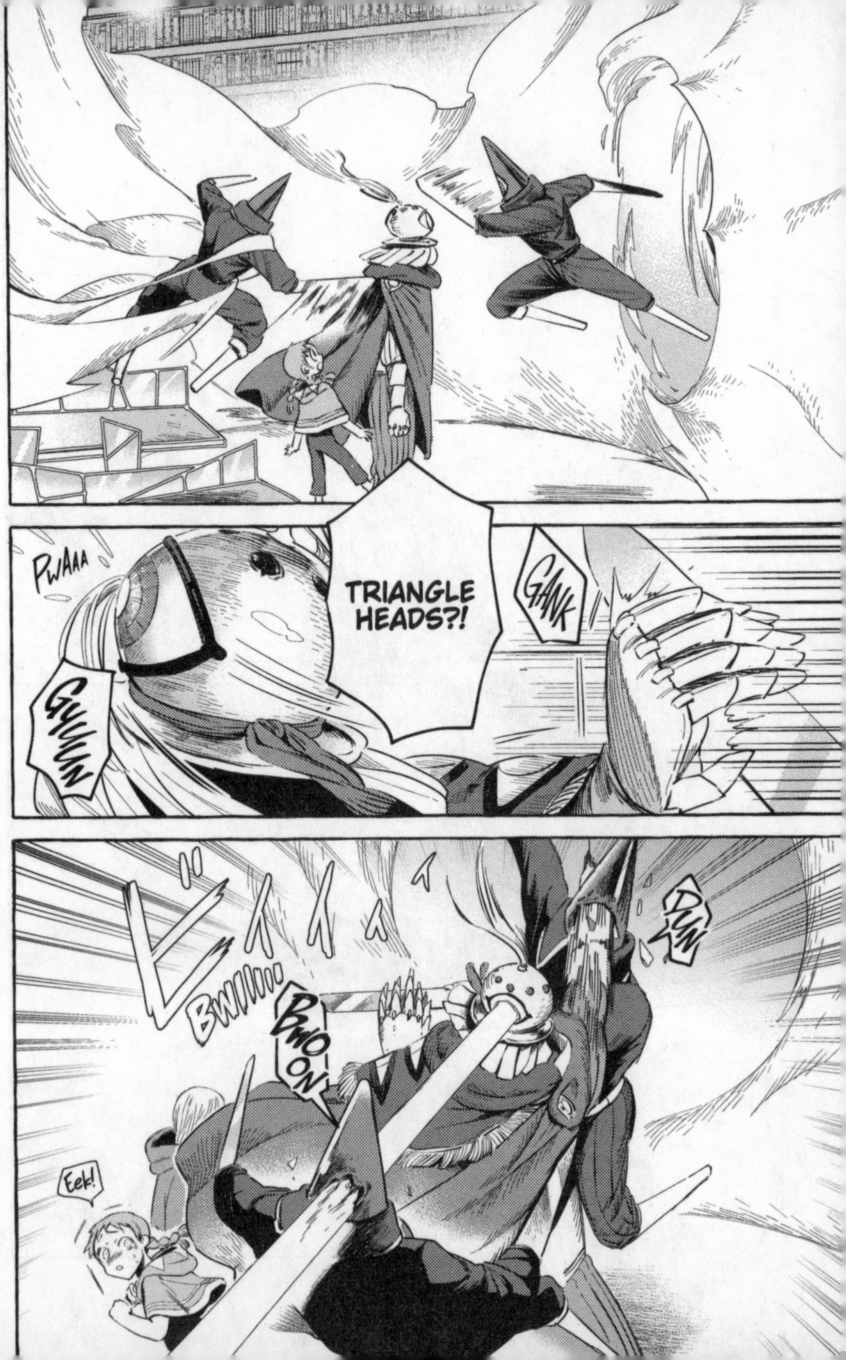
GANK
TRIANGLE HEADS?!
GYUUUN
PWAAA
DUN
BWIIIII
BWOOON
Eek!

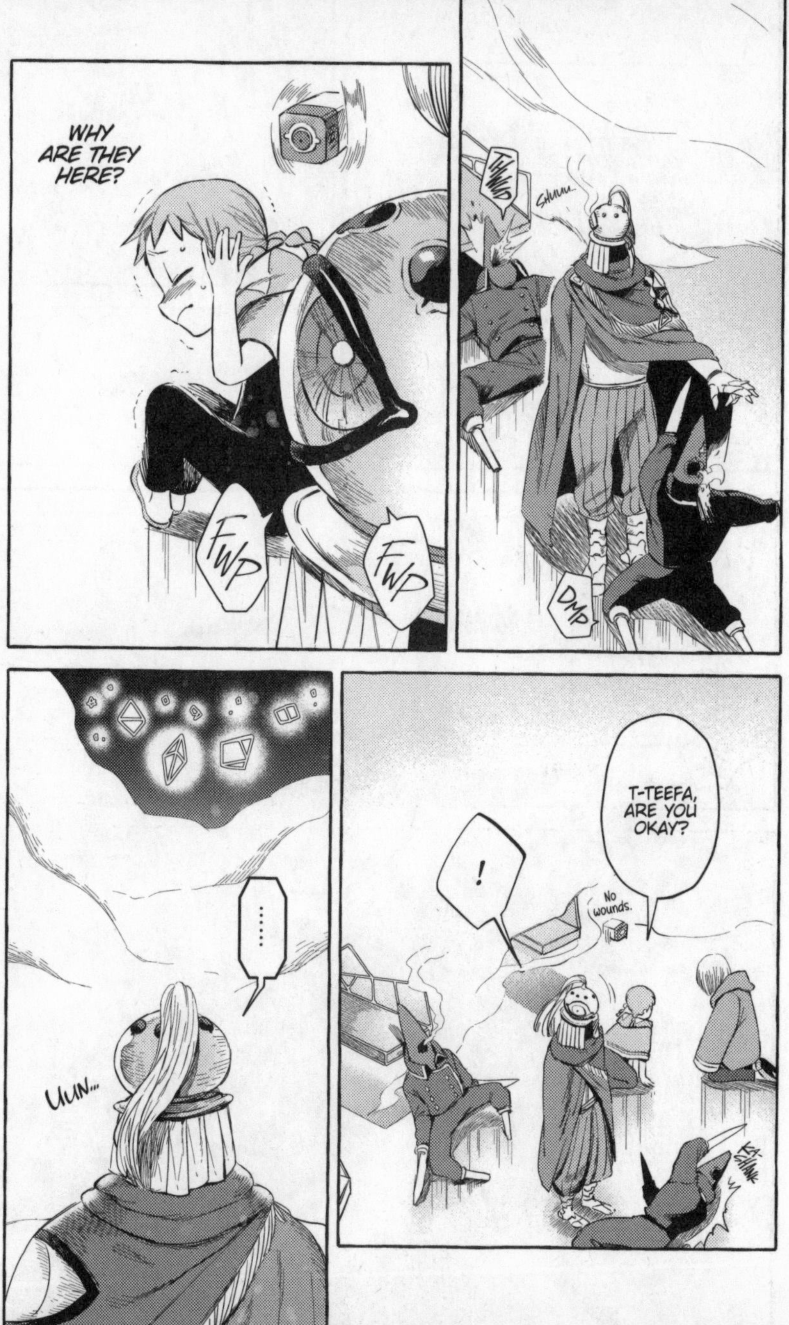
THWMP
SHUUU...
DMP
WHY ARE THEY HERE?
FWP
FWP
T-TEEFA, ARE YOU OKAY?
!
No wounds.
KA-SHANK
......
UUN...

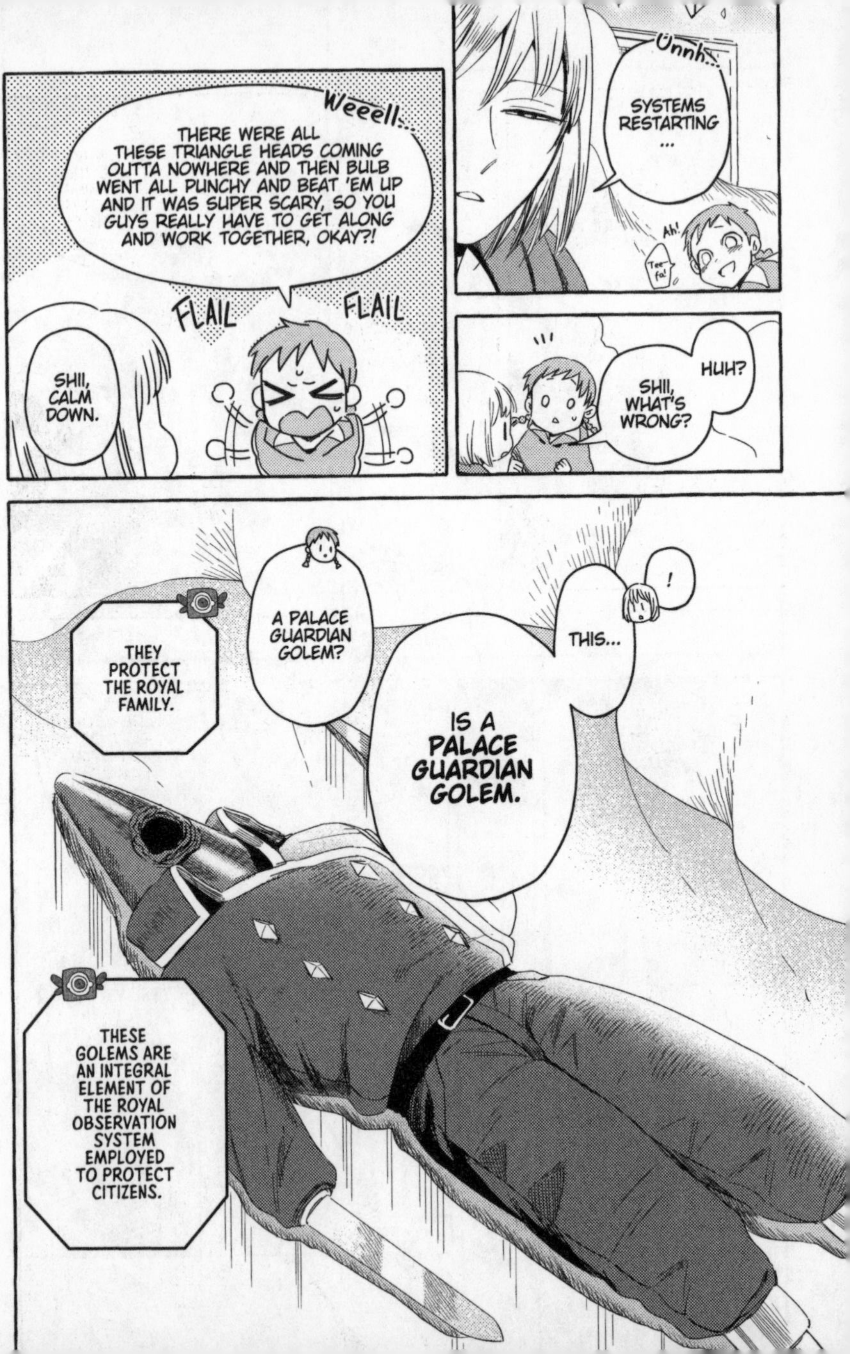
Unnh...
SYSTEMS RESTARTING ...
Ah!
Tee-fa!
HUH?
SHII, WHAT'S WRONG?
Weeell...
THERE WERE ALL THESE TRIANGLE HEADS COMING OUTTA NOWHERE AND THEN BULB WENT ALL PUNCHY AND BEAT 'EM UP AND IT WAS SUPER SCARY, SO YOU GUYS REALLY HAVE TO GET ALONG AND WORK TOGETHER, OKAY?!
FLAIL
FLAIL
SHII, CALM DOWN.
!
THIS...
IS A PALACE GUARDIAN GOLEM.
A PALACE GUARDIAN GOLEM?
THEY PROTECT THE ROYAL FAMILY.
THESE GOLEMS ARE AN INTEGRAL ELEMENT OF THE ROYAL OBSERVATION SYSTEM EMPLOYED TO PROTECT CITIZENS.

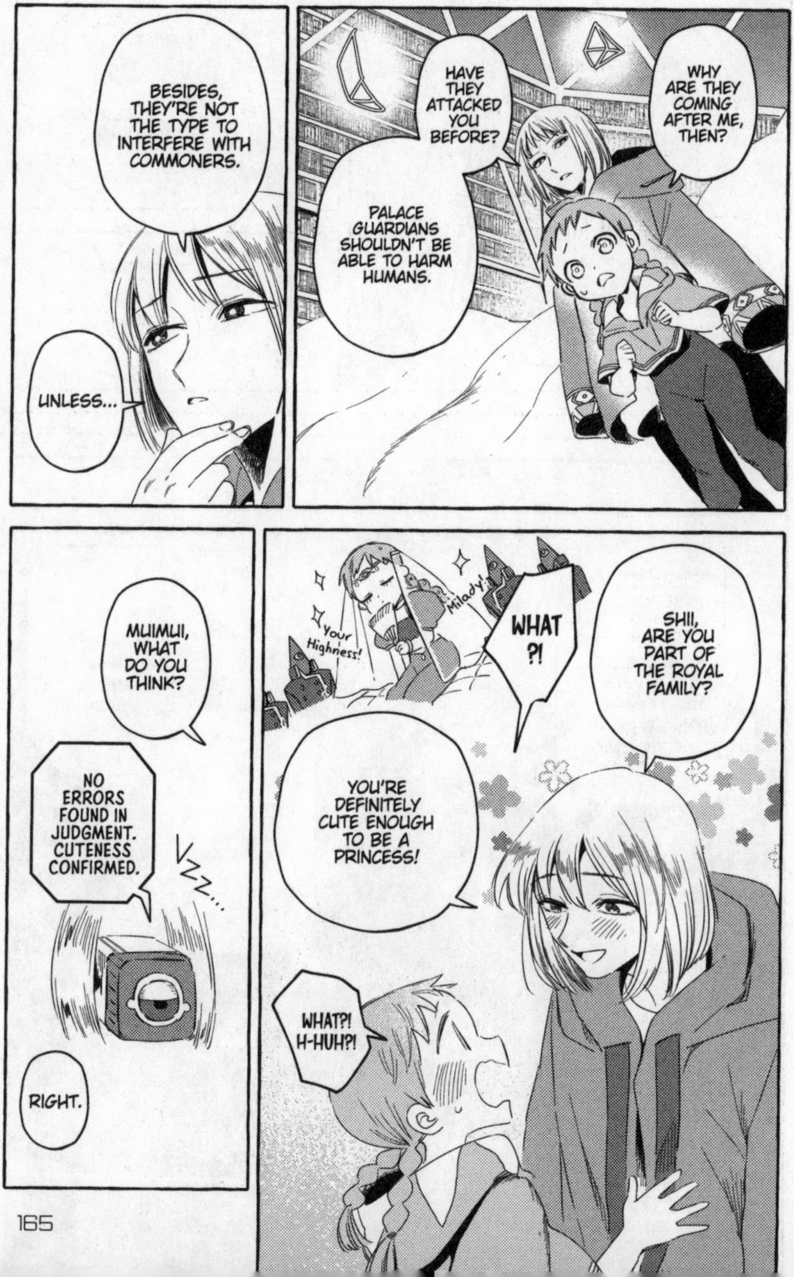
WHY ARE THEY COMING AFTER ME, THEN?
HAVE THEY ATTACKED YOU BEFORE?
PALACE GUARDIANS SHOULDN'T BE ABLE TO HARM HUMANS.
BESIDES, THEY'RE NOT THE TYPE TO INTERFERE WITH COMMONERS.
UNLESS...
SHII, ARE YOU PART OF THE ROYAL FAMILY?
WHAT ?!
Milady!
Your Highness!
YOU'RE DEFINITELY CUTE ENOUGH TO BE A PRINCESS!
WHAT?! H-HUH?!
MUIMUI, WHAT DO YOU THINK?
NO ERRORS FOUND IN JUDGMENT. CUTENESS CONFIRMED.
VZZ...
RIGHT.

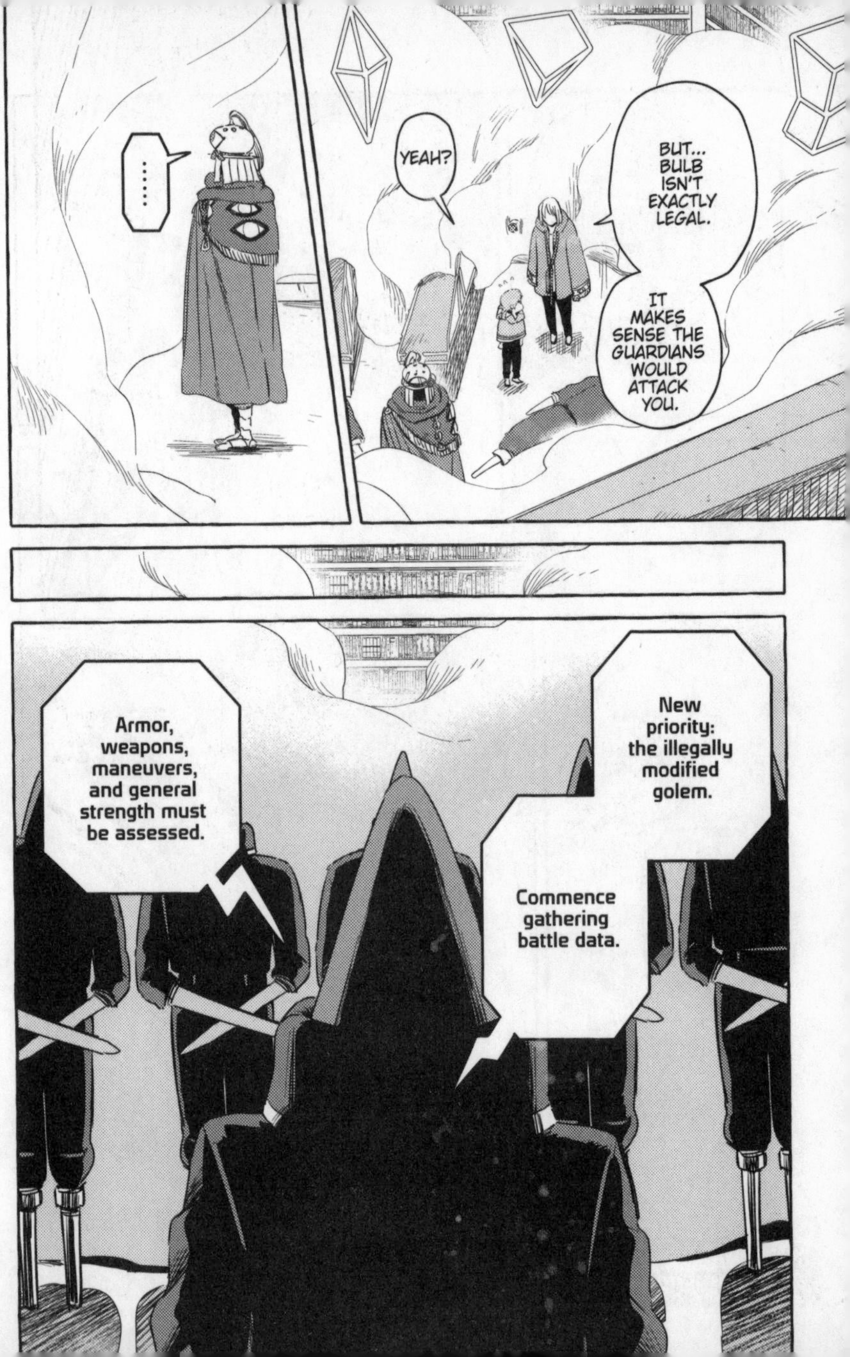
BUT... BULB ISN'T EXACTLY LEGAL.
IT MAKES SENSE THE GUARDIANS WOULD ATTACK YOU.
YEAH?
......
New priority: the illegally modified golem.
Commence gathering battle data.
Armor, weapons, maneuvers, and general strength must be assessed.

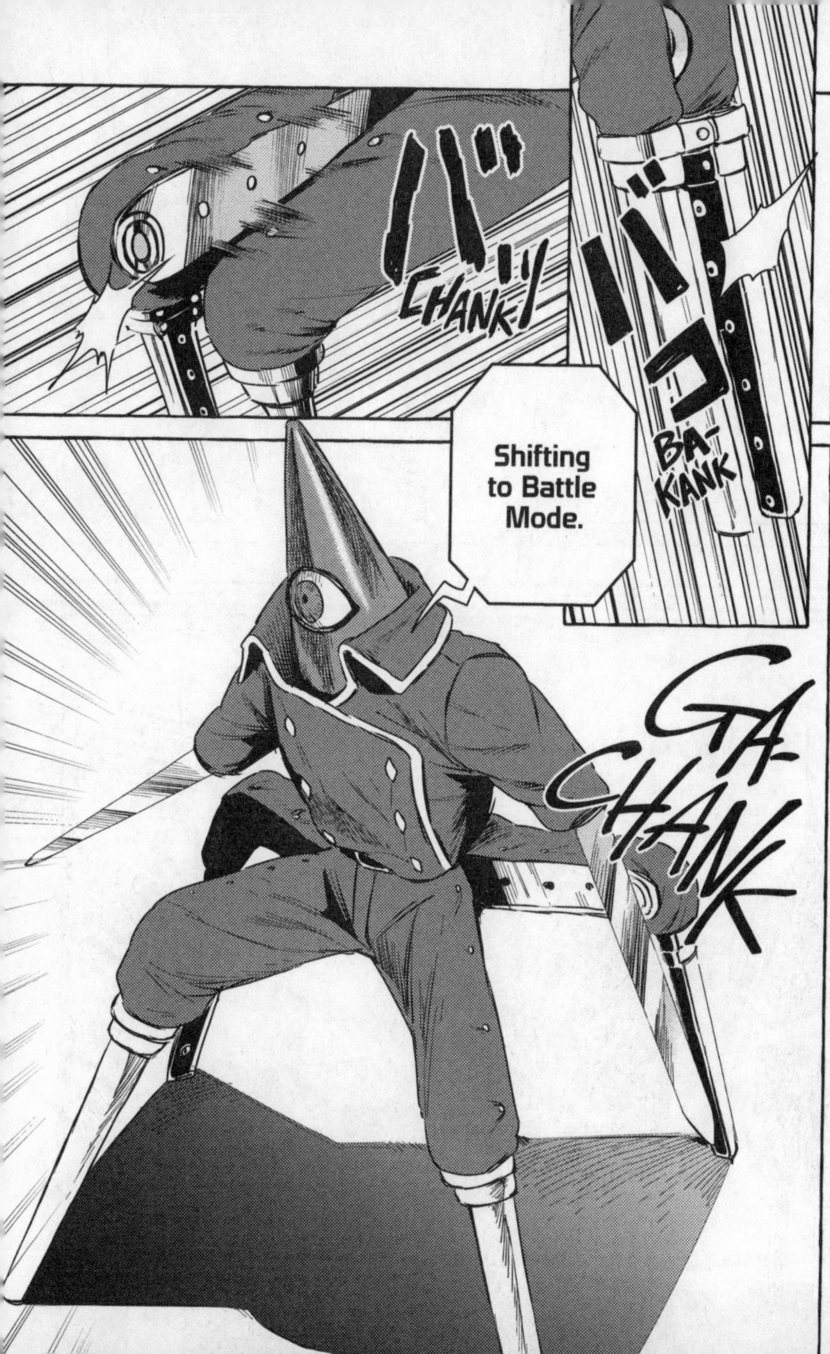
バコ
BA-KANK
バッ
CHANK!
Shifting to Battle Mode.
GA-CHANK

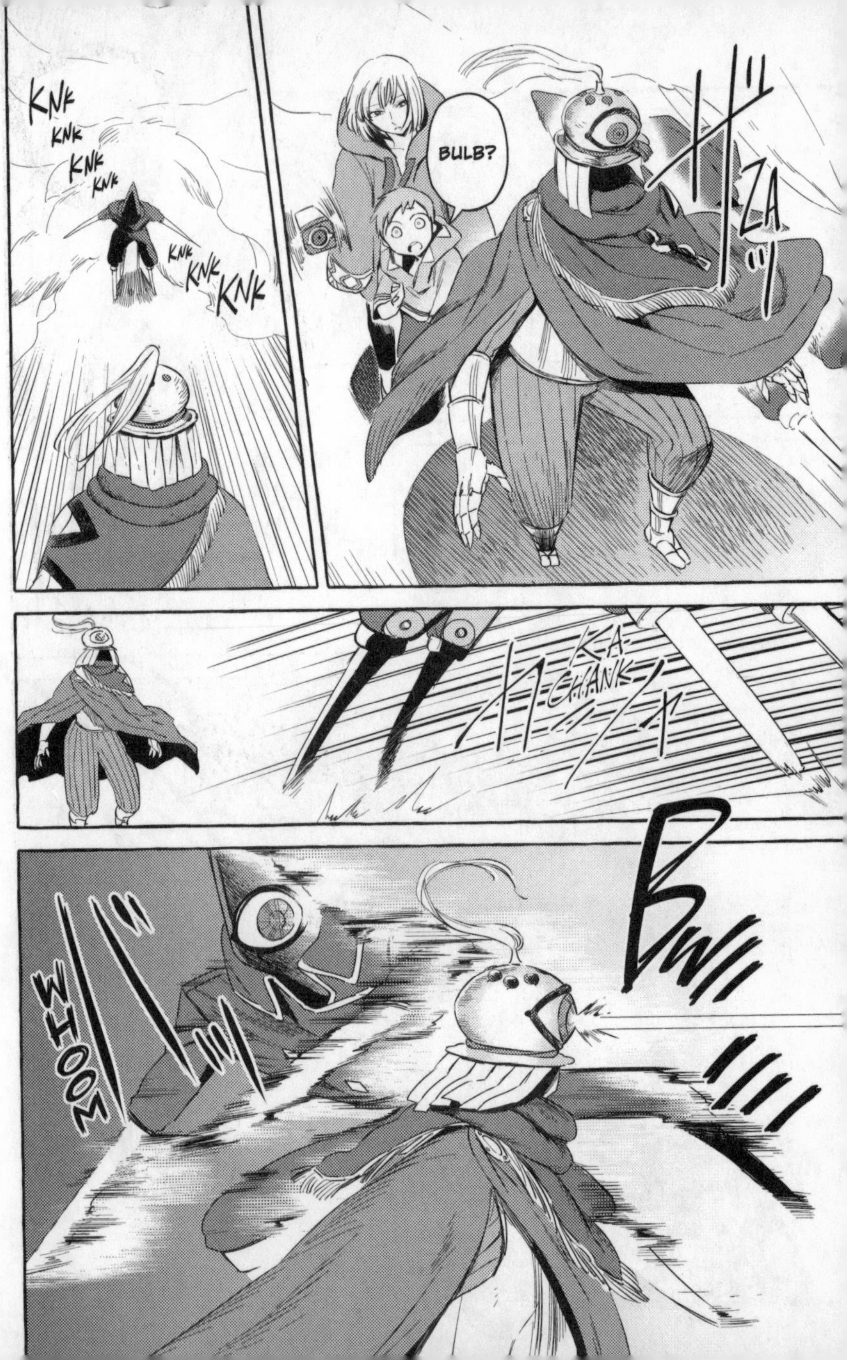
BULB?
ZA
KNK KNK KNK KNK
KNK KNK KNK
KA-CHANK
WHOOM

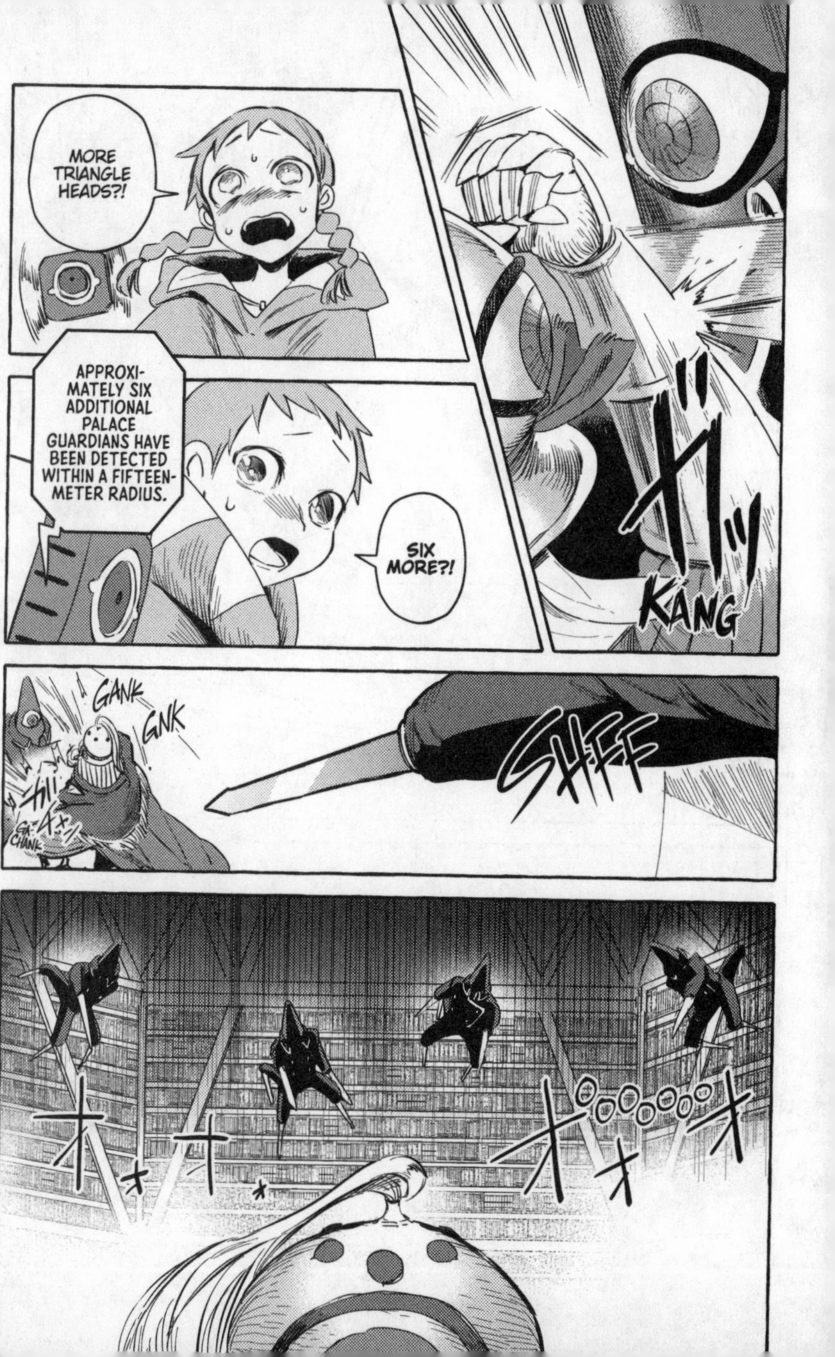
KANG
MORE TRIANGLE HEADS?!
APPROXI-MATELY SIX ADDITIONAL PALACE GUARDIANS HAVE BEEN DETECTED WITHIN A FIFTEEN-METER RADIUS.
SIX MORE?!
SHFF
GANK
GNK
GA-CHANK

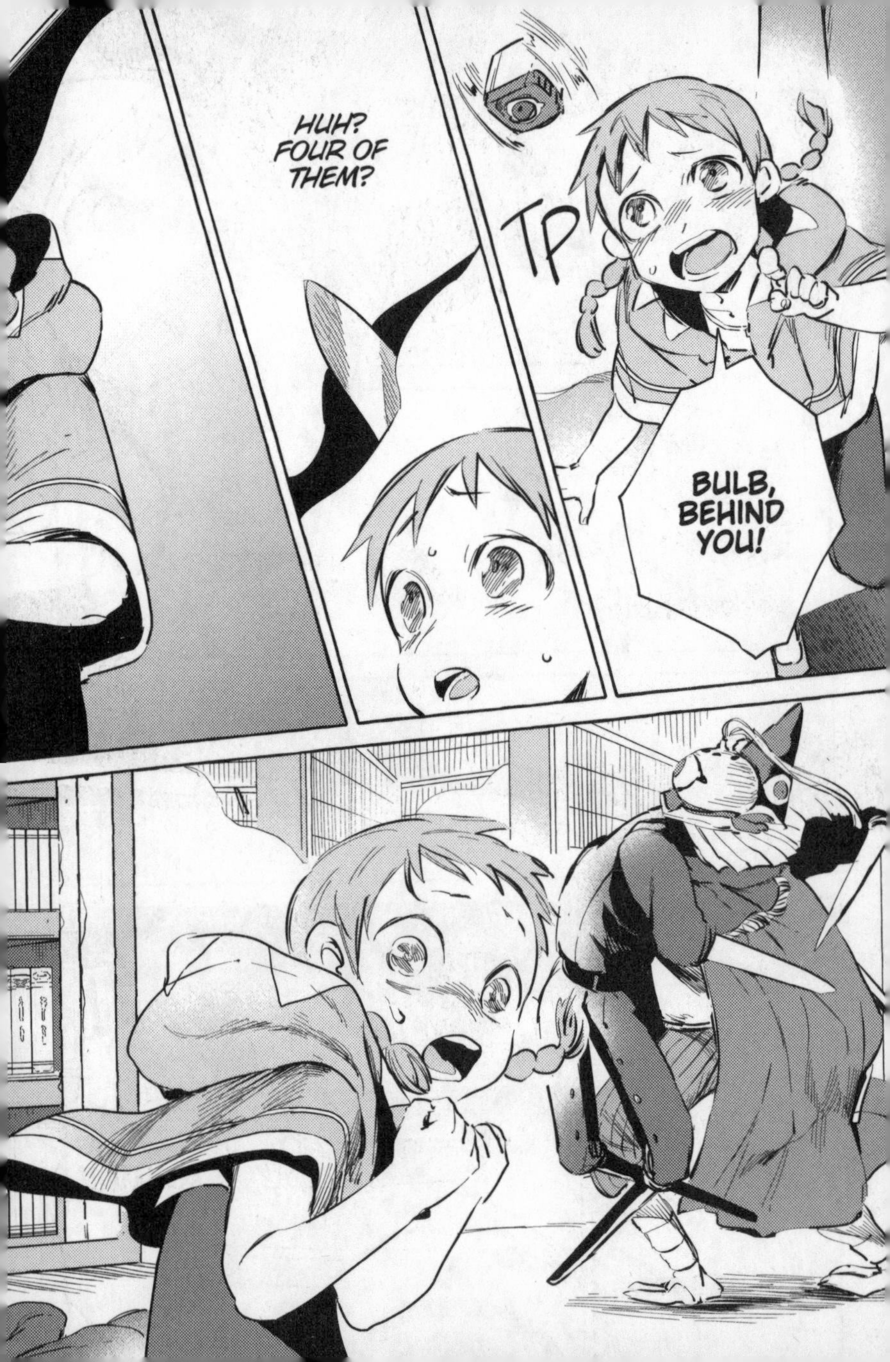
TP
BULB, BEHIND YOU!
HUH? FOUR OF THEM?

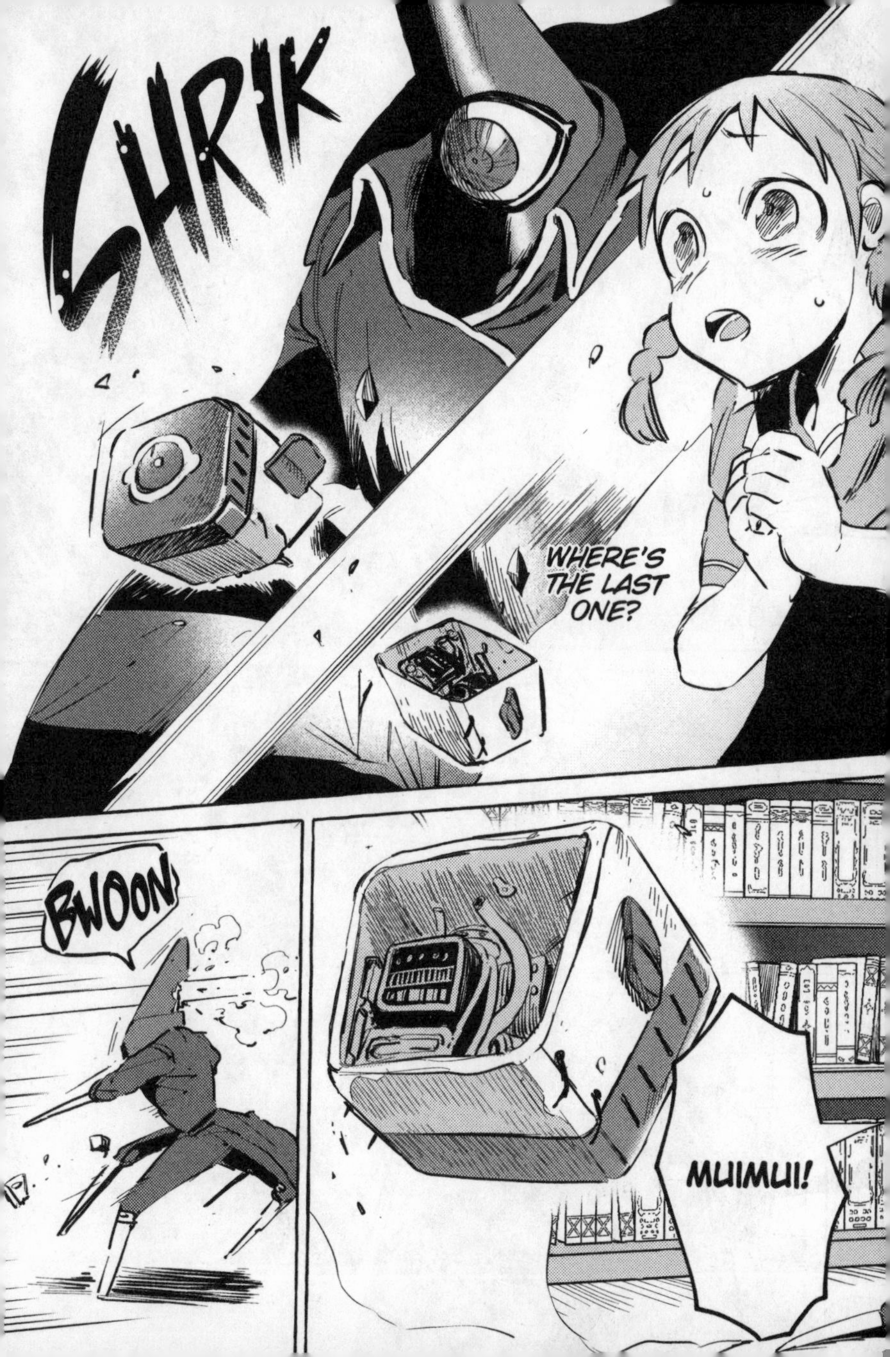
SHRIK
WHERE'S THE LAST ONE?
MUIMUI!
BWOON

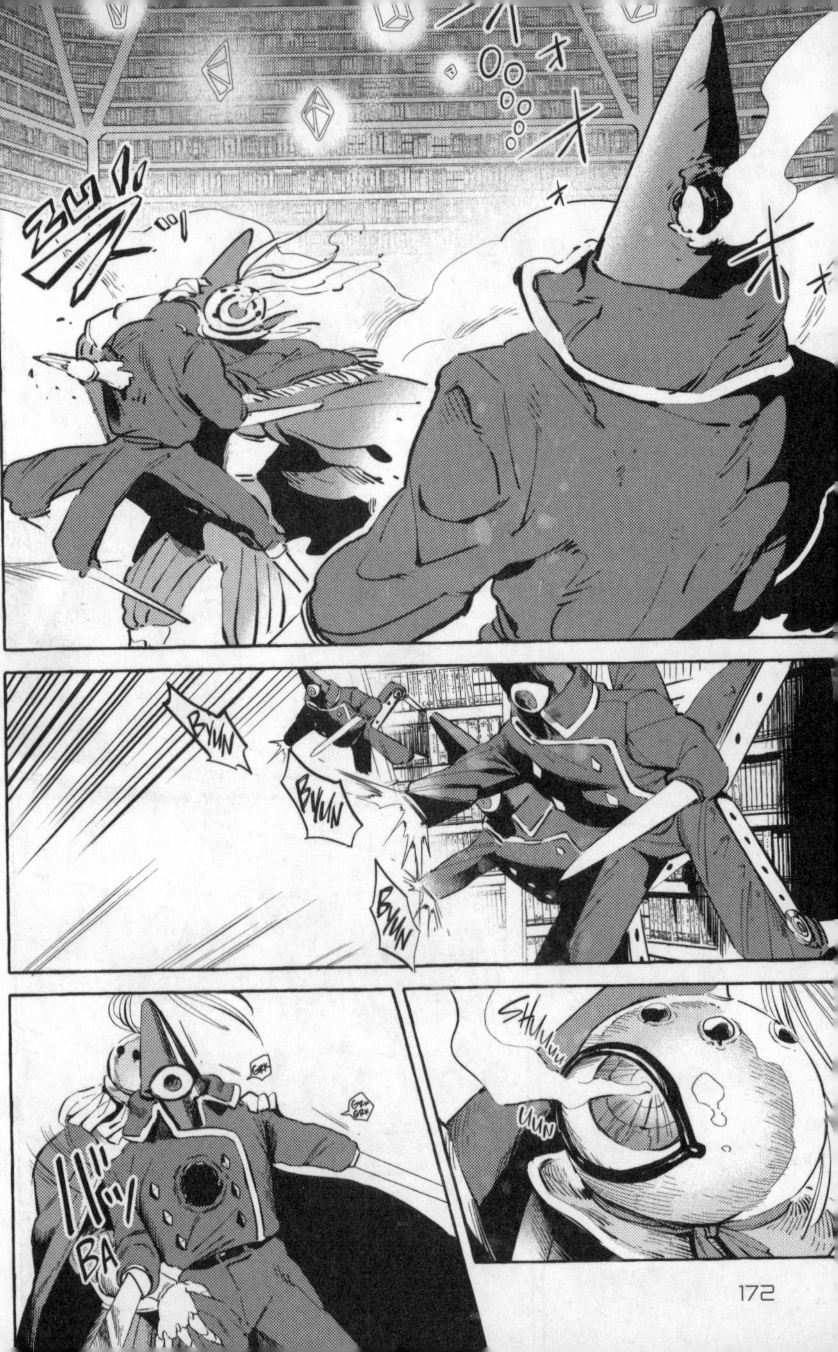
OOOOOO
ZU
BYUN
BYUN
BYUN
SHUuuuu
UUN
GRK
GRK GRK
BA

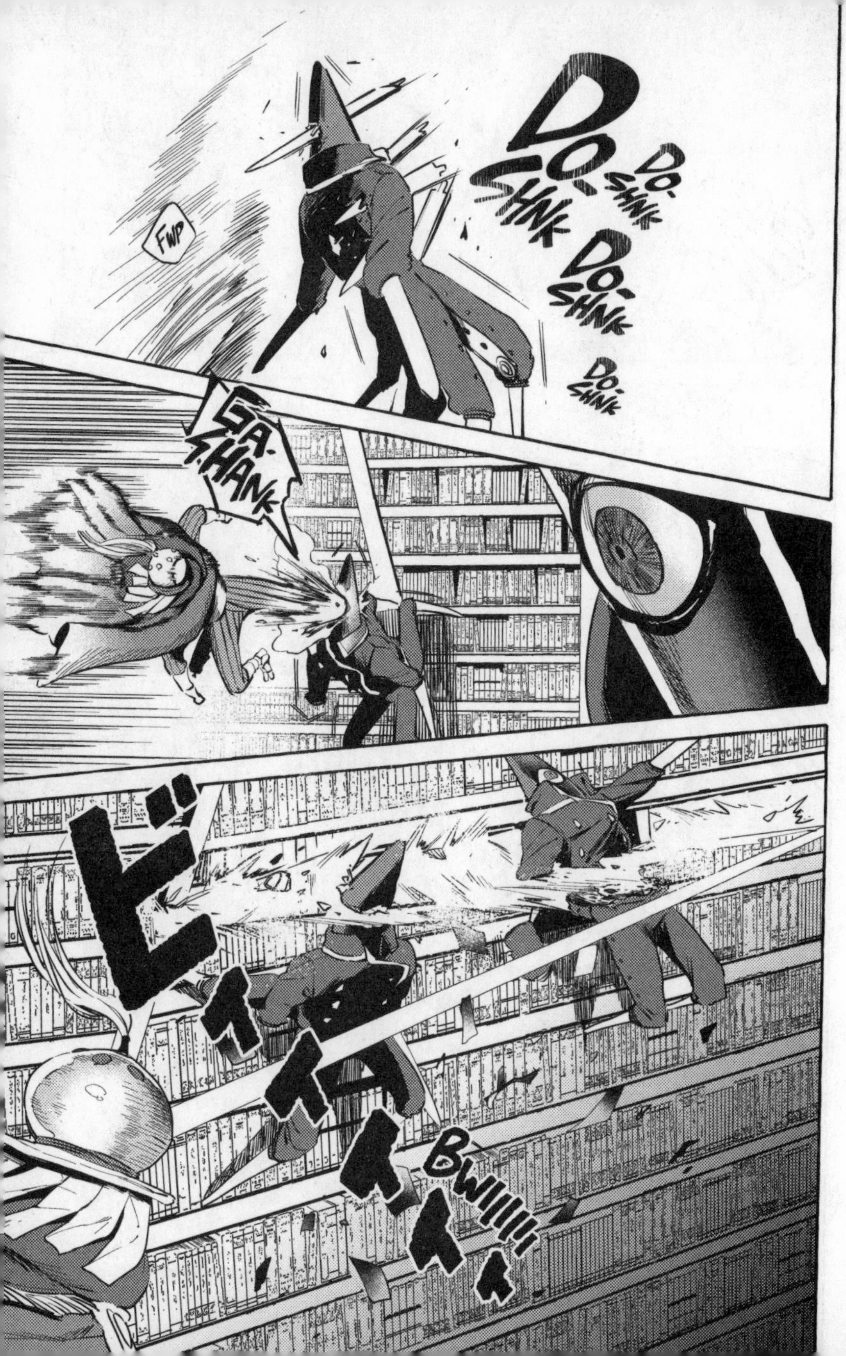
DO-SHNK
DO-SHNK
DO-SHNK
DO-SHNK
FWP
GA-SHANK
ビィィィィ
BWIIIIII

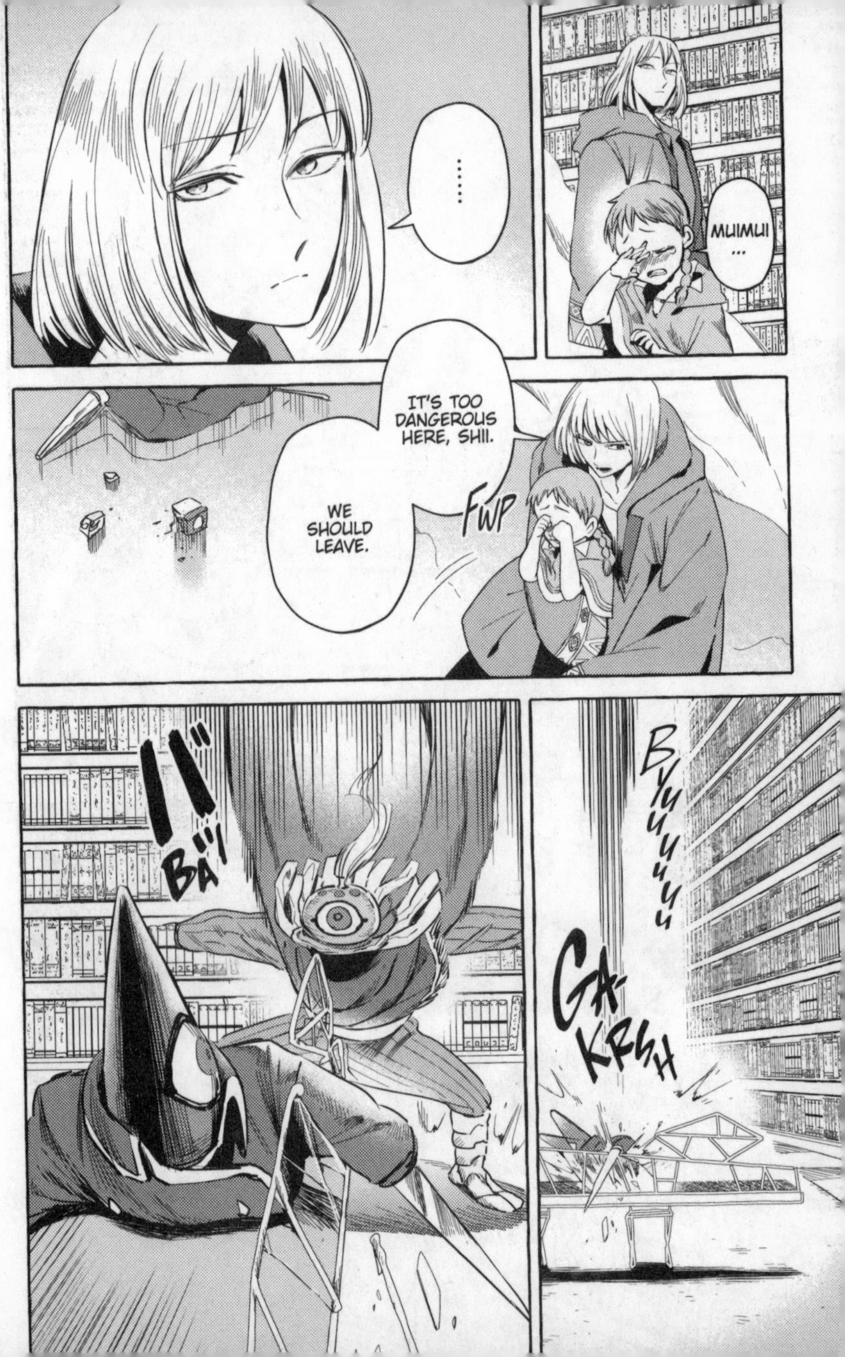

MUIMUI ...
......
IT'S TOO DANGEROUS HERE, SHII.
WE SHOULD LEAVE.
FWP
BYUUUUUUU
GA-KRSH
バ
BA

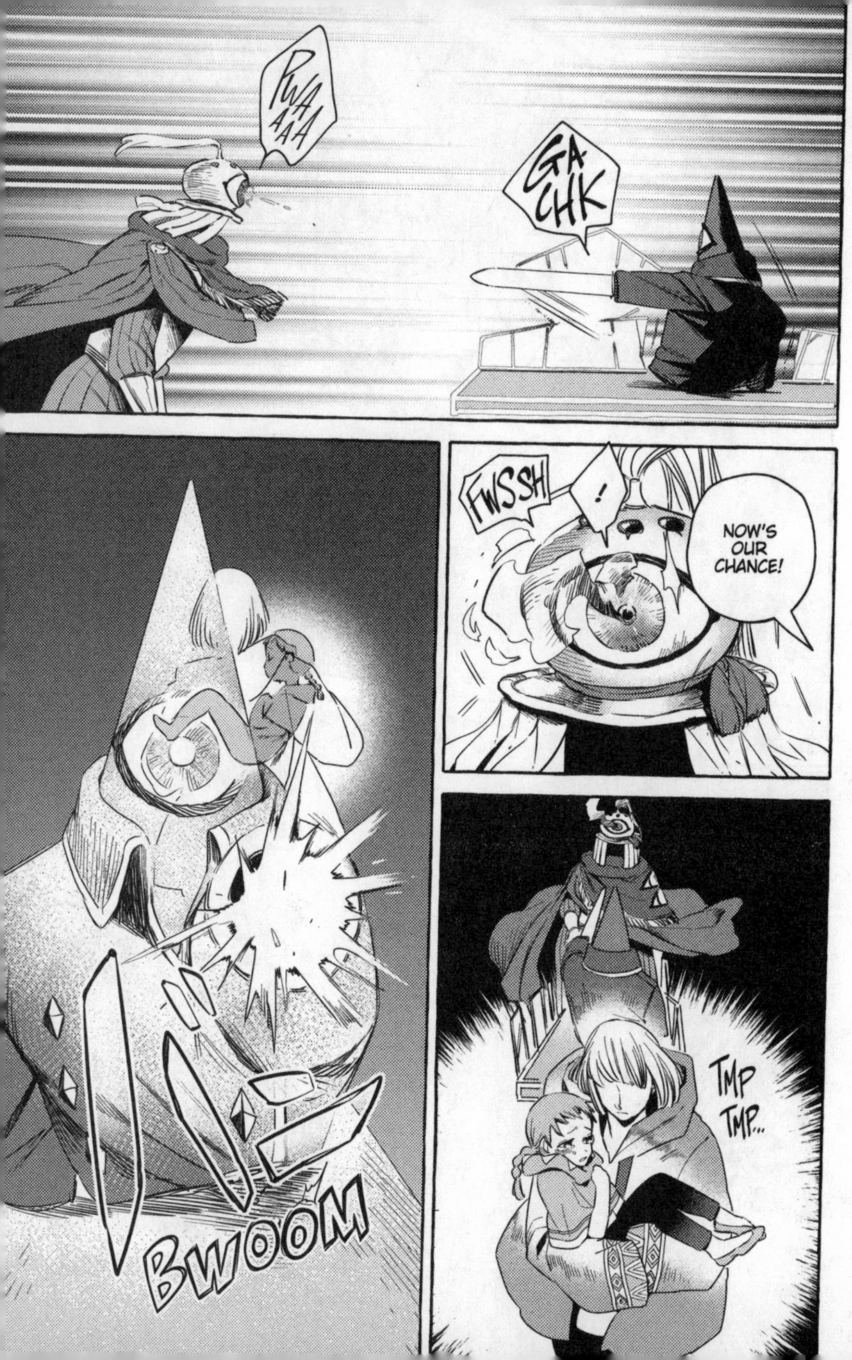
GACHK
PWAAAA
FWSSH
!
NOW'S OUR CHANCE!
TMP TMP...
BWOOM

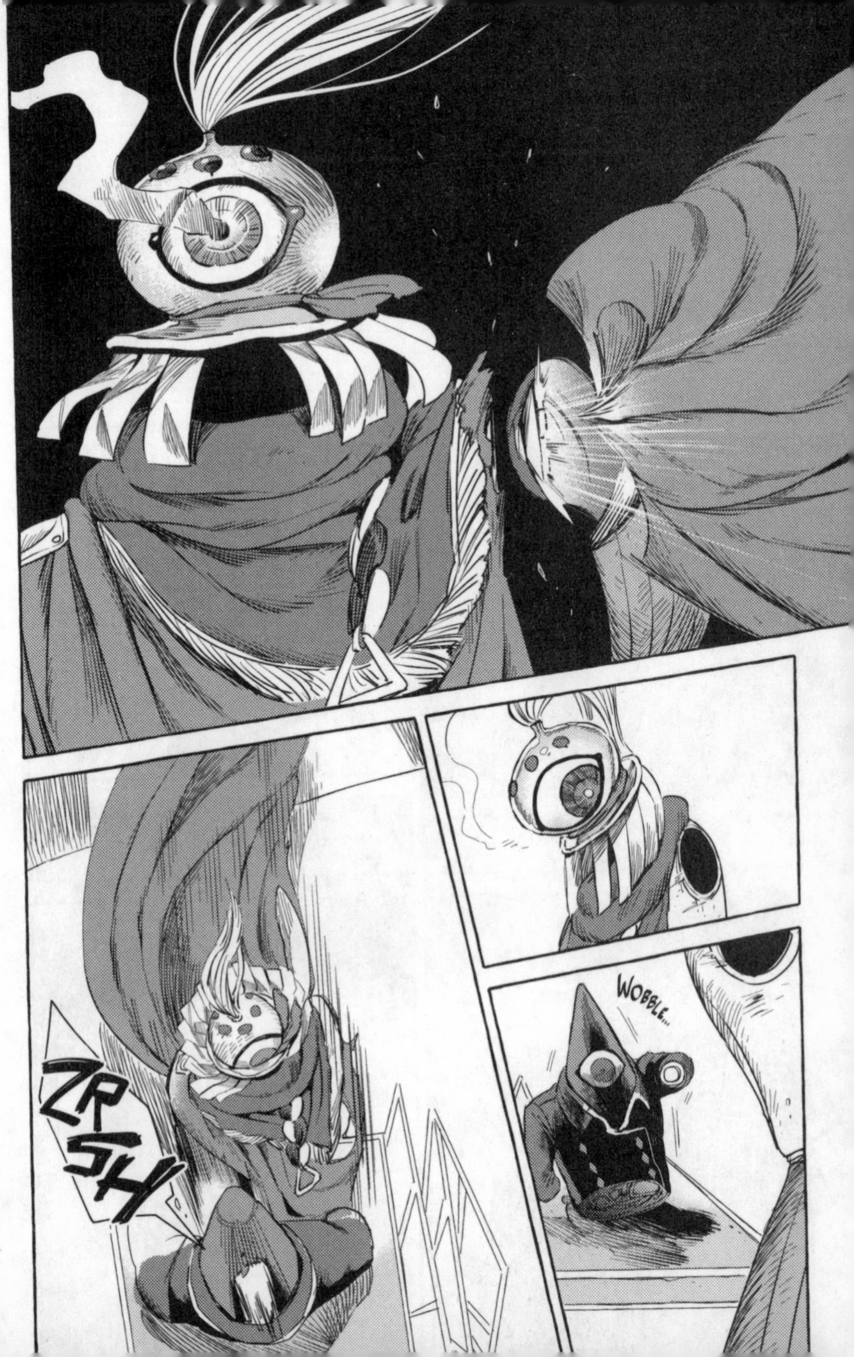
WOBBLE...
ZRSH

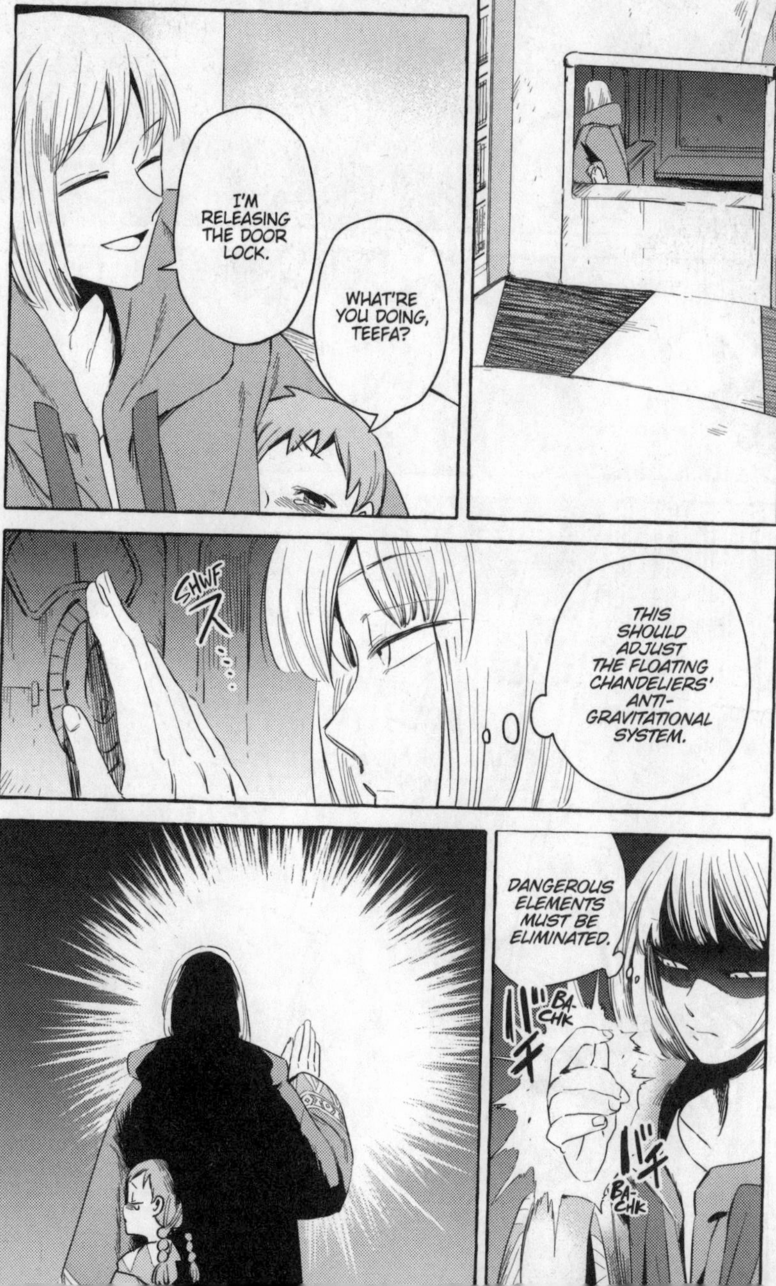
WHAT'RE YOU DOING, TEEFA?
I'M RELEASING THE DOOR LOCK.
THIS SHOULD ADJUST THE FLOATING CHANDELIERS' ANTI-GRAVITATIONAL SYSTEM.
SHWF
DANGEROUS ELEMENTS MUST BE ELIMINATED.
BA-CHK
BA-CHK

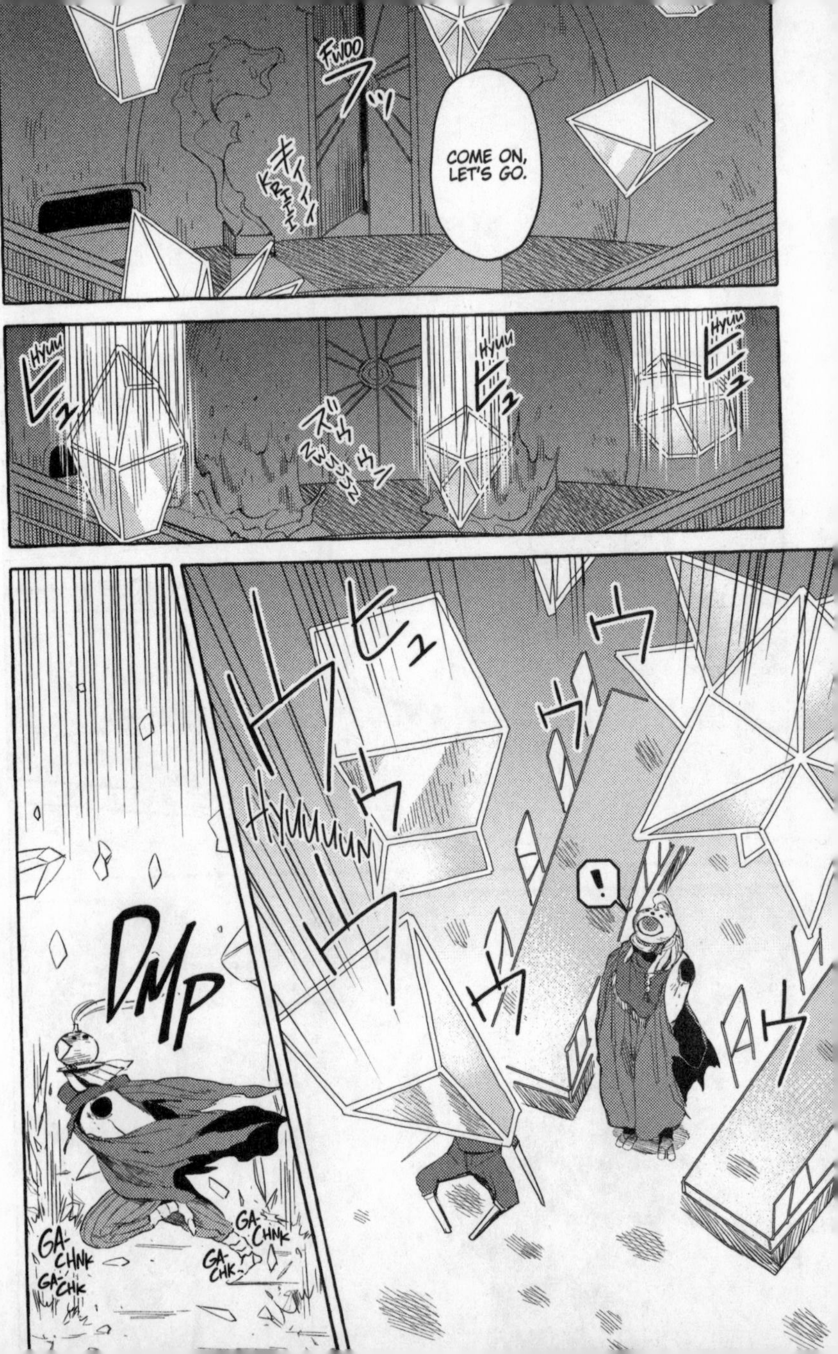
COME ON, LET'S GO.
FWOO
KREEE
HYUU
HYUU
HYUU
!
HYUUUUUN
DMP
GA-CHNK
GA-CHK
GA-CHNK
GA-CHK

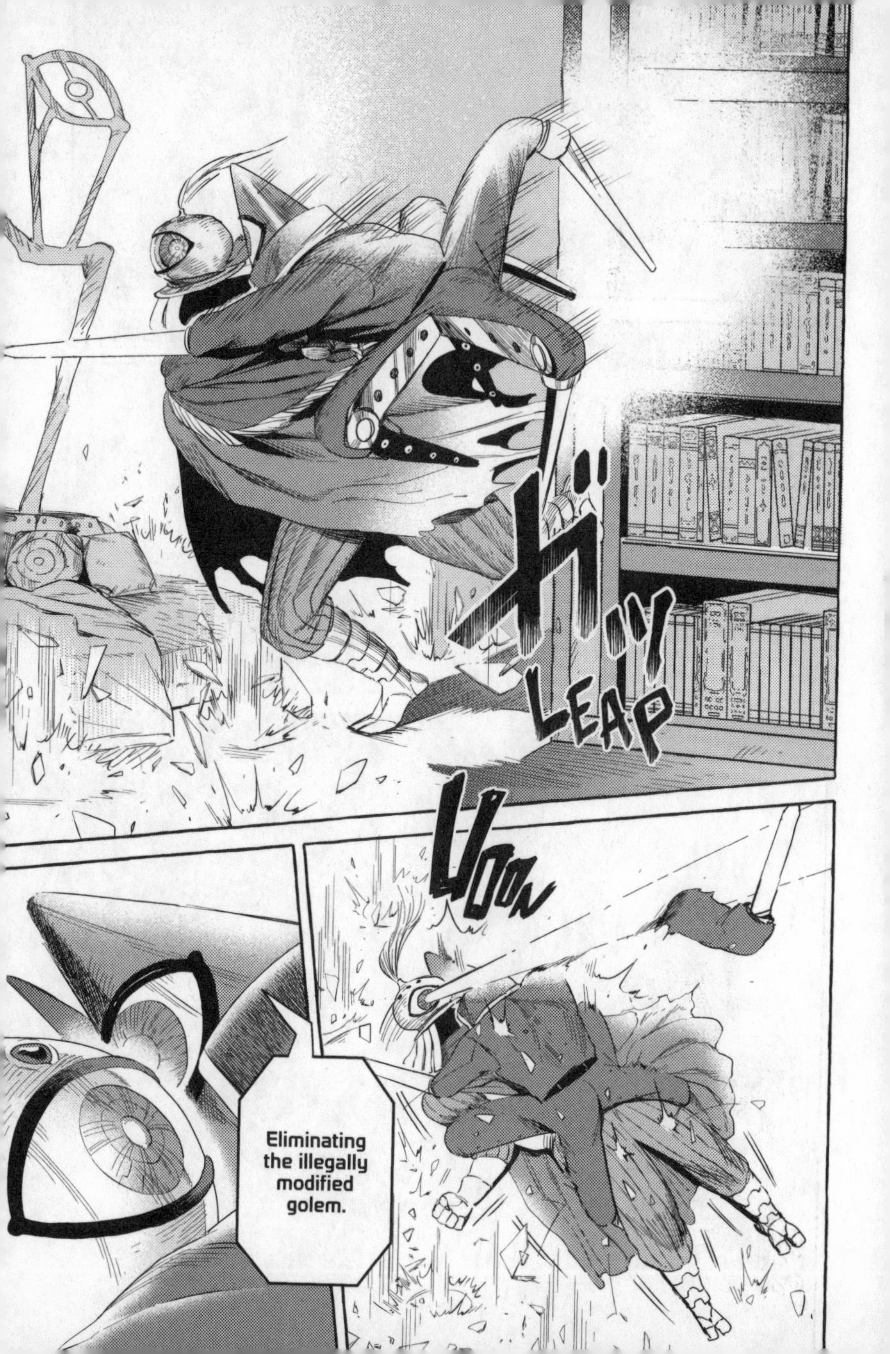
LEAP
Eliminating the illegally modified golem.

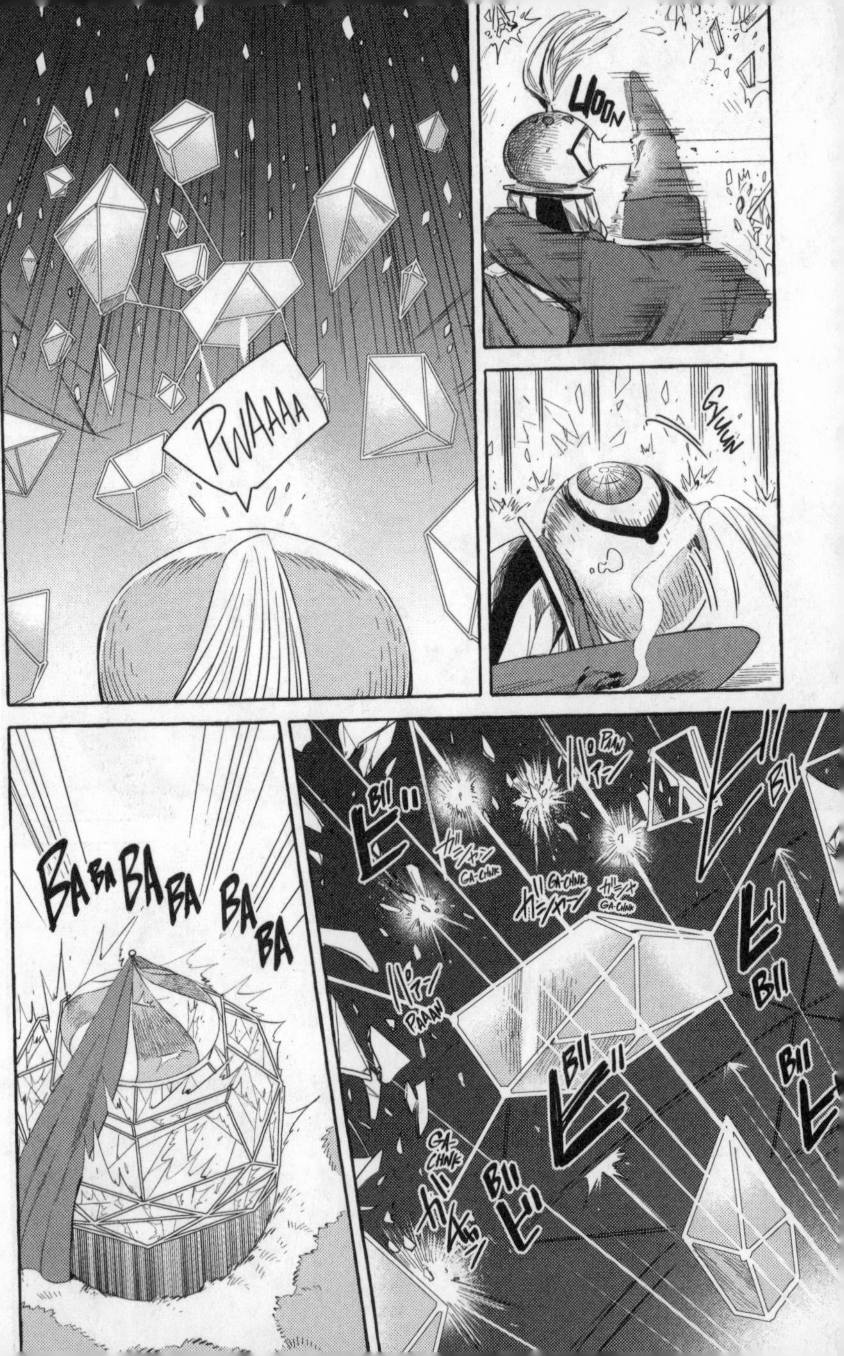
UOON
GYUUN
PWAAAA
PAN
BII
BII
GA-CHNK
GA-CHNK
GA-CHNK
PAAAN
BII
BII
BII
BII
GA-CHNK
BABABABABABA

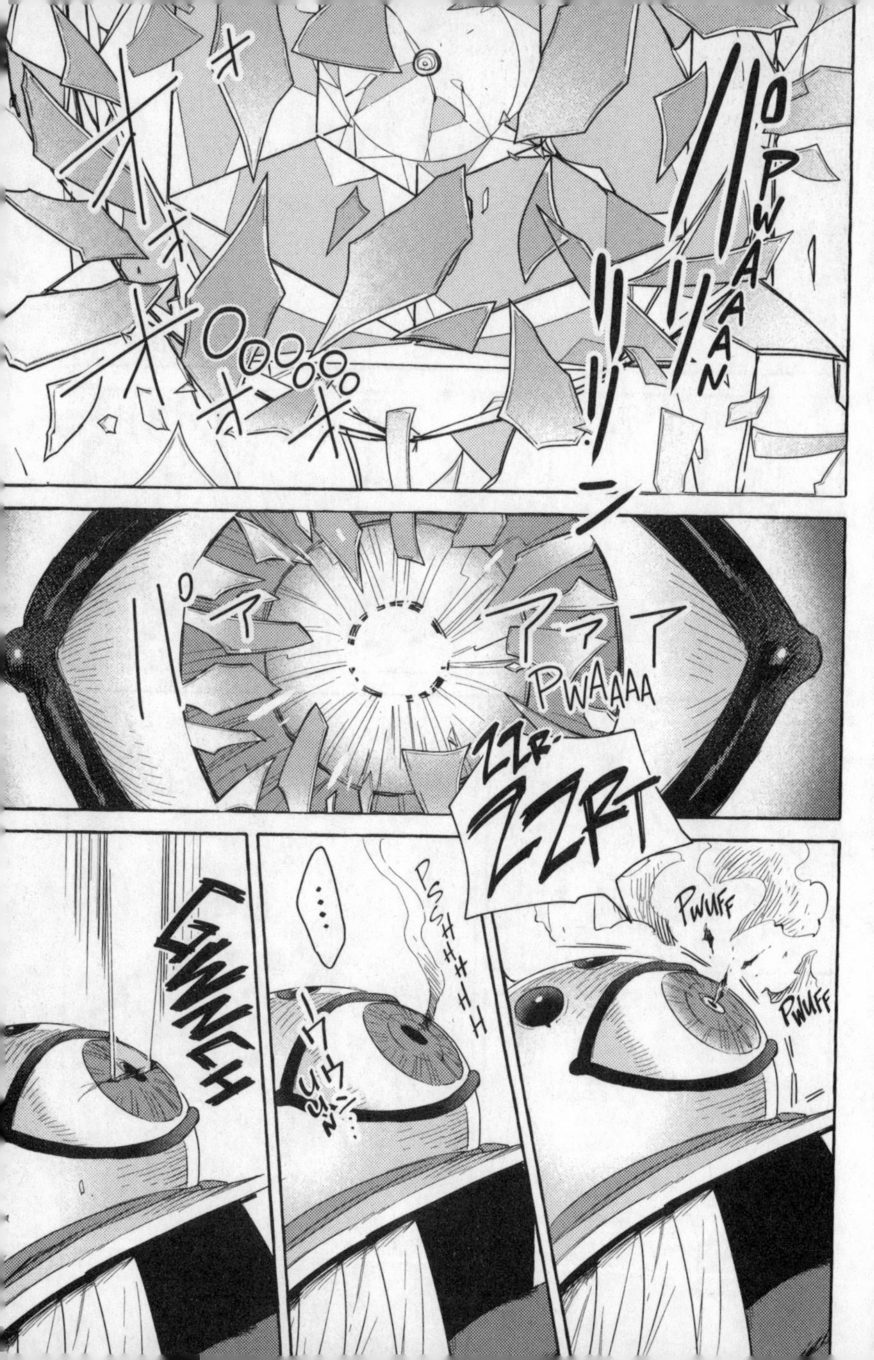
PWAAAN
OOOOOO
PWAAAA
ZZR
ZZRT
PWUFF
PWUFF
...
PSHHHHH
UGN...
GWNCH

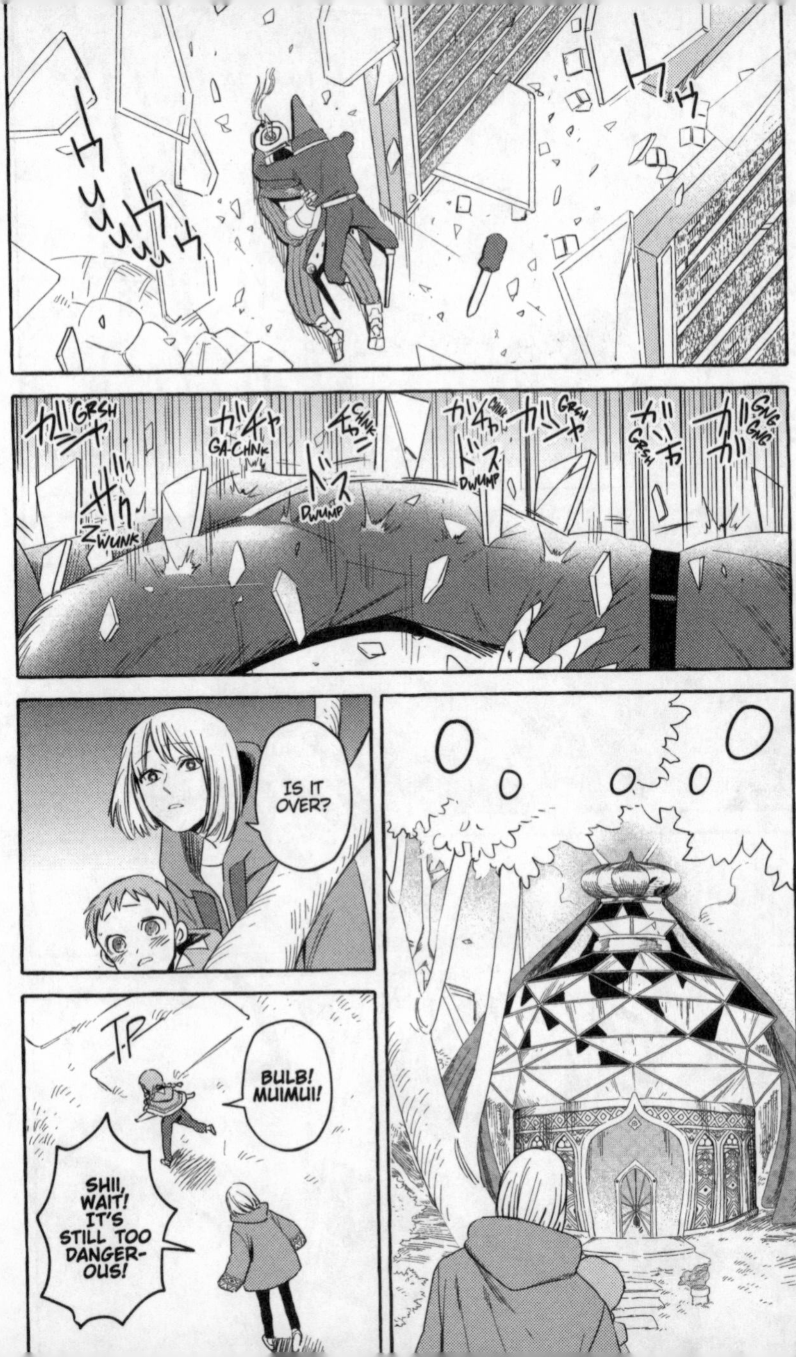
UUUUUUU
GNG GNG
GRSH
GRSH
DWUMP
CHNK
DWUMP
GA-CHNK
GRSH
ZWUNK
IS IT OVER?
T-P
BULB! MUIMUI!
SHII, WAIT! IT'S STILL TOO DANGER-OUS!

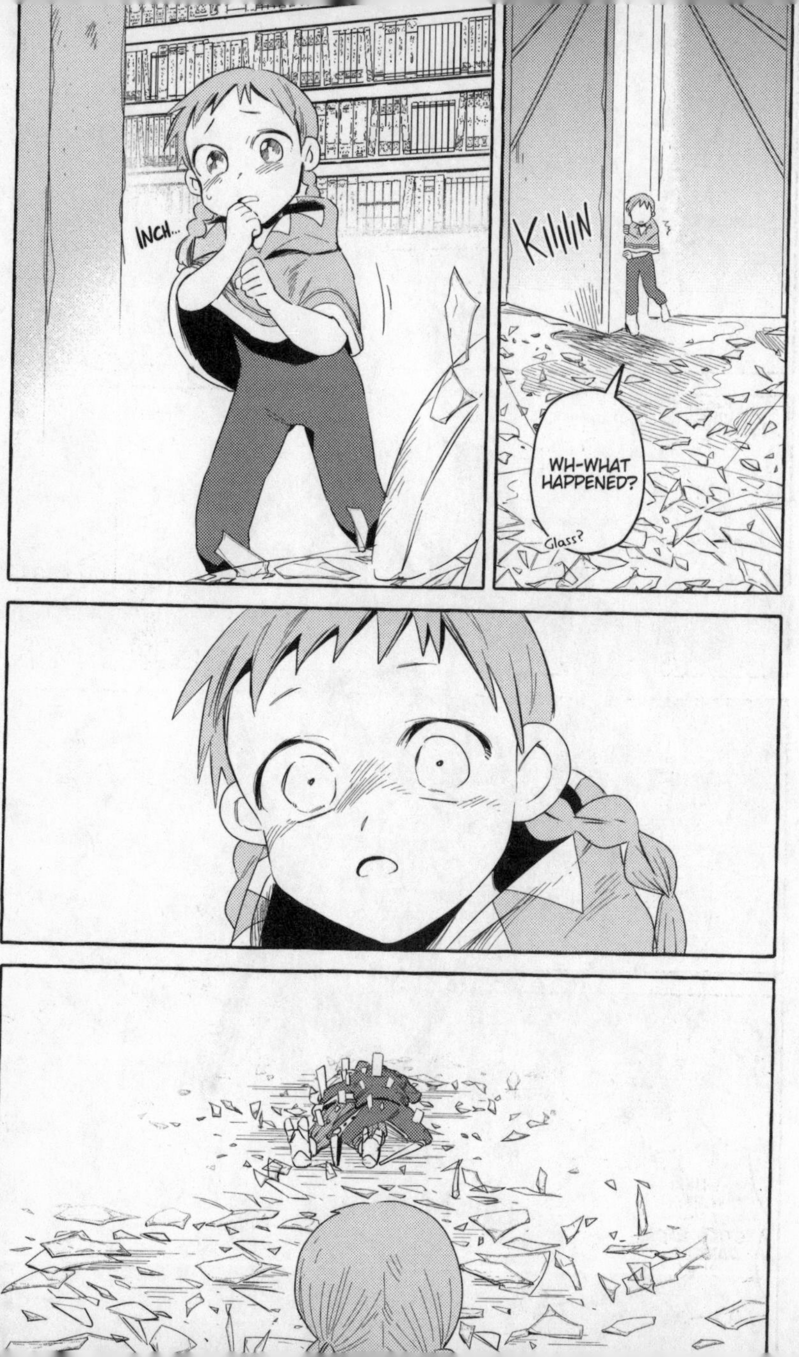
KIIIIIN
WH-WHAT HAPPENED?
Glass?
INCH...

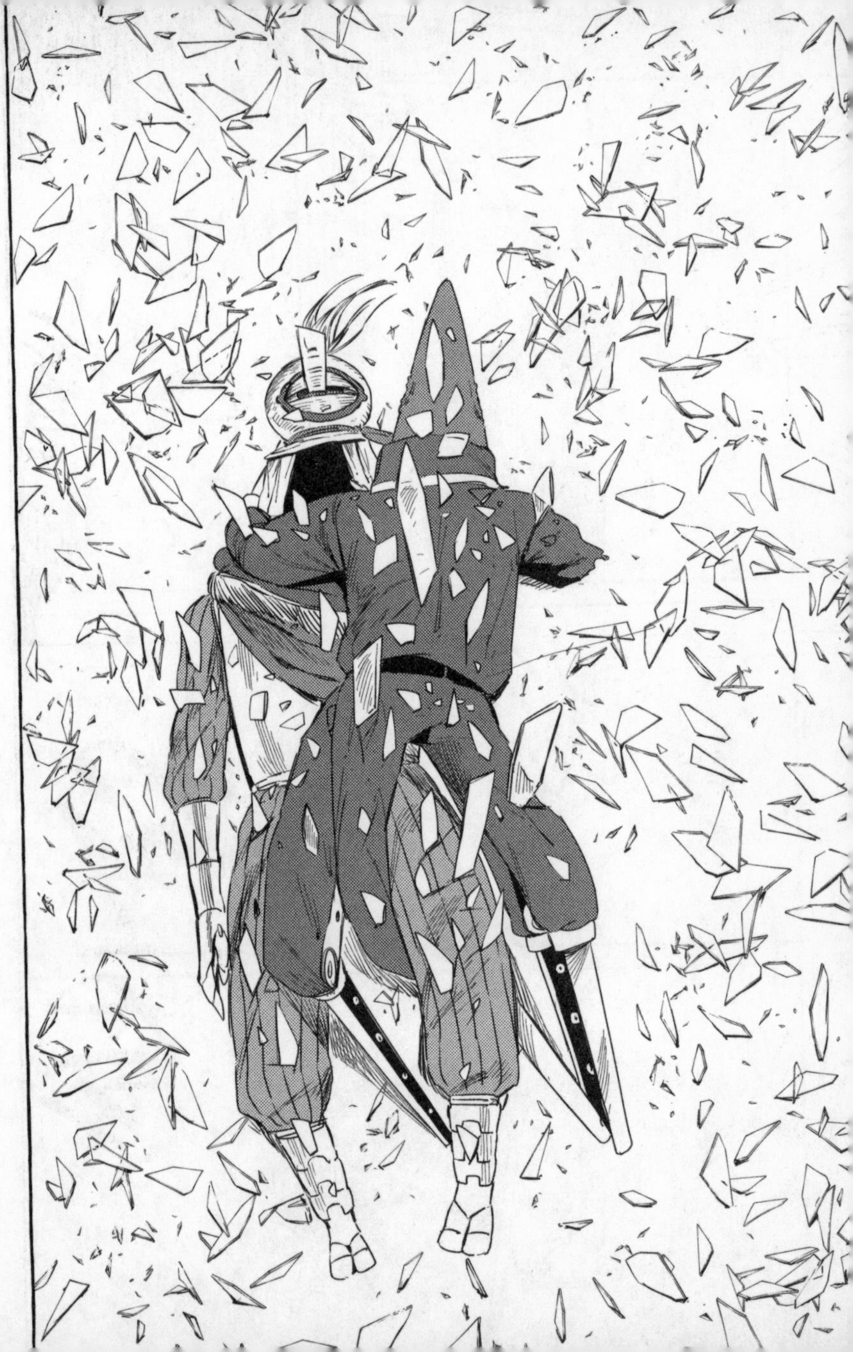

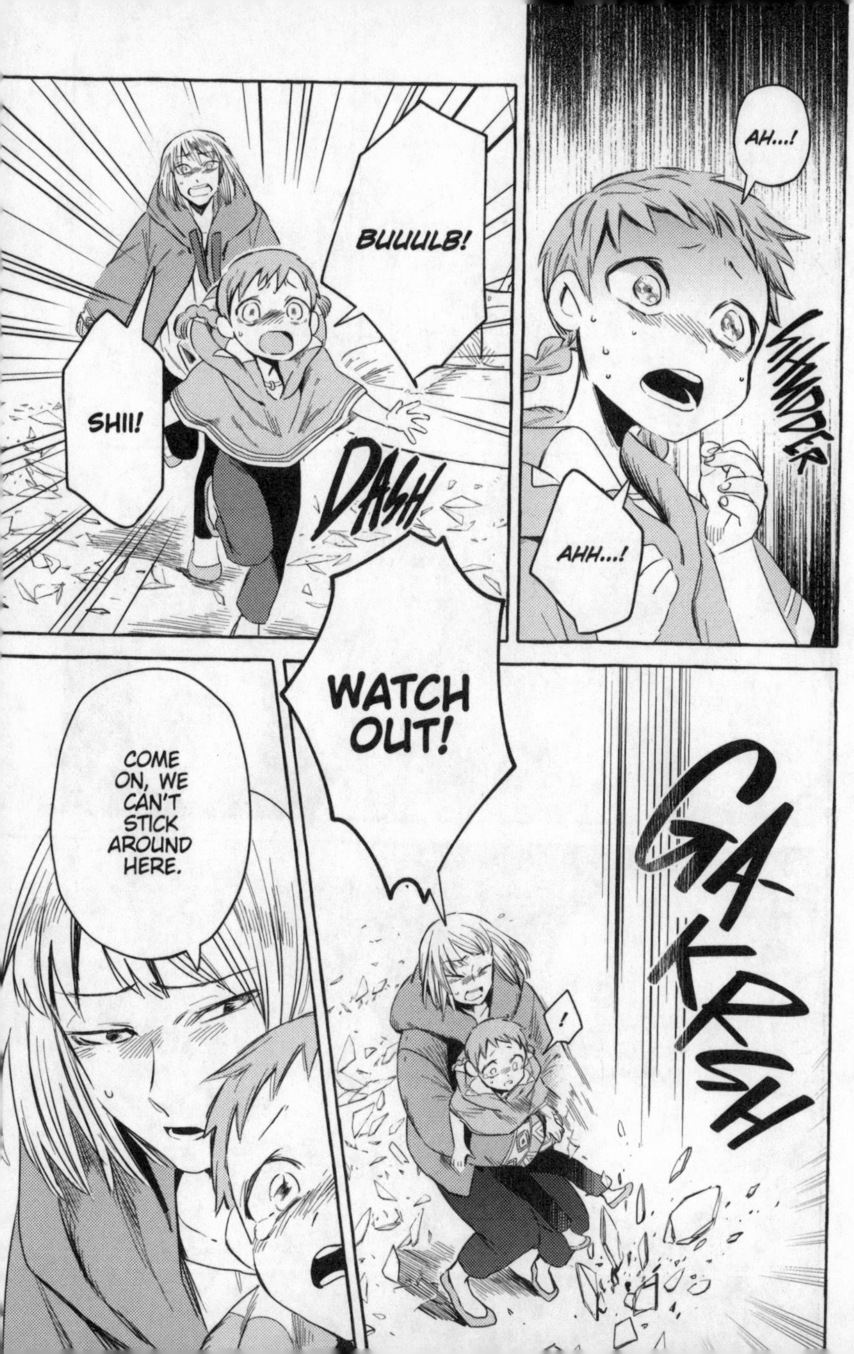
AH...!
SHUDDER
AHH...!
BUUULB!
SHII!
DASH
WATCH OUT!
!
GAKRSH
COME ON, WE CAN'T STICK AROUND HERE.

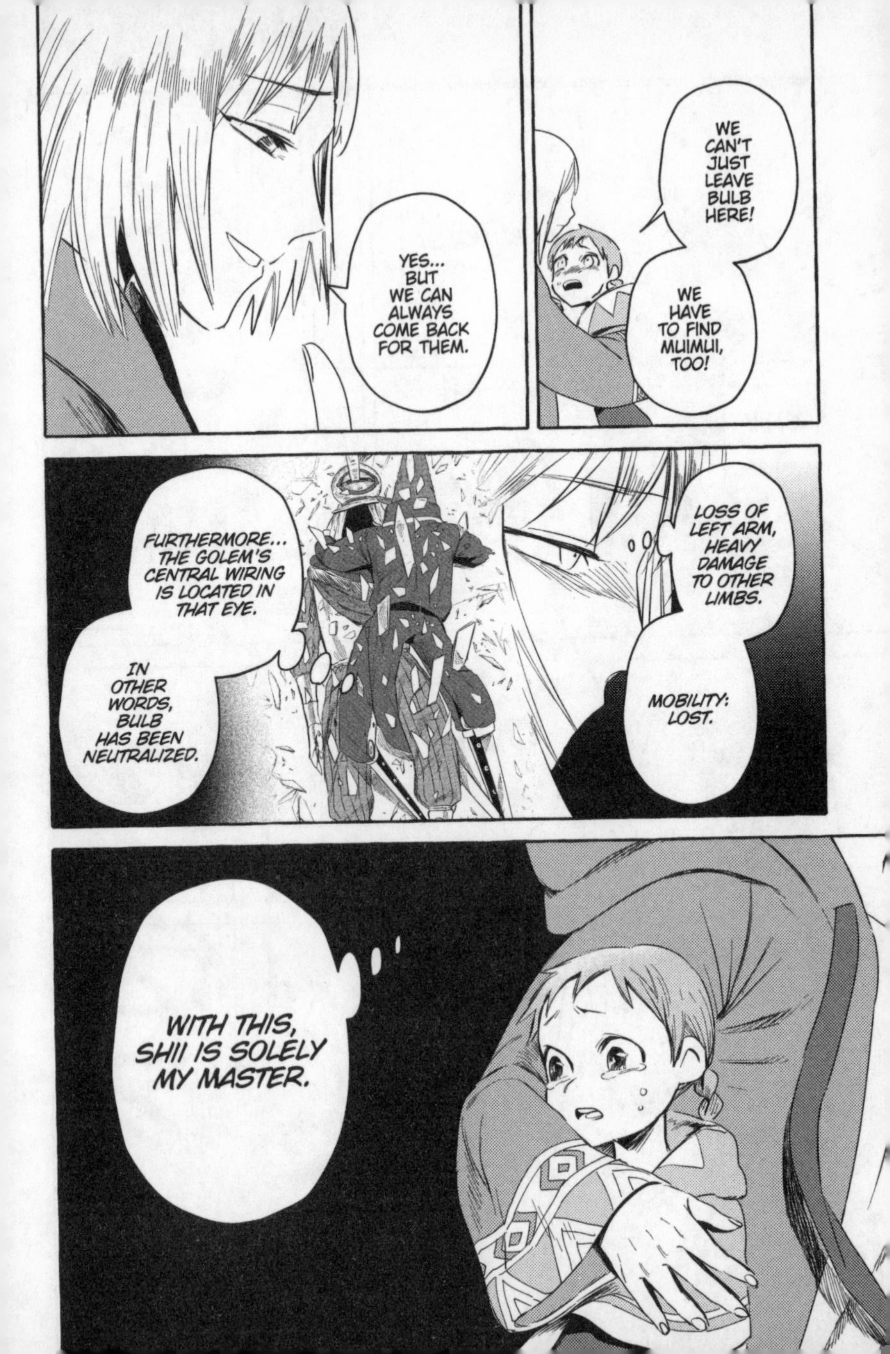
WE CAN'T JUST LEAVE BULB HERE!
WE HAVE TO FIND MUIMUI, TOO!
YES... BUT WE CAN ALWAYS COME BACK FOR THEM.
LOSS OF LEFT ARM, HEAVY DAMAGE TO OTHER LIMBS.
MOBILITY: LOST.
FURTHERMORE... THE GOLEM'S CENTRAL WIRING IS LOCATED IN THAT EYE.
IN OTHER WORDS, BULB HAS BEEN NEUTRALIZED.
WITH THIS, SHII IS SOLELY MY MASTER.

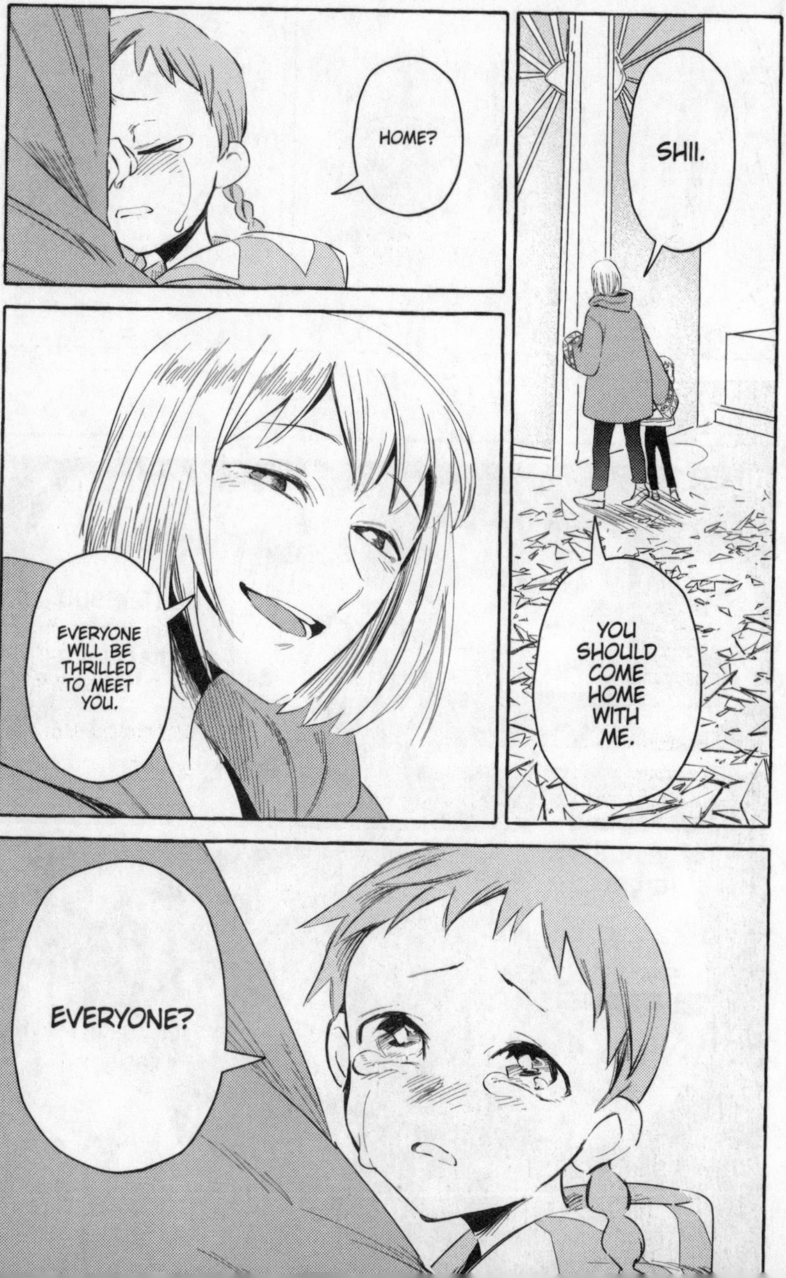
SHII.
YOU SHOULD COME HOME WITH ME.
HOME?
EVERYONE WILL BE THRILLED TO MEET YOU.
EVERYONE?

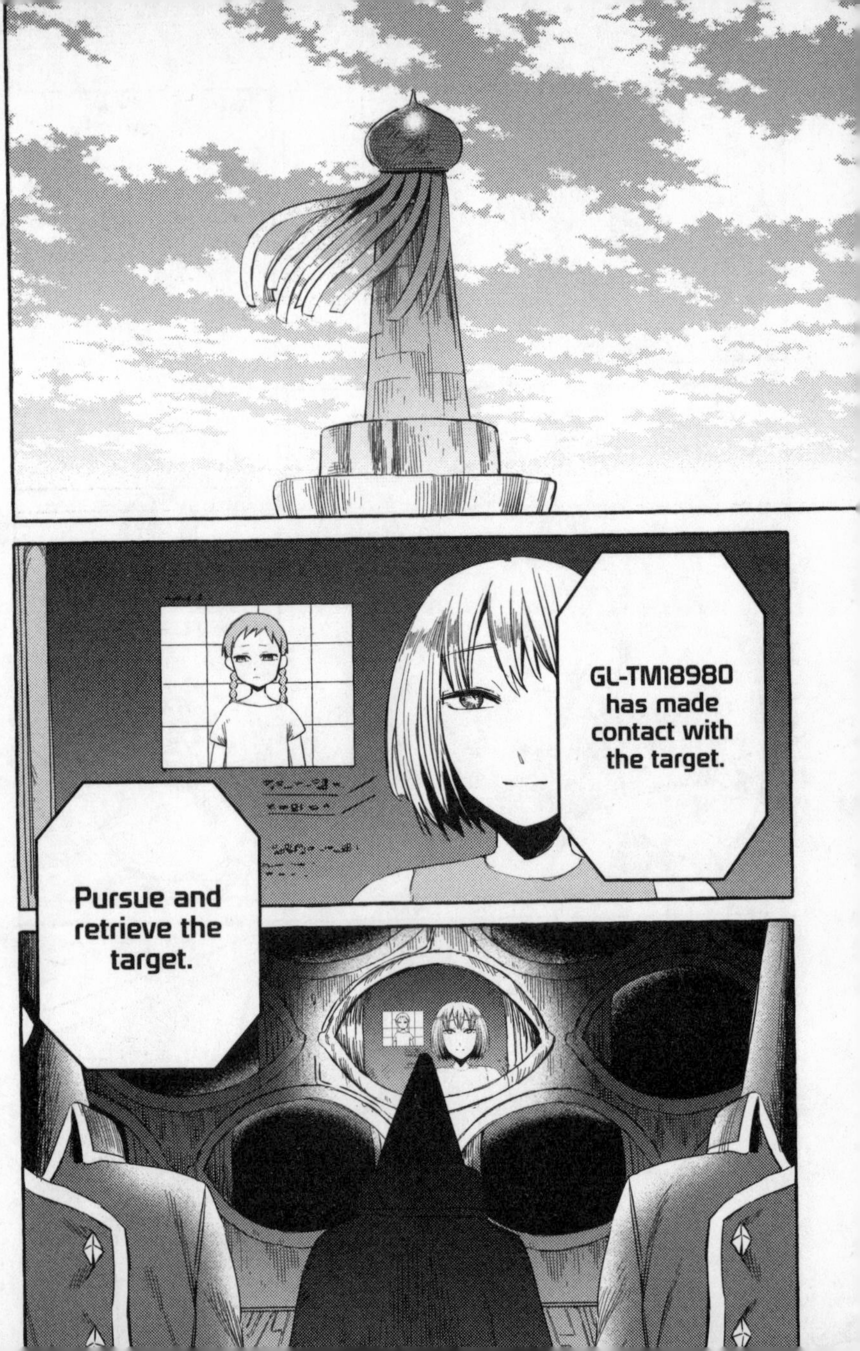
GL-TM18980 has made contact with the target.
Pursue and retrieve the target.

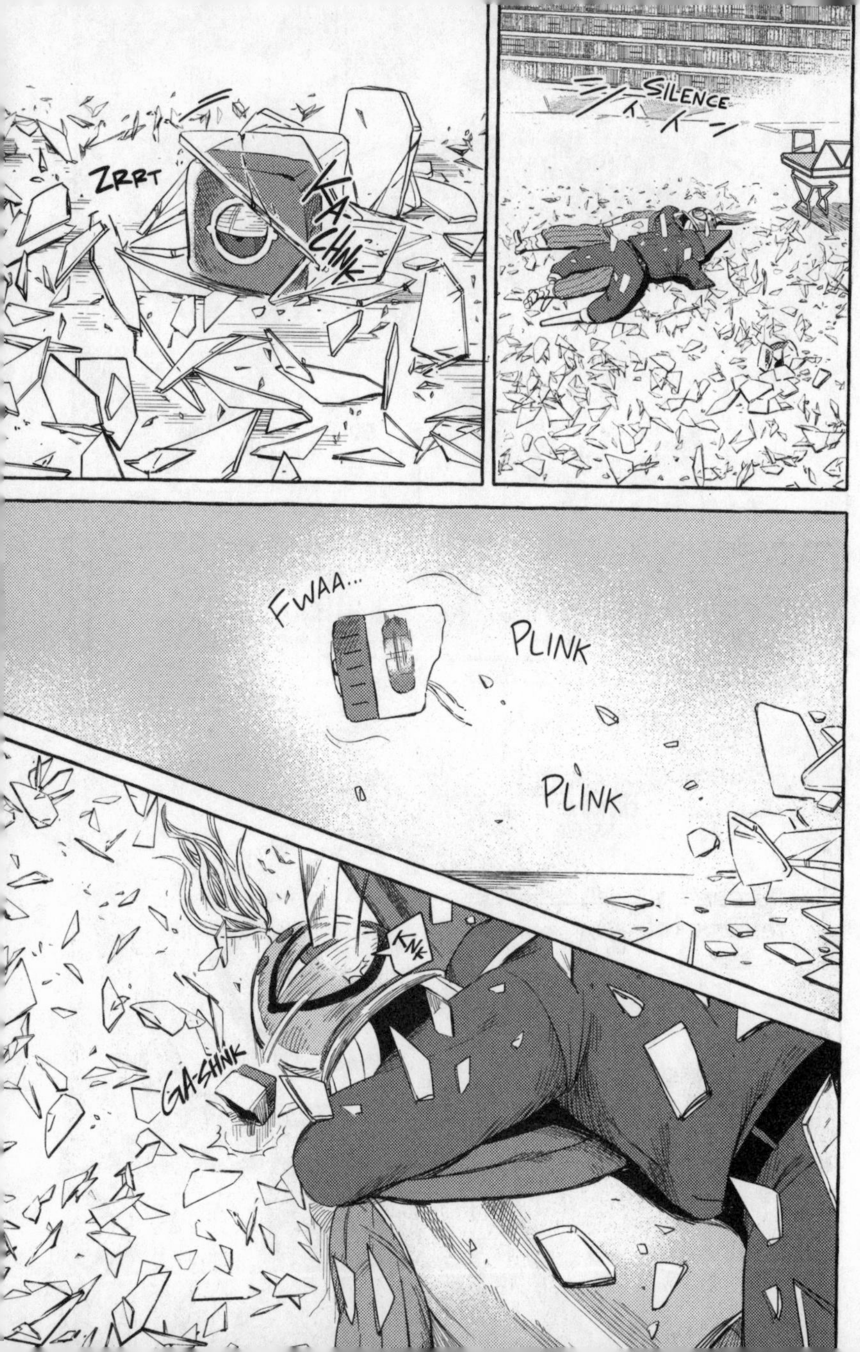
SILENCE
ZRRT
KA-CHNK
FWAA...
PLINK
PLINK
KNK
GA-SHNK

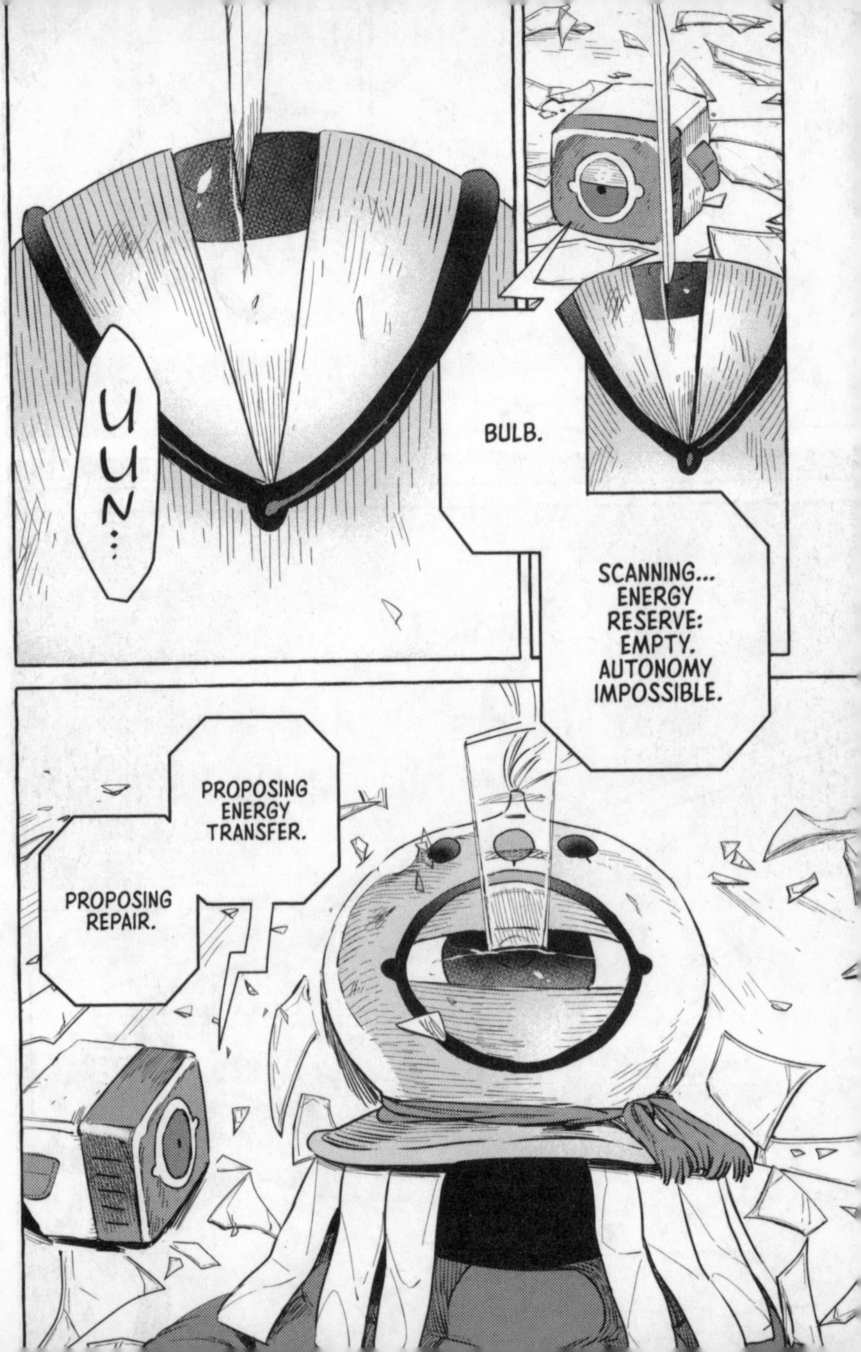
BULB.
UUN...
SCANNING... ENERGY RESERVE: EMPTY. AUTONOMY IMPOSSIBLE.
PROPOSING ENERGY TRANSFER.
PROPOSING REPAIR.

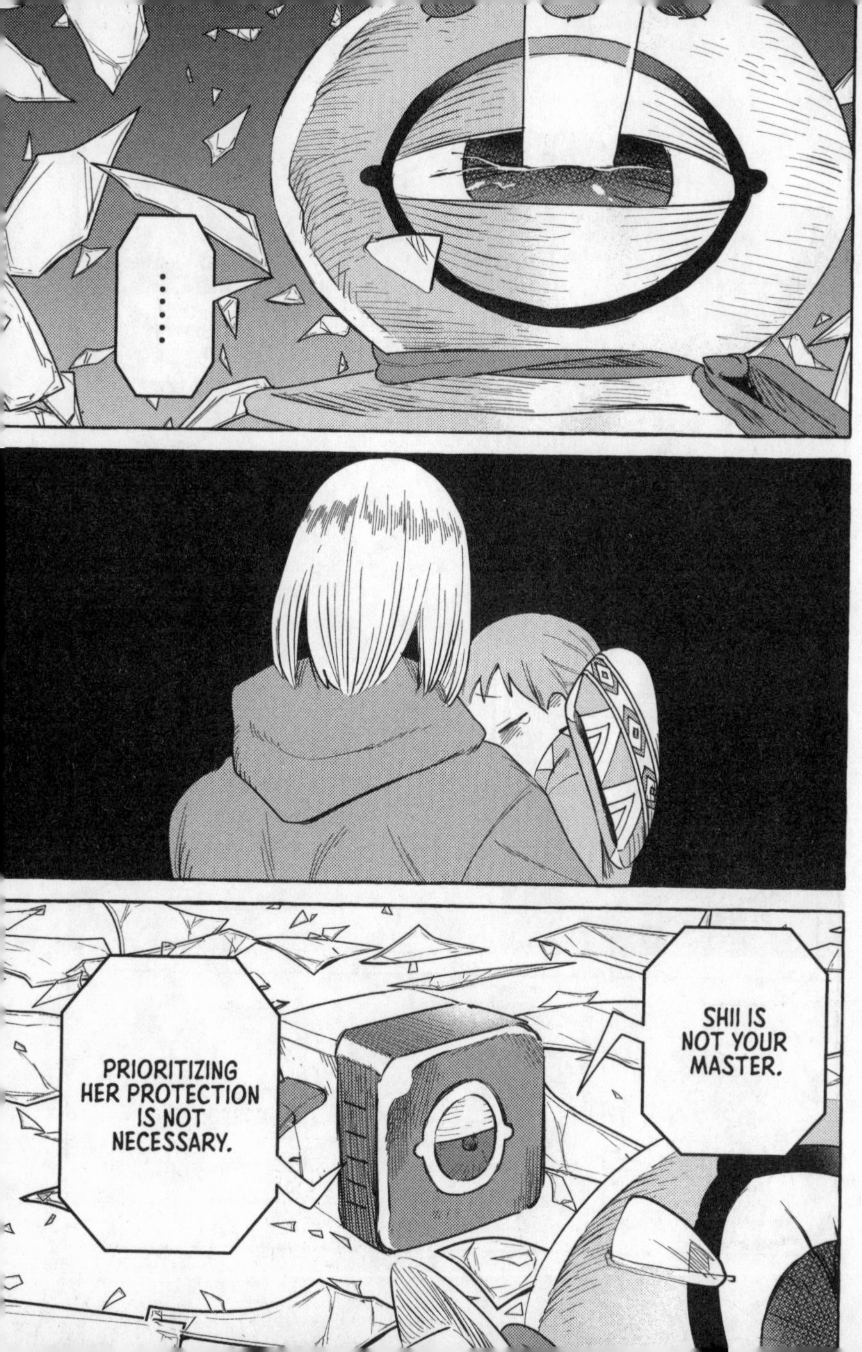
......
SHII IS NOT YOUR MASTER.
PRIORITIZING HER PROTECTION IS NOT NECESSARY.

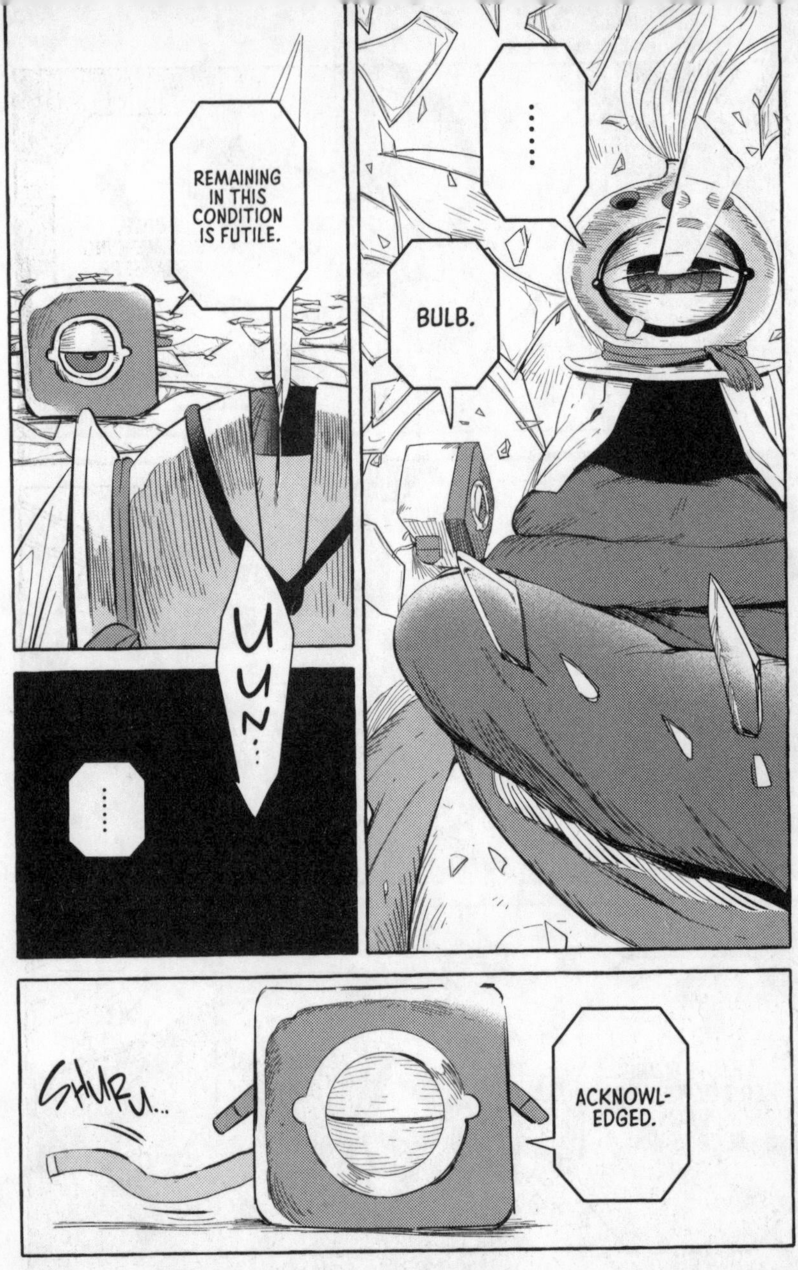
......
BULB.
REMAINING IN THIS CONDITION IS FUTILE.
UUN...
......
ACKNOWL-EDGED.
SHURU...

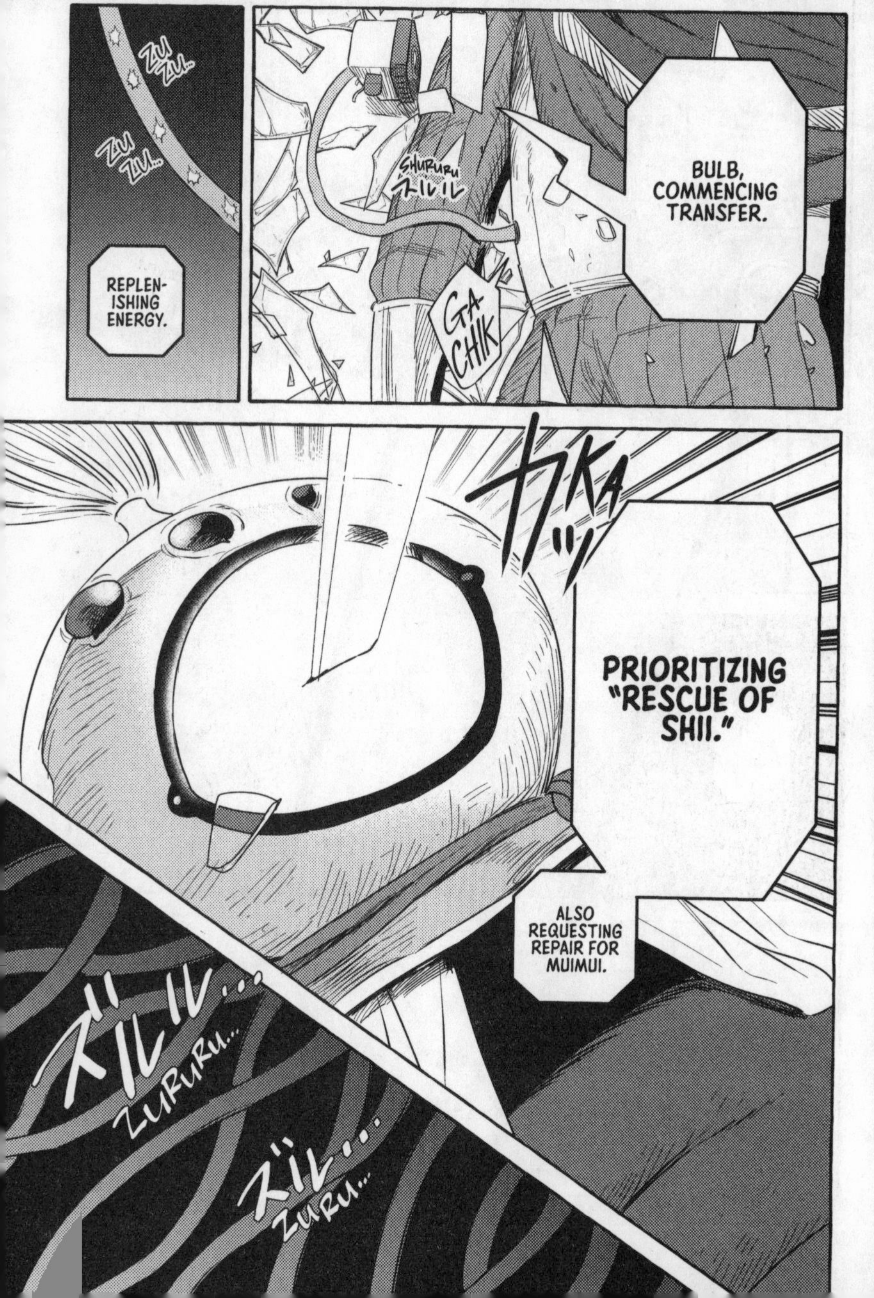
BULB, COMMENCING TRANSFER.
SHURURU
GA CHIK
ZU ZU...
ZU ZU...
REPLEN-ISHING ENERGY.
KA
PRIORITIZING "RESCUE OF SHII."
ALSO REQUESTING REPAIR FOR MUIMUI.
ズルル…
ZURURU...
ズル…
ZURU...

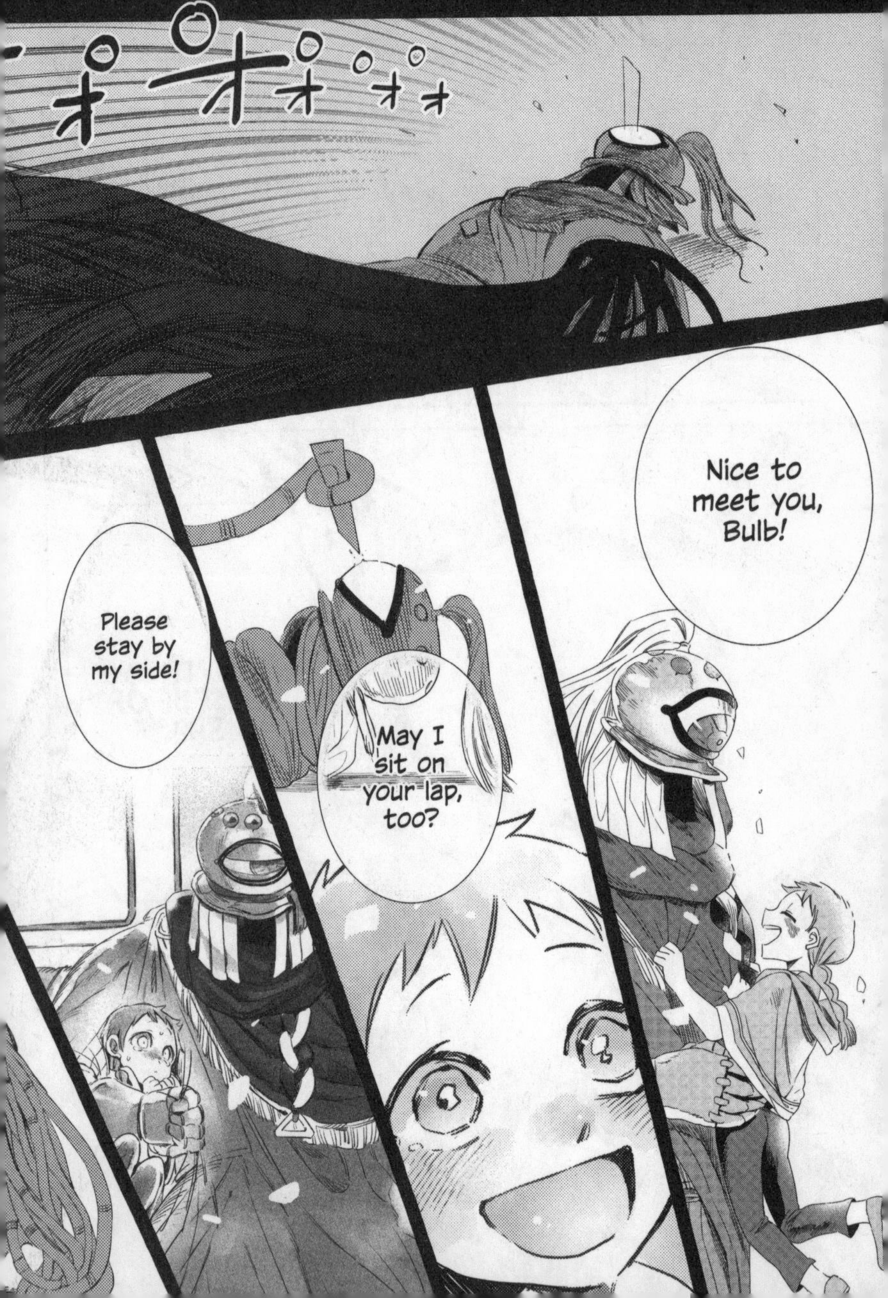
ーオ゚オ゚オ゚オ゚オ゚
Nice to meet you, Bulb!
May I sit on your lap, too?
Please stay by my side!

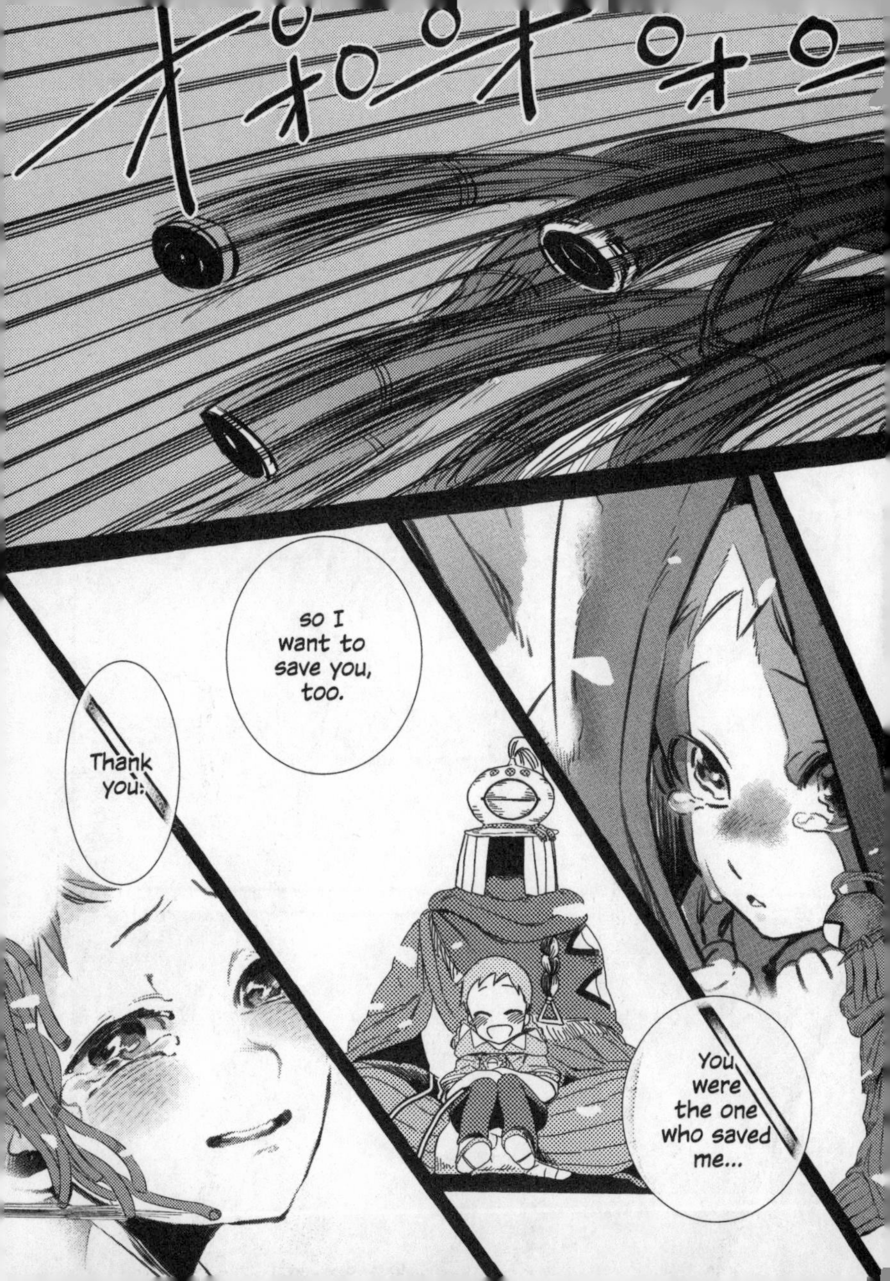

オォオォ
You were the one who saved me...
so I want to save you, too.
Thank you.

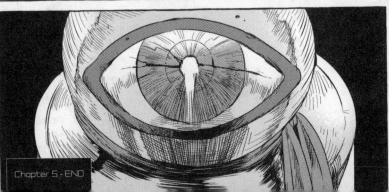

Chapter 5 - END